RECORDS OF CIVILIZATION

SOURCES AND STUDIES

EDITED UNDER THE AUSPICES OF THE

DEPARTMENT OF HISTORY, COLUMBIA UNIVERSITY

NUMBER V

THE LITERATURE OF THE OLD TESTAMENT

THE LITERATURE
OF THE
OLD TESTAMENT

BY

JULIUS A. BEWER

PROFESSOR IN
UNION THEOLOGICAL SEMINARY

REVISED EDITION

NEW YORK

COLUMBIA UNIVERSITY PRESS

Copyright 1922, 1933

COLUMBIA UNIVERSITY PRESS, NEW YORK

———

First printing, 1922
Second printing, 1924
Third printing, 1926
Fourth printing, 1928
Revised edition, 1933
Revised edition, second printing, 1938
Revised edition, third printing, 1940

Foreign agents; OXFORD UNIVERSITY PRESS, Humphrey Milford, Amen House, London, E.C. 4, England, AND B. I. Building, Nicol Road, Bombay, India; MARUZEN COMPANY, LTD., 6 Nihonbashi, Tori-Nichome, Tokyo, Japan

MANUFACTURED IN THE UNITED STATES OF AMERICA

To
MY DEAR MOTHER
IN GRATITUDE
AND DEVOTION

EDITOR'S PREFACE

THE plan of this volume needs a word of explanation. It was originally intended to publish translations of the most important texts of the Old Testament, grouped topically and edited in such a way as to show both their relation to each other and to that process of development into the work as a whole by which they found their place in the collection. Considerable progress had been made along these lines when the war interrupted the preparation of the series. After it was over, publishing conditions still presented sufficient difficulties to compel a modification in the original plan, since that would have involved reprinting large parts of the Old Testament which, with but slight textual variants, would be already accessible to any reader. It was therefore decided to shorten the quoted text to such an extent that it could be readily printed in the midst of the editorial comment, instead of as a body of documents by itself. Where necessary, the larger sections are summarized, and their significance is thus brought out at the same time. The book is obviously not any longer self-sufficing; it is a companion to the study of the Old Testament, rather than a repository of its texts.

And yet, by reason of his original treatment and strict application of the historical method, Professor Bewer has turned to advantage what at first seemed a loss. The volume now presents, much more clearly than would have been possible with a heavy mass of text, the way in which the makers of the Old Testament drew upon their sources and framed the miscellany into a canon. The chapters follow a general historical sequence; but the main thing in the formation of the Old Testament is less chronological antecedent than spiritual affiliation. Professor Bewer's contribution in this field, that of almost intuitive appreciation of the message of each part, is certainly not lessened by keeping text and comment so closely in touch. Yet, if, at some later time, it prove possible to revert to the earlier plan, the present volume may still stand as an introduction to the whole.

JAMES T. SHOTWELL

CONTENTS

INTRODUCTION

THE Old Testament is not a single book but a little library of thirty-nine books as we ordinarily count them. Originally there were even more, for several which were at first distinct and separate are now combined in one; and many more authors were responsible for their production than tradition allows. The Old Testament, as we now have it, is the result of a long literary process in which compilers and editors had a large share. It is in this final form that it has exerted its great influence on ancient and modern civilization alike. But each book, each component part indeed, had its special significance for its own time as well. Some of them were the direct cause of powerful religious and social movements; others contain the soul-stirring addresses that gave new direction to the life of the nation. Like tributary streams which give refreshment and inspiration in their individual courses before their waters mingle in the river adding to its greatness and power, so each part of the Old Testament gave refreshment and inspiration to the people before it became united with the Bible as a whole, whose greatness and power it now augments. To trace the origin and development of the individual contributions, to see how they sprang out of the life and thought of the people, how they influenced the cultural development of Israel, and how they in turn were influenced and modified, until finally the one great Sacred Bible resulted, is a fascinating story. If we read the Old Testament in the order in which its various parts originated, it takes on a new significance, for the warmly pulsating life of the people and of its leaders is felt much better at its sources. The common folk with their songs and stories, the poets and the prophets, the historians, lawgivers, and sages, all stand before us as we follow in our imagination the various phases of the great development and try to think ourselves into the different experiences with sympathetic understanding until we feel the power that moved them all and recreate in our own mind the times of long ago, when the pioneers of the Spirit blazed new paths for the moral and spiritual development of the race.

This we will attempt to do, and in order that we may really feel the throbbing life of the movement we will take the results of the special, detailed, and laborious literary investigations regarding the composition of the individual books, the separation of their various elements, their date, and authorship for granted and follow the historical development of the literature of the Old Testament unencumbered by technicalities. It is true that there is no consensus of critical scholars about the date and composition of not a few documents, but the main lines of the development are sure enough to warrant our weaving the single literary results together in a story, which in itself will be a means of judging their plausibility and validity.

The chronological sequence of the books which literary criticism has established differs greatly from their order in our Bibles. And not only is this true of the books as a whole but of their component parts as well, for most of the books are of composite authorship. The majestic story of Creation, for example, which now stands at the beginning of the Old Testament, is quite late as a literary composition. The stories of the Garden of Eden and of the Temptation which follow immediately upon it are several centuries earlier; and the history of Saul and David in the Books of Samuel is, from a literary point of view, older than the books themselves, older indeed than the oldest stories in the Book of Genesis. The earliest of all literary productions are the poems which are now incorporated in the historical books.

The order of historical development which we shall follow is this :

1. *The Pre-monarchic Period, before ca.* 1000 B.C. (topically arranged, not chronologically) :

   (a) *War and march songs:* Song of Lamech (Gen. 4 [23f.]). Song of Miriam (Ex. 15 [21]). Eternal War with Amalek (Ex. 17 [16]). Incantations to the Ark (Num. 10 [35f.]). List of Stations (Num. 21 [14f.]). Taunt Song on the Amorites (Num. 21 [27–30]). Song of the Well (Num. 21 [17f.]). Joshua's Appeal to the Sun and the Moon (Josh. 10 [12f.]). Song of Deborah (Judg. 5).

(*b*) *Proverbs, riddles, and fables:* David's Proverb (1 Sam. 24 [13]). Samson's Riddles (Judg. 14 [14.18]) and Taunt (Judg. 15 [16]). Jotham's Fable (Judg. 9 [7–15]).

(*c*) *Prophetic blessings and oracles:* The Blessing of Noah (Gen. 9 [25–27]) and of Jacob (Gen. 49). The Oracles of Balaam (Num. 23f.).

2. *The Time of David, Solomon, and Jeroboam I, from ca.* 1000–910 B.C.

(*a*) *Poems:* Pæan over David's victories (1 Sam. 18 [7] etc.). Sheba's War Cry (2 Sam. 20 [1]). David's Lamentation over Saul and Jonathan (2 Sam. 1 [19ff.]), and over Abner (2 Sam. 3 [33f.]). Nathan's Parable (2 Sam. 12 [1–4]). Solomon's Dedication of the Temple (1 Ki. 8 [12f.]). The Books of Yashar and of the Wars of Yahweh. The Blessing of Moses (Deut. 33).

(*b*) *Narratives:* The Story of the Founding and Establishment of the Kingdom by Saul, David, and Solomon (parts of 1 and 2 Sam and 1 Ki. 1f.). The Book of the Acts of Solomon (1 Ki. 3–11 in part). Beginnings of the Royal Annals and of the Temple Records.

(*c*) *Laws:* The Book of the Covenant (Ex. 20 [23]–23 [19]). The So-called Cultic Decalogue of Ex. 34.

3. *The Ninth and Eighth Centuries:*
The Elijah Stories (1 Ki. 17–19.21). The Elisha Stories (2 Ki. 2–8 in part, 13 [14–21]). The History of the Rise and Fall of the Dynasty of Omri (1 Ki. 20.22, 2 Ki. 3.6 [24]–7 [20] 8 [7–15] 9.10). The Yahwist (*ca.* 850 B.C.). The Elohist (*ca.* 750 B.C.). Amos (*ca.* 750). Hosea (from *ca.* 745–735). Isaiah (from 738–700 and perhaps later). Micah (from *ca.* 725 till perhaps the seventh century).

4. *The Seventh Century:*
Combination of the Yahwist and the Elohist. Deuteronomy (published in 621 B.C.). Zephaniah (*ca.* 627–626). Jeremiah (from 626 on). Nahum (*ca.* 615). The First Edition of the Books of Kings (between 620 and 608).

5. *The Sixth Century:*

Jeremiah (continued till after 585). Habakkuk (between 600 and 590). Ezekiel (593–571). The Holiness Code (Lev. 17–26). Lamentations (586–550). Isaiah 63 [7]–64 [12]. The Combination of the Yahwist and Elohist with the Deuteronomist in the Hexateuch. The Second Edition of the Books of Kings (*ca.* 550). The Deuteronomistic Editions of the Stories of Joshua, Judges, and Samuel. The Song of Moses (Deut. 32). Isaiah 13 [2ff.] 14 [4–21] 21. Deutero-Isaiah (Isa. 40–55, between 546 and 539). Haggai (520). Zechariah I–VIII (520–518 and after?). Isaiah 56 [9]–58 [12] 59 [1–15a] 65 [1–16] 66 [1–6.15–18a.24] (from 520 on). The Priest Code (*ca.* 500).

6. *The Fifth Century:*

Isaiah 59 [15b]–63 [6] 65 [17–25] 66 [7–14.18b–23]. Jeremiah 3 [14–18]. Isaiah 34f. Obadiah. Isaiah 15f. Amos 9 [8b–15]. Zephaniah 2 [7a.c 8–11]. Isaiah 11 [10–16]. Malachi (*ca.* 460). The Memoirs of Nehemiah (after 432), and of Ezra. The Book of Ruth. The Aramaic Story in Ezra 4 [8]–6 [18]. Joel (*ca.* 400).

7. *The Fourth Century:*

Joel (later elements). Isaiah 19 [1–15] 23 [1–14]. Proverbs (older portions). Job. Isaiah 24–27

8. *The Third Century:*

The Chronicler (300–250). Genesis 14. 1 Kings 13. Esther. Song of Songs. Proverbs 1–9.30f. Jonah. Isaiah 19 [18–25]. Ecclesiastes (*ca.* 200).

9. *The Second Century:*

Daniel (165–164). Zechariah 9–11.13 [7–9]. Isaiah 33. Zechariah 12.13 [1–6] 14.

Completion of the Psalter.

THE LITERATURE
OF THE
OLD TESTAMENT

CHAPTER I

EARLY POEMS

LONG before any one in Israel thought of writing in literary form, people sang songs and told stories, delighted in riddles and wise sayings, and handed them down from generation to generation in oral tradition. The few of these that have come down to us, embedded as quotations in our prose books, are all in poetry. They had been conceived in enthusiastic moods and had often been recited or sung on festive occasions, when the rhythmic form of some classes like the war songs and pæans of victory was accentuated by dancing and the accompanying clapping of the hands or by crude music. Certain men were especially interested in these folk songs. We read of ballad singers or reciters of poems in early Israel (Num. 21 27) and may be sure that in course of time they felt the need of committing their repertoire to writing. The names of two such early collections we know, the "Book of the Wars of Yahweh" and the "Book of Yashar" or the "Upright." The works themselves, the earliest books of Hebrew literature of which we have any record, are no longer extant, but some of the poems, which are quoted from them in the (later) prose narratives,[1] indicate that they were books of poetry.

Among the ancient poetic material that is still preserved in the books from Genesis to Samuel there are lyric songs, as well as didac-

---

[1] The fragment of the list of stations in Num. 21 14f. is quoted from the "Book of the Wars of Yahweh"; while Joshua's command to the sun and moon (Josh. 10 12f.), David's lamentation over Saul and Jonathan (2 Sam. 1 19–27), and Solomon's dedicatory sentence (1 Ki. 8 12f.) are from the "Book of Yashar."

tic, prophetic, and cultic poems.   Unfortunately, it is impossible to date them exactly.   Though some are very old, not a single song has come down from a time earlier than Moses, and whether any has from his own time is doubtful.   One of the oldest, in spirit if not in age or form, is the song of the terrible Lamech with its unquenchable thirst for revenge, its cruel lack of pity, and brutal boastfulness (Gen. 4 [23f.]).   It comes from a primitive civilization in which even the law of blood revenge exerted no restraint.   Proudly the reckless warrior utters his boast to his wives,

> Adah and Zillah, hear this voice of mine,
>   wives of Lamech, hearken to this speech of mine:
> I slay a man for wounds of mine,
>   and a young man for bruises of mine.
> If Cain takes vengeance sevenfold,
>   Lamech will truly seven and seventy fold!

The rhythm is perfect and the rhyme, which is rare in Hebrew poetry, enhances the wild beauty of the song.   Who can tell how old it is?   The form is polished, the contents are savage.   But poetic forms are ancient, and primitive savagery among desert tribes may have haunted the Israelites long after they had settled in Palestine.   The brutal boast of endless blood feud has many a parallel in Arab songs, where it is also addressed to the women.

From Moses' time, it may be, comes the original pæan of Miriam after the great deliverance at the Sea of Reeds (Ex. 15 [21]).   It was in just such manner that the ancient Arabs also celebrated their victories.   With music and dancing the women, led by Miriam, repeated ever again the exciting refrain,

> Sing to Yahweh,
>   for highly exalted is He,
> The horse and its rider
>   He has hurled into the sea.

It consisted only of these lines, just as the pæan of the women on David's victory over the Philistines.   A much later poet worked it out in more detail, beginning with this same refrain but unfolding its theme at length, and then attributing the whole not to Miriam but to Moses (Ex. 15 [1ff.]), the greater personality, as often happens in literary history.

There are some other interesting bits of poetry connected with this period. The brief distich which tells of Yahweh's eternal warfare against Amalek,

> A hand on the banner of Yahweh!
> Yahweh has war with Amalek forever (Ex. 17 [16]),

is our oldest literary witness to the immemorial enmity between Israel and Amalek. But whether it actually comes from this early time, it is impossible to tell.

The ancient cultic formulæ with which the Ark was addressed, when it was taken into battle and when it returned (Num. 10 [35f.]), are most probably from the time of the Exodus or of the Conquest. They give us the primitive conception of the Ark. In ancient times it was taken into battle, especially when the situation was critical, for in it Yahweh manifested His presence in visible form to His people. When it set out at the head of the army these words were spoken,

> Arise, Yahweh,
>   that Thine enemies be scattered,
>   and they that hate Thee flee before Thee!

when it came back from victory,

> Rest, O Yahweh,
>   Thou myriads of regiments of Israel!

For Yahweh was the god of battle, worth myriads of regiments of Israel. He brought victory and then returned to rest in His tent. The narrator understood these verses as referring to the beginning and the end of the day's march in the wilderness. When the Ark started, Israel broke camp; when it stopped, Israel did so too. Such cultic formulæ are frequently reinterpreted by later generations.

A list of names of places through which Israel had passed on its march to Canaan was handed down in poetry. It has its parallels in Arabic poetry where the recitation of lists is often enlivened by a reminiscence of one kind or another. We have only a little fragment of the list. It is quoted from the Book of the Wars of Yahweh, in which the Exodus from Egypt and the Conquest of Canaan appear to have been celebrated in poetry and song. And the particular point the narrator wished to prove by the quotation was that the Arnon was the border of Moab at that time.

> Waheb in Suphah (?) and the valleys,
>   Arnon and the cliff of the valleys,
> That slopes down to the dwelling of Ar,
>   And leans on the border of Moab. (Num. 21 [14f.])

Perhaps the little song of the well was also taken from this source, although this is not definitely stated.

> Spring up, O well; sing in response to it,
>   Well that the princes digged,
> The rulers of the people delved
>   With their sceptres and staves!
>   From the desert a gift! (Num. 21 [17f.])

It celebrates the festal opening of a well in the desert. And just as to-day Arabs on the borders of Moab, in the region where Israel's song is located, assert that the particular well has been dug by their respective chief and sing songs to the well,[1] so the Israelites claimed that their princes had delved it with their own staffs, although in reality their part was probably nothing but symbolical action. The narrator who inserted this song located its first recital at Beer in Moab, north of the Arnon; that is exactly the neighborhood where Musil found this custom still practised by the Arabs. The song belongs therefore to this locality, and Beer may be Beer Elim, that is, the well of the terebinths which is mentioned in Isa. 15 [8].

The taunt song on the Amorites (Num. 21 [27-30]) belonged to the repertoire of the ballad singers. It is inserted in the narrative to illustrate the assertion that Moab had been conquered by Sihon, king of the Amorites. If this is correct, we may see in the song a satire on the Amorites. The Israelites mockingly invite the Amorites to come and rebuild Heshbon, the stronghold of their king Sihon, that mighty victor, who had subdued all Moab. Ha! they

---

[1] Compare the song of the Arabs to-day,

> "Spring up, O well,
>   Flow copiously.
> Drink and disdain not,
>   With a staff have we dug it."
>   Musil, *Kuseyr Amra*, 1907, p. 298.

were strong enough to conquer Moab in the past, but now they
themselves have been terribly defeated by Israel! [1]

> Come to Heshbon, let it be built,
>   let the city of Sihon be restored!
> For a fire went forth from Heshbon,
>   a flame from the city of Sihon,
> It devoured the cities of Moab,
>   consumed the heights of the Arnon.
> Woe to thee, Moab!
>   thou art undone, O people of Kemosh:
> He gave his sons as fugitives,
>   and his daughters into captivity,
>   [to Sihon, king of the Amorites.]
> Their offspring (?) has perished
>   from Heshbon to Dibon,
> And their women (?) . . .
>   . . . unto Medeba (?). (Num. 21 [27-30])

The Book of the Upright contained also Joshua's famous prayer
during the battle of Gibeon, in which he begged that the day might
be long enough for a complete rout of the enemies,

> O Sun, stand thou still over Gibeon,
>   and Moon, over the vale of Aijalon!

And similarly the answer,

> And the sun stood still, and the moon stayed,
>   till the people were avenged on their foes.

This was expressed poetically by the author who lived some time
after the conquest had been completed. But the narrator, who
quoted it, interpreted it prosaically: a stupendous miracle was the
result!

And the sun stayed in the midst of heaven, and hasted not to go down
about a whole day. And there was no day like that before it or after it, that
Yahweh hearkened to the voice of a man. (Josh. 10 [12-14])

The finest and most elaborate of all early war songs, and generally regarded as the most ancient too, is Deborah's famous ode

---

[1] This interpretation is not quite certain. Some believe that the song celebrated
Israel's victory over Moab, and date it from the time of Omri (*ca.* 900 B.C.). But the
reference to the ballad singers suggests that it is older. And if our interpretation is
correct, this taunt may come from the time of the conquest or shortly thereafter and
may even be earlier than the Song of Deborah, which also ends in a taunt.

which celebrates Israel's victory over Sisera (Judg. 5). Composed either by the great prophetess herself or by some contemporary, the song is as invaluable for the history of the time as it is remarkable for its literary quality and poetic power. It begins with an imposing description of Yahweh's march from Sinai to battle for His people, and a sketch of the conditions of the time. The enthusiastic rally of the tribes who lived in or near the great plain of Esdraelon is then contrasted with the attitude of the more distant ones who kept aloof. A vivid picture of the mighty battle follows, with the flight of Sisera and his inglorious death at the hand of Jael, while a masterly portrayal of the anxious mother of Sisera and her ladies-in-waiting who are anticipating their share in Sisera's spoil, which will never come, concludes the song, to which a reader has added the "pious" wish, "So let all Thine enemies perish, O Yahweh!"

> Because the leaders took the lead in Israel,
>> because the people freely volunteered,
>>> bless ye Yahweh!
>
> Hear, O ye kings; ye princes give ear!
>> I will sing to Yahweh,
>>> I will sing praise to Yahweh, the God of Israel.
>
> Yahweh, when Thou wentest forth from Seir,
>> when Thou marchedst from Edom's field,
> The earth trembled, the heavens also swayed,
>> yea, the clouds poured water,
>>> the mountains quaked at the presence of Yahweh, God of Israel.
>
> In the days of Shamgar the son of Anath,
>> caravans ceased,
>>> and wayfaring men took roundabout ways.
> The rural population (?) had ceased,
>> in Israel they had ceased,
> Until thou didst arise, Deborah,
>> didst arise a mother in Israel.
>
> They chose new gods (?),
>> then was war in the gates (?).[1]
> A shield or spear was not seen
>> among forty thousand in Israel.
> My heart belongs to the rulers of Israel,
>> to those that freely volunteered among the people!

---

[1] The original text of these two lines is irrecoverable.

Bless ye Yahweh,
  ye that ride on tawny asses,
Ye that sit on rich carpets (?)
  and ye that walk by the way, sing!
(?) Hark the huzzahing (?) at the watering places!
  there they rehearse the victories of Yahweh,
The victories of his country folk in Israel,
  (how) at that time the people of Yahweh went down to the gates.

Rouse thee, rouse thee, Deborah;
  rouse thee, rouse thee, utter a song:
    arise, Barak, and lead forth thy captors, thou son of Abinoam.
Then marched down for him the nobles,
  and the people of Yahweh marched down for him as heroes.
From Ephraim they came down to the valleys (?),
  after them Benjamin with his hosts;
From Machir came down commanders,
  and from Zebulun they that wield the marshal's staff.
And the princes of Issachar were with Deborah;
  as was Issachar, so was Barak,
    into the valley they rushed forth at his heels.

Among the tribal divisions of Reuben
  were great searchings of heart.
Why didst thou sit still among the sheepfolds,
  to hear the flute calls of the flocks?
Gilead remained beyond the Jordan:
  and Dan sought the protection of (?) ships!
Asher sat still on the shore of the sea,
  and abode by his landings.
Zebulun is a people that jeoparded their lives to the death,
  Naphtali also, upon the heights of the field.

The kings came and they fought;
  then fought the kings of Canaan,
In Tannach by the waters of Megiddo:
  they took no gain of money.
From heaven fought the stars,
  from their courses they fought against Sisera.
The river Kishon swept them away,
  that onrushing river, the river Kishon.
O my soul, march on with strength (?).
  Then were battered the hoofs of the horses
    by the furious galloping of their chargers.

Curse ye Meroz, said the angel of Yahweh,
  curse bitterly its inhabitants,

Because they came not to the help of Yahweh,
  to Yahweh's help among the heroes.

Blessed above women be Jael,
  blessed above women in the tent.
Water he asked, milk she gave;
  she brought him curd in a lordly bowl.
She put forth her hand to the tent pin,
  and her right hand to the workman's hammer;
And with the hammer she battered Sisera, she crushed his head;
  yea, she shattered and struck through his temple.
At her feet he sank down, he fell, he lay still,
  where he sank down, there he lay slain.

Out of the window leaned Sisera's mother
  and looked through the lattice,
"Why is his chariot so long in coming?
  why tarry the hoof-beats of his horses?"
The wisest of his princesses answered her,
  yea, 'tis she that made reply to her,
"Surely they are finding, dividing the spoil,
  a damsel or two for each man;
Booty of dyed garments for Sisera,
  booty of dyed garments, embroidered,
    a dyed garment, two pieces of embroidered stuff for the neck of . . . . "
                        *   *   *
So let all Thine enemies perish, O Yahweh,
  but let them that love Thee be as the sun when he rises in his might. (Judg. 5)

This triumphal ode belongs in the judgment of critics to the finest odes in the literature of the world and is not excelled in poetic power by any of the later war poems of Israel. Its significance for our knowledge of the history of Israel greatly enhances its value. In the threatening crisis of a powerful offensive of Canaanite city kings against the Israelite invaders who had consolidated their gains in the mountains south and north of the Great Plain, the tribes Issachar, Zebulun, Naphtali together with Ephraim, Benjamin, and Machir were rallied by Deborah to the standard of Yahweh. Barak of Issachar assumed chief command. The battle itself with its victorious issue for Israel is clearly portrayed, but the further results we must infer. That it helped to weld Israel's tribes together is certain. It is noteworthy that the unifying element is the religion of Yahweh. The conviction that Reuben, Gilead, Dan, and Asher ought also to have followed the summons, and the bitter reproach for their failure to do so, show that in a crisis the feeling that they all belong together pervaded the people. It is all the more significant that Judah, Simeon, and Levi are not mentioned at all, the author did not consider them as part of Israel. For our knowledge of the conditions of Israel immediately preceding the attack, the power of the Canaanites, their control of the plains with their passes and caravan routes, their military forces with chariotry and cavalry, as well as for the strength of the religion of Yahweh, who comes from His sacred seat far in the south to the rescue of His people, Deborah's song is of singular importance.

Israel delighted also in proverbs, riddles, and wise sayings. Perhaps the oldest proverb that has come down to us in poetic form was once quoted by David.

> From the wicked comes forth wickedness,
>> but my hand shall not be upon thee. (1 Sam. 24 [13])

Even in his day it was a "proverb of the ancients." Many others must have circulated among the people, but they were not written down or collected at so early a date, and thus they are lost to us.

Riddles too were a favorite pastime of Israel in all ages. We still have the riddle which Samson propounded at his wedding,

> From the eater came forth the meat,
>> and from the strong one came forth sweet,

of which the guests gave their solution in the form of another,

> What is sweeter than honey,
>> and what is stronger than a lion? (Judg. 14 [14.18])

To this Samson sarcastically replied with a popular rhyme,

> Had ye not ploughed with the heifer of mine,
>> ye had not found out this riddle of mine.

Both riddles are older than the stories of which they now form a part, for they originally meant something altogether different, since the real answer to the second was "love." The narrator used it for his story with an entirely new meaning. What the first

one originally meant is uncertain; perhaps it was the lion in the
sky that brings the harvest.

Samson's taunt,

> With the jaw of an ass
>   I smashed them in mass,
> With the jaw of an ass
>   I slew a thousand men (Judg. 15 [16]),

was taken literally by the narrator, while originally the idiomatic
phrase "with a jawbone of an ass" expressed that Samson's astounding victory had been won with a most miserable, despicable
weapon (cf. Judg. 5 [8]).

There were also longer didactic poems.   The most remarkable
of them all is Jotham's fable of the trees' choice of a king, which
teaches that the good and useful people have too much to do to
accept the office of king;   only worthless and dangerous people are
willing to become monarchs.   Loyalty to them in the hope of gaining protection by them is sheer mockery, and disloyalty involves
ruin.

> Hearken to me, lords of Shechem,
>   that God may hearken to you!
>
> The trees went forth on a time
>   to anoint them a king,
> And they said to the olive, "Reign over us!"
>   But the olive said unto them,
> "Should I leave my fatness
>   which gods and men prize in me,
> And go to sway over the trees?"
>
> Then the trees said unto the fig-tree,
>   "Come thou, and reign over us!"
> But the fig-tree said unto them,
>   "Should I leave my sweetness
> And my good fruit
>   and go to sway over the trees?"
>
> Then the trees said unto the grape vine,
>   "Come thou, and reign over us!"
> But the grape vine said unto them,
>   "Should I leave my wine
> That cheers gods and men,
>   and go to sway over the trees?"

> Then said all the trees unto the thorn,
>   "Come thou, and reign over us!"
> And the thorn said unto the trees,
>   "If in truth ye anoint
> Me as king over you,
>   then come, take refuge in my shade,
> But if not, fire shall proceed from the thorn,
>   and devour the cedars of Lebanon." (Judg. 9)

This bitter judgment of kingship is applied by the narrator to Abimelech, whom the people of Shechem had made king. Whether the author himself composed the fable or whether it was taken from the people's fund of stories either by Jotham or by the author is a matter of debate. The latter seems a little more probable on the whole. The fable appears to voice the feelings of many free Israelites in the period shortly before the introduction of the monarchy. Only dire need made them ready for this new form of government. The fable is of great historical importance, even if it came from a much later time than we have assumed.

Another class of early poems is in the form of prediction: this is merely a literary form; for in reality they did not foretell the future, but explained the present as due to the magically potent word of the ancestor's blessing. These blessings were composed in poetry, because the inspiration of the vision of the future put the ancestors into an exalted mood in which speech assumes rhythmic form. The historian may use these poems as documents of the time which they predict, but not of that of the ancestors themselves, for they were not composed by them, but by the later poets who reflected on the causes of the conditions of their own times and found them in these magically effective blessings. The Blessing of Noah may be the earliest of them, but this is uncertain.

> Cursed be Canaan!
>   Meanest slave shall he be to his brothers!
>
> Bless, Yahweh, the tents of Shem,
>   and let Canaan be his slave!
>
> God enlarge Japheth,
>   and let him dwell in the tents of Shem,
> And let Canaan be his slave. (Gen. 9 [25-27])

The most striking feature is the curse on Canaan, which is reiterated in the blessings of Shem and Japheth. The historical allusions cannot be made out with certainty. But it seems quite probable that they refer to the time after David, when Canaan had been completely subdued and Israel and Philistia dwelt in the tents of Shem, when the recognition of each other's independence and territorial integrity had been finally won in the great Philistine wars, which David had brought to a successful termination.

In the Blessing of Jacob (Gen. 49) the ancestor, not speaking in his own name as an individual but representing the national consciousness of Israel, expresses the verdict on the historical condition and the future of the single tribes, beginning with Reuben and ending with Benjamin. We get here valuable information about the history of the tribes before and during the early monarchy. The various oracles were probably not all composed at the same time; most are earlier than the monarchy, but the blessing of Judah implies the rule of David as an accomplished fact, and the blessing of Joseph seems to date from the time of the divided kingdom, at least in its present form.

> JUDAH, thee shall thy brethren praise:
>> Thy hand shall be on the neck of thy foes,
>> Thy father's sons shall bow down before thee.
> Judah is a lion's whelp;
>> From the prey, my son, thou art gone up:
> He stoops down, he couches as a lion
>> And as a lioness; who shall rouse him up?
> The sceptre shall not depart from Judah,
>> Nor the ruler's staff from between his feet,
> Until he come to whom it belongs,[1]
>> And whose is the homage of the peoples.
> Binding his foal to the vine,
>> And his ass's colt to the choice vine;

[1] The ordinary translation of v.[10] is,

> The sceptre shall not depart from Judah,
> Nor the ruler's staff from between his feet
> Until *Shiloh* come,
> And unto him shall the obedience of the people be.

Shiloh has often been taken as a cryptic name for the Messiah. But it is more probable that we should read "until he comes *to whom it belongs*" and explain this as a reference to David. Judah will not lose its tribal independence until David comes, who is naturally not mentioned by name in the "prediction"; then David will become the ruler of nations, not only of the tribe Judah!

He washes his garments in wine,
  And his vesture in the blood of the grapes:
His eyes are red with wine,
  And his teeth white with milk. (Gen. 49 [8–12])

     *   *   *

JOSEPH is a young fruit tree,
  A young fruit tree by a fountain;
  His branches run over the wall (?).
The archers sorely provoked him,
  And strove with him and harassed him:
But his bow remained firm,
  And the arms of his hands were nimble.
By the hands of the Mighty One of Jacob,
  By the name of the shepherd of the children of Israel,
By the God of thy father, who shall help thee,
  And by the Almighty, who shall bless thee,
With blessings of heaven above,
  Blessings of the deep that couches beneath,
  Blessings of breast and of womb.
The blessings of thy father
  Surpassed the blessings of the everlasting mountains,
  The blessings of the everlasting hills,
May they be on the head of Joseph,
  And on the crown of the head of the prince of his brethren. (Gen. 49 [22–26])

The Blessing of Jacob is rhythmically more regular than the Song of Deborah, which is its companion in the elucidation of early tribal history.

The oracles of Balaam (Num. 23f.) belong here too, only in them a famous non-Israelite seer of antiquity utters those rhythmic verses that have the power to bring about all the glory proclaimed therein. The heathen prophet cannot pronounce a curse, when God has commanded a blessing. He must bless Israel, although Balak wants him to curse it, because in his vision he sees Israel's great future, Saul's victories, and David's splendid reign. These oracles are not real predictions, but poetic descriptions of the time of Saul and of David, during which they were composed. They are put into Balaam's mouth by the same literary device which ascribed the Blessings to the ancestors. The revelation of the divine purposes to a non-Israelite, the manner of Balaam's prophetic inspiration, and his emphasis on God's consistency are as important

for our understanding of the development of Israel's religion as
the political references are for the history of the early monarchy.

> From Aram has Balak brought me,
>> The king of Moab from the mountains of the East:
> Come, curse me Jacob,
>> And come, denounce Israel!
> How shall I curse, whom God has not cursed?
>> And how shall I denounce, whom Yahweh has not denounced?
> For from the top of the rocks I see him,
>> And from the hills I behold him:
> Lo, it is a people that dwells alone,
>> And that reckons not itself among the nations.
> Who can count the dust of Jacob,
>> Or number the myriads of Israel?
> Let me die the death of the righteous,
>> And let my last end be like his!

*　　*　　*

> Rise up, Balak, and hear;
>> Hearken to me, O son of Zippor:
> God is not a man that He should break His word,
>> Neither the son of man, that He should change His mind.
> Should He promise and not do it?
>> Or speak and not make it good?
> Behold, I have received orders to bless:
>> And He has blessed and I cannot reverse it.
> He has not beheld calamity in Jacob;
>> Nor seen trouble in Israel:
> Yahweh his God is with him,
>> And the shout for his king is among them.
> God who brought them forth out of Egypt,
>> Is for him like the horns (?) of the wild-ox.
> Now shall it be said of Jacob and of Israel,
>> What has God wrought!
> Behold, the people rises up like a lioness,
>> And like a lion it lifts itself up:
> It shall not lie down till it eat of the prey,
>> And drink the blood of the slain.

*　　*　　*

> The oracle of Balaam the son of Beor,
> Even the oracle of the man whose eye was opened,
> The oracle of him who hears the words of God,
> Who sees the vision of the Almighty,
> Falling down, and having his eyes opened:

How beautiful are thy tents, O Jacob,
   thy tabernacles, O Israel!
Like valleys are they spread forth,
   like gardens by the river-side,
Like cedars which Yahweh has planted,
   like palms beside the waters.

A man shall come from his seed (?)
   and shall rule over many nations,
And his king shall be higher than Agag,
   and his kingdom shall be exalted.
God who brought him out of Egypt;
   is for him like the horns of the wild-ox:
He shall devour the nations, his adversaries,
   and break their bones in pieces,
   and shatter their loins.
He couched, he lay down like a lion,
   and like a lioness, who shall rouse him up?
Blessed is every one that blesses thee,
   and cursed is every one that curses thee.

*   *   *

The oracle of Balaam the son of Beor,
Even the oracle of the man whose eye was opened,
The oracle of him who hears the words of God,
And knows the knowledge of the Most High,
Who sees the vision of the Almighty,
Falling down and having his eyes opened:

I see him, but not now;
   I behold him but not nigh:
A star has shone forth out of Jacob,
   a sceptre has risen out of Israel,
And it smites through the temples of Moab,
   and the skulls of all the sons of tumult (?).

And Edom shall be a possession,
   while Israel does valiant deeds,
And Jacob shall trample down his enemies,
   and destroy the survivors of Seir. (Num. 23 [7-10, 18-24] 24 [3-9, 15-19])

The time of David must have been rich in other forms of poetry too. One of the earliest poems of his time, which has been handed down to us, is the song of the women celebrating Saul's and especially David's victory over the Philistines (1 Sam. 18 [7] 21 [12] 29 [5]),

      Saul has slain his thousands,
       but David his myriads.

It is almost as brief as Miriam's Song, for it consists of only two lines which the women sang in ecstatic joy as they received the returning victor with music and dancing.   Over and over again they repeated the simple, expressive refrain.

Almost equally brief, but picturing entirely different emotions, was Sheba's rhythmic call to rebellion in David's old age.

> We have no portion in David,
>   nor have we heritage in Jesse's son!
> Every man to his tents, O Israel! (2 Sam. 20 [1])

It is the fierce war cry of a bold, embittered Benjamite, calling on the various tribes to forsake their allegiance to King David and resume once more their tribal independence, each to his own tribal tents!   Benjamin had lost the royal crown, Judah must not have it either!   Tribal jealousy was strong at the time.

David himself is celebrated in tradition as a minstrel and a poet. But unfortunately, almost everything he composed is lost.   Only two dirges remain; chief among them is the famous lamentation over Saul and Jonathan in which the sorrow and love of a great heart are poured out in moving words of beauty and sincerity.

> Thy glory, O Israel, is slain on thy heights,
>   how are the heroes fallen!
>
> Tell it not in Gath,
>   publish it not in Ashkelon's streets,
> Lest the Philistines' daughters rejoice,
>   lest the daughters of the uncircumcised triumph.
>
> Hills of Gilboa, no dew nor rain
>   be upon you, ye fields of death!
> For there lies defiled the shield of heroes,
>   the shield of Saul, not anointed with oil.
>
> From the blood of the slain,
>   from the fat of the mighty,
> Jonathan's bow never turned back,
>   nor did empty come back the sword of Saul.
>
> Saul and Jonathan, the beloved and dear,
>   in their lives and their death not divided!
> They were swifter than eagles,
>   they were stronger than lions!

Daughters of Israel, weep ye for Saul,
  who clothed you with scarlet and fine linen wrappers,
  who put ornaments of gold upon your apparel.

How are the heroes fallen in the thick of the battle!
  O Jonathan, slain on thy heights,
I am in anguish for thee, O Jonathan, my brother!
  Very dear hast thou been unto me:
Thy love to me was wonderful,
  passing the love of women.

How are the heroes fallen,
  and the weapons of war perished! (2 Sam. 1 [19-27])

This lamentation was taken from the Book of Yashar. The metre is not regular, but whether this was due to textual corruption or to the strong, passionate sorrow that would not be forced into the rhythmic regularity of the lamentation metre, although it sometimes finds utterance in it, we do not know. The sombre refrain is full of sadness. The dirge does high credit to the poet as well as the man. David's noble soul shines forth from it in immortal beauty.

The second dirge, over Abner, is much briefer.

Must Abner die as a fool dies?
Thy hands were not bound,
Thy feet not put in fetters.
As one falls before knaves, so thou didst fall! (2 Sam. 3 [33f.])

Its very brevity shows David's sincerity. There is nothing artificial in this lamentation, no love is expressed, only honor for the hero whose foul murder has jeopardized David's secret diplomacy.

These poems are secular, there is nothing religious in them. But a poet of such high order, as the lamentation over Saul and Jonathan exhibits, and of such profound religious feelings, as we know David to have been, probably composed also religious hymns and psalms.[1] But if any of these are really contained in our Psalter, we can no longer point them out. Even Psalm 18, if it was actually written by him, is no longer in its original form; and Psalm 24 [7-10], which is still regarded by some as Davidic, is now a part of a later psalm, whose religion is far in advance of that of David and his time.

[1] Cf. Chap. XX.

But the beautiful parable of Nathan (2 Sam. 12 [1-4]) with its remarkable religious lesson we may attribute to David's time, although some believe that it was composed much later. It is not in metric form, but it is highly poetic in its diction and wonderfully effective in its contents. Who can forget the rich man who had so many flocks and herds and who nevertheless rudely seized the one little ewe lamb of his poor neighbor that was as dear to him as a daughter, when a guest came whom he had to entertain? Who is not startled by the terrible application "thou art the man!" that Nathan thundered into David's ears? It is one of the finest poems in prose that has come down to us from antiquity.[1]

From Solomon we still have his original dedicatory sentences at the dedication of the temple. They are quoted, the Greek text tells us, from the "Book of Song," which was probably the same as the "Book of Yashar." The Hebrew, and therefore the English, text has omitted the important first line.

> Yahweh has set the sun in the firmament,
>> but declared He Himself would dwell in deep darkness.
> I have built now for Thee a lofty abode,
>> a place for Thy dwelling forever. (1 Ki. 8 [12f.])

From the time of Jeroboam I (932–911 B.C.) most likely, comes the Blessing of Moses (Deut. 33). It is the Ephraimite counterpart of the Blessing of Jacob. While Joseph receives a long eulogy and prediction in the Judæan Blessing of Jacob, only little space is given to Judah in this Ephraimite poem.

> Hear, Yahweh, the voice of JUDAH,
>> and bring him to his people.
> Thy hand contend for him
>> and be Thou a help against his adversaries. (Deut. 33 [7])

Contrast this with:

> The precious things of heaven above,
>> and the deep that couches beneath,
> And the precious things of the fruits of the sun,
>> and the precious things of the growth of the moons,
> And the chief things of the ancient mountains,
>> and the precious things of the everlasting hills,

---

[1] The last words of David (2 Sam. 23 [1-7]) were composed by a later poet who put these wise sayings about true and successful royal rule into the mouth of the aged king.

And the precious things of the earth and its fulness,
    and the favor of him that dwelt in the bush.
Let come upon the head of JOSEPH,
    and upon the crown of the head of the prince of his brethren.
For the strength of a bull and majesty are his,
    and his horns are the horns of the wild-ox:
With them he pushes peoples,
    all of them, even the ends of the earth:
These are the myriads of Ephraim,
    and these are the thousands of Manasseh. (Deut. 33 $^{13-17}$)

In its present form the blessing of Moses has a much later poetic introduction, which depends on the Song of Deborah, and a late conclusion, which contains the beautiful lines,

The eternal God is thy dwelling place,
    and underneath are the everlasting arms. (Deut. 33 ^{27})

The historical situation of this blessing is later than that of Jacob's. With the change of historical conditions came a new formulation of the single parts. Simeon is not mentioned at all, Reuben is dying out, Levi is no longer a secular but a priestly tribe, the temple is already built. Judah is in difficulties, but Joseph is prosperous and powerful. We seem to be in the time of Jeroboam I, although many think that the reign of Jeroboam II does more justice to the description of Joseph's opulence and power. But the form of the poem with its "blessings" for the individual tribes presupposes a strong tribal consciousness which was still awake at the time of Jeroboam I, but hardly as late as that of Jeroboam II when the national consciousness had developed. The theocratic tone of the poem contrasts strikingly with the secular tone of Gen. 49. It is quite likely that a priest of the Northern Kingdom was its author. Again the historian can learn much from this blessing for the time of the early monarchy, but not for that of Moses.

In these ancient poems we find already the balancing of the lines, called parallelism of the members, which is characteristic of Hebrew as of Babylonian poetry. Rhyme we meet but rarely, the song of Lamech is quite exceptional in this. It is the rhythmic accents of the lines that produce their poetic form. The accents, not the length or number of syllables, are measured. Frequently the first half contains three, occasionally two, beats and is balanced by an equal number.   In the so-called Qinah, or lamentation metre, the second half is shorter, the whole line is usually a pentameter. The power of the refrain was also known, as was the effective grouping into strophes.   Like their Arab kinsmen the ancient Israelites delighted in lyric poetry and practised its art.   The few poems that have been preserved and some suggestions in later poetry show that there were almost innumerable occasions which lent themselves to song and poetry.   The high development of the art of poetic expression which we find in these early poems indicates that a long training must have preceded the earliest literature.   Long before poems were committed to writing, they had been sung and recited orally and thus handed down from generation to generation as true folk poetry.   It is greatly to be regretted that not more of them have come down to us, because tradition in poetic form is better remembered and more exactly passed on to the succeeding generations.

CHAPTER II

EARLY NARRATIVES

ISRAEL'S first great literary production in prose was, in all probability, the Story of the Founding of the Kingdom. The splendid career of David, which introduced a new era of national life, stimulated the beginning of historical literature in Israel. Some time after David's death, while Solomon still reigned, one of the men who had known David well and who possessed first-hand knowledge of the affairs of his time wrote the story. He did it with intimate knowledge, great clearness, and without bias, and produced a narrative which is the joy of historical and literary critics alike. None is so likely to have been the author as David's priest and friend Abiathar, although this is, of course, but a guess.

He began with the dire need of the tribes under the Philistine oppression. The Philistines had invaded Canaan not long after Israel. They had come from Asia Minor and the islands of the Mediterranean and had made themselves masters of the maritime plain south of Mount Carmel. But gradually this was not enough for them, so they attacked the Israelites in their mountain seats, and proved a formidable peril to them. For the political history this is the most important element. For our knowledge of the religion of the period the magic conception of the ark in this story is significant, for it corresponds to that of the march signals of Num. 10 (cf. p. 3). Yahweh, the war god of Israel, went with them into battle in the ark which had been kept at Shiloh on Mount Ephraim, the central sanctuary of the tribes. But in the fateful battle at Aphek it was captured by the Philistines. Yet they could not keep it long. The overthrow of the statue of Dagon in his temple at Ashdod, where the ark had been placed, as well as a plague of tumors in one city after another whither they brought it, were attributed to Yahweh, and it was decided to send it away to Israel with votive offerings of five golden tumors and five golden mice [1] to pacify Yahweh.   After some mishap it was finally quartered at Kiriathjearim (1 Sam. 4 [1b]–7 [1]).

The Philistine danger grew greater.   They conquered the mountains and put garrisons in various strong places.   Divided as Israel's tribes were, they could never hope to end their subjection under the Philistines.   The situation seemed hopeless.   Only in union was strength enough for the task.   But for this a great leader was needed, around whom all could rally, and he was not there, — until the seer Samuel in the little town of Ramah discovered him in the person of the mighty Saul, whose gigantic stature and wild, contagious enthusiasm carried the people with him.   In the form of a folktale we are told how Saul went out to seek his father's asses and found a royal crown (1 Sam. 9 [1]–10 [6]).   This story retained the historically certain connection between Samuel and Saul, and made it plain that Samuel saw the need of the people and provided the leader, but it was the popular rather than the historical account of it.   The occasion which actually showed Saul's capacity for leadership was presented by the Ammonite attack upon Jabesh in Gilead.   Saul rose to it and it was this that won him the kingship (1 Sam. 11 [1–11.15]).

Saul set himself at once to the high task of freeing Israel from Philistine rule.   He was ably seconded by his great son, the lionhearted Jonathan, than whom no braver warrior ever lived.   He gave the signal for the bitter war by slaying the Philistine prefect at Gebah (1 Sam. 13 [2–6.15b–18.23]).   One of his exploits is told in detail.   Accompanied only by his armor bearer he climbed up into the Philistine camp, succeeded in killing twenty men in combat, and gave by this initial success to Saul the opportunity for a telling victory, which brought many that had hitherto been fearful to his side.   Saul almost marred the glory of this triumph by insisting that Jonathan should be killed, because he had unwillingly violated the ban that Saul had placed on food that day, by tasting some honey which greatly refreshed him and his aide.   But the people saved the victorious hero, "for he has wrought with God this day" (14 [1–46.52]).[2]

[1] The custom of presenting as votive offerings images of the members of the body that are afflicted with disease is connected with sympathetic magic.   The mice were symbols of the bubonic plague.   The ancients knew already that mice and other rodents are the carriers of this disease.

[2] In this story the Greek version has preserved the original text, which shows the method of the casting of the lot through which Jonathan's guilt was discovered.   After

Well might Israel rejoice over this success, but Saul saw clearly that the power of the Philistines was by no means broken and that he faced a long struggle. Full of enthusiasm as he was at times when nobody could resist him and the fanatic power of his inspiring personality, he was also visited by seasons of terrible mental depression when fits of melancholia threatened to darken his mind forever. It was to counteract this that there was brought to him that most wonderful figure in Israel's history, young David, who by his skilful playing was to charm away the dark spirit from Saul's mind. At once he came under the spell of David's fresh beauty and grace. His music laid its healing touch on Saul's sad spirit, but in the end the young warrior-minstrel thrust his soul into a deeper gloom from which none could save him. For David was destined to put the most celebrated heroes, Saul and Jonathan, in the shade by his skill, prowess, and success in battle. One story especially was told of him, — how he killed a mighty Philistine giant in single combat. The tale was elaborated later on, and the Philistine warrior was identified with the famous Goliath of Gath,[1] whom in reality not David but Elhanan of Bethlehem had slain as we know from 2 Sam. 21 [19]. David's great name attracted this deed to itself and as so often happens in history the more famous person was credited with what was accomplished by a lesser man. When the women came out to meet the returning victors, singing and dancing, they sang to the accompaniment of timbrels and cymbals over and over again in antiphony,

> Saul has slain his thousands,
> and David his myriads!

It was only natural that Saul should honor the young hero and wish to bind him closer to himself and his house. Our author did not

Saul and Jonathan had placed themselves on one side and the people on the other, Saul said, "Yahweh, God of Israel, why hast Thou not answered Thy servant to-day? If the guilt be in me or in my son Jonathan, Yahweh, God of Israel, give Urim; but if Thou say thus: the guilt is in Thy people Israel, give Tummim." And Jonathan and Saul were taken, but the people escaped. And Saul said, "Cast between me and Jonathan, my son! Whom Yahweh will take, he shall die." And the people said to Saul, "It shall not be so!" But Saul prevailed over the people. And they cast between him and his son Jonathan, and Jonathan was taken. The Urim and Tummim were a lot oracle.

[1] The Greek version contains already this identification of the warrior with Goliath, but it has the story in a much shorter and earlier form (17 [1–11. 32–40. 42–48a. 49. 51–53]).

look at it from this side, but presented David's advancement and honors and even his marriage to Saul's daughter Michal from the viewpoint of Saul's later jealousy. But we may be sure that it did not vitiate Saul's every motive from the outset. It is certainly true that nobody could withstand the charm of David's personality; Saul and Jonathan, Michal and the people all felt it and responded to it. It was natural that it awakened in Saul a restless spirit of envy. His kingship was too recent, his hold on the people only due to his valor and leadership, and here was a greater man, already put by the people above him as victor, constantly growing in influence and power. His sick mind felt those sinister forces working. Whether David thought of becoming king, as Saul feared, we do not know. That he should actually have plotted at this time, seems to be excluded by Jonathan's stanch friendship for him. But sometimes men like Saul see such things more clearly than men like Jonathan with his healthy mind and loyal heart. At any rate, in a fit of anger Saul threw his spear at David, who now fled for his life. Jonathan made sure that Saul had actually intended to kill David and then told him in secret.

David now led the life of a fugitive, whom Saul pursued with relentless rigor. Gradually all sorts of lawless elements gathered about him, and he became the captain of this band of outlaws. Finally escape seemed impossible and he resorted to a step which was really high treason: he went with his men over to Israel's merciless foes, the Philistines, and became the vassal of King Achish of Gath! He stayed four months[1] with him. Then came the day when he was summoned to fight against Saul and Jonathan. Nothing is said of the tragic conflict in his soul, when he saw no way of escape. But fate smiled once more upon him; he was spared the crowning shame of battling against his own people by the distrust of the other Philistine princes who refused to have him and his men in their army. So he was sent back. When he arrived at his residence town Ziklag, he was told that the Amalekites had made a raid upon the city during his absence, burnt it down, and taken the women and children into captivity, among them David's wives Ahinoam and Abigail. He quickly pursued them, attacked them unawares and defeated them, rescued all the women and children,

[1] Not one year and four months, as the Hebrew says.

and returned with much booty.   With fine tact he set the precedent
for the law of booty, deciding "as his share is that goes down to the
battle, so shall his share be that tarries by the baggage : they shall
share alike."   Then he sent, with much diplomatic skill, portions
of the booty to the princes of the various Judæan townships in the
Southland in order to ingratiate himself with them.   Meanwhile
the tragic fate of Saul and Jonathan fulfilled itself.   They fought
their last battle against the hated oppressor ; heroes to the end, they
did not survive their crushing defeat.   When David learned of
their death, he was moved with bitter sorrow, and sang the noble
lamentation that has touched so many generations by its beauty,
sincerity, and pain.   Sorrow and love mingle therein, but there is
no word of God, no thought of immortality, no hope of ever seeing
them again (see p. 16f.).

After Saul's and Jonathan's death, David offered himself to the
Judæans, who chose him as their king at Hebron, the great city of
the South.   But the Northerners, more specifically Abner, Saul's
commanding general, set Eshbaal,[1] one of Saul's sons, on the throne.
His residence was on the other side of Jordan at Mahanaim, for
Canaan was in the hands of the Philistines.   After two years of
state of war, during which David in wise self-restraint did not press
his advantage, Abner was murdered by Joab, David's commander-
in-chief, as a result of a blood feud, for he had killed Joab's brother
Asahel.   Abner's death came at a most inopportune moment for
David, for he had just made a pact with Abner, which had as its aim
the overthrow of Eshbaal.   All this was jeopardized, but David
succeeded in convincing the people that he was innocent of the
crime.   Child of luck that he was, he gained his end nevertheless.
Two Israelitish captains murdered Eshbaal soon afterwards.   Now
David was without rival for the throne of all Israel.   And all the
tribes came and made him their king.   Two decisive political events
marked his early reign, the final, definite defeat of the Philistines and
the capture of the strong fortress of Jerusalem, which hitherto had
been in the hands of the Jebusites.   It was a rare piece of insight

---

[1] The corruption of Eshbaal (= the man of Baal) to Ishbosheth (= the man of
shame) is due to the later custom of substituting *bosheth = shame* for Baal, based on
Hosea's prediction that the Baals should no more be mentioned by their names
(Hos. 2 [17]).

that led David to make Jerusalem the national capital. Not only its central situation and natural strength, but also its hitherto neutral character (it had belonged neither to the North nor to Judah) made it the city which would rouse no antagonism and around which all tribes could rally. Most cleverly David made Jerusalem also the religious centre of Israel by bringing the ark of Yahweh to it in solemn procession during which David performed a cultic dance which displeased his wife Michal. The far-reaching significance of this act of making Jerusalem the political and religious capital of Israel cannot be overestimated (2 Sam. 2–6).

Now comes the most remarkable part of the whole story, which has been the delight of the historian and the literary student alike, the story of the court at Jerusalem with its intimate details, its intrigues and crimes (2 Sam. 9–20; 1 Ki. 1f.). David's magnanimity towards Meribbaal,[1] the son of Jonathan, begins the series (2 Sam. 9). Then comes the war against the Ammonites and Aramæans, in which the sad story of David's adultery with Bathsheba and the murder of her husband Uriah is the most famous episode (2 Sam. 10–12). Amnon's rape of Tamar, his half sister, followed in that strange series of events in which one sin was always the cause of another. However strong David may have been as a warrior and king, he was weak as a father in his own family. His unwillingness to punish Amnon for the rape of his stepsister Tamar was the cause of her brother Absalom's fearful revenge; and his indecision in dealing with his beautiful son, who had inherited all of David's personal charm and diplomatic sagacity, brought about in the end Absalom's rebellion which almost cost David his throne, but which, thanks to the extraordinary diplomacy of the king's old friend and councillor Chushai and Joab's ruthless military measures, ended in Absalom's defeat and death. The spirit of rebellion, once awake, seized the Benjamite Sheba, who summoned the tribes to secede from David. A quick military expedition under Joab put down this movement which threatened the existence of the Union (2 Sam. 13–20). All this is told by a man who had been present at all these situations, with all the variety of graphic and intimate detail that bears the stamp of veracity on its face. He brings us finally into

[1] This and not Mephibosheth was his real name. For the corruption cf. footnote on p. 25.

the sick chamber of David and tells of the momentous things that were worked out there: Adonijah's and Solomon's struggle for the throne, and the last provisions of David, his testament in which he told his son how to deal with his enemies and his friends. The brutal measures by which Solomon established his throne by ridding himself most mercilessly of his opponents bring this story of the founding of the monarchy to a close, shedding at the end a most unexpected light on Solomon, the prince of peace of whom a later age believed that he shed no blood! (1 Ki. 1f.)

This story of the founding of the kingdom is an extremely able literary composition, well rounded and complete in itself, beginning with the conditions that necessitated a kingship in Israel and ending with its secure establishment under Solomon. If the priest Abiathar was its author, as has been suggested, he could draw on family history for the earlier portions, since he was a descendant of Eli, the last unhappy priest of Shiloh. For the Saul story he had his father Ahijah as authority, who as Saul's priest could tell him of Saul from direct, personal knowledge. But most vivid and detailed are the parts which he himself witnessed as David's priest, ending with Solomon's measures for securing his throne, of which he himself was a victim. The author told the story simply and plainly, he had no theory to propound or to prove, his interest was historical and biographical. The institution of the monarchy was to him a divine blessing in which he rejoiced. He loved David, but was not blind to his faults, and pictured not only the bright but also the dark side of his life. He never had any word of blame for David, nor for any of the others, everywhere he withheld his personal judgment. Perhaps this absence of historical criticism was a lack, but it was better that the facts interested him and that he told them without giving his own opinion of them than that he should have misled us by his criticism. Thus he could be so eminently fair to Saul and so objective in his story of David. Of course, in the selection of his material he shows to some extent his own convictions, but he does not force them on the reader. It was evident to him that there was a real connection between Amnon's rape and Absalom's rebellion. He showed how one led to the other. And he was right in this, but history, even political history, was all a matter of personal history to him. The great nexus of the social movements, the tribal and

separatist tendencies in this story and the driving forces in national
and international relations in other parts were not so important to
him as the story of the persons that made the history.   That he
wove the anecdotal together with the strictly historical was inevitable with such a view of historiography as his.   It does not
detract from his work, however, for most interesting material, embodying the views of the people of those days, has thus been preserved which illumines and vivifies the story.   That he had no
chronological system he could not help, for that was a later achievement.   One thing that strikes us in connection with his objective
manner is the unobtrusiveness of his religion.   The writer was a
pious man, to whom God and His righteous rule were realities.
Though He did not directly intervene by miracles, He was there
nevertheless, the silent background of all events, unobserved yet real.
This makes this author's history so attractive.   The innumerable
fascinating details in the many different situations which he tells
so well are true to life, and therefore so valuable.   His sense of
reality is refreshing.   One seeks in vain among the Babylonians
and Egyptians for a historical work of similar power and charm.
Only the Greeks have something equal to this.

A splendid beginning had thus been made for the prose literature
of Israel.   Its first historical narrative was of the highest value.
Others were sure to follow.   And indeed we learn from 1 Ki. 11 [41]
that there was a Book of the Acts of Solomon.   It was written by
an admirer of the king.   Well might the splendor, wealth, and power
of Solomon call forth an enthusiastic description of his reign.   Had
he not by his reorganization of the internal administration of the
kingdom; his wise utilization of the control of the caravan routes
that led from Egypt and Arabia to Phœnicia and Syria; his great
commercial undertakings as middleman and carrier; his commercial and political treaties with Egypt and Phœnicia, laid the foundation of the vast national wealth?   Had he not strengthened the military power by important fortifications, and given to the world an
exhibition of magnificent splendor in the building of the temple and
the palaces and in the maintenance of a brilliant court and harem
at Jerusalem?   Had not his wisdom become famous beyond the
frontiers of his country?   Unfortunately, the Book of the Acts of

Solomon is lost, and we only know that besides "all that he did" it told of "his wisdom." We may infer that the author of the Book of Kings took most of his material from it, but he worked it over in the interest of his own religious theory, and we can no longer reconstruct his source. The story of Solomon's dream at Gibeon, in which he prayed, "Give Thy servant an understanding heart to judge Thy people, that I may discern between good and evil, for who is able to judge this Thy great people?"; the famous Solomonic judgment in which he decided the question to whom the baby, which two women claimed, belonged by asking for a sword and commanding, "Divide the child in two, and give half to the one, and half to the other," — thereby infallibly discovering the real mother by her love, which would rather suffer the loss of the baby than consent to its death; the visit of the Queen of Sheba and her astonishment at Solomon's wealth and wisdom, which had seemed incredible to her before, but of which she now confessed, "The half was not told me"; all these tales were probably in the Book of the Acts of Solomon, and besides, his ever memorable deed of building the temple, his other building operations, and his internal administration and political activities. Historically most reliable information such as Solomon's provincial organization and system of taxation, his cession of twenty Galilean cities to King Hiram of Tyre, the rebellion of Hadad, Rezon, and Jeroboam, is accompanied by legends and anecdotes that cluster around his wisdom, wealth, and power. Such tales grow so quickly, often even during the lifetime of a great man, that it is never safe to say that they must be from much later days, and in spite of them it is probable that the Book of the Acts of Solomon was written not long after Solomon's death. It was a literary composition by a man who still had first-hand knowledge of Solomon's time, but did not sift the historically reliable and important from the legendary and unimportant. He was a religious man, to whom Solomon's wisdom was explicable only as a gift of God; he may have been a priest, especially if the particular description of the temple which is now incorporated in the Book of Kings and which shows great familiarity with the details of the temple was by him, but that is not so likely, for the author of the Book of Kings used here more probably an extract from the Annals of the Temple (cf. p. 44).

CHAPTER III

EARLY LAWS

HEBREW tradition attributes to Moses, the great founder of Israel's religion, the authorship of its entire legislation in the Pentateuch. That is impossible, for laws as a rule embody customs and grow gradually in history. As conditions change and insight deepens, customs vary and laws are modified. If a leader like David decides a matter differently from the usual way, and it commends itself to the judgment of the people by its fairness, it becomes henceforth a precedent with all the force of a law. Thus David changed the custom of dividing the booty and made his own arrangement "a statute and ordinance for Israel unto this day" (1 Sam. 30 21–25; cf. p. 25). And yet in Num. 31 25ff. Moses is credited with this law! Of course, an element of truth underlies the tradition that Moses gave the whole law to Israel. He had given the fundamental principles on which the entire legislation was built, the insistence on the exclusive worship of Yahweh as Israel's only God and on obedience to His will which refers especially to social morality within the nation. The whole subsequent development of religion in Israel presupposes these principles from the beginning.

The most famous formulation of them is contained in the Decalogue in Ex. 20 2–17 and Deut. 5 6–21. The ten original pithy sayings were later expounded and elaborated, and this commentary material is not altogether the same in Ex. 20 and Deut. 5. It is printed here in small type.

I am Yahweh thy God, who brought thee out of the land of Egypt, out of the house of bondage.

Thou shalt have no other gods before Me.

Thou shalt not make unto thee a graven image,

nor any likeness of any thing that is in heaven above, or that is in the earth beneath, or that is in the water under the earth: thou shalt not bow down thyself unto them, nor serve them; for I Yahweh thy God am a jealous God, visiting the iniquity of the fathers upon the children, upon the third and upon the fourth generation of them that hate Me, and showing lovingkindness unto thousands of them that love Me and keep My commandments.

Thou shalt not take the name of Yahweh thy God in vain:

for Yahweh will not hold him guiltless that takes His name in vain.

Remember the Sabbath day, to keep it holy.

Six days shalt thou labor, and do all thy work; but the seventh day is a Sabbath unto Yahweh thy God : in it thou shalt not do any work, thou, nor thy son, nor thy daughter, thy man-servant, nor thy maid-servant, nor thy cattle, nor thy stranger that is within thy gates : for in six days Yahweh made heaven and earth, the sea, and all that in them is, and rested the seventh day : wherefore Yahweh blessed the Sabbath day, and hallowed it.[1]

Honor thy father and thy mother,

that thy days may be long in the land which Yahweh thy God gives thee.

Thou shalt not kill.

Thou shalt not commit adultery.

Thou shalt not steal.

Thou shalt not bear false witness against thy neighbor.

Thou shalt not covet thy neighbor's house,[2]

thou shalt not covet thy neighbor's wife, nor his man-servant, nor his maid-servant, nor his ox, nor his ass, nor anything that is thy neighbor's.

Whether Moses ever formulated the principles of the religion of Yahweh in such pithy sentences we can neither dogmatically assert nor deny, although it is more likely that some successors did the formulating. In their present form they are certainly much later. In any case, Israel entered upon its historical career with the fundamental obligations of monolatry, that is, of worshipping Yahweh alone as its God, and of obedience to the will of God, which was principally social morality.

When they had settled in Canaan and lived in close contact with the Canaanites, whom they had by no means driven out or exterminated, the civilization and religion of Canaan influenced

---

[1] For this religious reason Deuteronomy has a social reason: "that thy man-servant and thy maid-servant may rest as well as thou. And thou shalt remember that thou wast a servant in the land of Egypt, and Yahweh thy God brought thee out thence by a mighty hand and by an outstretched arm : therefore Yahweh thy God commanded thee to keep the Sabbath day." This is thoroughly in line with the humane character of the Deuteronomic legislation.

[2] Deuteronomy puts the command "thou shalt not covet thy neighbor's wife" before "thou shalt not covet thy neighbor's house," thereby singling out the wife and elevating her from her former position of mere property. This is in line with Deuteronomy's attitude to women and is the result of a long development.

Israel profoundly. They passed from their half nomadic stage to the settled life of agriculture with its different and superior civilization. With the new order came new customs and new laws. Israel had had her own civil laws before, and some of them may have been given to them as precedents by Moses' decisions (cf. Ex. 18), but they did not meet all the new conditions. Here the Canaanites became her teachers. They had been under the sway of Babylonian law for centuries, and that is at least part of the reason why the civil and criminal law of Israel that came to be formulated in this early period of conquest is so much like the ancient Babylonian law of Hammurapi. It is contained in the so-called Book of the Covenant (Ex. 20 ^{22}–23 ^{19}), of which it forms the largest part (21 ^{1}–22 ^{17}). In view of Solomon's interest in all phases of civilization it is not venturesome to ascribe to him, the wise judge, the suggestion or command of the codification of the existing laws. The law code which was thus made was well thought out and carefully planned and arranged according to fundamental subjects. It is especially noteworthy that the code was not written from a priestly point of view. Civil law precedes religious law, and takes up by far the largest space. Of course, just as in Babylonia Hammurapi was represented as receiving the law from the sungod Shamash, so in Israel Moses was represented as receiving the law, both the civil and criminal, directly from God, and giving it to the people whom he bound by a sacred covenant to obedience to it. A thoughtful reading of the law with the supplied headings will show the careful plan and the systematic carrying out of certain fundamental legal principles by one controlling purposeful will, which modified and corrected the ancient customs and laws.

NOW THESE ARE THE ORDINANCES WHICH THOU SHALT SET BEFORE THEM

I. LAWS CONCERNING PERSONS

1. Personal Rights during Slavery

a. Men

If thou buy a Hebrew slave, six years he shall serve: and in the seventh he shall go out free for nothing.

If he come in by himself, he shall go out by himself: if he be married, then his wife shall go out with him.

If his master give him a wife, and she bear him sons or daughters; the wife and her children shall be her master's, and he shall go out by himself.

But if the slave shall plainly say, I love my master, my wife, and my children; I will not go out free: then his master shall bring him unto God, and shall bring him to the door, or unto the door-post;[1] and his master shall bore his ear through with an awl; and he shall serve him for ever.

b. Women

And if a man sell his daughter to be a slave, she shall not go out as the male slaves do.

If she please not her master, who has espoused her to himself, then shall he let her be redeemed: to sell her to a foreign people he shall have no power, because he has dealt deceitfully with her.

And if he espouse her to his son, he shall deal with her after the manner of daughters.

If he take for himself another wife; her food, her raiment, and her conjugal rights shall he not diminish. And if he do not these three things to her, then shall she go out for nothing, without money.

2. Laws Safeguarding Life and Limb

a. Homicide, Murder, Kidnapping

He that smites a man, so that he dies, shall surely be put to death.

And if a man lie not in wait, but God deliver him into his hand; then I will appoint a place whither he shall flee.

And if a man come presumptuously upon his neighbor, to slay him with guile; thou shalt take him from Mine altar, that he may die.

And he that smites his father, or his mother, shall be surely put to death.

And he that steals a man, and sells him, or if he be found in his hand, he shall surely be put to death.

And he that curses his father or his mother, shall surely be put to death.[2]

b. Assault and Battery

And if men contend, and one smite the other with a stone, or with his fist, and he die not, but keep his bed; if he rise again, and walk abroad upon his staff, then shall he that smote him be quit: only he shall pay for the loss of his time, and shall cause him to be thoroughly healed.

And if a man smite his male or his female slave with a rod, and he die under his hand; he shall surely be punished. Notwithstanding, if he continue to live a day or two, he shall not be punished: for he is his money.

And if men strive together, and hurt a woman with child, so that her fruit depart, and yet no harm follow; he shall be surely fined, according as the

---

[1] Apparently two customs are combined, one places the rite at the sanctuary, the other in the home.

[2] This assumes the terrible efficacy of the curse.

woman's husband shall lay upon him; and he shall pay for the miscarriage. But if any harm follow, then thou shalt give life for life, eye for eye, tooth for tooth, hand for hand, foot for foot, burning for burning, wound for wound, stripe for stripe.[1]

And if a man smite the eye of his servant, or the eye of his maid, and destroy it; he shall let him go free for his eye's sake. And if he smite out his man-servant's tooth, or his maid-servant's tooth; he shall let him go free for his tooth's sake.

c. Accidents and Contributory Negligence

And if an ox gore a man or a woman to death, the ox shall be surely stoned, and its flesh shall not be eaten; but the owner of the ox shall be acquitted.

But if the ox was wont to gore in time past, and it has been testified to its owner, and he has not kept it in, but it has killed a man or a woman; the ox shall be stoned, and its owner also shall be put to death.

If there be laid on him a ransom, then he shall give for the redemption of his life whatsoever is laid upon him.

Whether it have gored a son, or have gored a daughter, according to this judgment shall it be done to him.

If the ox gore a male or female slave, there shall be given to their master thirty shekels of silver, and the ox shall be stoned.

II. Laws of Property

1. Accidents to Animals

And if a man shall open a pit, or if a man shall dig a pit and not cover it, and an ox or an ass fall therein, the owner of the pit shall make it good; he shall give the price of it to its owner, and the dead beast shall be his.

And if one man's ox hurt another's, so that it dies, then they shall sell the live ox, and divide the price of it; and the dead also they shall divide. Or if it be known that the ox was wont to gore in time past, and its owner has not kept it in; he shall surely pay ox for ox, and the dead beast shall be his own.

2. Theft of Animals

If a man shall steal an ox, or a sheep, and kill it, or sell it; he shall pay five oxen for an ox, and four sheep for a sheep.

If the thief be found breaking in, and be smitten so that he dies, there shall be no bloodguiltiness for him. If the sun be risen upon him, there shall be bloodguiltiness for him.

He shall make restitution: if he have nothing, then he shall be sold for his theft.

If the theft be found in his hand alive, whether it be ox, or ass, or sheep; he shall pay double.

[1] This is the classic formulation of the *lex talionis*.

3. Damage to Fields and Vineyards

If a man cause a field or vineyard to be burnt, and shall let the burning spread, and it burn another man's field; of the best of his own field, and of the best of his own vineyard, shall he make restitution.

If fire spread, and catch in thorns, so that the shocks of grain, or the standing grain, or the field are consumed; he that kindled the fire shall surely make restitution.

4. Loss of or Injury to Property

a. *Money or Other Property Held in Trust*

If a man shall deliver to his neighbor money or stuff to keep, and it be stolen out of the man's house; if the thief be found, he shall pay double. If the thief be not found, then the master of the house shall come near to God, to see whether he have not put his hand to his neighbor's goods. For every matter of trespass, whether it be for ox, for ass, for sheep, for raiment, or for any manner of lost thing, of which one says, This is it, the cause of both parties shall come before God; he whom God shall condemn shall pay double to his neighbor.

b. *Animals Kept for the Owner*

If a man deliver to his neighbor an ass, or an ox, or a sheep, or any beast, to keep; and it die, or be hurt, no man seeing it: the oath of Yahweh shall decide between them both, whether he has not put his hand to his neighbor's goods; and its owner shall accept it, and he shall not make restitution. But if it be stolen from him, he shall make restitution to its owner. If it be torn in pieces, let him bring it for witness; he shall not make good that which was torn.

c. *Borrowed or Hired Property*

And if a man borrow anything of his neighbor, and it be hurt, or die, its owner not being with it, he shall surely make restitution.

If its owner be with it, he shall not make it good, if it be a hired thing, it came for its hire.[1]

d. *Seduction of a Virgin*

And if a man entice a virgin that is not betrothed, and lie with her, he shall surely pay a dowry for her to be his wife. If her father utterly refuse to give her to him, he shall pay money according to the dowry of virgins.

In the next section (22 [18–31]) Social and Religious Laws are given. They are different in their formulation. While the civil law had been presented in the form of case law with the formula, "if" a man does so and so, then so and so shall be done to him, and similarly in

---

[1] *Or*, if it be a hired servant, it (the damage) goes to his hire.

the detailed specifications, if such and such a particular occurs in connection with the case, then such and such is to be done, the religious and social laws are phrased, as a rule but not always, in the categorical formula "thou shalt" or " thou shalt not," or "he that" does so and so.   The section is a little disarranged.   This may be an indication that it was added to the original law code later on, or the dislocation may have been purely accidental.   Certainly the religious laws belong together, that is to say, the prohibition of blasphemy should follow the law against sacrificing to any other god. And the law of kindness to the enemy's ox or ass belongs with the social laws.   In the following the original order has been restored.

III. Social Laws

1. Honest Administration of Justice

Thou shalt not take up (on thy lips) a false report; nor make common cause with him that is in the wrong by becoming an unrighteous witness (on his behalf).   Thou shalt not follow a majority to do evil; neither shalt thou bear witness in a cause to turn aside after a majority to wrest justice: neither shalt thou favor a poor man in his cause.

Thou shalt not wrest the justice due to thy poor in his cause.

Keep thee far from a false matter; and the innocent and righteous slay thou not: and do not justify the wicked.   And thou shalt take no bribe: for a bribe blinds the open-eyed, and perverts the cause of the righteous.

2. Justice to the Defenceless Classes

And a sojourner shalt thou not oppress: for ye know the heart of a sojourner, seeing ye were sojourners in the land of Egypt.

Ye shall not afflict any widow, or fatherless child.   If thou afflict them at all, and they cry at all to Me, I will surely hear their cry; and My wrath shall wax hot, and I will kill you with the sword; and your wives shall be widows, and your children fatherless.

3. Considerate Treatment of the Debtor

If thou lend money to any of My people with thee that is poor, thou shalt not be to him as a creditor; neither shall ye lay upon him interest.   If thou at all take thy neighbor's garment to pledge, thou shalt restore it to him before the sun goes down: for that is his only covering, it is his garment for his skin: wherein shall he sleep? and it shall come to pass, when he cries to Me, that I will hear; for I am gracious.

4. Kindness to the Enemy's Animals

If thou meet thine enemy's ox or his ass going astray, thou shalt surely bring it back to him again.   Thou shalt not see the ass of him that hates thee lying under his burden, and forbear to help him; thou shalt surely help him.

The conditions to which this law corresponds are those of the premonarchic period. Israel was settled in Canaan and had passed on to the stage of agriculture; they raised of course also cattle and asses and sheep. The land was not communal but individual property. Workmen hired themselves out, and cattle also were rented for agricultural purposes. Money was not yet the common means of exchange, although it was used; natural products were given and taken as a rule. The king is nowhere mentioned. The judicial function lay in the hands of the community of all free citizens. There were no professional judges, usually the elders served as arbiters. The law warns against intimidation or bribery by the rich and powerful, and favoritism towards them, but also against partiality for the poor. There were no police or prisons in those days. The punishment was either corporal or the imposition of a fine. The execution of the judgment was left to the winning party. In cases of murder the *goel* or next-of-kin was obliged to secure vengeance. Revenge in its ancient, unrestricted form, as we saw it in the Song of Lamech (p. 2), has given way to the so-called *lex talionis*, the law which decrees like for like, " an eye for an eye," etc. The right of asylum is granted to the man slayer but refused to the murderer, who may even be torn from the altar. Some fines are fixed by the injured party, but in some cases arbitration is resorted to, in order that an excessive fine be avoided. If any cases could not be decided by evidence or testimony, they were settled by an oath of the accused at the sanctuary. The efficacy of the oath or curse (for an oath involved cursing oneself in case of guilt) was not doubted by any one. The curse was believed to have terrible power. He that cursed his father or mother was put to death, for he had set free forces that would accomplish the desired end in a magic but very real way. It was not necessary to state expressly what would be done to a man who refused to accept the judicial verdict, because he could not remain in the fellowship of the community. The band of outlaws of whom David became captain was composed of such fugitives from justice. They could not be apprehended and thrown into prison, because there were no prisons, but they had punished themselves by their flight and their self-imposed excommunication. It is significant that such social laws as those of kindness to debtors or justice to and kind treatment of widows, orphans, and strangers were left to the individual conscience.   The only sanction behind them is religious, Yahweh is the protector of these defenceless classes.   There is nobody else to enforce such laws.   Yet they belong to the finest parts of the entire law code, especially also the prohibition against taking interest on loans from poor fellow Israelites.   This was not due to sentimentalism, for the consistent upholding of this law also in the later law codes of the Old Testament shows that Israel was deliberately opposed to the custom of taking interest from fellow tribesmen.   It is therefore not an indication of the primitive stage of civilization in which all tribesmen are brothers and as such obliged to help each other in need.   In their marital relation, however, the Israelites were on a low plane.   The fact that the marital law in this code is immediately joined to the slave law is in itself significant. There was only one distinction between selling a girl to a man as a wife or as a slave, for the latter was expected to share his couch too. It was that the man could sell the slave again to other Israelites, but not the wife, whom he could divorce at any time he pleased but not sell.   A wife was part of a man's property, which he acquired by buying.   The deflowering of a virgin is therefore treated in connection with offences against property.   The seducer must either pay the dowry and marry her, or if the father refuse, he must simply pay the dowry, as a compensation of the lessened value of the girl![1]

The final section (23 $^{10-19}$) forms an appendix which contains the religious laws.   The laws dealing with idolatry and the altar, which are now prefixed to the Book of the Covenant in 20 $^{23-26}$, belong with these.   It is significant that they are now so arranged as to frame the code on either side, so that the religious laws enclose the others. But that was not the intention of the original codifiers.   In the parallel Ex. 34 $^{17ff.}$ the prohibition of making molten gods is directly connected with the cultic laws (cf. also 23 ^{13}).

IV. RELIGIOUS LAWS

1. Images

Ye shall not make other gods with Me; gods of silver, or gods of gold, ye shall not make to you.

---

[1] This indicates the immense progress that was made by Deuteronomy in treating the wife not as a part of a man's property but as a person, when it put the commandment "thou shalt not covet thy neighbor's wife" by itself (cf. p. 31).

2. The Altar

An altar of earth thou shalt make for Me, and shalt sacrifice thereon thy burnt-offerings, and thy peace-offerings, thy sheep, and thine oxen: in every place where I record My name I will come unto thee and I will bless thee. And if thou make Me an altar of stone, thou shalt not build it of hewn stones; for if thou lift up thy tool upon it, thou hast polluted it. Neither shalt thou go up by steps to Mine altar, that thy nakedness be not uncovered thereon.

3. Sorcery, Perverseness, Sacrifices to other Gods, Blasphemy

Thou shalt not suffer a sorceress to live.
Whosoever lies with a beast shall surely be put to death.
He that sacrifices to any god, except to Yahweh only, shall be banned.
Thou shalt not revile God, nor curse a ruler of thy people.

4. Cultic Laws

a. *Firstfruits and Firstborn*

Thou shalt not delay to offer the firstfruits of thy threshing floor and of thy winepress.
The firstborn of thy sons shalt thou give to Me.
Likewise shalt thou do with thine oxen, and with thy sheep: seven days it shall be with its dam; on the eighth day thou shalt give it to Me.

b. *Unclean Food*

And ye shall be holy men to Me: therefore ye shall not eat any flesh that is torn of beasts in the field; ye shall cast it to the dogs.

c. *The Sabbath Year*

And six years thou shalt sow thy land, and shalt gather in its increase: but the seventh year thou shalt let it rest and lie fallow, that the poor of thy people may eat: and what they leave the beast of the field shall eat. In like manner thou shalt deal with thy vineyard, and with thy oliveyard.

d. *The Sabbath*

Six days thou shalt do thy work, and on the seventh day thou shalt rest; that thine ox and thine ass may have rest, and the son of thy handmaid, and the sojourner, may be refreshed.

5. Monolatry

And in all things that I have said to you take ye heed: and make no mention of the name of other gods, neither let it be heard out of thy mouth.

The parallel to the concluding laws (23 [14-19]) which is found in Ex. 34 [10-26] has received much attention since Goethe thought that he had discovered here another decalogue, which some have regarded not only as older than the moral decalogue of Ex. 20, but even

as going back to Moses himself. It is now introduced and interwoven by commentary matter which in the following is printed in
small type. At the end the parallels appear side by side.

And He said, Behold, I make a covenant: before all thy people I will do marvels,
such as have not been wrought in all the earth, nor in any nation; and all the people
among which thou art shall see the work of Yahweh; for it is a terrible thing that I
do with thee.

Observe thou that which I command thee this day: behold, I drive out before
thee the Amorite, and the Canaanite, and the Hittite, and the Perizzite, and the Hivite,
and the Jebusite. Take heed to thyself, lest thou make a covenant with the inhabitants
of the land whither thou goest, lest it be for a snare in the midst of thee: but ye shall
break down their altars, and dash in pieces their pillars, and ye shall cut down their
Asherim,

for thou shalt worship no other god:

for Yahweh, whose name is Jealous, is a jealous God; lest thou make a covenant
with the inhabitants of the land, and they play the harlot after their gods, and sacrifice unto their gods, and one invite thee and thou eat of his sacrifice; and thou take of
their daughters for thy sons, and their daughters play the harlot after their gods, and
make thy sons play the harlot after their gods.

Thou shalt make thee no molten gods.

Three times thou shalt keep a feast
unto Me in the year:

The feast of unleavened bread shalt thou keep: seven days thou shalt eat unleavened bread, as I commanded thee, at the time appointed in the month Abib, for in it thou camest out from Egypt.	The feast of unleavened bread shalt thou keep. Seven days thou shalt eat unleavened bread, as I commanded thee, at the time appointed in the month Abib; for in the month Abib thou camest out from Egypt.
	All that opens the womb is Mine; and all thy cattle that is male, the firstlings of cow and sheep. And the firstling of an ass thou shalt redeem with a lamb: and if thou wilt not redeem it, then thou shalt break its neck. All the firstborn of thy sons thou shalt redeem.
And none shall appear before Me empty:	And none shall appear before Me empty.
	Six days thou shalt work, but on the seventh day thou shalt rest: in ploughing time and in harvest thou shalt rest.

and the feast of harvest, the first-fruits of thy labors, which thou sowest in the field: and the feast of ingathering, at the end of the year, when thou gatherest in thy labors out of the field.

Three times in the year all thy males shall appear before the Lord Yahweh.

Thou shalt not offer the blood of My sacrifice with leavened bread; neither shall the fat of My feast remain all night until the morning.

The first of the firstfruits of thy ground thou shalt bring to the house of thy God.

Thou shalt not boil a kid in its mother's milk.

And thou shalt observe the feast of weeks, even of the firstfruits of wheat harvest, and the feast of ingathering at the year's end.

Three times in the year all thy males shall appear before the Lord Yahweh, the God of Israel.

For I will cast out nations before thee, and enlarge thy borders: neither shall any man desire thy land, when thou goest up to appear before Yahweh thy God three times in the year.

Thou shalt not offer the blood of My sacrifice with leavened bread; neither shall the sacrifice of the feast of the passover be left unto the morning.

The first of the firstfruits of thy ground thou shalt bring to the house of Yahweh thy God.

Thou shalt not boil a kid in its mother's milk.

The sentences immediately following have been the cause of the never ending search for the original decalogue in the foregoing, although in the nature of the case there can be no agreement on the ten laws which are believed to constitute it.

And Yahweh said to Moses, Write thou these words: for after the tenor of these words I have made a covenant with thee and with Israel.

And he was there with Yahweh forty days and forty nights without eating bread or drinking water. And he wrote upon the tables the words of the covenant, [the ten commandments].

The final words "the ten commandments" are a later addition by one who believed that it was the decalogue that was originally written on the two tables of stone and not, as the author of Ex. 34 held, the Book of the Covenant.

The law against image worship may originally have been intended as a protest against the golden bulls which Jeroboam made for the temples at Bethel and Dan, and the law of the primitive altar against the artificial altars in Solomon's temple. But the laws may also be earlier, for the temptation to idolatry and to beautiful altars was present from the beginning of Israel's stay in Canaan. The Canaanites influenced the religion of Israel as well as their civilization. Some of their customs and beliefs Israel could not accept. But they took over from them the various sacred places, where the deity was believed to dwell and which had been hallowed by age-long worship, with the paraphernalia of worship, and the great annual agricultural festivals, the feast of Unleavened Bread at the beginning and the feast of Weeks at the end of the grain harvest in the spring and early summer — Easter and Pentecost, and the feast of Tabernacles at the end of the vintage and fruit harvest in the fall — the great thanksgiving feast. Only the first, the Maṣṣoth festival, is reinterpreted in our code and connected with the exodus from Egypt, when the haste of the departure prevented the Israelites from leavening their bread. Originally the unleavened bread had nothing to do with this; it was the firstfruit of the new harvest eaten before God. The new barley must not be mixed with any leaven of the old because there must be no trace of decay in the new gift of life.

The law of the altar, given above as the second of the religious laws (p. 39) is of fundamental importance for the true understanding of the development of Israel's religion. There was at first not one single sanctuary which alone was legitimate, but there were many local sanctuaries, which were called "high places" and which everybody frequented. They had formerly been the sacred places of the Canaanites, now they belonged to Israel, who worshipped Yahweh there. In spite of all these adoptions from Canaanite religious elements the religion of Yahweh remained victorious; it assimilated Canaanite religion as far as it was not altogether incompatible with Yahwism, the rest it rejected and overcame. It was too strong to be conquered in this fight between the two religions. This ancient cultic law is evidence of its triumphant strength.

CHAPTER IV

THE GROWTH OF HISTORICAL LITERATURE

THE institution of a royal and national government necessitated the keeping of the records of all important events. Already under David the royal scribe and the king's "remembrancer" are mentioned, and they may have been in charge of the Royal Annals. After the division of the kingdom, Israel and Judah kept separate annals. How much more we would know of the history, if they had been preserved to us, for they would be the most valuable historical sources! One of the later historians, the author of the Books of Kings, made use of them and incorporated a number of excerpts from them in his own work.[1] These annals recorded the events of the various reigns from year to year, very much like the Assyrian and Babylonian Royal Annals. The style was that of the actuary, dry, careful, and reliable, as the following extract from the Annals of Judah indicates:

And it came to pass in the fifth year of King Rehoboam, that Shishak king of Egypt came up against Jerusalem; and he took away the treasures of the house of Yahweh, and the treasures of the king's house; he even took away all: and he took away all the shields of gold which Solomon had made. And King Rehoboam made in their stead shields of brass, and committed them to the hands of the captains of the guard, who kept the door of the king's house. And it was so, that, as oft as the king went into the house of Yahweh, the guard bore them, and brought them back into the guard-chamber. (1 Ki. 14 [25-28])

The collection of such facts in these annals was not historical literature, but it supplied the sources for the historian. It enabled him to grasp the trend of the history of successive periods and provided the materials for a chronology which had hitherto been lacking. We shall see how the author of the history of the kingdoms of Israel and Judah used these annals in connection with the Books of Kings.

[1] He took from them such statistics as the summary of the wars of David in 2 Sam. 8; the catalogue of his generals and courtiers in 2 Sam. 20 [23-26] 21 [15-22] 23 [9-39]; and the list of his wives and sons in 2 Sam. 3 [2-5] 5 [13-16]. For Solomon and the other kings there were similar lists and brief summaries of the important events.

A parallel book of official records was prepared by the priests of the temple in Jerusalem. From the beginning they chronicled year after year the important events of the temple. And they were many, for the temple stood in the centre of the religious life of the nation; all great undertakings and especially all wars were consecrated here, trophies were brought to it, tribute was taken from it. Like the Royal Annals the records of the Temple Annals rested on contemporaneous knowledge, and they were therefore invaluable for the history and administration of the temple. But they also perished in the great conflagration that destroyed the temple and city in 586 B.C. Not long before, the author of the Books of Kings had made some excerpts from them, as we judge from certain of his stories that reveal such intimate knowledge of the temple that we may well believe that they were taken from these contemporaneous records of the priests who were most deeply interested in them: the stories of the building of the temple by Solomon (1 Ki. 6f.) ; of the rebellion in the temple against Athaliah (2 Ki. 11) ; of the repairs of the temple under Jehoash (2 Ki. 12 4–16) ; of the new brazen altar which Ahaz imported from Damascus (2 Ki. 16 10–18) ; and probably of Josiah's reformation (2 Ki. 23 3ff.). They do not differ from the stories excerpted from the Royal Annals except in subject matter, and they might all have been taken from them rather than from special Temple Records, for the temple occupied a large place in the life of the little Kingdom of Judah ever since Solomon's reign, and the Temple Records are nowhere referred to by the author of the Book of Kings. But there are good reasons for assuming their existence.

Extremely valuable as the Royal Annals and the Temple Records were, they did not treat of all the phases of the life of the people. They probably did not even mention the religious crisis of the ninth century about which a prophetic author wrote in the Elijah Stories soon after the death of the great prophet.[1] And yet this crisis was the result of politics and was destined to lead to the overthrow of the dynasty of Omri. The stories themselves are of the greatest possible significance. Ahab had married the princess Jezebel of Tyre in order to cement the political and commercial

[1] They are now incorporated in 1 Ki. 17–19. 21.

relations between Israel and Phœnicia.   It was an act of political wisdom.   But Jezebel, a woman of strong personality, had not
given up her native religion, but had brought Baal priests and
prophets with her in order that she might worship the Baal of Tyre
in her accustomed manner in the sanctuary which Ahab erected for
her in Samaria.   She seems to have used her influence over the court
so effectually that a number of people worshipped the Tyrian Baal
with her.   But that she made her royal husband an apostate from
the religion of Yahweh, as the author of the Books of Kings would
have us believe, is opposed to our best information.   The danger
of Baalism had always been present with Israel in Canaan, and the
religion of the local deities had strongly influenced them.   But they
were insignificant compared with the national God Yahweh.   Now,
however, with the introduction of the powerful Baal of Tyre, the
crisis came, for it meant either Baal or Yahweh in the end.   This
was at least the conviction of the champion of Yahweh, whose very
name Elijah (= *Yahweh is God!*) rang out the challenge and embodied the watchword of the fight.   Suddenly, like a bolt out of a
clear sky, he appeared before Ahab and announced in the name of
Yahweh, the God of Israel, a drought that would last three years.
As abruptly as he had appeared, he vanished.   And the drought
came and reduced the land to terrible straits.   This in itself was a
sign of Baal's impotence, for if he really were God, and more especially the God of Fertility, he could have averted the calamity quite
easily.   Yet no use is made of this argument, apparently in order
that the decisive contest between Yahweh and Baal might be presented with the greatest possible effectiveness in the Carmel story
of which Elijah's announcement of the drought forms only the prelude.   But that is skilfully retarded by the interesting miracle tales
of Elijah which fill the three years of drought: his feeding by the
ravens at the brook Cherith; his reward of the widow at Zarephath
in Phœnicia by providing that "the jar of meal did not waste nor the
cruise of oil fail"; and his raising of her son who had died during the
prophet's stay at the widow's home.   Such miracle tales do not add
for us anything at all to the moral and spiritual grandeur of Elijah,
but they show how the people of his time were impressed by the
tremendous power of his personality: to this man of God nothing was
impossible, he could even restore the dead to life, God worked His

miracles through him and for him! When the drought was nearing its end, Elijah met King Ahab, who greeted him with the words, "Is it thou, thou troubler of Israel?" but did not dare to touch him although he had tried for three years to apprehend him! Brushing aside this accusation, Elijah proposed that all Israel and the four hundred and fifty prophets of Baal (and of Asherah, Baal's consort) should meet on Mount Carmel. What followed is told with such dramatic power that only the ancient narrator's own words can do justice to it. When the people were all assembled, Elijah reproved them.

How long go ye limping between the two sides? If Yahweh be God, follow Him; but if Baal, then follow him. And the people answered him not a word. Then said Elijah to the people, I, even I only, am left a prophet of Yahweh; but Baal's prophets are four hundred and fifty men. Let them therefore give us two bullocks; and let them choose one bullock for themselves, and cut it in pieces, and lay it on the wood, and put no fire under; and I will dress the other bullock, and lay it on the wood, and put no fire under. And call ye on the name of your god, and I will call on the name of Yahweh: and the God that answers by fire, let him be God. And all the people answered and said, It is well spoken.

And Elijah said to the prophets of Baal, Choose one bullock for yourselves, and dress it first; for you are many; and call on the name of your god, but put no fire under. And they took the bullock, and they dressed it, and called on the name of Baal from morning even until noon, saying, O Baal, answer us! But there was no voice, nor any that answered. And they limped [1] about the altar which they had made.

And it came to pass at noon, that Elijah mocked them, and said, Cry aloud; for he is a god: either he is musing, or he is gone aside, or he is on a journey, or peradventure he sleeps and must be awaked.

And they cried aloud, and cut themselves after their manner with swords and lances, till the blood gushed out upon them.[2] And it was so, when midday was past, that they raved in prophetic ecstasy until the time of the offering of the evening oblation; but there was neither voice, nor any to answer, nor any that regarded.

And Elijah said to all the people, Come near to me; and all the people came near to him. And he repaired the altar of Yahweh that was thrown down. And with the stones he built an altar in the name of Yahweh; and he made a trench about the altar, as great as would be sown with two measures of seed.

---

[1] They performed a cultic dance.

[2] A primitive rite in which the suppliant offers of his own blood to the deity whether as a substitute for human sacrifice, or to come into more intimate union with the deity, or to awaken pity depends on the circumstances. Here probably the last.

And he put the wood in order, and cut the bullock in pieces, and laid it on the wood. And he said, Fill four jars with water, and pour it on the burnt-offering, and on the wood; and they did so. And he said, Do it the second time; and they did it the second time. And he said, Do it the third time; and they did it the third time. And the water ran round about the altar; and he filled the trench also with water. And it came to pass at the time of the offering of the evening oblation, that Elijah the prophet came near, and said, O Yahweh, the God of Abraham, of Isaac, and of Israel, let it be known this day that Thou art God in Israel, and that I am Thy servant, and that I have done all these things at Thy word. Hear me, O Yahweh, hear me, that this people may know that Thou, Yahweh, art God, and that Thou hast turned their heart back again. Then the fire of Yahweh fell, and consumed the burnt-offering, and the wood, and the stones, and the dust, and licked up the water that was in the trench. And when all the people saw it, they fell on their faces: and they said, Yahweh, He is God; Yahweh, He is God! And Elijah said to them, Take the prophets of Baal; let not one of them escape. And they took them; and Elijah brought them down to the brook Kishon, and slew them there.

And Elijah said to Ahab, Get thee up, eat and drink; for there is the sound of abundance of rain. So Ahab went up to eat and to drink. And Elijah went up to the top of Carmel; and he bowed himself down upon the earth, and put his face between his knees. And he said to his servant, Go up now, look toward the sea. And he went up, and looked, and said, There is nothing. And he said, Go again. And the servant went seven times. And it came to pass at the seventh time, that he said, Behold, there arises a cloud out of the sea, as small as a man's hand. And he said, Go up, say to Ahab, Make ready thy chariot, and get thee down, that the rain stop thee not. And it came to pass in a little while, that the heavens grew black with clouds and wind, and there was a great rain. And Ahab rode, and went to Jezreel: and the hand of Yahweh was on Elijah; and he girded up his loins, and ran before Ahab to the entrance of Jezreel. (1 Ki. 18 $^{21-46}$)

Yahweh had triumphed. He alone is God. To Elijah the struggle between the gods was a conflict of principles, between the nature religion of Baal and the moral religion of Yahweh. Baal was no real God to Elijah; a man who could mock Baal, as he did, could not believe in his reality and power. This fundamental principle of Moses was here reiterated with extraordinary power and effectiveness: Yahweh alone is to be worshipped in Israel! But not only because He is Israel's God, but because He alone is real, because He alone demonstrates His reality by His activity. This had become clear to Elijah by contrasting Yahweh and Baal. The question of other gods besides Baal did not present itself to him. If it had, we may be sure that his answer would have been the same, for in principle the question had been decided. Thus Elijah had passed beyond Moses. He was far on the way to monotheism, although he did not yet reach it.

The next story is not the sequel but really a parallel to this, although it is at present connected by Jezebel's threat to Elijah that she would kill him for his slaughter of Baal prophets.[1] The great man fled for his life and hastened to Mount Horeb to seek Yahweh where He had appeared of old to Moses. There was no trace of victory in his soul, only utter despair. In the strength of miraculously provided food he walked through the wilderness forty days and nights until he came to the cave on Mount Horeb, and stood upon the mountain.

> And, behold, Yahweh passed by, and a great and strong wind rent the mountains, and broke in pieces the rocks before Yahweh; but Yahweh was not in the wind: and after the wind an earthquake; but Yahweh was not in the earthquake: and after the earthquake a fire; but Yahweh was not in the fire: and after the fire the sound of a soft stillness. And when Elijah heard it, he wrapped his face in his mantle, and went out, and stood in the entrance of the cave. And, behold, a voice came to him, and said, What doest thou here, Elijah? And he said, I have been very jealous for Yahweh, the God of hosts; for the children of Israel have forsaken Thy covenant, thrown down Thine altars, and slain Thy prophets with the sword; and I, even I only, am left; and they seek my life, to take it away. (1 Ki. 19 [11-14])

The tempest, earthquake, and fire were the heralds of Yahweh, the awe-inspiring, terrible God. The deep calm that ensued was not symbolic of the gentleness of God, for He spoke to Elijah not kindly, gentle, gracious words of love but words of fearful import that were far more like the tempest, earthquake, and fire than like the gentle stillness.

> And Yahweh said to him, Go, return on thy way to the wilderness of Damascus: and when thou comest, thou shalt anoint Hazael to be king over Syria; and Jehu the son of Nimshi shalt thou anoint to be king over Israel; and Elisha the son of Shaphat of Abelmeholah shalt thou anoint to be prophet in thy room. And it shall come to pass, that him that escapes from the sword of Hazael shall Jehu slay; and him that escapes from the sword of Jehu shall Elisha slay. Yet will I leave seven thousand in Israel, all the knees which have not bowed to Baal, and every mouth which has not kissed him. (1 Ki. 19 [15-18])

Yahweh is terribly jealous, He will not tolerate the worship of Baal. He will punish His apostate people unsparingly through Hazael,

---

[1] Probably the Greek version has preserved the original beginning, "If thou art Elijah, I am Jezebel!"

Jehu, and Elisha, until only a faithful remnant is left. The loyalty of His people is more important to Him than its power and prosperity. Moreover, to this prophet's thought Yahweh's dominion is not confined to Israel. Thus Elijah broke down part of the national limitations of Yahweh. He sees the God of Israel using as His instrument Syria, where His agent is to be enthroned. To Elijah Yahweh directs the movements of history and not only those of Israel. But God's purpose has not yet been achieved, Elijah has not yet won a decisive victory for Him, nor will this prophet be the instrument of victory after all. Nevertheless in the end the divine purpose will be accomplished, and Elijah is to summon the human agents to complete the work. On his return from Horeb he met Elisha ploughing with twelve oxen and threw his mantle over him, thereby compelling him with magic power to follow him. Elisha could only say good-by to his parents and eat a farewell meal with his people from the oxen, which he quickly slaughtered; then he left everything and everybody dear to him and became Elijah's servant. Renunciation of family ties was a prerequisite for his discipleship! The other two agents, Hazael and Jehu, were not secured by the great Tishbite, but by Elisha and one of his disciples.

In another story Elijah appears as the champion of social justice. Naboth, a prominent citizen of Jezreel, had a vineyard adjoining the royal palace. Ahab wanted it but could not prevail upon Naboth to sell or exchange it, because it was an ancient family possession. Jezebel, with diplomatic skill and cold-hearted cruelty, had the elders of Jezreel proclaim a fast, put Naboth at the head of the people, accuse him through bribed witnesses of blasphemy against God and the king, and stone him to death, so that Ahab could confiscate the vineyard for the crown. Just as the king was about to take possession of it, Elijah appeared, the incarnate conscience of Israel, the spokesman of Yahweh. Impatiently Ahab exclaimed, "Hast thou found me, O mine enemy?" And he answered, "I have found thee! Hast thou killed and also taken possession? Thus says Yahweh, In the place where dogs licked the blood of Naboth shall dogs lick thy blood, even thine." [1] Yahweh's

---

[1] This brief prophecy was later expanded (1 Ki. 21 20b–26) to include the whole family of Ahab, and a still later hand added that Ahab humbled himself before Yahweh and that therefore this threatened extermination occurred not in Ahab's but in his son's days.

demand of righteousness is absolute, it is binding on king and peas-
ant alike.   That was a principle which had been written into the
very foundation of Yahweh's religion by Moses.

The other principle that Yahweh was to be worshipped alone,
Elijah once more reiterated, when King Ahaziah sent to the famous
healer Baalzebub [1] the god of Ekron for help after he had fallen
through the window of his upper chamber.   Elijah met the messengers with the stern command,

> Go, turn again to the king that sent you, and say to him, Thus says Yahweh,
> Is it because there is no God in Israel, that thou sendest to inquire of Baal-
> zebub, the god of Ekron? therefore thou shalt not come down from the bed
> whither thou art gone up, but shalt surely die.[2]   (2 Ki. 1 6)

All these Elijah stories are legends which the people told about
this spiritual hero, whom tradition ranks only second to Moses among
all the great ones of Israel.   That does not mean that they were
simply invented, for they contain many historical elements, although
it is often difficult to draw the line between fact and fiction, and they
give us perhaps a truer picture of the greatness of the prophet
than a strictly historical, matter-of-fact presentation could have
done.   Here the impression that this moral and spiritual giant made
upon his people is given; their enthusiasm and admiration have
idealized, heightened, and enlarged his personality, and yet their
interpretation showed the deepest insight, because it was born out
of affection and awe.   Such was the prophet as he lived in their memories.   And truly, the moral and spiritual insight revealed in these
tales, the emphasis on exclusive worship of Yahweh, who in contrast
to Baal was the only real God; the insistence on the demand of
social justice as absolute; and the enlargement of the dominion of
Yahweh, who directs history and uses even foreign nations for His
purposes, these truths belonged to the master before the disciple

---

[1] Baalzebub was the god of flies, as his name shows (*baal* = lord, *zebub* = fly).
Flies, just as mice (cf. p. 22), were regarded by the ancients as carriers of diseases.
The fly god brought them on or drove them away, he brought diseases and healed them.
In the time of Jesus Baalzebub or Beelzebub had become so important that he had
attained the rank of the prince of the demons.

[2] A later hand added the strange story of Elijah's sending fire upon two companies
of fifty soldiers with their captains who had been despatched to apprehend him.   The
third captain implored him for his own and his soldiers' lives, whereupon he went with
him and told the king the same that he had told the messengers.

wrote them down.   We may be sure that the pupil was not greater than his teacher.

Some decades later a collection of Elisha Stories was made which is now incorporated in 2 Ki. 2–8. 13 [14-21]. In the first of these Elijah has grown to almost superhuman stature.   He was too great to die!   Elijah and Elisha were walking for the last time together.

> And Elisha said, I pray thee, let a double portion of thy spirit be upon me. And he said, Thou hast asked a hard thing: nevertheless, if thou see me when I am taken from thee, it shall be so unto thee; but if not, it shall not be so. And it came to pass, as they still went on, and talked, that, behold, there appeared a chariot of fire, and horses of fire, which parted them both asunder; and Elijah went up by a whirlwind into heaven.   And Elisha saw it, and he cried, My father, my father, the chariots of Israel and the horsemen thereof! (2 Ki. 2 [10-12])

Elisha had seen and became chief heir!   The mantle of Elijah was his too, and with it he smote the waters of Jordan so that he could pass through!   To the other prophets who had seen it, this was proof enough that Elijah's spirit rested on Elisha.   With a miracle he had begun his career and soon one followed upon another.   The Saint endowed with heavenly power walked among the people who told story after story of this great man of God: how he healed the water at Jericho by throwing salt into it, saying, "Thus says Yahweh, I have healed these waters: there shall not be from thence any more death or miscarrying"; how he punished young lads, who had called after him, "Go up, thou bald head!" by bringing two she-bears upon them out of the woods through his curse; how he helped a poor widow from the fate of having her two children sold because of her debts by miraculously filling vessel after vessel with the oil of a single pot; how he rewarded a kindly and rich but childless Shunamite woman for her hospitality to him by promising her a son and later by restoring the little lad to life when he had died from sun-stroke; how he averted death from some sons of the prophets, who had eaten poisonous pottage, by throwing some meal into the pot; how he fed a hundred men with but twenty loaves of bread; how he healed Naaman the Syrian general from his leprosy; how he helped some disciples of his to recover an axe-head that had fallen into the Jordan by making the iron to swim; how horses and chariots of fire protected him from the Syrian soldiers who had been sent to apprehend him and how upon his request Yahweh smote the Syrians with blindness so that he could lead them into a trap; how he foresaw and magically influenced the future when he told King Jehoash to shoot arrows and to stamp upon the ground and how the king smote only three times when he should have done so five or six times, with the result that he could now defeat Syria only three times but not completely and decisively; and finally how even after his death, when men in their sudden fright of Syrian raiders threw a corpse that they were going to bury into the grave of Elisha, the life-giving power of the prophet's bones was so great that the man at once revived. Miracle upon miracle! Here was wonderland indeed! It is as if we were reading the story of the life of one of the saints, including all the legends and miracle tales that are so similar the world over, whether the saint be Jew or Christian, Buddhist or Mohammedan. Some of these stories had been told of Elijah also. They are invaluable for the history of popular religion in Israel. But we learn nothing of Elisha's message from them. His personality pictured in them is that of a saint, a miracle man, kindly, gentle, humane, always ready to help in time of need, but conscious of his power and insistent on the honor due to him as a prophet of Yahweh. But if this were all we knew of him, we should only think of him as a holy man, honored and revered by the people, but of no special significance for the development of religion.

But fortunately, there is another source of great historical value, which in addition corrects the impressions of Ahab in the Elijah Stories. It is a History of the Rise and Fall of the Dynasty of Omri. It has not all been preserved, because not all of it fitted in with the scheme of the author of the Books of Kings, as we shall see. Although the writer was interested in the part the prophets played in the history, he was concerned primarily with the political movements and wrote from a political point of view and subordinated, without underestimating, the prophets. His story of Omri is lost. This is all the more to be regretted, because Omri was a really great king, as the Assyrian inscriptions show when they still call Israel "the house of Omri" a century after its fall. But the story of Ahab's Syrian wars is preserved in 1 Ki. 20. 22. Syria, under the leadership of Damascus, was at that time in her period of power. She was pushing westward to gain access to the sea and to control the great caravan routes.   Omri, Ahab's father, had been defeated by Benhadad I, had lost a number of Israelite cities in the East Jordan territory, and had been compelled to grant to the Syrians a city district in his newly founded capital Samaria with bazaar privileges.   To counteract this strong Syrian power Omri had entered into family relations with Phœnicia, and arranged the marriage of his son Ahab with the Tyrian princess Jezebel.   Our author does not speak of this, but only of the siege of Samaria by Benhadad II and his defeat by Ahab.   He says nothing of the reason for the resumption of warfare by Syria, but tells of the advice of an unknown prophet of Yahweh, which brought victory to Ahab.   The renewal of the war in the following year was also predicted by the prophet later on, and so was the crushing defeat of Benhadad, before the battle had commenced.   After the decisive victory it was again a prophet who denounced the lenient terms which Ahab had imposed on Benhadad when he only demanded the return of the cities which his father had lost and bazaar privileges in Damascus, such as the Syrians had gained in Samaria.   The prophet voiced here the people's indignant dissatisfaction with the treaty of peace (1 Ki. 20). One does not gain the impression that Ahab was an apostate who would have nothing to do with Yahweh; on the contrary the prophets of Yahweh play an important rôle in his decisions.   But it developed that Ahab was not able to compel the execution of the terms of the treaty.   So he decided to resort to force.   His vassal king Jehoshaphat of Judah went with him.   But first they inquired of Yahweh's oracle from his prophets.   They one and all declared, "Go up; for Yahweh will deliver it into the hand of the king." When Jehoshaphat asked whether there was not another prophet, Ahab replied there was still one other, "Micaiah the son of Imlah, but I hate him, for he does not prophesy good concerning me, but evil."   However, he sent for him.   Meanwhile the leader of the other prophets, Zedekiah, brought two horns of iron and said, "Thus says Yahweh, with these shalt thou push the Syrians until they are destroyed."   And all joined him in saying, "Go up to Ramoth Gilead and prosper, for Yahweh will deliver it into the hand of the king."   The messenger who had gone to fetch Micaiah asked him to give a good oracle, but the prophet replied, "As Yahweh lives, what Yahweh says to me, that will I speak." But he repeated at first to the kings the message of the other prophets, in a sarcastic tone we presume, for Ahab rebuked him and demanded that he tell nothing but the truth. Then he said,

> I saw all Israel scattered on the mountains,
> as sheep that have no shepherd:
> And Yahweh said, "These have no master,
> let them return every man to his house in peace." (1 Ki. 22 ^{17})

It was a dramatic picture of the defeated people and their slain king in the characteristic poetic form which is so common with the great literary prophets. In explanation of the discrepancy between his oracle and that of the other prophets Micaiah continued,

> Therefore hear thou the word of Yahweh: I saw Yahweh sitting on His throne, and all the host of heaven standing by Him on His right hand and on His left. And Yahweh said, Who shall entice Ahab, that he may go up and fall at Ramoth-gilead? And one said on this manner; and another said on that manner. And the spirit came forth and stood before Yahweh, and said, I will entice him. And Yahweh said to him, Wherewith? And He said, I will go forth, and will be a lying spirit in the mouth of all his prophets. And He said, Thou shalt entice him, and shalt prevail also: go forth, and do so. Now therefore, behold, Yahweh has put a lying spirit in the mouth of all these thy prophets; and Yahweh has spoken evil concerning thee. (1 Ki. 22 $^{19-23}$)

Zedekiah full of rage struck Micaiah on the cheek, exclaiming, "Which way went the Spirit of Yahweh from me to speak to thee?' To which he replied, "Behold, thou shalt see on that day, when thou shalt go into an inner chamber to hide thyself," and to the king who sent him back to prison till his return he said, "If thou return at all in peace, Yahweh has not spoken by me." Then Ahab went into battle. He disguised himself, but in the battle an arrow sent at a venture mortally wounded him. In spite of his wound, he stayed with his chariot in the fight till evening, when he died. Who can withhold his sympathy from so brave and noble a king and warrior? The story is important not only in correcting our estimate of Ahab, but also in giving us the remarkable episode of the prophet Micaiah with his picture of the catastrophe so exquisitely phrased in metric language and with his view of prophetic inspiration, which does not doubt either the sincerity or the actual inspiration of the opposing prophets, but carries back the deception to Yahweh Himself who in a solemn throne council had planned to lead Ahab astray through a spirit of falsehood! For a true historical understanding of the professional prophets Micaiah's judgment of them is as important as his view of inspiration is valuable for the development of religious reasoning. Jeremiah judged his opponents more sharply and explained the discrepancy between their message and his own quite differently (Jer. 23). Jeremiah's theology may be better, but Micaiah's judgment was fairer.

After Ahab's death, Moab under its king Mesha revolted against Israelite suzerainty. In Mesha's famous memorial monument[1] details about the revolt are given. But Ahab's son and second successor Jehoram tried to restore Israelitish supremacy. Our author describes in 2 Ki. 3 how Jehoram with his vassals, the kings of Judah and of Edom, advanced against Moab from the south through Edom and how the prophet Elisha obtained water for the suffering army by making use of his knowledge of the country in which the rain water is retained under the surface of the soil by the rocky substratum and procured by the digging of trenches. It is of great interest to learn that Elisha induced his prophetic ecstasy by the music of a minstrel. We never find that the great prophets used external stimulants in order to transport themselves into the trance, but of the prophets of Baal we learned in the Elijah stories that they danced and raved and shouted and cut themselves with knives till the blood gushed forth and of the Israelitish prophets who roved in companies through the land in Saul's time we may assume the same. The dervishes to-day still use the same means. Elisha gave to the kings also the prediction of victory over Moab. When on the next morning "the sun shone upon the water, the Moabites saw the water against them as red as blood: and they said, "This is blood; the kings are surely destroyed, and they have smitten each man his fellow: now therefore Moab, to the spoil!" This was the Israelite view. We may be sure that the Moabites were not deceived by those pools of water nor by their red color, for both were familiar sights to them. But they were defeated and their land was devastated. Then, as his last resort, King Mesha took his eldest son, the crown-prince, and offered him

---

[1] "The Moabite Stone" was erected by Mesha at Dibon on the Arnon. An English translation is given in Barton's *Archaeology and the Bible*, p. 363 f.

upon the wall of his capital as a burnt-offering to his god Kemosh. It was a desperate means to gain help, but it succeeded. "And there was a great wrath [of Kemosh] against Israel, and they departed from him, and returned to their own land." Moab remained free, Jehoram's attempt to subdue it again had proved vain. This is in accord with Mesha's inscription. The Israelites, we see, still believed in the real existence and power of the god of Moab. We hear of no protest by Elisha either. But then Elisha is not of primary interest in this story, but more like Micaiah in Ahab's story. Differently from the Elisha Stories which we have considered, he is here opposed to the king of Israel and pays attention to him only because of his regard for King Jehoshaphat. Nevertheless he had followed him on his campaign !

In the next story (2 Ki. 6 ^{24}–7 ^{19}) Elisha is also opposed to the king, but again he gives him a hopeful prediction. The war with Syria continued under Jehoram. Benhadad of Damascus besieged Samaria until a famine raged whose terror is brought home to the reader by the experience of the king as he inspected the wall. A woman called out to him for help and said in answer to his question,

> This woman said to me, Give thy son, that we may eat him to-day, and we will eat my son to-morrow. So we boiled my son, and ate him: and I said to her on the next day, Give thy son, that we may eat him; and she has hidden her son. And it came to pass, when the king heard the words of the woman, that he rent his clothes as he was standing upon the wall; and the people looked, and, behold, he had sackcloth within upon his flesh. Then he said, God do so to me, and more also, if the head of Elisha the son of Shaphat shall stand on him this day. (2 Ki. 6 $^{28-31}$)

Why Elisha was held responsible for the distress, we are not told. From the sequel we may deduce that he had counselled the king not to capitulate, but to trust in the help of Yahweh. Elisha knew instinctively, the author proceeds, that the king had planned his murder and told the elders who were with him, "See ye how this son of a murderer has sent to take my head?" So they bolted the door against the assassin. When the king himself appeared soon afterwards and said, "Behold, this evil is of Yahweh; why should I wait for Yahweh any longer?" Elisha declared in an oracle of Yahweh that by this time to-morrow the famine in Samaria would be at an end, and warned the king's aide, who doubted the truth of this, "Behold, thou shalt see it with thine eyes, but shalt not eat thereof." Meanwhile the Syrians had received news of the intended invasion of a powerful confederation of enemies. The author speaks of the Hittites and the Egyptians, but that was the mistaken popular notion; in reality the Assyrians were menacing Damascus. Four famishing lepers, who had gone to the camp of the Syrians to get food, discovered that it was forsaken, and after eating and drinking and taking spoil they told the Samaritans the good news, which seemed to them too good to be true. They investigated and then all poured out of the city to plunder the Syrian camp. The press at the gate was so great that the king's aide, who was the officer in charge there, was trampled to death, as the prophet had foretold.

In the next two stories Elisha is the executor of Elijah's testament. In Damascus he told Hazael, who inquired about the outcome of Benhadad's serious illness,

Go, say to him, Thou shalt surely recover; howbeit Yahweh has showed me that he shall surely die. And he settled his countenance steadfastly upon him, until he was ashamed: and the man of God wept. And Hazael said, Why does my lord weep? And he answered, Because I know the evil that thou wilt do to the children of Israel: their strongholds wilt thou set on fire, and their young men wilt thou slay with the sword, and wilt dash in pieces their little ones, and rip up their women with child. And Hazael said, But what is thy servant, who is but a dog, that he should do this great thing? And Elisha answered, Yahweh has showed me that thou shalt be king over Syria. (2 Ki. 8 [10-13])

On the next day Hazael murdered Benhadad and became king in his stead. The narrator shows exquisite tact in this fateful interview: the prophet was on a terrible errand, his heart was full of grief and tears streamed down his cheeks, he had to tell Hazael, but he did not tell him directly but only suggested, and Hazael understood the suggestion all too well. Did Elisha actually show such delicacy? Or was this only his disciple's way of telling the terrible tale?

The anointing of Jehu followed. Jehoram had been wounded in a fierce battle for the defence of Ramoth Gilead against the Syrians and had gone home to nurse his wounds. Elisha took this opportunity of sending one of his disciples to anoint Jehu, a general at Ramoth Gilead, who was at once proclaimed king by his fellow officers when they learned what "this mad fellow" had done. This epithet shows what impression the ecstatic behavior of these prophets made on the people, who nevertheless acknowledged their divine inspiration and authority.   Jehu must have been one of the fanatical Yahweh party, whom Elisha could use for his purpose of overthrowing the dynasty of Omri which was religiously too tolerant of other cults and not enthusiastic enough for Yahweh.   The wars with Syria, in which questions of political power and commercial control were decided, had pushed aside for these rulers the great religious matters which concerned the prophetic party.   Ahab had incurred their hatred for his marriage with Jezebel, and for his judicial murder of Naboth.   Jehu now rode at a furious pace to Jezreel and murdered his king and the visiting Judæan king Ahaziah. He felt himself to be the avenger of Naboth and the fulfiller of Elijah's oracle to Ahab.   After killing Joram,

> He said to Bidkar his adjutant, Take up, and cast him in the portion of the field of Naboth the Jezreelite; for remember how that, when I and thou rode together after Ahab his father, Yahweh uttered this oracle against him: Surely I have seen yesterday the blood of Naboth, and the blood of his sons, says Yahweh; and I will requite thee in this plot, says Yahweh.   Now therefore take and cast him into the plot of ground, according to the word of Yahweh. (2 Ki. 9 [25f.])

Queen Jezebel too, who defied the regicide, he commanded to be thrown out of the window; seventy royal princes in Samaria were executed at his suggestion, although he later on disclaimed all responsibility for this; forty-two royal princes of Judah he slew on their way to a visit of the princes in Samaria.   The horror of it all sent a shudder through both countries, yet none dared to resist the brutal usurper, who knew so well how to cloak his acts with religious devotion.   He compelled Jonadab, the son of Rechab, to ride with him in his chariot in order that he might be seen with the head of this fanatic Yahweh party, who in their violent opposition to Baal worship rejected not only the religion but also the civilization of Canaan with its vine culture and its cities.   The final stroke, by which he exterminated all the adherents of Baal, was struck at a feast of Baal which they were all compelled to attend, and where they were all cut down.   The words "Thus Jehu destroyed Baal out of Israel," end the story which is so dramatically told in this on the whole reliable document.   The author approved of Jehu, though he does not say so outright, but a hundred years later the prophet Hosea shuddered as he foretold the fall of Jehu's dynasty because of these cruel crimes.   Conscience had a history in Israel as elsewhere.   What Elisha's conscience approved, Hosea's condemned!

The Elisha of this history is quite different from the kindly and humane man of God in the Elisha Stories.   But this presentation is more historical.   Even so we do not gain the impression that he had a double portion of his master's spirit or that he was at all comparable to Elijah in personal greatness or historical significance. But we learn that his political activity and importance were considerable.   The few of his messages which are embodied in the stories do not contain any thought that was higher than the thought of the people about him.

The History of the Rise and Fall of the Dynasty of Omri, as we have called it, is one of the most valuable historical sources that we possess.   It was written in Israel during the reign of Jehu (842–815 B.C.) by an author who, in spite of his predilection for the prophets, had no prejudice against the dynasty, but described Ahab so as to evoke our deep interest in him, if not our admiration for him, and Joram also, in spite of Elisha's opposition to him, as a man who was unobtrusively religious, as his hidden sackcloth proved, and desirous of waiting for Yahweh's help, if he could only be sure that the calamity was not purposed by Him.   This author maintained the standard of fairness and objectivity set by the early History of the Founding of the Monarchy.

CHAPTER V

THE YAHWIST

THE legends of the past had been handed down from age to age with astounding tenacity of memory. Some had come from hoary antiquity, repeated by one generation to another. The priests had recited the stories connected with their particular sanctuaries; the shepherds had told their tales of pastoral life, the peasants of agricultural, the city dwellers of urban life. They were all at first single stories, complete in themselves, independent of others. Minstrels and story-tellers had collected and narrated them to the people in camp or at the festivals, and the parents had told them in turn to their children. Yet, in course of time, with the development of settled life the need for writing them down came to be felt, and certain groups of stories were thus preserved. It was inevitable that by the time we come to literate records, the tales should have been more or less modified in the long oral process of tradition. Stories that were originally not Israelitish but Canaanitish or Babylonian had been made Israelitish. Thus religious tales, originally connected with the Canaanitish god Baal or the Babylonian god Marduk or with some other deity, were now told of Yahweh. How far this transforming process had gone by the time of Elijah, we do not know. But about that time (*ca.* 850 B.C.) an author gathered the various stories and groups together for a great work, in which he told the story of Israel from its origin to the conquest of Canaan and showed why and how his people came into the possession of the land.

He went back to the beginning of time and told the story of man's creation; how Yahweh had formed him from the dust of the ground and breathed the breath of life into his nostrils, then placed him in the garden of Eden and built a companion for him from one of his ribs. That is the reason, he observed, why "a man leaves his father and his mother and cleaves to his wife and they become one flesh"; they belonged originally together! "And the man called his wife's

name Eve, because she became the mother of all living." Deep
questions of never ceasing interest to the human mind are answered
in these early tales. The golden age lay at the beginning. Men
were happy and care-free in the wonderful garden of Eden. Why
did it not last? Why did misery come into this world and all pain
and suffering and labor? Because of man's disobedience! Yahweh
had forbidden them to eat of the fruit of a tree in the midst of the
garden, but, tempted by the wily serpent, they transgressed this command and were punished, the woman with the fearful pain of child-
bearing and her ever renewed desire with its ever following pangs;
the man with hard and endless labor for the fruit of the soil, which
had hitherto been his without work. The serpent too was cursed,
that is why it now crawls on its belly and why there is perpetual
enmity between it and man! A variant story had told also of the
tree of life, by the eating of whose fruit man would become immortal.
Israel in common with other nations believed that knowledge and
eternal life could be procured by the eating of certain food. Our
author took from this latter tale the motivation of man's expulsion
from the garden of Eden, of which the other story had said nothing.
Yahweh feared that man might eat from the tree of life also, so He
drove him out and barred the way to the garden by Cherubim and
an ever turning glittering sword. The Eden story was originally
told by a man of agriculture. Quite unconcerned about its origin,
the author, who had told of man's first disobedience, now followed it
with a story of the first murder, which was originally told by a shepherd, for Cain the murderer was "a tiller of the ground" and his
cereal offering was not acceptable to Yahweh, but Abel was "a
keeper of sheep" and "Yahweh had respect to Abel and to his offering." To our author this was of no significance any more; to him
the reason for Yahweh's non-acceptance of Cain's gift was moral,
for Yahweh, who sees the heart, warned Cain,

Why art thou wroth? and why is thy countenance fallen? If thou doest
well, shall it not be lifted up? and if thou doest not well, sin couches at the door,
and unto thee is its desire; but do thou rule over it. (Gen. 4 [6])

Nevertheless Cain slew Abel, but was punished with a fearful
curse which drove him away from his home "a fugitive and wanderer
in the earth." As a protection against murder Yahweh gave him a
sign, the tribal sign of the Cainites, by which he was recognized

everywhere as a member of a tribe which was famous for its terrible blood revenge. Our author placed this early institution of law at the beginning of human history, quite unconcerned that in reality it came much later and that with all its terrors it was a great step in advance, safeguarding life through family or tribal action before a strong government could take the execution of justice in hand. That this story presupposed the existence of many people besides Adam and Eve and their sons, did not concern our author either, for he had no intention of telling the story of the whole human race in detail. He proceeded to speak of Cain's building of the first city and of his descendants who were the ancestors of the nomadic cattle raisers, of the musicians, and of the smiths, and he incorporated here the terrible song of Lamech which celebrated his brutal, unrestrained blood feud (cf. p. 2). Civilization had advanced through Cain and his descendants, but so had murder and sin! Side by side with the Cain line the author shows how in the Seth line religion arose. After the birth of Seth's son Enosh, "men began to call upon the name of Yahweh." [1] The fabulous giants of old,"the Nephilim," the offspring of heavenly beings and fair daughters of men, are placed by the author in this period, but only a fragment remains of what must have been in earlier forms a longer story, for Israel, like other peoples, had tales about such demigods, which our author could not use. As the brief reference to them now stands, it seems to have been intended to serve as an illustration of the growing sinfulness in the world. For directly afterwards we read,

And Yahweh saw that the wickedness of man was great in the earth, and that every imagination of the thoughts of his heart was only evil continually,

wherefore He determined to destroy them all. Only "Noah found favor in the eyes of Yahweh," and was saved in an ark which he had made, with seven pairs of every clean and two pairs of every unclean beast, from the terrible flood which Yahweh brought on by a rain lasting forty days and forty nights. When Noah offered burnt offerings after his deliverance,

Yahweh smelt the sweet savor, and Yahweh said in His heart, "I will not again curse the ground any more for man's sake, for the imagination of his

[1] Our author calls God Jahveh (or phonetically spelled, Yahweh) and is named therefore Jahvist or J.

heart is evil from his youth; neither will I again smite any more everything living as I have done.

> While the earth remains,
> seedtime and harvest, and cold and heat,
> and summer and winter, and day and night
> shall not cease. (Gen. 8 [21f.])

This profound observation of human sinfulness is at once illustrated in the shameful behavior of Canaan towards his father Noah who had drunk too much of the wine which he had been the first to make. The story must once have been much more drastic than it is now in J's version of it. Noah's curse on Canaan and his blessing of Shem and Japheth (see p.11) contains the theme of J's whole history, Canaan is to be subject to Shem and Japheth. This is the program of the future, whose realization J traces through the succeeding ages, until Israel (Shem) becomes at last the lord of Canaan. The curse and the blessing of the ancestor have, according to ancient belief, a magic potency to set free forces that work for their fulfilment. In spite of all obstacles that may ever again rise to frustrate the great hope, the final outcome is assured. With this end clearly in view, J proceeds to tell the remarkable story. After quickly giving a genealogy of the sons of Noah, in which he showed how they repeopled the earth, and narrating of the tower of Babel that men built in their overweening pride and for which they were scattered over all the earth,[1] J commenced the story of Abraham, the father of the chosen race.

At the beginning J placed the great promise,

Now Yahweh said to Abram, Get thee out of thy country, and from thy kindred, and from thy father's house, to the land that I will show thee: and I will make of thee a great nation, and I will bless thee, and make thy name great; and be thou a blessing: and I will bless them that bless thee, and them that curse thee will I curse: and in thee shall all the families of the earth be blessed. (Gen. 12 [1-3])

But this was for the distant future. Homeless, Abram wandered on, without knowing his destination, until he came to Shechem in Canaan, where the divine promise was given, "to thy seed will I give this land." But soon afterwards a severe famine compelled him to leave this promised land and to seek food in Egypt. There the

[1] The primeval story of J is in Gen. 2 [4b]-4 [25] 5 [29] 6 [1-8] 7 [1-5.7-10.12.16b.17b.22f.] 8 [2b.3a.] [6-12 13b.20-22] 9 [18-27] 10 [8-19.21 24-30] 11 [1-9].

beauty of his wife Sarah got them into trouble, but they emerged safely and returned to Canaan with great wealth which the Pharaoh had given him for Sarah when he took her into his harem. But again the reader is kept in suspense, for Abram almost lost the land through his generosity,— as would actually have happened if Lot had not chosen the marvellously fertile territory of Sodom, which later, through a judgment of God, was turned into a desolation on account of Sodom's fearful wickedness. At Hebron, where Abram now settled, Yahweh gave him the promise of a son, but Sarah was barren! The promise seemed unfulfillable, and especially when Hagar her handmaiden, whom Sarah had given to Abram as a concubine, fled into the wilderness because of the intolerable harshness of the jealous Sarah before she had borne her son. At last, when he and his wife were so old that they could no longer expect children, Yahweh promised an own son to them as a reward for their hospitality on His visit with two angels at Abram's tent.[1] And true enough, at the predicted time Isaac was born! When he had grown up, Abram sent his trusted steward to his homeland in Syria that he might procure a wife from the daughters of his kinsmen for him, for he should not marry a Canaanite maiden. After a successful trip he came back with Laban's sister, Rebekah, whom Isaac gladly took as his wife.[2] But she also was barren! And only after Isaac's earnest entreaty did Yahweh grant to her children, the twin-brothers Jacob and Esau. While still in her womb, they struggled together. The oracle of Yahweh interpreted this as prophetic of the strife of the two nations, Israel and Edom, whose ancestors they would be, and the prediction was given, "the elder shall serve the younger." The full significance of this appeared, when Esau = Edom was born first, and Jacob = Israel second. The first-born should ordinarily be the heir. But Jacob had the promise! And he got by fraud his father's potent blessing, which had been intended for his favorite son, Esau: fertility and lordship! Yet in spite of all this, the fulfilment seemed again impossible, for Jacob had to flee from Esau's vengeance. But it turned out to his good fortune. He went to Laban, his mother's brother, married his two daughters,

---

[1] J's story of Abram is in Gen. 11 $^{28-30}$ 12 (except $^{4b.5}$) 13 $^{1-5.6b. 7-11a. 12b. 13. 18}$ 15 $^{1-11* 17. 18a}$ 16 $^{1b. 2. 4-8. 11-14}$ 18 $^{1-16. 20-22a}$ 19 except ^{29}.

[2] J's story of Isaac is in Gen. 21 $^{1a. 2a. 7. 33}$ 22 $^{20-24}$ 24. 25 $^{1-5. 11b. 18a}$ 26 $^{1-33*}$.

Leah and Rachel, and came back with immense wealth, which he
had gotten by his work and by his tricks, accompanied by his wives
and twelve sons, most of whom he had by Leah, whom he had at
first not wanted! All obstacles were removed, Laban's pursuit
and Esau's encounter, however threatening they were at the time;
and Jacob settled once more in Canaan. The time for the possession of the promised land seemed to have come.[1] But again his
favorite son, Joseph, was removed from the land and sold to Egypt
as a slave, and thrown into prison, but there he rose to the position
of viceroy! Jacob with all his sons left the land too and emigrated
to Egypt, where he died after blessing his sons (cf. p. 12f.) Once
more the promise seemed frustrated.[2] And yet in Egypt they
became a very numerous people and part of the promise was being
fulfilled. Yet this growth filled the Egyptians with anxiety, so
they oppressed and enslaved them. A champion arose for them
in Moses, but soon he had to flee after killing an Egyptian who had
slain a Hebrew. Once again this apparent misfortune turned out
to be of a decisive significance for Israel's fate. For in Midian,
whither Moses had fled and where he had married the priest's
daughter, Zipporah, Yahweh appeared and said to him that He had
heard the cry of His people in Egypt and that Moses must go, in
spite of his remonstrance, as His agent to Egypt to effect His people's release, and for this He endowed him with miracle-working
power. On Moses' return to Egypt with his wife and son, Yahweh,
for no reason given, attacked him at a khan in the wilderness, but
Zipporah saved him by applying the magically potent blood of her
son whom she circumcised. In Egypt his mission with Pharaoh
was at first unsuccessful and only resulted in harsher oppression of
the people.[3] But by a series of plagues,[4] which Moses announced

---

[1] J's story of Jacob and Esau is in Gen. 25 [21—26a. 28] 27 [1—10. 14f. 17. 18a. 20. 24—27a.]
[29b—32. 35—39a. 40a. 41—45] 28 [10. 13—16. 19a] 29 [2—14. 26. 31—35] 30 [9—16. 20b. 21. 24b. 25. 27. 29—40 ac. 41—43]
31 [1. 17. 18a. 25. 27. 31. 43f. 46. 48. 51—53] 32 [3—7a. 13b—22a. 23b—29. 31f.] 33 [1—17a] 34* 35 [21f.] 36 [15—19.]
[31—39.] 38.

[2] J's story of Joseph is in Gen. 37 [3f. 12. 13a. 14b. 18b. 21. 23a. 25—27. 28b. 31a. 32f. 35] 39 [1ac. 2ff.]
42 [2. 4b—7. 27. 28a. 38] 43 [1—13. 14b—23a. 24—34] 44. 45 [1a. 2. 4b. 5a. 9—11. 13f. 19. 28] 46 [1a. 28—34] 47 [1—5a.]
[6b. 12—27a. 29—31] 48 [2b. 8a. 9b. 13f. 17—19] 49 [2—27. 33a*] 50 [1—11. 14. 18. 21. 24.]

[3] Ex. 1 [6. 8—12. 14a] 2 [11—23a] 3 [2—4a. 5. 7—9a. 16—18] 4 [1—16. 19. 20a. 24—26. 29—31] 5 [3. 5—23] 6 [1.]

[4] J has seven plagues, 1. the Nile was made foul (Ex. 7 [14. 16. 17a. 18. 21a. 24f.]); 2. frogs
(8 [1—4. 8—15a]); 3. flies (8 [20—32]); 4. murrain (9 [1—7]); 5. hail (9 [13. 17f. 23b. 24b. 25b—29a. 33f.]);
6. locusts (10 [1a. 3—11. 13b. 14b. 15ac—19. 24—29]); 7. death of the first-born (11 [4—8]).

in Yahweh's name, Pharaoh was finally compelled to let the people go in order that they might celebrate the feast to Yahweh at the sacred mountain in the wilderness. At the last they could not leave Egypt too quickly for him. In great haste, without having time to leaven their dough, they departed in the month Abib. As a memorial of this exodus Moses ordered that they should keep the feast of unleavened bread every year in Abib, and give to Yahweh the first-born males, animal and human. The great throng of 600,000 (!) men, besides children and a mixed crowd of foreigners, went southward, Yahweh marching before them in a pillar of cloud by day and of fire by night. But suddenly the whole deliverance was endangered, for Pharaoh had changed his mind and pursued them with his chariotry. There seemed to be no way of escape, but Yahweh "caused the sea" (which extended at that time far up inland and which hindered the Israelites from crossing to the wilderness) "to go back by a strong wind all night, and made the sea dry land" and thus enabled them to pass through safely, while the pursuing Egyptians stuck fast with their chariot wheels in the soft ground and were miserably overtaken and drowned by the incoming tide. A mighty deliverance had been won! Full of joy Israel sang to Yahweh,

> I will sing to Yahweh,
>   for He has triumphed gloriously,
> The horse and its rider
>   has He hurled into the sea.

This was the foundation of all their great historical experiences, a never-to-be-forgotten deed of Providence. Yahweh had overthrown the Egyptians. He had shown that He could save His people from all perils.[1]

In the desert He cared for them and provided them with water and food, in spite of their ungrateful murmurings. In the great vision Yahweh had told Moses that He would bring them out of Egypt to the fertile land of Canaan, and this destination he constantly kept in mind.[2]

[1] Ex. 12 21a. 27b. 29—34. 37—39 13 3a. 4. 6. 10—13. 21f. 14 5f. 10a. 11—14. 19b. 20b. 21b. 24a. 25. 27b. 28b. 30 15 1.

[2] Ex. 15 22—25a. 27 17 3. 2b. 7ac 18 7. 9—11. J did not tell of their going to Yahweh's mountain in the wilderness. Yahweh Himself was present with them all along. The assertion made to Pharaoh that they must go a three days' journey into the wilder-

Moses secured his brother-in-law Hobab as a guide. At last they were at the southern border of the land and sent spies to reconnoitre the southern part. But when they returned and reported that the land was indeed flowing with milk and honey, but that the inhabitants were strong, some of them veritable giants in stature, and that their cities were fortified, the people were afraid and refused to attempt the invasion. So near their destination, so near the fulfilment of the prophecy, and again it had to be postponed! Yahweh declared that the present generation would not see it.[1]

When they finally attempted to invade Canaan from the East, they attacked and defeated the Ammonites and Amorites who blocked their way. King Balak of Moab, fearing invasion and defeat by Israel, sent for the famous prophet Balaam, the son of Beor, that he might curse Israel and thus destroy it. But when he came, he could not curse, because Yahweh compelled him to bless. And in his oracles (cf. p. 14f.) he foretold not only the future prosperity of Israel, but also the coming of David "the star out of Jacob, — the sceptre out of Israel," and his conquest of Moab and Edom. The horizon of the ancient prediction was widened and it was sure to be fulfilled. Moab was not attacked, indeed some Israelites joined the Moabites in sacrificial festivals in honor of their gods, but Yahweh demanded in great anger that the ringleaders should be hanged for this. The occupation of the East Jordan territory by the Manassites was quickly told, and the conquest of Palestine apparently also, for we have only a few stories concerning it from J in the Book of Joshua : the fragment of the meeting of Joshua, the captain of the Israelite army, with "the prince of Yahweh's host," the covenant with the tricky Hivvites, and perhaps the quotation from the Book of Yashar where Joshua commanded the sun and moon to stand still (cf. p. 5).[2] Certain passages in Joshua[3] and especially the first chapter of the Book of Judges give a most

ness to celebrate a feast there to Yahweh was merely a pretext. J had originally no covenant or legislation at Mount Sinai. That part of the story was inserted in J later.

[1] Num. 10 $^{29-33}$ 11 $^{4-13.\ 15.\ 18-24a.\ 31-35}$ 12 ^{16} 13 $^{17b.\ 18b.\ 19.\ 22.\ 27a.\ 28.\ 30f.}$ 14 $^{1c.\ 3.\ 8.\ 9b.\ 31.}$ $^{41-45.}$

[2] Num. 21 $^{16-20.\ 24b.\ 25-32}$ 22 $^{3b.\ 4.\ 5ac-7.\ 11.\ 17f.\ 22-36a.\ 37b.\ 39}$ 23 ^{28} 24. 25 $^{1b.\ 2.\ 3b.\ 4}$ 32 $^{39-42}$ Josh. 5 $^{13-15}$ 9 $^{6f.}$ 10 $^{12-14.}$

[3] Josh. 13 ^{13} 15 $^{13-19.\ 63}$ 16 ^{10} 17 $^{11-18}$ 19 ^{47}.

valuable summary by J of the results of Israel's battles for the possession of Canaan. According to J, Israel conquered the land, but not all of it; especially the cities and the plains remained in the hands of the Canaanites, because the cities were too strongly fortified, and in the plains Israel could not prevail against their chariotry. The Canaanites were therefore neither completely driven out nor exterminated. Israel settled among them and learned the art of war from these experienced warriors (Judg. 3 [2]). Nevertheless (in the end) the Canaanites " became subject to taskwork." The great prediction had been fulfilled: Canaan was Israel's slave !

J may have concluded his story here. But if the promise to Japheth was an original part of the blessing of Noah, he must have continued in order to show how this also was fulfilled. Besides, the wonderful prophecy of the king out of Israel, the star out of Jacob, pointed forward to David, and thus J's story could not be complete until he had told of David too and the splendor and power of his kingdom. In the period of the so-called Judges J recited the story of the left-handed Benjamite Ehud, who assassinated King Eglon of Moab and defeated the Moabites; incorporated the Song of Deborah; told of Gideon the champion of Manasseh and his victory over the Midianite raiders; of Abimelech and his abortive attempt to establish a kingship; of Jephthah the Gileadite, and his war against Ammon with his fierce attack upon the Ephraimites who had quarrelled with him, and his slaughter of the fugitives at the Jordan fords where he recognized them by their pronunciation of Shibboleth for which they said Sibboleth; he wrote of Samson and the pranks he played upon the Philistines; of Micah and his idol and the migration of the Danites; and of the outrage at Gibeah and its expiation.[1]

The conclusion and climax of J's story dealt with the Philistine danger, already touched on in the Samson tales, and with the founding of the monarchy which secured Israel's hold on the land, the completion of her subjection of the Canaanites and her final deliverance from the Philistine peril. For all this the Yahwist made use of the David story (cf. p. 21ff.). Now at length the whole of

---

[1] Judg. 3 [16-27a. 28] 5 [2-31a] 8 [4-21. 24-27a] 9 [26-41] 11 [1-11a. 29. 33b] 12 [1-6] 13-16 (except 13 [1. 5b] 15 [20] 16 [31b]) 17-20[*]. 21 [15-23].

Noah's prediction was fulfilled, Canaan was the slave of Shem and of Japheth! In his tents Japheth dwelt. The Philistine danger was past for Israel; but significantly enough, no hope was expressed for Israel's subjection of the Philistines, but their permanent stay in the country and their independence were assumed. The divine promise to Abram was fulfilled, Israel was now a mighty people, happy and prosperous, envied and admired by the peoples of the earth. Jacob's blessing had come true. And Balaam's prediction was realized: the star out of Jacob had come, David ruled the nations!

It was a wonderful work, this story of J. It was the first comprehensive history that had ever been written; even the Greeks had nothing like it till centuries later. The history of Israel was set in the framework of the history of the world! The vast horizon which takes in the nations of the world in its sweep, together with the comprehensive grasp of the history from the creation of mankind to the time of David, was a historiographical achievement of the first order. And equal in importance was the marshalling of the whole movement of history under one great idea which is stated in the blessing of Noah and realized in spite of all sorts of obstacles that ever retarded and often threatened to frustrate it, — because it was a divine idea. Here was a master mind at work, who thought of history as the working out of the purpose of God. For He was behind the great movements and He ordered events according to His plan. That the worldwide horizon was not maintained all through the story lay in the nature of the author's task. Later when the great world movements inaugurated by Assyria and Babylonia came, the prophets, especially the so-called Deutero-Isaiah, thought in universal terms. But the beginning we have in J, who deeply influenced the great prophet of the exile. Of course, he had the material for his history before him, partly in oral, partly in written form. But he ordered it as we have it now. Whether this order corresponds to history we do not always know; in some cases we can tell that certain stories belong elsewhere. For instance, in the period of the Judges we know that the migration of the Danites took place before the war under Deborah, for at that time they were already in their new northern seats. Whether the various heroes, who were deliverers of their respective tribes not of all Israel, lived in the order given or not, whether some were contemporaries or not, we can no longer tell.

The historical value of J's material varies. In the primeval period J had of course only myths and legends, for nobody had been present at the creation, and the story of the deluge was originally part of the Babylonian Gilgamesh epic,[1] as a comparison demonstrates. We expect no history in this first period, but stories woven by the poetic imagination of the people. The story of the creation and of the deluge came originally from Babylonia, perhaps also the story of the tower of Babel; whether they had come to Israel through the mediation of the Canaanites or more directly when Solomon opened the avenues of commercial and intellectual intercourse with the East, is not of great importance. In the second or patriarchal period we are still in the epic period. The stories embody valuable reminiscences of tribal history, but these are not always easy to extract. The whole period is described in legends and it is impossible to reconstruct any real history from them. J brought order into the stories by arranging them as he did, making Abram the ancestor, Isaac his son, Jacob his grandson, and Joseph his great grandson. In the Mosaic period there is more historical foundation and we may say that the oppression in Egypt, the deliverance by Moses, and the marvellous escape at the Sea of Reeds are historical facts, although the history is woven about with wreaths of legends. For the period of the conquest J's material is quite reliable. In the time of the Judges also good historical material on the whole underlies his stories, with the exception of the poetic tales about Samson, although even here the background of the beginning Philistine oppression is historical.

The stories are told with great literary art. J was not only a master in planning, arranging, and grouping the whole material, but also in the narration of the individual story. He is an acknowledged master of story-tellers. His literary art is exquisite. Fresh, lifelike, concrete, and graphic, the persons are sketched with the sureness of a great artist, the stories move swiftly and are full of

---

[1] The Gilgamesh epic describes the friendship and adventures of the famous ancient heroes Gilgamesh and Engidu, and Gilgamesh's search for eternal life after the death of his friend, in the course of which he comes to his ancestor Utnapishtim, the Babylonian Noah, who tells him the story of the flood. This part is translated in George A. Barton, *Archæology and the Bible* (1916), pp. 273–277, from tablets of the library of King Ashurbanipal (668–626 B.C.), which were copies of more ancient texts. Another account of the flood written before 2000 B.C. is given there on pp. 280f.

interest. No wonder that they have delighted the readers of more than two millenniums. We must not forget that the stories as J had received them in oral or written form had been polished for generations, but nevertheless he impressed his literary stamp upon them. In their present form they are J's property.

More important than this literary art was the transformation of the popular tales into truly Israelite narratives in which the spirit of the religion of Yahweh dwelt. One of the best illustrations of the moulding and transforming activity of the Israelite mind is the story of the deluge, for a comparison with its Babylonian prototype shows not only the remarkable similarity of the two, even in details, but also the striking difference. In the Hebrew story every trace of polytheism and mythology is omitted; it is a pure, moral, monotheistic tale. If we understand J correctly, he was not only a superb historian and a wonderful literary artist, but also a great teacher of religion. He taught by means of his stories. Yahweh was to him the one great God, the Creator, the only God for Israel. He controlled the forces of nature, as the creation and deluge stories show, and also the forces of history, as the whole trend of his tales prove. He is a moral God who demands righteousness, rewards faith and kindness, innocence and unselfishness, but punishes wickedness and oppression, and this not only in Israel, but in the whole earth, in Babel, in Egypt, etc. Such is Israel's God and to Him the people must be loyal, for He had done everything for them, so that they have finally become a great and prosperous nation. Now it is noteworthy that in telling the ancient stories J did not reject the various Canaanite elements that had been introduced into Israel's religion, but he transformed them. Thus the ancient local sanctuaries of the Canaanites were not sacred to Israel, because Baal had lived and received his worshippers' homage there, but because Yahweh had appeared there to the ancestors, who thereupon had built altars to Him there. The sacred places were not the only places where Yahweh dwelt and worked, for He was not bound to them. He dwelt in heaven. The sacred trees were not God's dwelling place, but some were planted by Abram, and the sacred wells were dug by Isaac. The deity did not live in them, as the Canaanites thought. When Yahweh appeared to Abram at Hebron, He did not come out of the tree ; nor out of the well at Beerlahairoi when he appeared to

Hagar. The sacred pillars of stone were not Bethels or houses of God, but memorial or grave stones. There was no open fight against these paraphernalia of Canaanite worship but a quiet reinterpretation, which displaced their old meaning and made them harmless. Of course, unassimilable ideas were discarded, *e.g.* polytheistic notions and female deities. In the story of the visit of the three men to Abram, anthropomorphic as it is, there are no longer three deities, as there must have been in the older narrative, but Yahweh and two angels. It is not surprising to find that occasionally J did not quite succeed in eliminating every non-Israelite trace. In the story of the temptation the serpent is no longer a deity, but something uncanny still clings to it so that even now it is not quite like a mere serpent; in the marriage of the angels with human women the mythical is still shining through. In the jealousy of God lest men become immortal; in His fear that men might become too powerful in their union; in Jacob's wrestling with God; in Yahweh's sudden attack upon Moses in the wilderness khan; in all these there are elements which cannot easily be harmonized with J's exalted idea of God. But after all, how very little there is of all this! and what a wonderful energy and success in the tranformation of religious ideas are manifest all through J's work! That J deepened also the purely Israelite ideas in these stories is manifest, *e.g.* from the story of Cain, where the older conflict between the non-acceptability of cereal sacrifices and the legitimacy of animal sacrifices is thrown into the background entirely, and the moral idea of harboring sinful thoughts and the subsequent mastery of sin in the heart are emphasized, together with man's social obligation of being his brother's keeper. It is true that there is a very pronounced anthropomorphism in some stories, *e.g.* when God walks in the garden, or visits Abram in the tent and eats a meal there. This does not easily conform to the grand conception of the Creator. But it is a question whether J felt an incongruity here, and we must not forget that anthropomorphic ideas are often a sign of vital religion. More serious is, to our mind, that J did not disapprove of Abram's lie; that he told with evident joy the stories of Jacob's deception of his father and his fraudulent tricks upon Laban; and that he did not omit the story of Lot's incest. True enough, these are elements which belong to a lower level of ethics according to our ideas. But they are quite incidental and cannot dim the glory of this man, to whom we owe admiration and gratitude as historian, literary artist, and religious teacher.

Later some variant or new traditions were inserted in suitable places, so the story of Rebekah in the harem of Abimelech in Gen. 26 and of Judah and Tamar in Gen. 38. More especially certain religious additions were made to heighten the religious quality of the story: the promise was repeated to Abram in Gen. 13 [14-17] and to Jacob in Gen. 28 [13-16. 19a]; in the story of the plagues a series of insertions was made which showed that they were manifestations of Yahweh's power and designed to prove His deity and make His name known in all the earth.[1] The most beautiful of these additions are Jacob's prayer at the river Jabbok (Gen. 32 [10-13]) and Moses' intercession in Num. 14 [11-24], where some of the finest religious convictions are expressed. The most significant of them all are Abram's plea for Sodom, in which the problem of solidary responsibility and the saving effect of even a small remnant is discussed,[2] and the story of the stay at Sinai and the giving of the law.[3]

---

[1] Ex. 7 [17a] 8 [6b. 18b] 9 [14-16. 29b] 10 [1b. 2].

[2] Gen. 18 [17-19. 22b-23a].

[3] Ex. 19 [11b-13. 18. 20-25] 24 [1f. 9-11] 32 [25-29] 33 [1. 3. 4a] 34 [1-5. 10a. 14. 17. 18a. 19-23. 25-28].

CHAPTER VI

THE ELOHIST

In the northern kingdom a work quite similar to the Yahwist's great history was prepared in the first half of the eighth century. Here a prophetic mind, influenced by the prophet Elijah, wrote the story from a northern point of view, emphasizing the Israelitish tradition more strongly than the Judæan, and presenting it from the standpoint of a convinced theocrat. He did not have the vast sweep of J nor did he give his story the universal setting in which J had so effectively placed his history of Israel, but he made it more definitely the vehicle of his religious ideas. His name is lost, but he is now generally known as the Elohist, or abbreviated E, because he used in his stories Elohim for God and avoided the proper name Yahweh until the time of Moses, for he believed that it was first revealed to Moses and had been altogether unknown to the patriarchs.

E's story is parallel to J's, but it does not begin until Abram. In three stories which are preserved of Abram we discern at once the peculiar character of E. There is a distinct advance in his theological and ethical views. The story of Sarah in Pharaoh's harem as told by J had left an unfavorable impression of Abram upon the reader. E corrected this in his version (Gen. 20 $^{1-17}$), which placed her in the harem of King Abimelech at Gerar and emphasized that nothing had happened to her, because God had warned the king early enough in a dream. But E's special concern was that in J's story Abram had told a lie when he said that Sarah was his sister. E pointed out in his version that he had not really lied, because Sarah was indeed his sister, the daughter of Abram's father, though not of his mother. Again, the great wealth which Abram had gotten from the king is here definitely declared to be for her "a covering of the eyes to all that are with" her. Abram is thus cleared of every stain, and even declared to be a prophet, at whose intercession

74

Abimelech and his harem were healed! In J's story of Hagar's flight Abram had not acted admirably either. E therefore showed in his version (Gen. 21 $^{8-21}$) how much Sarah's demand to expel Hagar and her son pained the patriarch; how he was comforted by God, who told him to obey Sarah and promised that He would greatly bless Hagar's son; and how Abram gave Hagar a bottle of water and bread for the journey when he sent her away! The finer feeling of E shows itself also in the moving way in which he describes Hagar's despair in the desert, when the water was gone and the boy cried, and she did not know what to do. This beautiful sympathy is also manifest in E's wonderful story of the sacrifice of Isaac (Gen. 22 $^{1-14.19}$). But most important here is the teaching that while God demands absolute obedience, even if it involve the sacrifice of the dearest that a man possesses, He will not have human offerings at all. His demand of Abram that he sacrifice Isaac was only for the purpose of testing him. For the redemption of the first-born sons He had provided an animal substitute. The story clearly opposes the inhuman practice of sacrificing the first-born son, which seems to be presupposed even in the ancient law of Ex. 22 ^{29}. E was a teacher, who knew the effectiveness of a well-told story in religious education.

Of Isaac E had no special tales besides the sacrifice and his part in the Jacob and Esau stories. But here we note again the correction of offensive passages. In J Jacob and Esau had struggled even in their mother's womb, Jacob trying to get the upper hand in order to become the first-born. Undoubtedly the right of the first-born had passed to Jacob, so E told how Esau sold his birthright to Jacob, who thus became legally the first-born (Gen. 25 $^{29-34}$)! In J the eating of mandrakes had enabled Rachel to conceive. But E said it was due to God's favor (Gen. 30 ^{22}). E could not tolerate the sharp practices of Jacob which J had told so gleefully and as a result of which Jacob had become so wealthy. So he took pains to point out that it was God's special blessing which took the sheep from Laban and gave them to Jacob, and he had even Leah and Rachel testify that they were fully convinced of this (Gen. 31 $^{4-16}$). How honest Jacob was! and with what righteous indignation he could scold Laban as a consequence! Yet here a contrary motive, stronger than the desire to present the ancestors in the purest light, led E to tell of a deception that Rachel practised upon her father (Gen. 31 [19. 32—35]). She had stolen her father's teraphim! And when he later demanded them back from Jacob and searched for them all through the camp, Rachel sat on them and excused herself for not rising by saying that she was not well! Here E wanted to throw contempt on these household gods, which a woman had stolen and upon which she sat in her impurity! The humor of the situation was effective. Having laughed over the teraphim that had thus been treated, the reader could no longer take them quite so seriously as before. One of the most effective arguments, humor, was thus used by E, when it served to gain his end. But Rachel was no longer a saint! She had stolen and lied in addition. But that did not matter so much after all! E has no word of censure for her. As for Jacob, before he came to Bethel, he collected all the idols and amulets in his camp and buried them under the oak near Shechem (Gen. 35 [1—4]). E had no antagonism to the local sanctuaries. Jacob set up a pillar at Bethel and poured oil upon the top of it (28 [18]) and later he built an altar there (35 [7]). He buried Deborah under the oak below Bethel (35 [8]). But pillars and trees or posts were only memorials for E, he did not believe that they were the seats of the deity. God to E dwelt in heaven, His angels ascend to it by a stairway (28 [12]). E wanted to supersede the popular belief by his own higher view. We perceive his method of teaching and admire him for it.

E's masterpiece is the Joseph Story. It is a well-knit novel, finely conceived and worked out; the theme is stated in the words of Joseph to his brothers,

> Ye meant evil against me, but God meant it for good, to bring to pass, as it is this day, to save much people alive (50 [20]). And now be not grieved, nor angry with yourselves, for God sent me before you to preserve life. For these two years has the famine been in the land: and there are yet five years, in which there shall be neither ploughing nor harvest. And God sent me before you to preserve you a remnant in the earth, and to save you alive by a great deliverance. So now it was not you that sent me hither but God (45 [5—8]).

This is a fine statement of belief in the silent activity of God in the affairs of men, guiding and controlling all in accordance with His purpose. God's providence rules and overrules in the life of the individual, for to E Joseph was here an individual; he was not the tribe, even though tribal memories are contained in the story.

In the Moses Story E preserved a number of traditions that J did not give. After the recital of God's overruling providence which saved the child Moses from certain death and put him into the care of Pharaoh's daughter (Ex. 1 [15]–2 [10]) the most significant story is told of God's self-revelation to Moses at Horeb, the mountain of God in Midian, where Moses learned for the first time God's name Yahweh, who had chosen him as His agent in the deliverance of Israel, from Egypt.[1] To E the Yahweh religion of Israel began with Moses, he did not believe that the fathers had worshipped Yahweh before. In this he was probably correct; their religion had been an "El" religion or polydemonism. With Moses the religion of Yahweh commenced. To J, as we saw, Yahweh worship had begun with Adam's grandson Enosh. We have here the differing traditions of the Leah and of the Rachel tribes. Judah had known Yahweh from of old, Joseph learned to know Him through Moses. On his way to Egypt Moses met his brother Aaron, who became his associate in the work of deliverance according to E (4 [27f.] 5 [1.2.4.]). At the time of his first vision Yahweh had given to Moses a miracle-working rod, which he used in bringing on the plagues and for the crossing of the Sea of Reeds,[2] where E ascribed the song of Moses to Miriam, Aaron's sister (15 [20f.]) whom J had not mentioned. At Horeb Moses smote the rock with his rod and procured water for the people, and at Rephidim he held his rod in his hand all during the battle against the Amalekites until Joshua, who was the commanding general here and who also elsewhere in E is of great importance, had won the victory. Aaron and Hur had steadied Moses' arm. There was no word of intercession spoken, the miracle-working rod alone had won the victory![3] Moses' father-in-law, Jethro, visited him here, offered sacrifices to Yahweh, shared in the communion meal with Moses, Aaron, and the elders, and on the morrow showed Moses how to organize the administration of justice (Ex. 18 except [3.9–11]). This is one of the most important traditions of E, and especially

[1] Ex. 3 [1. 4b. 6. 9b—15. 19—22] 4 [17f. 20b.]

[2] Ex. 7 [15. 17b. 20b. 23] 9 [22. 23a. 24a. 25a. 31. 35] 10 [12. 13a. 14a. 15b. 20—23. 27] 11 [1–3] 13 [17—19] 14 [7. 9a. 10b. 15a. 16a. 19a. 20a. 24b.]

[3] Ex. 17 [1b. 2a. 4—6. 7b*. 8—16.]

noteworthy in that it showed that judicial organization in Israel
went back ultimately to Jethro, the Midianite priest, and not to
Moses.   Immediately following this is E's story of the great legislation at Mount Horeb and the giving of the Decalogue.   The code
of laws embodied in the Book of the Covenant on the basis of which
the people made a solemn covenant with Yahweh (Ex. 20 ^{22}–23 ^{19})
was probably not in the original story of E, but only inserted later
on.   In the story of the Golden Calf, which Aaron made of the
golden ear-rings of the people, E made splendid use of the opportunity of showing the heinousness as well as the folly of worshipping
gods made with hands and of attributing to such a calf the great
act of deliverance from Egypt (Ex. 32 $^{1-6.\ 15-24}$).   In his anger Moses
broke the sacred tables of the law and E has no word of rebuke for
this, because his anger was justified.   E's keen irony is seen in the
answer of Aaron to Moses,

> Let not the anger of my lord wax hot, thou knowest the people that they
> are set on evil.   For they said to me, "Make us gods, which shall go before us:
> for as for this Moses, the man that brought us up out of the land of Egypt, we
> know not what has become of him."   And I said to them, "Whosoever has any
> gold, let them break it off."   So they gave it me, and I cast it into the fire, and
> there came out this calf.   (Ex. 32 $^{22-24}$)

Forsooth, all by itself!   One literally sees it coming out!   Again
the readers or hearers laughed, and having once laughed at the
golden calf, they found it hard to take the golden calves in the
temples at Bethel and Dan as seriously as before.   E's humor had
spoiled their sacred significance for them, and that was his intention!
Sent away from Mount Horeb by the indignant God, the people were
led by the ark of Yahweh in which His presence manifested itself.
E has preserved the ancient signals used with it (Num. 10 $^{33-36}$; cf.
p. 3).   Murmurings of the people were punished at Taberah (Num.
11 $^{1-3}$) and the rebellion of Miriam and Aaron was terribly visited, at
least upon Miriam, but on Moses' intercession her leprosy was
removed (12 $^{1.\ 9-15}$).[1]   After cravenly fearing at first to invade Canaan on the report of the spies, but stung by the reproof of Yahweh,
who declared that none of the present generation except Caleb
would see the land, the people attacked the Amalekites and Ca-

---

[1] Originally Aaron must have been punished too, but that is now omitted because
of his eminence among the priests.

naanites against Moses' command and were terribly defeated
(14 $^{39-45}$). Obedience to Yahweh and to His prophet is one of E's important teachings. Dathan and Abiram also with all their families suffered death, because they dared to rebel against Moses' authority (Num. 16).[1] Israel's request for permission to pass through
Edom's territory was refused, so they turned south to skirt the land
of Edom (20 $^{14-18.\ 21a.\ 22a}$). On the way from Kadesh fiery serpents
were sent among them because of their murmurings against God
and Moses. But Moses interceded for them, when they repented,
and was instructed to make a serpent of brass, which would heal
every one who looked at it when he was bitten (21 $^{4b-9}$). This was a
case of healing by sympathetic magic, a practice well known among
many peoples. The significant part of the story however is that E
here tried to counteract the worship of the brazen serpent, an
ancient idol which had found its place in the temple at Jerusalem, by
reinterpreting its meaning. It was indeed quite old, he admitted,
for it went back to Moses. But he only made it as a symbol. It
was not divine, nor did it represent a god. Yahweh used it as a
means of healing those that had been bitten by serpents in the
wilderness. There was therefore no reason whatever to pay homage
to it. E's reinterpretation did not have the desired effect, it still
permitted the people to look upon it in the expectation of being
healed from their present ills, and they continued to offer incense to
it. The spell was broken only by its destruction under King Hezekiah (2 Ki. 18 ^{4}). For Israel's march E gave extracts from the Book
of the Wars of Yahweh (cf. p. 4) and told of the defeat of Sihon,
King of the Amorites, and the occupation of his country; and of
Balak's fruitless attempt to destroy Israel through the prophecies
of the famous Balaam (Num. 21–24 in part). In the punishment
of those that had taken part in Moabite sacrificial festivals, E demanded that every one who had joined himself to Baal Peor, not
only the ringleaders, should be executed (25 $^{3a.\ 5}$). E's loyalty to
Yahweh was intense, his antagonism against other gods most bitter.
At last the days of Moses drew to an end. Joshua was made his
successor (Deut. 31 $^{14.\ 15.\ 23}$), but before his death Moses blessed the
Israelites with the so-called blessing of Moses which E incorporated

[1] The analysis of J and E in this story is not certain. Probably vv $^{1b.\ 2a.\ 12.\ 14b.}$ $^{25.\ 27b.\ 32a.\ 33b.\ 34}$ are from E.

here (Deut. 33). Then he died in the land of Moab. Nobody knows his grave. But his fame has lived on.

> There has not arisen a prophet since in Israel like unto Moses, whom Yahweh knew face to face. (Deut. 34 [5. 6. 10f.])

This high judgment of Moses was also written, in the spirit of E but probably not by himself, into the story of Miriam's and Aaron's rebellion against Moses,

> Hear now My words,
> If there be a prophet among you,
> I Yahweh make Myself known to him in visions,
> I speak with him in dreams.
> My servant Moses is not so;
> He is entrusted with all My house,
> With him I speak mouth to mouth,
> Plainly, and not in dark speeches,
> And the form of Yahweh he beholds. (Num. 12 [6ff.])

Quite in line with this is the story of the seventy elders who received something of the spirit of Moses and began to prophesy, and of the two elders that had remained in the camp and prophesied too. The ideal of E is voiced by Moses,

> Would that all Yahweh's people were prophets, that Yahweh would put His spirit upon them![1] (Num. 11 [16f. 24b—30])

The story of the conquest of Canaan under Joshua, beginning with the spying out of Jericho, the crossing of the Jordan, the setting up of memorial stones, and Jericho's and Ai's capture, was told by E in his usual interesting, swiftly moving manner. The covenant which Joshua had been tricked into making with the Hivvites of Gibeon was the cause of the war of a confederation of southern city-kings under Adonizedek of Jerusalem against Gibeon which resulted in their terrible defeat by Israel at Gibeon. The southern confederacy was broken, its power was destroyed. But in the North a confederacy under King Jabin of Hazor fought against Joshua and was defeated by him at the waters of Merom. These two decisive victories in the North and the South secured Israel its foothold in the land. After assigning Hebron to Caleb and allotting

---

[1] Since this story tells of Moses' installing these elders as judges at the command of Yahweh, while E himself had told of the judicial organization as introduced by Moses at the suggestion of Jethro his father-in-law, it was probably inserted later.

territory to those tribes that were not yet settled[1] Joshua made his solemn farewell address at Shechem (24) and bound the people in sacred covenant to the exclusive worship of Yahweh :

Now therefore fear Yahweh, and serve Him in sincerity and in truth; and put away the gods which your fathers served beyond the River, and in Egypt; and serve ye Yahweh. And if it seem evil unto you to serve Yahweh, choose you this day whom ye will serve; whether the gods which your fathers served that were beyond the River, or the gods of the Amorites, in whose land ye dwell : but as for me and my house, we will serve Yahweh.

And the people answered and said, Far be it from us that we should forsake Yahweh, to serve other gods; for Yahweh our God, He it is that brought us up out of the land of Egypt, from the house of bondage, and that did those great signs in our sight, and preserved us in all the way wherein we went, and among all the peoples through the midst of whom we passed; and Yahweh drove out from before us the Amorites that dwelt in the land : therefore we also will serve Yahweh; for He is our God.

And Joshua said to the people, Ye cannot serve Yahweh; for He is a holy God; He is a jealous God; He will not forgive your transgression nor your sins. If ye forsake Yahweh, and serve foreign gods, then He will turn and do you evil, and consume you, after that He has done you good. And the people said to Joshua, Nay; but we will serve Yahweh. And Joshua said to the people, Ye are witnesses against yourselves that ye have chosen you Yahweh, to serve Him. Now therefore put away, said he, the foreign gods which are among you, and incline your heart to Yahweh, the God of Israel. And the people said unto Joshua, Yahweh our God will we serve, and to His voice will we hearken. (Josh. 24 [14-24])

In this long address E laid down the principle that was so close to his heart. Here he used the method of direct teaching and preaching, and sought to win a decision from his readers that coincided with that of Joshua's hearers. This was a real sermon by E.

The history of the Judges E viewed entirely from this point of view. In an introduction he made this plain :

And Joshua the son of Nun, the servant of Yahweh, died, a hundred and ten years old. And they buried him in the border of his inheritance in Timnath-heres, in the hill-country of Ephraim, on the north of the mountain of Gaash.

And also all that generation were gathered to their fathers : and there arose another generation after them, that knew not Yahweh, nor yet the work which he had wrought for Israel. And they forsook Yahweh, and served Baal and the Ashtaroth. And the anger of Yahweh was kindled against Israel; and He said, Because this nation have transgressed My covenant which I commanded their

[1] Josh. 14 [6-15] 16 [1-3. 9] 17 [1b. 2. 8. 10b] 18 [2-6. 8-10].

fathers, and have not hearkened to My voice; I also will not henceforth drive out any from before them of the nations that Joshua left when he died. And they were left, to prove Israel by them, to know whether they would obey the commandments of Yahweh, which he commanded their fathers by Moses.[1] (Judg. 2 [6–11. 13. 20f. 23])

The individual stories of the Judges were brought together in a history which is dominated by the thought that Israel's dwelling among the Canaanites constituted a test of their fidelity and that any apostasy from Yahweh was punished by national calamity. The local heroes became for E champions and leaders of all Israel. Theocrat as he was by profound conviction, the Judges were for him the representatives of the divine King, who really was ruling and controlling the affairs of His people. The stories of J were amplified and new ones were added, so that E's treatment comprised all the major and minor Judges and the appendices.[2] In the story of Gideon he made plain that this great hero refused to become king, when his people offered the kingship to him : "I will not rule over you, neither shall my son rule over you : Yahweh shall rule over you"(Judg. 8 [22f.]). In the fable of Jotham (cf. p. 10f.) the institution of kingship was derided, and the miserable fate of Abimelech who had made himself king in Shechem proved to E the correctness of his judgment (Judg. 9). Israel was intended as a theocracy not as a monarchy; Yahweh Himself was its King and not a mortal man.

In his treatment of the founding of the monarchy E brought out his theocratic point of view with the greatest preciseness. In the story of Samuel, which is the introduction to it, E showed how from childhood up Samuel had been God's favorite and how he had been chosen as His instrument, the champion and leader of Israel. But when he was old and his sons, whom he had made judges, proved recreant to his high ideal, the elders of Israel demanded of Samuel that he should make them a king "to judge us like all the nations." But he was displeased with this, and only after God had told him to hearken to them "for they have not rejected thee, but they have rejected Me, that I should not be King over them," and only after he had told the people quite solemnly that kingship would involve

[1] Cf. also 6 [7–10] 10 [10. 11a. 12b–16].

[2] In the story of Micah and his idol E added a few characteristic interpolations in order to cast contempt upon the image.

for them the loss of individual liberty, since the king would use them all as his servants, did he yield to their repeated demand for a king and called a popular assembly at Mizpah. There he told them once more,

Ye have this day rejected your God, who Himself saves you out of all your calamities and your distresses; and ye have said to Him, "Nay, but set a king over us." (1 Sam. 10 ^{19})

Then Saul, the son of Kish, was chosen by lot and acclaimed as king. Whereupon Samuel, laying down his theocratic office, demanded and received from the people the approval of his administration and then warned them and their king to be loyal to Yahweh in a solemn address in which he briefly reviewed the history of the theocracy from Moses to the demand for a king. As a sign that it was a great wickedness to ask for a king, he called on Yahweh, who sent thunder and lightning. But when the people, greatly fearing and confessing "we have added to all our sins this evil, to ask for a king," begged Samuel to intercede for them, he promised that he would never cease doing this and instructing them in the good and right way, and exhorted them to serve Yahweh in truth with all their hearts. Although Samuel had abdicated, he nevertheless retained, as it were, supreme command. For it was he that ordered Saul to attack and exterminate the Amalekites, "spare them not, but slay both man and woman, infant and suckling, ox and sheep, camel and ass." When Saul had defeated the Amalekites but spared King Agag and the choice animals, Samuel absolutely refused to accept his excuse that the people had spared these animals for a sacrifice to Yahweh and asked in truly prophetic manner,

Has Yahweh as great delight in burnt-offerings and sacrifices,
    as in obeying the voice of Yahweh?
Behold, to obey is better than sacrifice,
    and to hearken than the fat of rams.
For rebellion is as the sin of witchcraft,
    and stubbornness is as idolatry and teraphim.
Because thou hast rejected the word of Yahweh,
    He has also rejected thee from being king. (1 Sam. 15 $^{22f.}$)

Saul's rejection was irrevocable, in spite of his humble plea. Samuel himself hewed the Amalekite king to pieces before Yahweh in Gilgal; then he went home and never saw Saul again in his life. But after his death he appeared once more to him, when Saul, having sought God's oracle in vain, went in utter despair to the witch at Endor to cite through her Samuel's ghost that he might give him counsel. But he only received the confirmation of his rejection and the prediction of his and his sons' death and of Israel's defeat in the battle on the morrow. Stunned by the terror of these words Saul suddenly fell down unconscious. He was utterly exhausted by this experience and his fast. Hardly could they persuade him to eat. Then he went away, — to his doom. On Gilboa's height his sons were slain, and he himself was severely wounded as he fought his last fight. To escape ignominious death at the hand of the Philistines he fell upon his own sword. Thus ended the first king of Israel.[1] A dark premonition comes upon the reader, what will the history of the kings of Israel be, that began so ominously with Saul? E knew the story of murder and bloodshed that disgraced the monarchy in Israel, and was convinced that the people had sinned in asking for a king.

E was a wonderful teacher. These stories were the means of his instruction. Like J, he was an ardent worshipper of Yahweh and a thorough believer in Israel's obligation of exclusive loyalty to Him. That spirit he wished to inculcate in his hearers and readers too. He attacked the worship at the local sanctuaries as little as J, and accepted the various festivals and cultic practices and all sorts of Canaanitish implements. Indeed E was quite friendly to the priesthood, as his interest in Aaron shows. But to him the sacred pillars and posts were only memorials. The brazen serpent he reinterpreted as a symbol. But the golden calf he rejected and all images, including the teraphim. Sacrifices are well-pleasing to Yahweh, but obedience is more important. In his finest story, the sacrifice of Isaac, E showed that willingness to obey God to the uttermost was what He desired more than anything else. Similarly in the story of Saul's rejection. As for the law of the first-born son, he expounded it as meaning not human sacrifice but a redemption by the substitution of an animal sacrifice. In the transformation of the ancient material E went further than J. His moral consciousness was more sensitive and refined, so he qualified Abram's deliber-

---

[1] E's story is contained in 1 Sam. 1. 2 $^{11-26}$ 3. [4 ^{1} –7 ^{2}] 7 $^{3-17}$ 8. 10 $^{17-25}$ 12. 15. 16 $^{1-13}$ 28 $^{3-25}$ 31.

ate lie and explained Jacob's wealth as not due to his sharp practices but to the blessing of God. His more advanced theology made him shun the naïve anthropomorphic methods of God's revelation that J still used in his stories. In E God no longer appeared in person, but revealed Himself in a vision or a dream, or by one angel or more. He had His special organs of revelation. Abram was a prophet, Miriam a prophetess, the seventy Elders were endowed with the spirit of prophecy, and Samuel was a prophet too. But the greatest of them all was Moses, with whom alone God spoke face to face; there was none like him. To E there was a progress of divine revelation in history. The forefathers beyond the River were idolaters. Abram became God's prophet. But the full revelation of God was not given till Moses, to whom God revealed for the first time His name Yahweh. Thus E did not use this name before Moses. In this he rightly held fast the memory of the polydemonistic character of the religion before Moses. He told history not for its own sake merely, but as a means of religious instruction, made it more definitely than J had done the vehicle of religious truth and inserted therefore more of a distinctly religious character and more of the miraculous. He was a thorough believer in the theocratic form of government and showed the inherent wickedness of the monarchy. Great teacher that he was, E used not only the story but also the direct method of command and prohibition by law, and the argumentative and hortatory method of prophetic address. If only he could instil the truth in his people's minds, if only he could make his people more loyal to Yahweh!

It is impossible to overestimate the importance of J and E for the development of the religion of Israel. E prepared his work about 750 B.C. After the fall of the Northern Kingdom in 722, Judah fell heir to her greater brother's name and literary treasures. Sometime in the early part of the seventh century, these were adapted to the needs of the Judæans and published in Judæan editions. For E they had however their own parallel Yahwist history. But E had so much additional material and especially such a strong prophetic tendency that it was felt that it must be preserved by all means. And yet it was out of the question that the Elohist should displace, even in a Judæan edition, the popular Judæan Jahvist. So it was decided to combine them in a single history JE. For the period from the creation to Abraham there was only the Judæan document. From Abraham on both documents were woven together. For the Abraham stories J served as the basis and the E stories were inserted; but as the editor proceeded he made more and more use of E; thus in the Joseph story E is the basis, and while in the Exodus story J and E are at first almost equally used, E becomes more and more predominant in the Sinai sections and especially in the story of the conquest and the time of the Judges. It is also prominent in the Samuel stories. This was only natural, for the prophetic element is stronger in E and its pedagogic value seemed to the editor to be greater than that of J. But in the Saul and especially in the David stories the Judæan source took the lead, as was to be expected. The work of compilation was done with great skill. Sometimes both stories were placed side by side without abridgement, as, *e.g.*, the stories of Sarah's danger and Abraham's deception (Gen. 12 J; 20 E); sometimes they were woven together into a single story, now J now E forming the basis into which the variant traditions were worked, as, *e.g.*, in the story of how Joseph came to Egypt (Gen. 37). Occasionally it was necessary for the editor to add certain sentences of his own in order to make room for the variant story or to harmonize both, *e.g.* Gen. 16 [9] in J's story of Hagar's flight, for Hagar had to be brought back for E's story (Gen. 20), or 1 Sam. 10 [8. 25b. 26. 27] 11 [12–14] in the story of the founding of the kingdom. Again, the editor added matter of his own in order to emphasize certain ideas, *e.g.* by reiterating the promise of Israel's great future (Gen. 22 [15–18] 26 [3b. 4f.]). But for all this he treated the stories both of J and of E with much reverence and left them pretty much as they had been handed down. This is fortunate for us and remarkable for him, for his own religious ideas were in several respects more advanced even than those of E. If he had radically revised the stories in the interest of his own higher religious conceptions, many valuable and interesting survivals of earlier stages of religious development would have been altogether lost to us. The new book JE was destined to supplant the separate editions of J and E, but it did not succeed in this immediately.

CHAPTER VII

AMOS AND HOSEA

A NEW epoch not only in literature but in religion began with the rise of the literary prophets, for they did not merely produce a new class of literature, but ushered in the greatest movement in the spiritual history of mankind. It was a great day for religion, when at a harvest feast in Bethel about 750 B.C. Amos chanted before a vast assembly the funeral song of Israel:

> The virgin of Israel is fallen,
>   she shall no more rise,
> Prostrate she lies on her ground,
>   none raises her up. (5 [1])

Nothing could have been more startling and absurd, if not blasphemous, than the quickly following announcement that Yahweh Himself would deal the deathblow to His people. How could He, who was so completely bound together with Israel that His very existence depended on that of His people, destroy them? It would have meant His own destruction too, for He would no longer be known and worshipped, His religion would be extinct with Israel's death. But Amos asserted, with irresistible spiritual authority, that in spite of her national prosperity under Jeroboam's splendid reign Israel was doomed by Yahweh Himself.

How did Amos gain this conviction? He was not a professional prophet but a plain shepherd and dresser of sycamore trees in Tekoa, Judah. His mind was wonderfully clear, his moral nature finely developed, his spiritual sensitiveness singularly alert. He lived in the solitude of the steppe. In the silence of the desert he meditated on important problems, pondered till a great fear came upon him, a dark presentiment of impending disaster; he brooded over it until he was in the ecstatic state, where his feelings crystallized into a vision in which Yahweh would have destroyed Israel by a locust plague, if Amos had not interceded for them.

87

Thus the Lord Yahweh showed me: and, behold, there was a brood of locusts in the beginning of the shooting up of the latter growth; and lo, it was the
latter growth after the king's mowings. And it came to pass that, when they
were about to devour completely the herbage of the land, then I said, O Lord
Yahweh, forgive, I beseech Thee: how shall Jacob stand? for he is small. Yahweh repented concerning this: It shall not be, said Yahweh. (7 $^{1-3}$)

Again it came, his fear would not be quieted: another vision of
destruction! Once more it was averted by his intercession.

Thus the Lord Yahweh showed me: and, behold, the Lord Yahweh called
to contend by fire; and it devoured the great deep, and would have eaten up
the land. Then said I, O Lord Yahweh, cease, I beseech Thee: how shall
Jacob stand? for he is small. Yahweh repented concerning this: This also
shall not be, said the Lord Yahweh. (7 $^{4-6}$)

These were great experiences, but they did not yet make Amos
a prophet. Still in the light of them many things assumed a different aspect. As he went to the markets of North Israel to sell the
wool of his sheep and the fruits of his trees, he saw the fearful social
corruption of the people, the oppression of the poor, the revelries
of the rich, the debasing immoral practices carried on in connection
with the worship of Yahweh at the various sanctuaries, and with it
all a sense of shamelessness and arrogance. The conscience of the
plain shepherd revolted, hot anger rose in his heart. Again he
mused in the desert, again the dark fear came upon him, mingled
with the clear memory of the things he had witnessed in North
Israel, when suddenly there burst upon him the vision that made him
a prophet of Yahweh.

Thus He showed me: and, behold, the Lord stood beside a wall made by a
plumb-line, with a plumb-line in his hand. And Yahweh said to me, Amos,
what seest thou? And I said, A plumb-line. Then said the Lord, Behold, I
am setting a plumb-line in the midst of My people Israel; I will not again pardon them any more; and the high places of Isaac shall be desolate, and the
sanctuaries of Israel shall be laid waste; and I will rise against the house of
Jeroboam with the sword. (7 $^{7-9}$)

As a wall that is crooked *must* fall, so a nation that is corrupt *must*
perish. It was not until the awful presentiment of coming danger
became blended with the sense of the sin of the people and the revelation of the moral character of Yahweh in one overmastering experience that Amos knew that he must go and prophesy to Israel.

He would never have gone, had not Yahweh Himself compelled him
to prophesy. But

> Does a lion roar in the forest,
>   when he has no prey?
> Does a young lion cry out of his den,
>   if he has taken nothing?
> Does a bird fall upon the earth,
>   where no gin is set for him?
> Does a snare spring up from the ground,
>   and has taken nothing at all?
> Is the trumpet blown in the city,
>   and the people are not afraid?
> Does evil befall a city,
>   and Yahweh has not done it?
> The lion has roared,
>   who will not fear?
> The Lord Yahweh has spoken,
>   who can but prophesy? (3 [4-6. 8]) [1]

Two final visions confirmed him in his conviction.

Thus the Lord Yahweh showed me: and, behold, a basket of summer
fruit. And He said, Amos, what seest thou? And I said, A basket of summer
fruit. Then said Yahweh to me, The end is come upon My people Israel; I
will not again pardon them any more. (8 [1f.])

I saw the Lord standing beside the altar: and He said, I will smite the
capitals, that the thresholds shake; and I will kill with a crash all of them; and I
will slay the last of them with the sword: there shall not one of them flee away,
and there shall not one of them escape. Though they dig into Sheol, thence
shall My hand take them; and though they climb up to heaven, thence will I
bring them down. And though they hide themselves in the top of Carmel, I
will search and take them out thence; and though they be hid from My sight
in the bottom of the sea, thence will I command the serpent, and it shall bite
them. And though they go into captivity before their enemies, thence will I
command the sword, and it shall slay them: and I will set Mine eyes upon them
for evil, and not for good. (9 [1-4])

How often Amos appeared in public we do not know. We have a graphic account of his meeting with the priest at Bethel after one of his addresses to the people.

Then Amaziah the priest of Beth-el sent to Jeroboam, king of Israel, saying,
Amos has conspired against thee in the midst of the house of Israel: the land
is not able to bear all his words. For thus Amos says, Jeroboam shall die by

---

[1] A negative answer is expected to each question.

the sword, and Israel shall surely be led away captive out of his land. Also
Amaziah said to Amos, O thou seer, go, flee thou away into the land of Judah
and there eat bread, and prophesy there : but prophesy not again any more at
Beth-el ; for it is the king's sanctuary, and it is a royal house. Then answered
Amos, and said to Amaziah, I am no prophet, nor prophet's son ; but a herds-
man, and a dresser of sycamore-trees : and Yahweh took me from following the
flock, and Yahweh said to me, Go, prophesy to My people Israel. Now therefore hear thou the word of Yahweh : Thou sayest, Prophesy not against Israel,
and drop not (thy word) against the house of Isaac ; therefore thus says Yahweh :

> Thy wife shall be a harlot in the city,
> And thy sons and thy daughters shall fall by the sword,
> And thy land shall be divided by line ;
> And thou thyself shall die in a land that is unclean,
> And Israel shall surely go into exile away from his land. (7 $^{10-17}$)

Amaziah drove him from Bethel, but the message burnt still in his
soul ; it was too great to be left unsaid. In the silence of the steppe
whither he returned, Amos wrote his mighty book and sent it forth
to preach where he himself could no longer be heard.

It was a short book, clear, easily understood, arranged in three
sections. After the brief motto comes an address on Yahweh's
judgment of the neighboring nations and of Israel which is a rhetorical masterpiece of great power (ch. 1f.). The middle section (3–6)
contains a series of addresses, grouped according to identical introductions, "Hear this word" and "Woe to," all dealing with Yahweh's
absolute righteousness and Israel's certain doom on account of her
social corruption. The last section (7–9 ^{8a}) presents a sort of defence of Amos' prophetic office in the record of his visions and his
experience at Bethel, besides various addresses.[1]

We note with astonishment Amos' literary style. All his addresses are in clear rhythmic lines, usually grouped in strophes.
This is characteristic of all the great prophets, not only of Amos.
In the exaltation of the prophet's spirit the words flow from his lips
in rhythmic regularity. It is a well-recognized experience not
confined to the Hebrews, which makes the prophet and the poet
akin. In Amos poetic power was combined with rhetorical skill.
In his great address against the foreign nations he used grave and
impressive refrains at the beginning and the end of each strophe.

---

[1] Later the book received several additions, an oracle against Judah among the
oracles against the nations (2 $^{4f.}$) ; a series of passages celebrating Yahweh's rule in
nature (4 ^{13} 5 $^{8f.}$ 9 $^{5f.}$) ; and a prediction of the glorious future of Judah (9 $^{8b-15}$).

With consummate skill he began with the hostile neighbors, scored their sins, and predicted punishment to one after another, when suddenly, after intoning the same terrible opening refrain, he turned on Israel, denounced her social corruption, and foretold her certain doom:

> *Thus says Yahweh,*
> *For three transgressions of* ISRAEL,
> *yea for four, I will not revoke her punishment:*
> Because they have sold the righteous for silver,
> and the needy for a pair of shoes, etc. (2 [6])

Amos grasped with singular clearness a truth of fundamental importance: the righteousness of God. This brought him into conflict with popular religion along several lines. In the first place there was his emphasis upon upright conduct as opposed to mere cult. The priests and the people believed that Yahweh's requirement was the cult and that He would be pleased with them, if they fulfilled this. Amos insisted that God's sole requirement was social justice. God had never required any sacrificial cult from His people at all, only righteousness, nothing else! As for the cult,

> I hate, I despise your feasts,
> and I take no delight in your solemn assemblies.
> Yea, though ye offer Me your burnt-offerings
> and meal-offerings, I will not accept them;
> neither will I regard the peace offerings of your fat beasts.
> Take away from Me the noise of thy songs,
> for I will not hear the melody of thy viols:
> *But let justice roll down as waters,*
> *and righteousness as an overflowing stream!*
> Did ye bring unto Me sacrifices and offerings in the wilderness
> forty years, O house of Israel? (5 [21-25])

The answer is, of course, No! Even in the wonderful days of the early love union between Yahweh and Israel no sacrifices were brought. Well, then, Yahweh cannot be found in mere external worship with all its magical devices. His grace can be only experienced in the steady pursuit of the moral ideal. The emphasis is altogether on the moral element in religion. "Seek *good*, and not evil, that ye may live" stands side by side with "Seek ye *Me* and ye shall live."

This extreme rejection of the entire cult was due to polemics. The question never came to Amos how, from his point of view, religion should be organized. He saw the injustice and oppression, the greed and brutality, the luxury and debauchery, in short, the violation of the common moral law by a people who were most zealous in the performance of all religious rites and ceremonies, giving much to God in order to get much from Him. He revolted against this practice, attacked the cult which had benumbed the moral feeling and perception of the people. Not gifts to God, but justice to men! was his cry. How can men be so bare of all feeling of delicacy and shame as the father and son are who carry on their debauch in the name of religion at the cost of the suffering poor (2 [7f.])? How can Yahweh endure a nation whose fat rich women spur their husbands on to oppress the poor and to grind out of them the means for frivolous and luxurious banquets (4 [1-3])? Yahweh is righteous and punishes injustice with relentless anger.

The second point in Amos' message was that Yahweh's requirement of righteousness is universal. Not only Israel but all the nations of the world are bound to observe the fundamental laws of humanity and social morality. Else they will be terribly punished by the righteous Yahweh, who visits everywhere the violations of the moral law. Yahweh is not only Israel's God, but the God of the whole world and interested in all the nations. "Are ye not as the children of the Ethiopians unto Me, O children of Israel?" says Yahweh. "Have not I brought up Israel out of the land of Egypt?" Yes, but also "the Philistines from Caphtor, and the Syrians from Kir!" (9 [7]) The national history of Israel's hated enemies also has been guided by Yahweh! We note with glad amazement how broad Amos' idea of God has become. Moab, he declared, would be punished, because they had "burned the bones of the king of Edom into lime!" (2 [1]) A nationalist would have rejoiced over this brutality that violated deep-rooted instincts of humanity, for Edom was Israel's enemy. Of course, Amos ran counter to the cherished popular belief in Israel's peculiar connection with Yahweh. He knew it well. But assuming for a moment that "you only have I known of all the families of the earth," he drew this startling consequence, "*therefore* I will visit upon all your iniquities!" (3 [1]) If Israel claims the prerogative of special intimacy, it must bear special responsibility. The relation between Yahweh and Israel is entirely moral and will be dissolved, if the moral conditions are not fulfilled.

In the third place, along with this universal outlook went Amos' reaction against the popular hope of the "Day of Yahweh." Ardently the people looked for the day, when Yahweh Himself would triumph over all His and Israel's enemies. Amos rudely shattered this belief.

> Woe to you that desire the day of Yahweh!
>   Wherefore would you have the day of Yahweh?
> It is darkness and not light! (5 18)

There is a sternness in Amos which was born out of moral indignation. He was a man of steel, whose indomitable spirit no opposition could break. But we must not forget that he pleaded twice with Yahweh for little Jacob (7 2.5). And we may well ask whether he actually had no hope for Israel, although his messages contain nothing but unrelieved doom. Only once he refers to the possibility that a few might perhaps be saved.

> Hate the evil, and love the good,
>   and establish justice in the gate:
> *it may be* that Yahweh, the God of hosts,
>   will be gracious to *the remnant* of Joseph. (5 15)

Did he ever spin out this hope? It may be! But if he did, he never published it. He had not been commissioned to it. He was a prophet of doom. It is to a later age that we owe the conclusion (9 8b−15) which now follows upon his messages like the dawn upon the gloomy night.

Amos may justly be called the prophet of righteousness, for that expresses his great contribution to religion. The moral character of Yahweh had, of course, been recognized before. Amos himself did not believe that he had said anything new. He assumed the knowledge of the moral law in all men, and its implications as well. But nobody had ever seen so clearly what it involved or dared to be so thoroughgoing in the application of this truth. Significantly enough, it is this moral principle on which Amos' practical monotheism was based. Not because Yahweh is almighty, nor because He is the one great Cause behind the phenomena of the world, but because He is righteous and visits unrighteousness everywhere, did He come to be regarded as the one God. This is the so-called ethical monotheism of the prophets, of which Amos was the first exponent.

Only a few years after Amos, Hosea began to prophesy, *ca.* 745–735 B.C. Gentle and tender, warm-hearted and loving, Hosea stood in sharp contrast to the rugged, mighty prophet of the South. But he ranks with him among the greatest by reason of his spiritual insight. At first he also was a prophet of doom. The dynasty of Jehu, founded on blood, will fall! Yahweh will no longer pity His people but reject them forever! Thus he proclaimed, in harmony with Amos. But then came the tragedy that changed him and made him the prophet of love. He had married Gomer, the daughter of Diblaim; she had borne him three children, to whom he had given symbolical names which were to be perpetual sermons to Israel, warning them of the coming doom. They outline his message during the first years of his ministry. Here is the record:

Yahweh said to Hosea, Go, take to thee a wife. So he went and took Gomer the daughter of Diblaim; and she conceived, and bore him a son. And Yahweh said to him, Call his name Jezreel; for yet a little while, and I will avenge the blood of Jezreel upon the house of Jehu, and will cause the kingdom of the house of Israel to cease. And it shall come to pass at that day, that I will break the bow of Israel in the valley of Jezreel. And she conceived again, and bore a daughter. And He said to him, Call her name Lo-ruhamah,[1] for I will no more have mercy upon the house of Israel, that I should in any wise pardon them. Now when she had weaned Lo-ruhamah, she conceived, and bore a son. And He said, Call his name Lo-ammi,[2] for ye are not My people, and I will not be your God. (Hos. 1 2a. 3–6. 8)

Not yet had Hosea known that his wife was unfaithful. When he discovered it, there was but one course open to him according to Israelite law and custom. His heart might break, now that its idol had fallen, but he must deal with her as was customary with adulteresses:

She is not my wife,
　　and I am not her husband!
And her children I do not pity,
　　because they are children of harlotry,
For their mother has played the harlot,
　　she that conceived them has done shamefully.
And now will I uncover her shame
　　before the eyes of her lovers,
And no man shall save her out of my hand. (2 2a. 4. 5a. 10)

[1] This means, she that has not obtained mercy.
[2] This means, not My people.

He does not tell us of his anguish and his grief, of his yearning love, his rage and shame, as he went to mete out full punishment to her. He tells only that which happened at the decisive moment: "And Yahweh said to me, Go, still love a woman, beloved of her paramour and an adulteress" (3 ¹). An unheard-of command! He must love her still, although she loves another and is an adulteress! And this is the reason for the strange order: "Even as Yahweh loves the children of Israel, though they turn to other gods." Yahweh is in an entirely similar condition with His wife, Israel, who also is unfaithful. Hosea could not but believe that Yahweh would cast her off; in fact, he had proclaimed this rejection for years. But now comes this startling message: Yahweh loves Israel still, He cannot bear to cast her off forever; and Hosea is to symbolize in his life, hard as that may be, this deathless love in spite of cruel faithlessness: love Gomer still, for Yahweh loves Israel still! The love of God is to be incarnate in Hosea. Yahweh then goes on to tell Hosea that he is to speak earnestly to Gomer, saying to her that he will keep her in confinement so that she will have no chance to see her lover, but that he himself will still be her own. For this will be Yahweh's treatment of Israel too, "for the children of Israel shall abide many days without king, and without prince, and without sacrifice, and without pillar, and without ephod or teraphim" (3 ⁴). The story breaks off here. It is in the nature of its purpose that we are not told with what success Hosea tried to woo back the love of his erring wife and to build a new happiness on the ruins of that of his youth, for his experience has become symbolic of Yahweh's experience. Like Hosea, Yahweh will take Israel away from the influence of the terrible temptation. He will allure her into the wilderness and there, where they had spent the time of their first love, will He woo for her heart again, and when she turns to Him again and comes to know Him really and to see how vain and empty her love for others has been, He will restore her to her own land and wonderful fertility will accompany the reëstablishment of the love relationship between Yahweh and Israel. Hosea still believed in the necessity of punishment; Israel will have to go into exile, but it will not be due to Yahweh's punitive justice but to His redemptive purpose: her sin will not merely be punished, but inwardly conquered. The stern prophet of doom has become the prophet of love, a love that is faithful in spite of the loved one's faithlessness, a love that punishes but in order to redeem and restore! Henceforth he preached the deeply moral love of God, His inexorable moral demands, and His certain punishment of sin. But through all and in spite of all, love will triumph in the end, and the hope of the future is assured.

When Hosea came to write down his messages, he began in ch. 1-3 with his own sad story, but he wove it so completely together with Yahweh's story that we can separate it only with difficulty (1 2a. 3-6. 8 2 2a. 4. 5a. 10 3 1-3). He now interpreted the divine purpose of his tragedy, and believed that Gomer had been a licentious woman from the beginning and that her children were not really his own. In the second part of his book (4-14) Hosea collected his prophetic utterances, although not all, we may be sure.[1] They are mostly brief strophes, put together without any definite scheme of arrangement. The whole passion of his heart speaks in them. Sometimes it is doom, sometimes it is hope. In one of the most moving passages he does not shrink from transferring the terrible struggle of his own heart to the heart of the Eternal:

> How shall I give thee up, Ephraim?
>   how shall I cast thee off, Israel?
> How shall I make thee as Admah?
>   how shall I set thee as Zeboim?
> My heart is turned within Me,
>   My compassions are kindled together.
> I will not execute the fierceness of Mine anger,
>   I will not return to destroy Ephraim:
> For I am God, and not man,
>   the Holy One in thy midst, and not mortal. (11 8f.)

The whole second part of the book is in poetry. Hosea was a great lyrical poet. His imagination was vivid, his style most picturesque. At times he moves us by the exquisite tenderness of his feelings, at times he carries us away in his passionate anger, again he startles us by the originality and unexpected beauty of his thought and diction.

---

[1] We have the book of Hosea in a Judæan edition. Two Judæan editors made slight modifications and additions. The earlier one made the messages to apply to Judah as well as to Israel (5 10. 12. 13. 14 6 4. 11 8 14 10 11 12 2). The later one added hopeful words for Judah (1 7. 10) and some favorable references (3 5 "and David their king" 4 15a 11 12b).

There is a restlessness of spirit in the book, a nervousness, and an ever present sadness. But at the end the yearning hope finds rest in the divine promise of harmony and restoration.

Hosea conceived the relation between Yahweh and Israel after the analogy of the marital relation. Israel is Yahweh's wife. He had fallen in love with her in the wilderness and had given her blessings of every sort. But she, in base ingratitude, became faithless and turned to other lovers, the local nature deities of the Canaanites, the so-called Baalim, from whom she claimed to have received the blessings of agriculture. In wild and shameful cult she gave them her love. The Israelites themselves did not look upon their worship thus, they thought they were worshipping Yahweh in this cult, they called Him their Baal, their owner, possessor, husband. But while they might think that it mattered not whether they followed this nature cult, Hosea perceived its soul-destroying power, saw more deeply than they that it undermined the spiritual character of the religion of Yahweh. Its base, licentious practices deadened the moral and spiritual sensibility of the people. So he fought against it with all his might, and no less against the image worship which went with it. With bitter sarcasm he scorned the idols as the work of men's hands and ridiculed the practice of kissing the calves, those images in the sanctuaries that were to represent Yahweh! As if Yahweh, the spiritual deity, could be represented by an image at all! Hosea did not succeed in his determined attack upon the local shrines. He incurred the enmity of the priests and of others. They taunted him, "The prophet is a fool, the man that has the spirit is mad," passionately he retorted, "For the abundance of thine iniquity, and because the enmity is great!" (9 [7]). But his work was not in vain, a century later his principle won out in the great reformation of Josiah.

Although Hosea laid most stress on the religious corruption of the people, he did not overlook the moral iniquities, which he condemned no less than Amos (4 [1ff.]), with whom he agreed that God demanded only morality not sacrificial cult. He also went into a field that Amos had not touched, politics both home and foreign, attacked the monarchy and showed the folly of making alliances. He foresaw the clash between Assyria and Egypt, warned the pro-Assyrian as well as the pro-Egyptian party, and showed that

Yahweh's plan would be carried out, no matter what these politicians might do to hinder it. For the political history of the last years of the Northern Kingdom Hosea's book, with its invaluable information and its keen judgment, is as important as for the religious.

Religiously, socially, politically the people had been faithless to Yahweh. Unfaithfulness was their fundamental sin. The keen reader of the human heart probed more deeply. Unfaithfulness was grounded in ignorance. If the people only knew Yahweh, they would not worship Baal or confound Yahweh with Baal or worship images; they would not commit the terrible social sins and violate all the moral law; they would not choose kings or enter political alliances with foreign nations, for Yahweh is spiritual and moral and the only real saviour. Oh, if Israel but knew Yahweh! But "my people perish for lack of knowledge." There rings through these words all the pathos of Hosea's sad heart. He knew the value of the knowledge of God, he knew it is life indeed. Righteousness and love and trust, all spring from it. And thus says Yahweh:

> I desire loving kindness and not sacrifice,
>   and the knowledge of God rather than burnt offerings. (6 [6])
> Therefore turn thou to thy God,
>   keep kindness and justice,
>   and wait for thy God continually. (12 [6])

Hosea knew that sin had become a habit with the people, a tendency, from which they could not free themselves, "their doings will not suffer them to turn unto their God, for the spirit of whoredom is within them and they know not Yahweh" (5 [4]). And yet he hoped that through the awful suffering, which they would have to undergo, they would come to know Yahweh, repent with all their hearts, and be restored again.

We miss in Hosea the monotheistic emphasis of Amos with its universal implications. He was interested in his own people, he wanted to bind Yahweh and Israel together in a union of whole-hearted affection. Never before had the relation between God and Israel been comprehended with such strong emotional passion. Love is the keynote of this relation. Yahweh alone for Israel, and Israel alone for Yahweh. Hosea deepened and intensified religion, but he also narrowed it in this exclusive possession of one by the other.

The spiritualization and refinement of religion is his great contribution. His joining of love with righteousness also in the relation of man to man meant much for social ethics, for the healing of society is possible only by righteousness and love. His profounder interpretation of the nature of sin and his union of hope with moral discipline by his faith in the love of God as a redeeming and regenerating power exerted great influence on religious thought, while his insistence on the knowledge of God as absolutely essential points forward to his spiritual kinsman John who wrote, "This is life eternal that they might know Thee the only true God, and him whom Thou didst send, even Jesus Christ."

CHAPTER VIII

ISAIAH AND MICAH

WHILE Hosea was still prophesying in the North, there arose in Judah the most majestic of the prophets, Isaiah of Jerusalem. For forty years or more he was God's spokesman to his people, *ca.* 738–700 B.C. or even later. The splendor of his diction, the wealth of his imagery, the amazing variety of his style, now grand and majestic, powerful and sweeping, now gentle and sweet, moving as if full of silent tears, mark him out as the prince of Hebrew orators. But he was greater than his style and his words. He had penetrated through outward appearances to the underlying reality, had seen the One who directs all movements of history, had understood His character and purpose, and thus was enabled to interpret Him to his people and to unfold His plan in the events of the nations. One day in the year that King Uzziah died (738), he was in the temple in deep meditation; we can but imagine his thoughts, his hopes and his fears, for he does not tell us of them. Suddenly his inner eye was opened and there came to him the vision that burnt itself indelibly into his soul and ever after controlled his thought and life. He saw the divine King on His throne. Filled with awe, he only dared to look at the vast flowing garment that filled the temple, and at the mysterious winged seraphim, from whose lips pealed forth the mighty antiphonal song that expressed to him ever after the true nature of Yahweh:

> Holy, holy, holy is Yahweh of hosts,
> the whole earth is full of His glory.

At the vision of holiness Isaiah was shaken by fear. In the swift realization of his own and his people's sinfulness he cried out in utter dismay. He had seen the divine mystery, he knew he must die. But a seraph flew to him and purified his lips with a glowing stone from the altar and pronounced him clean. By this act of consecration he was enabled to see the true significance of the scene and to hear Yahweh Himself as He asked His throne-council, "Whom shall I send, and who will go for us?" In quick, glad readiness Isaiah cried, "Here am I, send me!" At once he got his commission. He must go and speak to "this people," as they are scornfully called, he must continually make clear to them Yahweh's will, continually interpret to them the true significance of all events; they shall listen to him all the time but never grasp the inner meaning of his words, and as they hear without understanding and without following the light thus revealed, they will grow more and more callous, lose their spiritual sensibilities and their very capacity of repentance and moral restoration, and thus they will be prepared for destruction — by Isaiah's ministry:

> Go, and tell this people:
> Hear ye continually, but understand not,
>   and see ye continually, but perceive not!
> Make the heart of this people fat
>   and their ears heavy, and shut their eyes,
> Lest they see with their eyes, and hear with their ears,
>   and understand with their heart, and return and be healed!

When Isaiah, full of anguish, asked, "Lord, how long?" Yahweh replied,

> Until cities are waste without inhabitant,
>   and houses without man,
>   and the land becomes utterly waste,
> And Yahweh has removed men far away,
>   and the forsaking be great in the land.
> And if there be yet a tenth in it,
>   it also shall in turn be consumed,
> As a terebinth and as an oak
>   whose stump has remained after they are felled. (6 $^{9-13a}$)

Their destruction is to be complete. If a remnant should be left in the awful visitation, it too shall be destroyed, until nobody remains of all the sinful people.[1] No prophet ever received a more terrible commission. But Isaiah performed it in the strength of this vision of God's holiness, which dominated henceforth all his thought.

God's holiness, His physical majesty, had to him as its corollary man's insignificance. It behooves man to be humble before the

---

[1] The addition at the end "a holy seed is its stump" expresses the later conviction of Isaiah regarding the remnant that is to be converted and saved.

high God. In his earliest prophecies (2 $^{6ff.}$) Isaiah described how Yahweh, in His hatred of everything proud, would sweep in a fearful tornado on His great day over the country, breaking the cedars of Lebanon, shattering the oaks of Bashan, tearing down every high building, crashing into the ships on the ocean, leaving wreck and ruin in His path, while above it all there rings out the triumphant refrain,

> And Yahweh alone shall be exalted in that day!

With this is joined another prophecy of the Day of Yahweh, in which Isaiah turns upon sorcery and wealth, horses and chariots, and the idols made by men's hands, all of which alienate men from God, and warns his people in the refrain,

> Go into the caverns of the rocks,
>   and into the clefts of the ragged rocks,
> From before the terror of Yahweh,
>   and from the glory of His majesty,
> When He arises to shake mightily the earth!

Isaiah's eyes were sharpened by his prophetic activity among the people. He had witnessed the downfall of Jehu's dynasty in the North that Hosea had prophesied, he knew that Zechariah's murderer Shallum had in turn been assassinated by Menahem and that intolerable conditions prevailed in the country. He came to foresee a revolution in Judah too, for here also social conditions were unbearable, the king was a child and a tool in the hands of the women. The revolution was to be the judgment of Yahweh. The injustice and grinding oppression of the people by the leaders and princes, and the haughty, coquettish wantonness of the Jerusalem women were the reason why He must intervene (3 ^{1}—4 ^{1} 32 $^{9-14}$).

Isaiah made quite an impression on the people, though not of the kind he wanted. For they seem to have avoided the dark prophet of woe. So, one day, he appeared in the market place as a minstrel, for he wanted the people to listen to his message. He began by singing in melodious rhythm,

> I will sing now of my beloved,
>   a love-song concerning his vineyard.

Vineyard was a term of endearment for sweetheart (cf. Cant. 8 $^{11f.}$). So he sang of his "vineyard" for which he had done everything he could, only to be bitterly disappointed at the harvest. Here the singer stopped and asked his hearers to judge between his friend and his vineyard. But as nobody replied, he went on to tell of the severe but just treatment that he would mete out to it. His hearers all agreed, not thinking of anything extraordinary until he said, "I will also command the clouds that they rain no rain upon it." No ordinary man could say that! But before they could recover from their astonishment, Isaiah had thundered the application of his love song into their ears,

> For the vineyard of Yahweh of hosts is the house of Israel,
>> and the men of Judah his pleasant plant:
> And He looked for justice (*mishpaṭ*), but behold oppression (*mispah*);
>> for righteousness (*ṣedhakah*), but behold a cry (*se'akah*). (5 1-7)

An unforgettable word-play! Likely enough, Isaiah took this occasion to pronounce his series of woes, that have come down the avenues of time with none of their power lost, the woes upon them that buy up houses and fields until they alone are in possession of the land; upon the drunkards; the frivolous mockers; the swindlers; the self-conceited; and the unjust judges (5 8-24). Woe to them all, their punishment is certain, for

> Yahweh of hosts is exalted in justice,
>> and God the Holy One shows His holiness in righteousness.

At another time Isaiah mourned over the deterioration of Jerusalem in the characteristic rhythm of the dirge.

> How is the faithful city become a harlot!
>> she that was full of justice!
> Righteousness lodged in her,
>> but now murderers.

The princes and judges are companions of thieves, grafters, and perverters of justice. But Yahweh will avenge Himself on them all. He will remove the wicked elements and thoroughly purge the city.

> And I will restore thy judges as at the first,
>> and thy counsellors as at the beginning:
> Afterward thou shalt be called,
>> The city of righteousness, a faithful town. (1 21-26)

All of a sudden a ray of hope had come into Isaiah's message! The punishment is only for the wicked; after their removal the ancient righteousness of Zion will once more be restored by Yahweh Himself, not by introducing a new system but by installing righteous men as office-holders.

From now on Isaiah's message was no longer unrelieved gloom. His words had fallen on fruitful ground, a group of earnest people had gathered about him. It was at this time that he gave the pregnant name "Shearjashub" to a little son who was born to him, in the glad hope that after all "a remnant shall return" to Yahweh and be saved.

So far Isaiah had not yet mentioned the Assyrians, although the advance of Tiglathpileser against Syria had already begun and King Menahem of Israel had been forced to pay tribute to him in 738. The Syrians perceived the fateful danger, and under the leadership of Rezin of Damascus a confederacy was effected between the erstwhile enemies, Damascus and Samaria. It was of the utmost importance that this alliance be strengthened. When King Ahaz of Judah refused to join it, the confederates were so deeply concerned about it that they resolved to compel Judah by force of arms to overthrow Ahaz and to join them. It was at the beginning of this Syro-Ephraimitic war (735), when Ahaz went out to inspect the fortification of the city in view of the impending siege, that Isaiah met him in one of the most memorable interviews of history. He had his little son Shearjashub with him, whom the king knew as the embodiment of Isaiah's sermons, for Isaiah belonged to a high family and was familiar at court, well acquainted with the king and the leading people. With intense conviction the prophet assured the king in the name of God Himself that he need not fear the contemptible confederacy of Syria and Ephraim; God's plan was to frustrate its purpose. Let Ahaz believe and rely on Yahweh, for "if ye will not believe, surely ye shall not be established!" To Isaiah who had seen the great vision of the Heavenly King it was easy to believe that He was the sole ruler and director of all the affairs of men, that He alone controlled all the movements of history, and that His will alone mattered. He had declared that the allies' plan would be frustrated, and of course it would. If Ahaz believed, Yahweh would do the rest. But Ahaz did not reply; he did not believe. He had probably already sent to Assyria for aid and become Tiglathpileser's vassal. Isaiah, desperate in his desire to win him, offers to him any sign in heaven or hell in confirmation of his message. But the king evades with a pious phrase, whereupon Isaiah burst forth full of indignation,

Hear ye now, O house of David: Is it a small thing for you to weary men, that ye will weary my God also? Therefore the Lord Himself will give you a sign: behold, a young woman shall conceive, and bear a son, and shall call his name Immanuel [*i.e.* with us is God]. For before the child shall know to refuse the evil, and choose the good, the land of whose two kings thou art so terribly afraid shall be forsaken. (But) curd and honey shall he eat, when he knows to refuse the evil and choose the good. (For) Yahweh will bring upon thee, and upon thy people, and upon thy father's house, days such as have not come, from the day that Ephraim departed from Judah. (7 1–17)[1]

This is the sign: the young woman (the Hebrew does not say a virgin but a young woman of marriageable age) who now becomes pregnant shall in her hour of crisis cry out in glorious joy "*Immanuel* = with us is God," and call her new-born baby thus, for then already the divine deliverance will be manifest, and in two or three years the countries of the enemies will be devastated. Ahaz will remember this hour in which God offered His grace to him in vain, but the name "Immanuel" will not be to him pure joy, for the result of his unbelief will be that Judah also will have to pass through an unprecedented calamity (7 1–17). For Ahaz this hour meant little, for mankind it was of incalculable value, for it put faith into the center of religion, and this interview has therefore been called the birth-hour of faith, which for Isaiah was the conviction of the reality and supremacy of the spiritual world, of God.

Isaiah brought these messages also to the people. In a spectac-

---

[1] V. 15 "Curd and honey," etc., has been transposed. It belongs not to the hopeful but to the threatening part of the announcement. The country of Judah will also be devastated, there will be no harvests and the inhabitants will have to eat the food of nomads at that time. Isaiah makes this meaning plain in 7 21–25 :

And it shall come to pass in that day, that a man shall keep alive a young cow, and two sheep; and it shall come to pass, that (because of the abundance of milk which they shall give) he shall eat curd: for curd and honey shall every one eat that is left in the midst of the land.

And it shall come to pass in that day, that every place, where there were a thousand vines at a thousand silverlings, shall be for briers and thorns. With arrows and with bow shall one come thither, because all the land shall be briers and thorns. And all the hills that were digged with the mattock, thou shalt not come thither for fear of briers and thorns; but it shall be for the sending forth of oxen, and for the treading of sheep.

ular manner he wrote upon a large tablet in easily legible letters "*Maher shalal hash baz* = the spoil speeds, the prey hastens," in the presence of two unimpeachable witnesses of high rank. And to a little son who was born at this time he gave this strange name Maher shalal hash baz, in order to have a double attestation that he foretold at this time that "the riches of Damascus and the spoil of Samaria shall be carried away before the king of Assyria" (8^{1-4} $17^{1-6.\ 9-11}$). In his high ecstasy he even defied the whole world,

> *With us is God!*
> Know, ye peoples,
> and give ear all ye of far countries:
> Gird yourselves, and be broken in pieces!
> Gird yourselves, and be broken in pieces!
> Take counsel together, and it shall be brought to nought,
> speak the word, and it shall not stand,
> *for with us is God!* ($8^{9f.}$)

He did not conceal from the people the danger for Judah in the invasion of Israel by Assyria. He judged Ahaz's policy rightly; it would not bring deliverance in the end. He foresaw that the clash between Egypt and Assyria would take place in Palestine and engulf Judah too, since the people had not put their trust in the softly flowing waters of Siloam, *i.e.* in Yahweh's silently working power. With God no confederacy of human forces could prevail against them, without Him they were lost ($7^{18-25}\ 8^{5-8}$).

During the exciting days of the Syro-Ephraimitic war Isaiah the patriot felt the strong power of the war psychosis from which the people suffered. When they denounced men as traitors and conspirators, aiding and abetting the enemy, he felt like joining them in patriotic fervor but Yahweh held him "with the strong pressure of the hand," by an irresistible psychic constraint, and warned him that there was only one plotter to be taken into account — Yahweh Himself, the arch-conspirator who was planning the ruin of His people! (8^{11-15})

Soon Isaiah found himself in such fatal opposition to the king and the people that he withdrew from his public ministry and devoted his attention to the training of his disciples. Quietly he worked, conscious that also for the public he himself and his children with their symbolical names were still witnesses of Yahweh, howbeit

silent for a time. Patiently he would wait for a better time, for his
hope was in Yahweh who dwelt in Mount Zion (8 16–18).

Events moved too quickly to permit him to be quiet very long.
In 734 the most northern and the East Jordan tribes had been carried into Assyrian captivity, Israel had become a vassal; in 732
Damascus had fallen. And now after the death of the great conqueror Tiglathpileser in 726, Israel, under King Hosea, revolted
against her new sovereign Shalmaneser. Isaiah predicted what was
bound to come. Yahweh had tried to save them by discipline after
discipline, but all in vain, they did not repent; after the recital of
each act Isaiah concluded with the refrain,

> For all this His anger is not turned away,
> and His hand is stretched out still,

until he announced the final punishment, the end, in the famous description of the Assyrian advance.

> And He will lift up an ensign to the nation from far,
> and will hiss to it from the end of the earth,
> And, behold, it comes swiftly with speed,
> none is weary or stumbles among them,
> none slumbers nor sleeps.
> The girdle of their loins is not loosed,
> nor the latchet of their shoes broken;
> Their arrows are sharp,
> and all their bows bent;
> Their horses' hoofs are accounted as flint,
> and their wheels as a whirlwind.
> Their roaring is like a lioness,
> they roar like young lions;
> Yea, they roar, and lay hold of the prey,
> and carry it off safe, and there is none to deliver. (5 26–29)

The same social iniquities of which Judah was guilty are the cause
of Israel's doom. The Assyrians are the instrument of punishment
in the hand of Yahweh, who controls all nations in His righteous
rule (9 7–10 4 5 25–29 28 1–4). In 722 Samaria was taken and Israel
was carried into captivity. Above the fallen city we seem to hear
again the dirge which Amos had sung some thirty years before:

> The virgin of Israel is fallen,
> she shall no more rise;
> Prostrate she lies on her ground,
> none lifts her up.

And in its empty streets and places the heart-breaking words of Hosea seem once more to sound with all their mingled sternness and grace, their justice and love, awaking a wistful yearning in us, a hope which can never be fulfilled. For Israel had gone into exile, never to return.

In the next decades there were repeated attempts by the subject nations to throw off the Assyrian yoke. Merodachbaladan the artful Babylonian rebel instigated them ever again and Egypt always promised her help. In 711 popular opinion in Jerusalem was strongly in favor of joining the Philistines, who were aided by Egypt, against Sargon. Isaiah perceived the folly and peril of it, and for three years he walked in the streets of Jerusalem like a prisoner of war "naked and barefoot" in order to give weight to his impassioned warnings. Thus all the Egyptians and Ethiopians would be carried away into exile by the Assyrians, if they rebelled against them; Judah would be bitterly disappointed if she trusted the allies (ch. 20). This time Isaiah succeeded, Judah remained neutral. All through the following years he tried in many addresses to convince his countrymen of the profound truth that their national salvation could only be secured through faith in Yahweh, but all without avail. When Sennacherib ascended the throne of Assyria in 705, the whole country was in rebellion. Ambassadors from Philistia appeared in Jerusalem to urge the Judæans to join the anti-Assyrian alliance. They found them eager and ready. Isaiah alone saw more deeply than they all, perceived the utter hopelessness of the undertaking, and addressed an oracle to Philistia, in which he correctly foretold the fate that awaited her from the new king who would be even more cruel to her than Sargon had been.[1]

> Rejoice not, O Philistia, all of thee,
>   because the rod that smote thee is broken,
> For out of the serpent's root shall come forth an adder,
>   and his fruit shall be a fiery flying serpent.
> And the first-born of the poor shall feed,
>   and the needy shall lie down in safety;

[1] The original text of 14 [28] was, "in the year that the king died I saw this oracle." The king was Sargon. A copyist, missing the proper name, took the next word *waa-hazeh* as containing it = Ahaz, and read, "in the year that King *Ahaz* died was this oracle."

> And I will kill thy root with famine,
>> and thy remnant shall be slain.
> Howl, O gate; cry, O city!
>> thou art melted away, O Philistia, all of thee;
> For there comes a smoke out of the north,
>> and there is no straggler in his ranks!

To the question directly put to him by the people Isaiah replied,

> What then shall one answer the messengers of the nation?
> That Yahweh has founded Zion,
>> and in her shall the afflicted of His people take refuge! (14 $^{28-32}$)

Trust in Yahweh alone, not trust in any political alliance, is the guarantee of salvation, it alone can insure national permanence. But the people would not listen. Popular enthusiasm had been inflamed. King Hezekiah was unable to resist the pressure and joined the anti-Assyrian alliance, especially as it was certain that Egypt would this time support the movement with all her strength. Isaiah never receded from his position. Here also he saw more clearly than the others and denounced the pact with Egypt as bringing only disappointment and woe.

> Woe to them that go down to Egypt for help,
>> and rely on horses,
> And trust in chariots because they are many,
>> and in horsemen because they are very strong,
> But they look not to the Holy One of Israel,
>> neither seek they Yahweh! (31 ^{1})

There is only one real helper, Yahweh! All human and material forces are of no avail, the battle is between the spiritual and the material world.

> The Egyptians are men, and not God;
>> and their horses flesh and not spirit:
> And when Yahweh shall stretch out His hand,
>> both he that helps shall stumble and he that is helped shall fall,
> And they shall all be consumed together. (31 ^{3})

On another occasion Isaiah summed up his counsel in the great words.

> In returning and rest shall you be saved,
>> in quietness and confidence is your strength. (30 ^{15})

Isaiah repeated his warnings so often that the people grew

tired of them. When he appeared one day in the temple just as sacrificial meals were celebrated and the participants, priests and prophets included, were so intoxicated with strong drink that "all tables were full of vomit and filthiness so that there was no place clean," he was greeted with scornful derision:

> Whom will he teach knowledge?
>   and whom will he make to understand the message?
> Them that are weaned from the milk,
>   and drawn from the breasts?
> For it is "precept upon precept, precept upon precept;
>   line upon line, line upon line;
>   here a little, there a little."

The Hebrew brings out most effectively their imitation of baby talk:

> Ṣaw laṣaw ṣaw laṣaw
> Ḳaw laḳaw ḳaw laḳaw
> Zᵉir sham zᵉir sham.

To which Isaiah retorted, that since they would not listen to God's plain message by which they could gain rest and refreshment, He would give to them this same "baby talk" in Assyrian with the fearful result that they would "go and fall backward and be broken, and snared and taken."

> Therefore hear the word of Yahweh, ye scoffers,
>   that rule this people that is in Jerusalem:
> Because ye have said,
> "We have made a covenant with death,
>   and with Sheol are we in agreement,
> When the overflowing scourge shall pass through
>   it shall not come unto us;
> For we have made lies our refuge,
>   and under falsehood have we hid ourselves":
> Therefore has the Lord Yahweh said thus,
> *"Behold, I lay in Zion for a foundation a stone,*
>   *a tried stone, a precious corner-stone of sure foundation:*
> *He that believes shall not be removed!*
> And I will make justice the line,
>   and righteousness the plummet;
> And the hail shall sweep away the refuge of lies,
>   and the waters shall overflow the hiding-place.

And your covenant with death shall be annulled,
  and your agreement with Sheol shall not stand.
When the overflowing scourge shall pass through,
  then ye shall be trodden down by it."
As often as it passes through,
  it shall take you;
For morning by morning shall it pass through,
  by day and by night:
And it shall be nought but terror
  to understand the message.
For the bed is too short for one to stretch himself on,
  and the covering too scanty for one to wrap himself in.
For Yahweh will rise up as in mount Perazim,
  He will be wroth as in the valley of Gibeon;
That He may do His work, His strange work,
  and bring to pass His act, His strange act.
Now therefore be ye not scoffers,
  lest your bonds be made strong!
For a decree of destruction have I heard
  from the Lord Yahweh of hosts
  upon the whole land. (28 7-22)

The most significant sentence in this strong address has been printed in italics. Isaiah penetrated through the outward events to the underlying spiritual realities. Faith was to him the eternal foundation. "He that believes shall not be removed," for he is allied with the mightiest power in the whole world, with God Himself. But the people did not see what Isaiah had seen and they did not believe. He knew it well. In a remarkable passage he has preserved a picture of the popular mood at that time. It was on a day when Jerusalem celebrated some little ephemeral triumph, perhaps the bringing in as prisoner of war of the pro-Assyrian King Padi of Ekron. The people were on the roofs to see the joyful spectacle, living only in the present, blind to the future. Their own ruin was impending, and they were celebrating a festival of joy!

What ails thee now that thou art wholly
  gone up to the house-tops?
O thou that art full of shoutings, a tumultuous city,
  a joyous town;
Thy slain are not slain with the sword,
  neither are they dead in battle;

> All thy rulers fled away together,
>   they fled afar off;
> All thy mighty men are captured,
>   captured without their bows!

As this terrible picture stood before Isaiah's mind, it filled him with such uncontrollable grief that he implored the people,

> Look away from me,
>   Let me weep bitterly;
> Labor not to comfort me
>   for the destruction of the daughter of my people!
> For it is a day of discomfiture, of treading down and perplexity
>   from the Lord, Yahweh of hosts,
> In the valley of decision a breaking down of walls,
>   and a crying to the mountains.
> And Elam has lifted up the quiver,
>   and Kir has uncovered the shield.
> Thy choicest valleys are full of chariots,
>   and the horsemen set themselves in array at the gate,
> And He has taken away the covering of Judah.

The measures which the people had taken for such a crisis were without avail, because they had neglected the moral and spiritual preparation. They had not looked to Him who had planned this catastrophe. They had not appeased Him with earnest repentance, but looked forward to the coming war with incredible lightheartedness and frivolity.

> The Lord, Yahweh of hosts, called
>   on that day
> To weeping and mourning and baldness,
>   and to girding with sackcloth:
> And, behold, joy and gladness,
>   slaying of oxen and killing of sheep,
> Eating of flesh and drinking of wine:
>   "Let us eat and drink, for to-morrow we shall die!"
> And Yahweh of hosts revealed Himself in mine ears,
>   "Surely this iniquity shall not be forgiven you till you die." (22 $^{1-14}$)

Events moved relentlessly onward. Sennacherib appeared in Judah and devastated the country. Egyptian help proved inadequate. At last the capitulation of Jerusalem was demanded.

Then Isaiah rose to the height of his great conviction. Although to the superficial reader he appears to contradict himself,[1] he was nevertheless true to his fundamental faith in the holiness of God and the obligation of humility on the part of men.   The Assyrian had been Yahweh's instrument again and again.   He had used him also against His own people, but now he had overstepped the limits of his commission.   Isaiah had long observed that the Assyrian was not conscious of being Yahweh's servant, that it was sheer lust of conquest that carried him on.   But now when he dared to boast in reckless arrogance that he would overthrow the city of Yahweh *and Yahweh Himself,* Isaiah replied with scornful irony,

> Shall the axe boast itself against him that hews therewith?
>   shall the saw magnify itself against him that wields it?
> As if a rod should wield them that lift it up,
>   or as if a staff should lift up him that is not wood! (10 [15])

The blasphemous folly of it all!   The Assyrian can no longer be Yahweh's instrument, but must himself be punished.   He shall not take Jerusalem, but will himself be broken by Yahweh.

> Surely, as I have thought, so shall it come to pass;
>   and as I have purposed, so shall it stand:

[1] Isaiah himself refuted any charge of inconsistency in the remarkable passage in which he showed that different conditions require different treatment, as they might have learned from the farmer.   We may well believe that it was first of all an answer to his own questionings:

> Give ear, and hear my voice;
>   hearken, and hear my speech!
> Does the plower continually plow for the sowing?
>   does he (continually) open and harrow his ground?
> When he has levelled its surface,
>   does he not cast abroad black cummel and scatter cummin,
> And put in the wheat in rows, and the barley in the appointed place,
>   and the spelt in its border?
> For his God instructs him aright
>   and teaches him.
> For black cummel is not threshed with threshing-sledges,
>   neither is a cart wheel turned about upon cummin;
> But black cummel is beaten out with a staff,
>   and cummin with a rod.
> Is bread-grain crushed?
>   nay, he will not be always threshing it;
> And though he drive the wheel of his cart over it,
>   he scatters it, but does not crush it.
> This also comes forth from Yahweh of hosts,
>   who is wonderful in counsel and excellent in wisdom (28 [23-29]).

> That I will break the Assyrian in My land,
>> and upon My mountains tread him underfoot:
> Then shall his yoke depart from off them,
>> and his burden depart from off their shoulders.
> For this is the purpose that is purposed upon the whole earth,
>> and this is the hand that is stretched out upon all the nations.
> For Yahweh of hosts has purposed, and who shall annul it?
>> and His hand is stretched out, and who shall turn it back? (14 $^{24-27}$)

The incredible happened. Sennacherib was compelled to march away, apparently a pestilence decimated his army. It was a great deliverance for the Jews, and constituted one of the most significant events in Judæan history, but it did not make upon the people the impression for which Isaiah had hoped. No moral renewal resulted, the old social abuses continued, together with great religious zeal. Once more the prophet appeared before the people and in a powerful reform sermon he appealed to them to repent whole-heartedly. It is the sermon that now stands at the beginning of his book (1 $^{2-20}$) in which he painted the graphic picture of the ravaged condition of the country, rejected all cult as strongly as Amos had done, including new moon and sabbath and prayer, summoned the people to a life of social justice, and pleaded with them,

> Come now, and let us reason together, says Yahweh,
> Though your sins be as scarlet,
>> they shall be as white as snow,
> Though they be red as crimson,
>> they shall be as wool. (1 ^{18})

One would like to believe that it was this sermon that set Hezekiah to work in reforming the cult of Judah. That Isaiah influenced him to it, there can be no doubt.

In the great joy over the deliverance from the Assyrian oppressor Isaiah described the jubilant happiness of the people over their new liberty and foretold, in words so beautiful and melodious that they are still music to our ears, the ideal king who would bring in the golden age.

> The people that walked in darkness have seen a great light,
>> on them that dwelt in the land of deep gloom has the light shined.
> Thou hast multiplied gladness, increased joy,
>> they joy before Thee according to the joy in harvest,
>> as men rejoice when they divide the spoil.

For the yoke of his burden, and the staff of his shoulder,
  the rod of his oppressor Thou hast broken as in the day of Midian.
For all the armor of the armed man in the tumult,
  and the garments rolled in blood,
  shall be for burning, for fuel of fire.
For unto us a child is born, unto us a son is given;
  and the government shall be upon his shoulder:
And his name shall be called Wonderful Counsellor,
  Mighty God, Everlasting Father, Prince of Peace.
Great shall be his government, and of peace there shall be no end,
  upon the throne of David and upon his kingdom,
To establish it and to uphold it
  with justice and with righteousness from henceforth even forever.
The zeal of Yahweh of hosts will perform this. (9^{2-7})

In another poem Isaiah described the endowment of the king with the spirit of God by which he would be enabled to rule as an ideal monarch in an age of peace:

And there shall come forth a shoot out of the stock of Jesse,
  and a branch out of its roots shall bear fruit.
And the Spirit of Yahweh shall rest upon him,
  the spirit of wisdom and of understanding,
The spirit of counsel and might,
  the spirit of the knowledge and fear of Yahweh.
He shall not judge after the sight of his eyes,
  neither decide after the hearing of his ears;
But with righteousness shall he judge the poor,
  and decide with equity for the meek of the earth;
And he shall smite the tyrant with the rod of his mouth
  and with the breath of his lips shall he slay the wicked.
And righteousness shall be the girdle of his waist,
  and faithfulness the girdle of his loins.
And the wolf shall dwell with the lamb
  and the leopard shall lie down with the kid;
And the calf and the lion and the fatling together;
  and a little child shall lead them.
And the cow and the bear shall feed,
  their young ones shall lie down together;
And the lion shall eat straw like the ox,
  and the sucking child shall play on the hole of the asp,
  and the weaned child shall put his hand on the adder's den.
They shall not hurt or destroy in all My holy mountain,
  for the earth shall be full of the knowledge of Yahweh,
  as the waters cover the sea. (11^{1-9})

In another poem (32 [1–8. 15–20]) the ideal reign is still further described. Isaiah had a childlike faith in the importance of the personality of the king. He expected an ideal age from the rule of the ideal monarch and the administration of righteous office holders. The golden age was to him the purification and glorification of the old order. That had been his hope in the early years of his ministry (1 [25f.]), but he had not painted it with the glowing colors of his riper age. Social justice and social peace, however, always remained fundamental with him.

As he worked out his hope of the future his vision grew larger. He saw the time coming when many nations, attracted by Judah's glory, would come to Mount Zion to inquire of the oracle of Yahweh about the conditions of national happiness and peace, and would bring all their international disputes to the arbitership of Yahweh and abide by His just and impartial decisions:

> And it shall come to pass in the latter days,
>> that the mountain of Yahweh's house shall be established
> On the top of the mountains,
>> and shall be exalted above the hills.
> And nations shall flow unto it,
>> and many peoples shall go and say,
> " Come ye, and let us go up to the mountain of Yahweh,
>> to the house of the God of Jacob;
> And He will teach us of His ways,
>> and we will walk in His paths!"
> For out of Zion shall go forth the law,
>> and the word of Yahweh from Jerusalem.
> And He will judge between the nations,
>> and will decide concerning many peoples;
> And they shall beat their swords into ploughshares,
>> and their spears into pruning-hooks;
> Nation shall not lift up sword against nation,
>> neither shall they learn war any more. (2 [2–4])

A vision of universal peace! Thus did the aged prophet look forward with longing eye into the future and formulate a hope for all mankind that makes men's hearts still beat faster, for these words still express humanity's longing for peace.

It is no wonder that these so-called Messianic passages have been regarded for many centuries as the most important contribution of Isaiah. As a matter of fact, this is not so; he was primarily the prophet of faith, and his greatest and most significant contribution was his teaching of faith in the holiness of God, which meant to him faith in His physical and moral majesty and supremacy, in His overwhelming reality and righteous rule of the world and in His direction of all history. If he wrote the messages of hope at all, which is seriously questioned, he gave them only to his disciples.

Isaiah was a man of affairs and an orator, not primarily a writer. It was due to the opposition he encountered that he felt impelled to write down his messages. The first little book (6–8) he probably wrote at the time of his withdrawal from the public ministry under Ahaz. Around this as a nucleus other early oracles were added (2 $^{6ff.}$ 3 ^{1}–4 ^{1} 5 $^{1-24}$ and 9 ^{7}–10 ^{4} 5 $^{25-29}$). Another little book Isaiah wrote during the time of Sennacherib, when the people would not hear any more of his attacks upon the Egyptian alliance. Yahweh commanded him then,

> Now go, write it before them on a tablet,
>   and inscribe it in a book,
> That it may be for the time to come
>   for ever and ever. (30 ^{8})

Those messages are contained mainly in ch. 28–31. We owe them in a sense to Isaiah's opponents.

The Book of Isaiah now contains many passages which are not from him. Not only the whole second part, ch. 40–66, most of the oracles against foreign nations in ch. 13–23, the so-called apocalypse in ch. 24–27, the biographical material in ch. 36–39, but a good many other passages were added later, so that we now have a great collection of oracles in his book, of which Isaiah's own are not even the largest part.[1]

Besides the majestic Isaiah the figure of his contemporary Micah appears small. But in reality he was one of the great prophets.

---

[1] The genuine passages may be arranged according to time as follows:
From his call to the Syro-Ephraimitic war (738–735): 6 2 $^{6-18}$ 3 ^{1}–4 ^{1} 32 $^{9-14}$ 5 $^{1-24}$ 1 $^{21-26}$. $^{29-31}$.
During the Syro-Ephraimitic war (735–734): 7. 8. 17 $^{1-6.9-11}$.
After the war but before the fall of Samaria (734–722): 9 ^{8}–10 ^{4} 5 $^{25-30}$ 28 $^{1-4}$.
During Sargon's siege of Ashdod (711): 20.
Before and during Sennacherib's invasion: 10 $^{5ff.}$ 14 $^{24-32}$ 17 ^{12}–18 ^{6} 22.28 $^{7-29}$ 29 $^{1-4}$. $^{6-16}$ 30 $^{1-17.27-33}$ 31.
After the deliverance of Jerusalem: 1 $^{2-20}$ 9 $^{1-7}$ 11 $^{1-9}$ 32 $^{1-8.15-20}$ 2 $^{2-5}$.

He belonged to the plain people in the little Judæan town of More-sheth-Gath near the Philistine border. Of his family and of his profession we know nothing. He left no record of the experiences that made him a prophet, for he scorned all external attestations of his authority and relied solely on the manifestation of the Spirit and of Power. Like another Amos he came, in the last decade of North Israel (730–722), and announced the certain fall of Samaria. Even then he feared that Jerusalem would be involved too. This became a certainty to him during Hezekiah's reign. With burning passion and scorching, smashing words of terrible power he arraigned the leaders of his people for all their moral iniquities and predicted the impending destruction. He was the spokesman of the poor, who were suffering in dumb submission from outrageous oppression and shameless perversion of justice. Princes, priests, and prophets, all were guilty, greed and avarice possessed them and poisoned the whole social and religious life of the nation.

> Therefore shall Zion for your sake be ploughed as a field,
>> and Jerusalem shall become heaps,
>> and the mountain of the house of the high places of the forest. (3 ^{12})

A hundred years later this prophecy was still remembered, so great had been its impression.

Perhaps the first three chapters (except 2 $^{12f.}$), in which Micah collected his memorable addresses, and the threatening passages in ch. 4 are all that he ever wrote, especially if he did not preach after Hezekiah's reign. But it is likely that he lived and worked also during the time of Manasseh. If he did, the great passages in ch. 6 ^{1}–7 ^{6} may have come from him too. It is true that there is an unexpected tenderness in the poem in which the prophet interprets the awful practice of child sacrifice, to which the people had been driven in their despair in Manasseh's time, as a sad mistake in their deep craving for reconciliation with God. He represents the people asking with great concern:

> Wherewith shall I come before Yahweh,
>> and bow myself before the high God?
> Shall I come before Him with burnt-offerings,
>> with calves a year old?
> Will Yahweh be pleased with thousands of rams,
>> with ten thousands of rivers of oil?

> Shall I give my first-born for my transgression,
>   the fruit of my body for the sin of my soul?

He answers,

> He has showed thee, O man, what is good,
>   and what does Yahweh require of thee,
> But to do justly, and love kindness,
>   and to walk humbly with thy God? (6 6–8)

What a wonderful passage this is! What insight it reveals! It gives the classical definition of prophetic religion. With what tenderness it is expressed! Age had mellowed the stern prophet. He understood and pardoned. But in his early ministry also Micah had shown how deeply he himself was moved by the prospect of Israel's certain destruction:

> For this will I lament and wail,
>   I will go stripped and naked;
> I will make a wailing like the jackals,
>   and a lamentation like the ostriches. (1 8)

He had known quite well even then that Yahweh was kind. "Do not My words do good to him that walks uprightly?" (2 7) But the social iniquity of the people necessitated their punishment. And that was his conviction still. With all the fire of his youth he scored the social wrongs. But it is not so exclusively the leaders that he now charged. Deceit, violence, injustice were rampant in all classes. Conditions were now worse than they had been before. "The godly man has perished out of the land, there is none upright among men. The best of them is a brier which is only straighter than the others in a hedge" (7 2.4). Nobody may trust his closest relation and dearest friend. "A man's enemies are they of his own house" (7 6).

If Micah wrote, directly following this arraignment of the general deterioration of the people, the words,

> But as for me, I will look unto Yahweh,
>   I will wait for the God of my salvation:
> My God will hear me (7 7),

we may ask whether he carried this hope silently in his heart or whether he published it. Were not some of the hopeful passages of his book written with reference to North Israel (2 12f. 4 6f.)? And does not Micah's characteristic preference for the country as opposed to the city appear in the addition to the famous prophecy of universal peace (4 ³) and in the prediction of the coming of the ideal king from the country town of Bethlehem (5 ²)? If we only knew! It seems rather that later writers inserted all the hopeful passages in his book. He himself was convinced that he was a prophet of doom. In sharp contrast to the venal professional good-weather prophets of his time he had exclaimed,

> But as for me, I am full of power
> and of judgment and of might,
> To declare to Jacob his transgression,
> and to Israel his sin. (3 ⁸)

As such Micah lived in the memory of the people. Not even Amos excelled him in his terrible arraignment of social ills. He shared Hosea's conviction about the demoralizing local cult, but went beyond him by predicting the extermination of the sacred pillars and posts (5 ¹³), and prepared thus even more directly the Deuteronomic reformation.

CHAPTER IX

DEUTERONOMY

WHATEVER may be the historical facts of the reformation of Hezekiah, whether 2 Ki. 18 [4] is correct in saying that "he removed the high places, and broke the pillars and cut down the Asherah," [1] or whether it was in the main a purification of the temple and the local sanctuaries from all their idolatrous implements, in any case it was short-lived. A reaction set in directly under his son and successor Manasseh (692-638), under whom Assyrian influence became dominant in Judah not only in politics and civilization but also in religion. The introduction of Assyrian worship, the cults of the sun, moon, and stars, especially of Ishtar, the queen of heavens (Venus), came inevitably with Assyrian suzerainty. Altars for these cults were built in both courts and on the roof of the temple, while horses and chariots of the sun were placed at the entrance, and other cultic implements were provided. With this went a recrudescence of the old forms of superstition, witchcraft, necromancy, and the like, and of the familiar worship of Baal and his consort Asherah in the especially heinous form of Moloch [2] worship with its human sacrifices on the Topheth in the valley of Hinnom. Manasseh himself is said to have caused his son to pass through the fire (2 Ki. 21 [3-7] 23 [4-6. 10-12]). It must not be supposed, however, that all this meant the giving up of Yahweh worship by Manasseh and his subservient priests. Yahweh retained His place — only not exclusively. In His holy temple there were now a number of other gods too, but not necessarily as His rivals, for we must assume that the priests interpreted Yahweh as the God of heaven who was supreme over all the other deities, the God of gods, the Lord of lords. Their

---

[1] Cf. also the words of the Assyrian officer to the people in 2 Ki. 18 [22], "But if you say to me, 'We trust in Yahweh our God,' is not that he, whose high places and whose altars Hezekiah has taken away and has said to Judah and to Jerusalem, 'You shall worship before this altar in Jerusalem'?"

[2] The original pronunciation was Melech = King. The Jews wrote it with the vowels of *bosheth* = shame.

religion was a form of monarchical monotheism. We may be sure that it did not pass without vigorous protest. It is quite likely that Micah wrote his wonderful prophecies (6 ¹–7 ⁷) at this time (cf. p. 118f). 2 Ki. 21 ¹⁰ff. speaks of prophets who announced doom to Manasseh, and v. ¹⁶ says that he "shed very much innocent blood, till he had filled Jerusalem from one end to another." The words of Jeremiah, "Your own sword has devoured your prophets like a destroying lion" (2 ³⁰), show that this meant not simply judicial murders by a high-handed government, which copied the despotic methods of Assyria, as Ahab and Jezebel had done with those of Tyre (Mic. 6 ¹⁶ 7 ¹⁻⁶), but religious persecution and martyrdom.¹ But the blood of the martyrs is ever the seed of the church.

The prophetic party, the disciples of Isaiah whom he had instructed in the great truths of religion and whom Micah also had influenced, worked in silence preparing for the future reformation. Their cardinal principle was an exclusive, ethical, and spiritual monotheism. Yahweh alone is God, He alone is to be worshipped, all foreign cults are to be exterminated; and His own cult is to be purged of all images and all other heathen elements, however much they may have become part of Israel's worship. History had taught the prophetic party in the fateful year 701 B.C., when all Judah was devastated by Sennacherib and Jerusalem alone was saved by Yahweh of hosts, that Jerusalem had been chosen by Yahweh as His habitation, who dwelt in Mount Zion as Isaiah had said. Here alone was His real sanctuary. The high places, those breeding spots of idolatry with its debasing practices, must therefore be removed; they were not dear to Yahweh; on the contrary, He had nothing to do with them. Micah (5 ¹³f.) had predicted the destruction of the pillars and posts, those ancient symbols of stone and tree worship, which Israel had adopted into her religion from the Canaanites. To these reformers it was clear that they had no place in the worship of Yahweh. The reinterpretation of them by J and E had not displaced the older views. Destruction alone promised to be effectual.

To their first principle of the unity of God these reformers added therefore the second, the unity of the sanctuary. It followed,

---

¹ A well-known legend tells of the sawing asunder of the prophet Isaiah under Manasseh (cf. Martyrdom of Isaiah 5 ¹¹, referred to in the Epistle to the Hebrews 11 ³⁷).

to their thinking, quite inevitably : if Yahweh was one, He had only one sanctuary where He might be worshipped and His oracle might be consulted. The great prophets had rejected the sacrificial cult of the people altogether and had insisted on social righteousness and spiritual religion as the only demands of Yahweh, who had never imposed any sacrifices and external ceremonies on His people. But when the practical side was considered, it became clear that a purely ethical and spiritual religion without external worship proved too exacting for the people and required too much concentrated spiritual endeavor. The cult was necessary, and for this not only a stated place, a sanctuary, but also certain rules and regulations, rites and ceremonies, and offerings were needed. Only, this worship must be pure, whole-hearted, and sincere, based on a true moral life, and free from all impure heathen elements. Thus these men, who had the interest of true religion at heart and who insisted on the prophetic interpretation of it, were convinced that the great end they had in view could be gained not by putting away all external forms of religion but by purging, regulating, spiritualizing them.

They emphasized therefore as their third cardinal principle the combination of the requirement of true social morality and whole-hearted worship in accordance with the purified sacrificial system. This was a distinct compromise between the prophetic and the priestly views.

The program of this party was laid down by a master-mind in the Book of Deuteronomy, more particularly in ch. 5–26. 28, of which 5–11 form the introduction and 28 the conclusion. Dt. 12–26 are a law code in which the demands of religion and life are formulated, for these men wanted to regulate the whole life of the nation by their fundamental principles. They believed that they were giving to the people nothing but the great principles of the religion of Moses. They thought they were only expounding these and bringing out more clearly and in a more modern form the inherent truths of Yahwism. They had no intention of deceiving the people by declaring that their work was by Moses in order to enhance the authority of these laws. For much of their work was really quite old, the basis of their code was the Book of the Covenant and other customary laws, in written or oral form. These they arranged in a *corpus iuris,* carefully planned by a legal mind, as the following summary will show.

[1] This belongs here, it is displaced in the Bible.

[1] This belongs here, it is displaced in the Bible.

The arrangement on the whole is clear, but some laws are not in their right places now (as 16 ¹⁸ᶠᶠ· 21 ¹ᶠᶠ·) and some groups are not arranged properly according to their subject. No. VI contains three groups not related to each other and the whole section intervenes awkwardly between V and VII. No. IX is not well arranged, and No. XI not at all. The lack of orderly grouping and arrangement is all the more striking, because in the greater part of the code it has been carried out so well. Whether this is due to the fact that the author found those laws partly arranged and partly not, or whether, *e.g.*, Nos. VI, IX, XI were inserted later, we do not know. Some laws of IX belong with X, and are characteristic of the spirit of humanity and equity that pervades the code.

At the beginning stands the law which was of prime importance to the reformers, the law of the single sanctuary which involved the destruction of all other sanctuaries and the centralization of all worship in one place. It was so important that we have it in three slightly different formulations in ch. 12, all of them saying the same as the first one which we quote:

> Ye shall surely destroy all the places wherein the nations that ye shall dispossess served their gods, upon the high mountains and upon the hills, and under every green tree: and ye shall break down their altars, and dash in pieces their pillars, and hew down their Asherim; and ye shall burn with fire the graven images of their gods; and ye shall destroy their name out of that place. Ye shall not do so to Yahweh your God. But to the place which Yahweh your God shall choose out of all your tribes, to put His name there, shall ye resort, and thither thou shalt come; and thither ye shall bring your burnt-offerings, and your sacrifices, and your tithes, and the heave-offering of your hand, and your vows, and your freewill-offerings, and the firstlings of your herd and of your flock: and there ye shall eat before Yahweh your God, and ye shall rejoice in all your undertakings, ye and your households, in which Yahweh thy God has blessed thee. (12 ²⁻⁷)

True Yahwism had been defiled by contact with the Canaanites and their religion. If Israel had obeyed the command of Yahweh to exterminate all the Canaanites without exception and to destroy all their sanctuaries and instruments of worship, this would not have happened, for then Israel would not have been tempted to fall away from Yahweh. The killing of all the Canaanites was of course only theoretical, but the demolition of the high places with their altars and sacred posts and pillars was most seriously meant; and with it the doing away of all worship of other gods, not only of Baal and Asherah, but also of the sun, moon, and stars, and of all the licentious and superstitious practices connected with it. Deuteronomy would have nothing to do with them and ordered therefore the strict regulation of clean and unclean food, as well as of other things that were related to foreign worship, *e.g.* the mixture of wool and linen, mourning customs, etc., in order that the worship of Yahweh might be pure, uncontaminated by any heathen element.

The reformers perceived quite well what was involved in the radical abolition of the local sanctuaries and advocated the measures directly necessitated by it. If all festivals, even the Passover, had to be celebrated at the central sanctuary and all sacrifices had to be brought there, it was no longer possible to kill, *i.e.* to sacrifice any animal at the local shrine, and the eating of meat was restricted to Jerusalem. So sacrifice and secular slaughter had to be separated and the latter was allowed anywhere, only the blood must not be eaten.

When Yahweh thy God shall enlarge thy border, and thou shalt say, I will eat flesh, because thy soul desires to eat flesh; thou mayest eat flesh, after all the desire of thy soul. If the place which Yahweh thy God shall choose, to put His name there, be too far from thee, then thou shalt kill of thy herd and of thy flock, which Yahweh has given thee, and thou mayest eat in thy home town, after all the desire of thy soul. Even as the gazelle and as the hart is eaten, so thou shalt eat of it: the unclean and the clean may eat of it alike. Only be sure that thou eat not the blood: for the blood is the life; and thou shalt not eat the life with the flesh. Thou shalt not eat it; thou shalt pour it out upon the earth as water. Thou shalt not eat it; that it may go well with thee, and with thy children after thee, when thou shalt do that which is right in the eyes of Yahweh. (12 [20-25])

Similarly tithes could not easily be brought to the distant central sanctuary. It was therefore permitted to convert them into money and to buy with it other material at the sanctuary.

And if the way be too long for thee, so that thou art not able to carry it, because the place is too far from thee, which Yahweh thy God shall choose, to set His name there, when Yahweh thy God shall bless thee; then shalt thou turn it into money, and bind up the money in thy hand, and shalt go to the place which Yahweh thy God shall choose: and thou shalt bestow the money for whatsoever thy soul desires, for oxen, or for sheep, or for wine, or for strong drink, or for whatsoever thy soul asks of thee; and thou shalt eat there before Yahweh thy God, and thou shalt rejoice, thou and thy household. (14 [24-26])

Again, the altars of the local sanctuaries had served as places of asylum for the man-slayer. After their removal cities of refuge were to be designated where one who had unintentionally killed someone might flee from the avenger of blood. But only such a one, not the intentional murderer, should find refuge there (19 $^{1-13}$). In place of the priests, who could no longer officiate at the local shrines in judicial cases as dispensers of the oracle, lay-judges had to be appointed in the various places. If these felt unable to decide a case, it was referred to the priests at the central sanctuary, who with a lay-judge were to form the supreme court of land (17$^{8ff.}$).[1] Of the local priests who had lost their places and their income care had to be taken. The law-giver decrees,

> And if a Levite come from any of thy gates out of all Israel, where he sojourns, and come with all the desire of his soul to the place which Yahweh shall choose; then he shall minister in the name of Yahweh his God, as all his brethren the Levites do, who stand there before Yahweh. They shall have like portions to eat, besides that which comes of the sale of his patrimony. (18 $^{6-8}$)

But this was a precarious living, and Deuteromony admonished the people again and again to take care of the Levites, since they had fallen among the poor and dependent classes (*e.g.* 12 ^{19} 14 $^{27.29}$ 16 $^{11. 14}$).

In all these matters the spirit of fairness and humaneness which characterizes the entire legislation is apparent. Righteousness and love are to be shown to all. The great prophetic teaching of social justice was applied in detail. The ideal for the law-giver was that there should be no poor in the land :

> Howbeit there shall be no poor with thee (for Yahweh will surely bless thee in the land which Yahweh thy God gives thee for an inheritance to possess it), if only thou diligently hearken to the voice of Yahweh thy God, to observe to do all this commandment which I command thee this day. For Yahweh thy God will bless thee, as He promised thee : and thou shalt lend to many nations, but thou shalt not borrow; and thou shalt rule over many nations, but they shall not rule over thee. (15 $^{4-6}$)

But he knew that this was utopian, and therefore he tried to inculcate the spirit of justice and kindness in the treatment of the poor.

---

[1] The addition of the lay-judge is striking. It shows the great influence which the lay-judges had had all through the country. The priestly oracle had been a final resort.

If there be with thee a poor man, one of thy brethren, within any of thy gates in thy land which Yahweh thy God gives thee, thou shalt not harden thy heart, nor shut thy hand from thy poor brother; but thou shalt surely open thy hand to him, and shalt surely lend him sufficient for his need. Beware that there be not a base thought in thy heart, saying, The seventh year, the year of release, is at hand; and thou be grudging against thy poor brother, and thou give him nothing; and he cry to Yahweh against thee, and it be sin in thee. Thou shalt surely give him, and thy heart shall not be grieved when thou givest to him; because for this thing Yahweh thy God will bless thee in all thy work, and in all that thou puttest thy hand to. For the poor will never cease out of the land: therefore I command thee, saying, Thou shalt surely open thy hand to thy brother, to thy needy, and to thy poor, in thy land. (15 7–11)

The orphan, widows, and resident foreigners (sojourners), to whom the Levites also are sometimes added because they belonged to the dependent classes, are to be dealt with justly and kindly (24 17 27 19). The gleanings in the fields are to be left for them (24 19–21). At the great festivals they are to be made happy at the sacrifices (16 11. 14). The tithes of the third year are for their benefit, for they are Yahweh's clients (14 28f. 26 12–15). The poor are to be assisted in every way. Money or victuals are to be lent to them without any interest in a spirit of glad helpfulness:

Thou shalt not lend upon interest to thy brother; interest of money, interest of victuals, interest of anything that is lent upon interest. (23 19)

Things absolutely necessary for the daily life must not be taken from them in pledge, e.g. the mill or the upper millstone (24 6). And when pledges must be exacted, great consideration for the feelings of the debtor was to be shown.

When thou lendest thy neighbor any manner of loan, thou shalt not go into his house to fetch his pledge. Thou shalt stand without, and the man to whom thou lendest shall bring forth the pledge without to thee. And if he be a poor man, thou shalt not sleep with his pledge; thou shalt surely restore to him the pledge when the sun goes down, that he may sleep in his garment, and bless thee: and it shall be righteousness to thee before Yahweh thy God. (24 10–13)

Every seventh year was to be a year of release, when the collection of all loans was forbidden, and an opportunity was afforded to the poor for material rehabilitation (15 1–11). The difficulties connected with such a law were felt by the law-giver, and he knew no other way to enforce it than by moral and spiritual appeal.

The laborers are to be treated justly and kindly too; they are to be paid promptly in the evening of the working day.

> Thou shalt not oppress a hired servant that is poor and needy, whether he be of thy brethren, or of thy sojourners that are in thy land within thy gates: in his day thou shalt give him his hire, neither shall the sun go down upon it (for he is poor, and sets his heart upon it); lest he cry against thee to Yahweh, and it be sin to thee. (24 [14f.])

For the slaves also there is to be justice and kindness. A runaway slave must not be returned to his owner (23 [15f.]). In the seventh year, when the Hebrew slaves were released, they were to be sent away not empty-handed but loaded with all sorts of products to enable them to make a fresh beginning in their new freedom (15 [13f.]). Deuteronomy went beyond the older law by specifying that this related also to women. In another connection D safeguarded the rights and feelings of a female prisoner of war (21 [10–14]).

This is in harmony with D's advanced conception of woman as a person. To him she was no longer merely a part of man's property. In his recension of the Decalogue she is singled out and separated from man's household (5 [21]). The law against kidnapping (24 [7]) applies not only to the male, as it did in Ex. 21 [16]. Deuteronomy defends the bride that has been unjustly accused, by punishing the man not only by a money fine but by public chastisement (22 [18f.]); the man who forces another's bride is to be put to death, and the seducer of an unbetrothed virgin must pay her father fifty shekels and marry her, but has forfeited the right of divorcing her (22 [25–29]). It was not sentimentalism but the sense of justice that actuated the law-giver in this, for if the woman was guilty, she was to suffer just punishment as well as the man.

In the family relation too the law-giver had the social values at heart. He regulated divorce (24 [1–4]); restricted the custom of the Levirate marriage to brethren who lived together and safeguarded the observance of the law (25 [5–10]); separated the inheritance of the first-born from sentiment and based it on justice (21 [15–17]); and limited the father's right to punish his disobedient son (21 [18–21]).

The administration of justice was ordered by the appointment of lay-judges in the various towns and of the supreme court in Jerusalem (16 [18–20] 17 [8–13]). Justice was to mark all proceedings.

Thou shalt not wrest justice: thou shalt not respect persons; neither shalt thou take a bribe; for a bribe blinds the eyes of the wise, and perverts the words of the righteous. That which is altogether just shalt thou follow, that thou mayest live, and inherit the land which Yahweh thy God gives thee. (16 ^{19f.})

The rights of the accused were carefully guarded. A full trial was to be made; nobody could be condemned save on the testimony of at least two witnesses.

One witness shall not rise up against a man for any iniquity, or for any sin, in any sin that he sins: at the mouth of two witnesses, or at the mouth of three witnesses, shall a matter be established. (19 ¹⁵)

In cases of capital punishment the witnesses had to be the first to lay hand on the condemned criminal in order that they might bear the full responsibility in case he had been condemned unjustly (17 ^{4–7}). To counteract the tendency to false testimony Deuteronomy decreed,

If an unrighteous witness rise up against any man to testify against him of wrong-doing, then both the men, between whom the controversy is, shall stand before Yahweh, before the priests and the judges that shall be in those days; and the judges shall make diligent inquisition: and, behold, if the witness be a false witness, and have testified falsely against his brother; then shall ye do to him, as he had thought to do to his brother: so shalt thou put away the evil from the midst of thee. And those that remain shall hear, and fear, and shall henceforth commit no more any such evil in the midst of thee. And thine eyes shall not pity; life for life, eye for eye, tooth for tooth, hand for hand, foot for foot. (19 ^{16–21})

The distinction between murder and manslaughter was strongly emphasized, and for the man-slayer cities of asylum were appointed in order that he might not be killed by the avenger of blood (19 ^{1–10}). Blood revenge was limited to the actually guilty person and the responsibility of the other members of his family repudiated.

The fathers shall not be put to death for the children, neither shall the children be put to death for the fathers: every man shall be put to death for his own sin. (24 ¹⁶)

This was one of the most significant advances in criminal law. The discovery of the value of the individual and of his separate rights and obligations was responsible for this. Although the execution of the blood feud lay still in the hands of the family, the community was strong enough to limit its extent. The next step must be that the community itself becomes the executor of the punishment. Deuteronomy was almost ready for this, but did not yet take it.

The spirit of humaneness and of regard for the personal dignity of the other appears also in the law which orders that the punishment of flogging must take place in the presence of the judge and must not be carried to such an extent that it degrades the "brother" too deeply (25 $^{2f.}$).

Justice and love, equity and humanity pervade this code of laws.[1] And these qualities are directly connected with God, for He is impartial and just, merciful and loving. Therefore Israel is to be like Him. Here we come upon the conviction which underlies everything else in Deuteronomy. It was not possible to bring this out fully in the laws, but in the introduction which D wrote for the law he exhorted the people with great warmth and urgency to love Yahweh and to do His will. There he summarized for them the law, not only in the Decalogue (5 $^{1-21}$) but in the famous *Shema*:[2]

> Hear, O Israel: Yahweh is our God, Yahweh alone: and thou shalt love Yahweh thy God with all thy heart, and with all thy soul, and with all thy might.
>
> And these words, which I command thee this day, shall be upon thy heart; and thou shalt teach them diligently unto thy children, and shalt talk of them when thou sittest in thy house, and when thou goest on a journey, and when thou liest down, and when thou risest up. And thou shalt bind them for a sign upon thy hand, and they shall be for frontlets between thine eyes. And thou shalt write them upon the door-posts of thy house, and upon thy gates. (6 $^{4-9}$)

Similarly D summarized the requirements of Yahweh in a form with which we are familiar from Mic. 6 ^{8}:

> And now, Israel, what does Yahweh thy God require of thee, but to fear Yahweh thy God, to walk in all His ways, and to love Him, and to serve Yahweh

---

[1] But note that the humanitarian laws are for Israelites, not for foreigners, (15 ^{3} 23 ^{20}). The resident foreigner (the sojourner) was included in Deuteronomy's large heartedness and the Israelites were urged to love him. But this does not refer to other foreigners, some of whom are excluded forever from citizenship in Israel (23 $^{1-8}$). There is no missionary spirit in the book or any thought of sharing the blessings of Israel's wonderful religion with others. Deuteronomy had not yet perceived the universal implications of monotheism. Its religion was still exclusive.

[2] *Shema* = *hear*, is the first word of the passage (6 $^{4-9}$) which Jesus quoted as the first and greatest commandment.

thy God with all thy heart and with all thy soul, to keep the commandments of Yahweh, and His statutes, which I command thee this day for thy good? Behold, to Yahweh thy God belong heaven and the heaven of heavens, the earth, with all that is therein. Only Yahweh had a delight in thy fathers to love them, and He chose their seed after them, even you beyond all peoples, as at this day. Circumcise therefore the foreskin of your heart, and be no more stiffnecked. For Yahweh your God, he is God of gods, and Lord of lords, the great God, the mighty, and the terrible, who regards not persons, nor takes reward. He executes justice for the fatherless and widow, and loves the sojourner, in giving him food and raiment. Love ye therefore the sojourner; for ye were sojourners in the land of Egypt. Thou shalt fear Yahweh thy God; Him shalt thou serve; and to Him shalt thou cleave, and by His name shalt thou swear. He is thy praise, and He is thy God, that has done for thee these great and terrible things, which thine eyes have seen. (10 $^{12-21}$)

In the conclusion (28 ^{47}) Deuteronomy spoke of serving God "with joyfulness and with gladness of heart, by reason of the abundance of all things." In the introduction (5 ^{11}) the law-giver emphasized especially the prohibition of serving foreign gods and the necessity of destroying all the inhabitants of Canaan lest by intercourse with them Israel be tempted to disloyalty to Yahweh. And in the conclusion (ch. 28) he set forth, in a series of blessings for obedience to this law and of curses for disobedience, his teaching of retribution, his pedagogical doctrine of eudæmonism which was so influential later on. All this is done most impressively in an "urgent and sonorous" style, one of the most distinctive in the Old Testament. It is the style of a preacher. The rhythm of its language, the particular phraseology of its well-formed sentences, and the distinction of its vocabulary are impressive. And the whole is pervaded by such a warm tone, the author's solicitude is so sincere, that the reader who has come under the spell of this great reform preacher is filled with admiration. His style and thought influenced many writers, among them Jeremiah, and the whole devotional language of the people, as the Psalter and the prayers in the books of Nehemiah (1 $^{5-11}$ 9 $^{6ff.}$) and of Daniel (9 $^{4.19}$) prove. A student who has once felt the charm and understood the quality of this style will never forget it and will always be able to detect it in other books with ease.

The book could not be published directly after it was written. But when after Manasseh's long (692–638 B.C.) and Amon's short reign (638–637 B.C.) Josiah became king, the time was more auspi-

cious. In the second decade of his reign the terrible Scythian invasion threatened and prophetic voices foretold Judah's destruction.
But it passed by safely and the people felt that Yahweh had once
more been gracious to them, although He had announced ruin by
His prophets. This was the moment of opportunity for the prophetic party, and in 621 the new law book was placed in the hand of
King Josiah. Hilkiah, the chief priest, had "found" it in the temple and gave it to the chancellor Shaphan, who had been sent by the
king on an errand to the temple. On his return he read it before
Josiah. "And it came to pass when the king had heard the words of
the book of the law that he rent his clothes." After Hilkiah, Shaphan,
and three others at the command of the king had secured the divine
attestation of the book through an oracle, which Huldah the prophetess gave to them, Josiah at once began to institute a reformation
of the cult in accordance with the demands of the Deuteronomic
law. In a convocation of the entire people at the temple the king
and the people adopted in a solemn covenant this code as the fundamental law of the state. Thereupon the temple at Jerusalem was
cleansed of everything connected with foreign worship; the sanctuaries outside of Jerusalem were destroyed and defiled; idolatry and
superstition all through the land were put away; and the Passover
was celebrated in Jerusalem as it had been directed in this law (2 Ki.
22f.). It was the most radical reformation imaginable and it was
carried out with relentless zeal. Its effects were not only immediate
but far-reaching. Religion now had an authoritative book around
which it centred more and more. It could be taught. Men were
exhorted to study it day and night, to think of it at home and abroad,
to teach it to their children. Religion was a reasonable thing.
There was nothing mysterious about it. One need not go far to
know it, as another deuteronomist phrased it,

> For this commandment which I command thee this day, it is not too hard
> for thee, neither is it far off. It is not in heaven, that thou shouldest say, Who
> shall go up for us to heaven, and bring it unto us, and make us to hear it, that
> we may do it? Neither is it beyond the sea, that thou shouldest say, Who
> shall go over the sea for us, and bring it to us, and make us to hear it, that we
> may do it? But the word is very nigh unto thee, in thy mouth, and in thy
> heart, that thou mayest do it. (30 11–14)

With Deuteronomy began the movement by which the religion of

Israel became the religion of a book. In this respect we feel the effect of Deuteronomy to this day, both in Judaism and Christianity.

After the reformation was over, the reformers had apparently gained their ends. But though they had insisted on wholehearted devotion to Yahweh, they concentrated their efforts on securing this in and through the cult. They tried to effect a spiritual reformation by the change of the cult, while it can be accomplished only by a change of the heart. With the best intentions and the purest enthusiasm they had failed. The critic had already risen in the person of the prophet Jeremiah. But before going to him we will treat his three lesser contemporaries.

CHAPTER X

ZEPHANIAH, NAHUM, AND HABAKKUK

ABOUT 626 the great Scythian invasion, of which Herodotus (Book I, §§ 103–106) tells us, threatened Palestine and roused Zephaniah and Jeremiah to interpret to their people the underlying significance of the impending catastrophe. To Zephaniah it was the coming of the Day of Yahweh, the awful day which Amos had painted as a day of darkness and judgment, and Isaiah as a day of earthquake and tornado. It was coming with ominous speed; horror and fright seized the heart of the prophet, and with compelling words of terrifying effect he described it to his people:

> The great day of Yahweh is near,
>   it is near and hastes greatly.
> Hark! the day of Yahweh;
>   the mighty man cries bitterly there.
> That day is a day of wrath,
>   a day of trouble and distress,
> A day of wasteness and desolation, ·
>   a day of darkness and gloom,
> A day of clouds and thick darkness,
>   a day of the trumpet and alarm,
> Against the fortified cities,
>   and against the high battlements.
> And I will bring distress upon men,
>   that they shall walk like blind men,
> And their blood shall be poured out as dust,
>   and their flesh as dung.
> Neither their silver nor their gold
>   shall be able to deliver them
> In the day of Yahweh's wrath,
>   in the fire of His zeal.
> For He will make an end, yea, a terrible end,
>   of all them that dwell in the earth. (1 14–18)

It was this passage whose terror inspired the famous mediæval hymn,

Dies irae, dies illa
solvet saeclum in favilla, etc.,

of which the English counterpart is still sung in the churches,

Day of wrath, O day of mourning !
See fulfilled the prophets' warning,
Heaven and earth in ashes burning !

To Zephaniah the day will be the day of universal judgment,

I will utterly consume all things,
   from off the face of the ground, — says Yahweh.
I will consume man and beast,
   I will consume the birds of the heavens,
   and the fishes of the sea.
I will cause the wicked to stumble,
   and I will cut off man
   from off the face of the ground, — says Yahweh. (1 $^{2-3}$)

The judgment will come especially upon Judah because of her social and religious corruption, the religious and moral indifference and materialistic scepticism of her people. Zephaniah singled out Philistia, Ethiopia, and Assyria too,[1] but he turned again his bitter accusations upon the oppressing and rebellious city with her corrupt princes and judges, prophets and priests, whom he knew so well. For he was of noble birth, his great great grandfather had been King Hezekiah, and he mingled freely among the great in the city of Jerusalem. One cannot expect that this born aristocrat should feel the sufferings of the poor as Micah the prophet of the poor had done, in whom their sorrows had become articulate. And yet he recognized in the poor people the hope of Israel. He had studied not only Amos and Micah but also Isaiah and knew his teaching of the pious remnant, on whom the hope of the future was built. So he called them to repentance and moral renewal in order that they might escape from the fearful judgment. The Day itself can no longer be averted, it must surely come, but "it may be that you will be hid in the day of Yahweh's anger" (2 ^{3}). Later this hope became a certainty to him and he prophesied,

---

[1] A later exilic reader added the Moabites and Ammonites in 2 $^{2-11}$, and inserted in 2 ^{7} the political hope, "and the coast shall be for the remnant of Judah," and "for Yahweh their God will visit them and bring back their captivity."

> I will leave in the midst of thee
>   an afflicted and poor people,
>   and they shall take refuge in the name of Yahweh.
> The remnant of Israel shall not do iniquity,
>   nor speak lies;
> Neither shall be found in their mouths
>   a deceitful tongue;
> For they shall feed and lie down,
>   and none shall make them afraid. (3 $^{11-13}$)

Faith, social justice, and peace characterize this plain and sombre picture of the future. It lacks all of Isaiah's brilliance and beauty, but it is quite in keeping with Zephaniah's sober, unadorned style. The religious community, independent of the political state, is here predicted by him who foresaw the destruction of the state and all its organization.

It may be that Zephaniah held out a similar hope to the nations, although this is doubtful. Was the final outcome of their judgment merely punishment and annihilation or was it also purification, as in Israel's case? If Zephaniah thought only of punishment (3 ^{8}), a later prophet with wider vision and universal sympathies saw what Zephaniah did not see and what was yet inherent in his message, and added

> For then will I turn to the peoples a pure language,
>   that they may all call upon the name of Yahweh,
>   to serve Him with one consent. (3 $^{9f.}$)

Another poet with national interest worked out sometime during the Exile the hope of Israel's restoration, which Zephaniah had treated so soberly, and wrote a poem of joy and hope so that the book now ends with a song (3 $^{14-20}$).

Perhaps at about the same time that Zephaniah prophesied, when Nineveh was besieged by the Medes under Cyaxares (625), but more probably about one decade later, shortly before the fall of Nineveh (612), Nahum began to prophesy. He is the least attractive of the prophets. He was a nationalist, and his heart was filled with vengeance for his country's foe. Full of enthusiasm, he welcomed Assyria's fall. At last the brutal despot will be overthrown. All the known world has had to bear his sinful tyranny. At last his cruelty and rapacity, his lying diplomacy are to be requited. Yahweh, the God of history, will judge him. He has ordered the affairs of the world to Assyria's undoing.   No other judgment will ever be needed, this one is to be final.

> There is no assuaging of thy hurt,
>   thy wound is grievous.
> All that hear the report of thee
>   clap their hands over thee,
> For upon whom has not thy wickedness
>   passed continually? (3 ¹⁹)

Nahum was a great poet.   His word-pictures are superb, his rhetorical skill is beyond praise.   In the description of the attack, destruction, and plundering of the city he exhibits such vivid imagination and such great power of poetic expression that we hardly dare to attribute to so bold and original a prophet the torso of the artificial alphabetical psalm with which his book now opens (1 ¹⁻⁸). Also 1 ¹³· ¹⁵ 2 ² are later additions.

In his own day Nahum may have been very popular and important; in the history of religion he holds an inferior place.   Were it not that the feelings of oppressed humanity found voice in him and that he was conscious of it, his message would have been one of unrelieved nationalism.

Nahum witnessed the triumph of righteousness in Nineveh's fall, which took place in 612.   But justice was not always victorious, and the experiences of life could not always be harmonized with faith in God's moral government of the world.   The problem of theodicy sorely troubled Nahum's greater contemporary Habakkuk. It was an axiom of prophetic religion that Yahweh is righteous. But in Judah a condition of social injustice and oppression had set in under Jehojakim (608–597) and Yahweh did not interfere.   Did He not care?   That could not be!   But why, oh why did the righteous God tolerate such wickedness in the world?   In words whose pathos still moves the reader's heart Habakkuk complained and appealed to Yahweh.

> O Yahweh, how long shall I cry,
>   and Thou wilt not hear?
> I cry out unto Thee "violence!"
>   and Thou wilt not save.
> Why dost Thou show me iniquity,
>   and look upon perverseness?

For destruction and violence are before me,
and there is strife, and contention arises.
Therefore the law is slacked,
and justice never goes forth;
For the wicked compasses about the righteous;
therefore justice goes forth perverted. (1 2-4)

Habakkuk neither doubted nor denied the reality or the righteousness of God, but he could not understand His silence in the presence of these terrible conditions. His faith was baffled by his experience. Ten thousand times his cry has been repeated by men whose anguish was deeper than his own and whose faith had given way to doubt. The problem of God's righteous government had grown too dark, their hearts were full of despair, and no reply ever came back from a leaden sky. But Habakkuk's appeal was answered. The solution came to him in the advance of the Chaldeans whom Yahweh had raised up as His instrument to establish justice in the world. Like Isaiah he interpreted the historic movements of his time as guided and controlled by Yahweh, and from this great predecessor and teacher he took the features of his vivid description of the foes whom he had never seen.

But after the Chaldeans had come under Nebuchadrezzar, the problem came back with redoubled force, for Habakkuk saw that their victory could not be the final answer, for they had turned out to be brutal and self-sufficient, caring naught for God or man. Without regard for Yahweh they overthrew and plundered nation after nation and "made their own might their god." The cruel injustice of the situation was even more glaring now than before. Again Habakkuk appealed to Yahweh,

O Yahweh, Thou hast ordained him for judgment,
and Thou, O Rock, hast established him for correction.
Thou that art purer of eyes than to behold evil,
and that canst not look upon perverseness,
Wherefore lookest Thou upon the treacherous and art silent,
when the wicked swallows up the man that is more righteous than he? (1 12f.)

The problem was harder than ever. It could not be solved in the same manner as before, for in the political constellations of the time there was no ray of hope. The Chaldeans were impregnable in the strength of their empire. But Habakkuk could not give up his faith in Yahweh's righteous government of the world; that was too deeply ingrained in the fibre of his religion. His only hope was in Yahweh and it was not disappointed, for the illumination finally came to his troubled mind in a vision of God. He saw with his inner eye a majestic theophany (3^{2-16}). Yahweh appeared as in times of old in all His awe-inspiring splendor and terrifying power to accomplish the deliverance of His people and the destruction of their foes. Habakkuk was overwhelmed by the power of the vision,

> I heard and my body trembled,
>> my lips quivered at the voice;
> Rottenness enters into my bones,
>> and I tremble in my place;
> Because I must wait quietly for the day of trouble,
>> when it comes to the people that invades us. (3^{16})

But the fulfilment of the vision tarried. Yahweh did not intervene. Conditions remained as before or grew worse. Once more the prophet sought an explanation:

> Upon my watch tower I will stand,
>> and take my place upon the rampart,
> Will wait to see, what He will say to me,
>> and what answer I shall get to my plea.

Patiently he waited till the answer came,

> Write the vision, and make it plain upon tablets,
>> that he may run that reads it.
> For the vision is yet for the appointed time,
>> and it hastes toward the end, and shall not lie:
> Though it tarry, wait for it,
>> because it will surely come, it will not delay. (2^{1-3})

The vision which he had seen is true and will certainly be fulfilled. Let Habakkuk publish it abroad! For Yahweh is in control of this world. His righteousness will surely be vindicated at the appointed time, all appearances to the contrary notwithstanding. Do not doubt, only believe! Be steadfast in your allegiance to Yahweh and in your faith in His righteousness, for

> The righteous shall live by his faith! (2^{4b})

After this Habakkuk could wait, and in the confident assurance that the vision would be fulfilled "at the appointed time" he pronounced his woes upon the Chaldean oppressor. His problem had been solved for him. He knew as never before,

Though the cause of evil prosper,
Yet 'tis truth alone is strong:
Though her portion be the scaffold,
And upon the throne be wrong, —
Yet that scaffold sways the future,
And behind the dim unknown,
Standeth God within the shadow,
Keeping watch above His own.

(James Russell Lowell)

The independent circulation of the vision was probably responsible for its present position at the end of the book in ch. 3, whereas
it really belongs between ch. 1 and 2.   It had its own literary history for it came to be used in public worship as a psalm.   For this
purpose several lines (3 [14b. 17–19]) as well as a heading and subscription, musical notes and *selah's* were added.[1]   It is of course not
impossible that Habakkuk's own vision was lost and that a later
editor who missed a record of it supplied it from some collection of
psalms which had headings and musical notations.   If he did, he
showed admirable insight, for its contents fit most remarkably
the requirements of Habakkuk's book.

If Habakkuk prophesied between 605 and 590, as is most probable, the fulfilment of his vision tarried for a generation, for Babylon
did not fall till 539.   We do not know how great Habakkuk's influence was upon his contemporaries, but on posterity it was far-
reaching.   Though he was but a spiritual disciple of the great
prophet of faith Isaiah, and by no means as great as he, the formulation of the result of his profound soul struggles was so simple and
pregnant that six centuries later Paul adopted it as most adequately
expressing the answer to his own deep problem, and after another
fifteen centuries Martin Luther found in it the light that illumined
and liberated his soul.   To each in his own way, as an answer to his
own particular problem, came with pregnant meaning, different in
each case, the great words,

The righteous shall live by his faith.

[1] Hab. 2 [8b.13a.14.18–20] are also later additions to the original book.

CHAPTER XI

JEREMIAH

ABOUT 650, during the reign of Manasseh, Jeremiah was born as the son of a devoted priestly family in the little country town of Anathoth, about four miles northeast of Jerusalem. He was trained by his saintly parents, whose piety had been intensified by the persecution under Manasseh, and grew up well versed in the traditions of his people, especially also of his exiled northern countrymen, for his family belonged to the North, to Benjamin rather than to Judah. He had studied the writings of Amos, Isaiah, Micah, and especially of North Israel's greatest prophet, Hosea, by whom he was profoundly influenced and to whom he was bound by a deep, spiritual kinship. By nature shy and sensitive, gentle and loving, with a beautiful poetic imagination, keen moral insight, and profound religious devotion, he was a unique personality even in his youth. In the year 626 he was called to the prophethood. He shrank at first from this high calling and pleaded his youth, but Yahweh persuaded and consecrated him in the great spiritual experience which gave to him a consciousness of prophetic mission unparalleled among the prophets. He knew himself to have been predestined and prepared, even before he was born, for his prophethood (1^{4-10}). Such visions are the result of long previous preparation. The great experiences of the soul come to a climax in the sudden illumination of the vision. But we do not know anything particular about the steps that led up to it in Jeremiah.

The immediate occasion for the beginning of his prophetic activity was the Scythian invasion which threatened Palestine in 626. Anxiously the young man looked to the north; in a second vision it became plain to him that a fearful calamity would break in on his people from there, that Yahweh had summoned the northern armies to attack Jerusalem and the other Judaean cities, because they had "forsaken Yahweh, burned incense to other gods and worshipped the work of their hands." Jeremiah must go and announce this to his people. He knew that it would not be easy, that it would bring him into sharp conflict with the leaders and the nation itself. But emboldened and empowered by Yahweh's own assurance of help, he spoke courageously his message in the face of persecution and death (1 ¹³⁻¹⁹). In a series of brief, vivid, and picturesque oracles he announced the coming of the wild northern hosts. The impression they made on him was profound. He heard them coming, saw them galloping over Palestine's hills irresistibly onward. He had no rest and peace, his visions tormented him, his auditions tortured him until he cried out in the despair of his soul,

> My anguish, my anguish, I am pained
>   at my very heart,
> My heart is disquieted within me,
>   I cannot hold my peace;
> Because thou hast heard, O my soul, the sound of the trumpet,
>   the alarm of war.
> Destruction upon destruction is cried,
>   for the whole land is laid waste:
> Suddenly are my tents destroyed,
>   and my curtains in a moment.
> How long shall I see the standard,
>   and hear the sound of the trumpet? (4 ¹⁹⁻²¹)

He looked at the fields and mountains, saw them in all their glory, listened to the birds and to the songs of men and of women, and — all of a sudden they had vanished!

> I beheld the earth, and, lo, it was waste and void,
>   and the heavens, and they had no light.
> I beheld the mountains, and, lo, they trembled,
>   and all the hills moved to and fro.
> I beheld, and, lo, there was no man,
>   and all the birds of the heaven were fled.
> I beheld, and, lo, the fruitful field was a wilderness,
>   and all its cities were broken down. (4 ²³⁻²⁶)

The astonishment is masterly portrayed by the repeated "I beheld" and the following "and, lo." As if he could not trust his eyes, he looked from one to the other: desolation round about and utter loneliness, even the birds had fled! Ah, destruction comes, it is inevitable, desolation, ruin, and death. And why? It comes from

Yahweh Himself because of the terrible religious corruption of
Judah. The northern hosts are but the agents of the offended
deity. Jeremiah had seen the fearful religious corruption at the
local shrines and was deeply offended by the base practices of the
people. He knew that was the reason for the awful ruin that was so
sure to come. He warned his people, pleaded with them to repent
and avert God's anger in this way. But their repentance must be
wholehearted,

> Break up your fallow ground,
>   and sow not among thorns.
> Circumcise yourselves to Yahweh,
>   and take away the foreskins of your heart! (4 [3f.])

It meant breaking with the past, beginning a new life; it meant
doing away with all the shameful practices at the local sanctuaries,
giving up the Baalim, whom Judah still worshipped, and turning
with heart and soul to Yahweh (2 [1-13. 20-35]). It meant also re-
nouncing the foolish policy of seeking international alliances with
Egypt or Assyria, which had brought nothing but national humiliation. The only helper, the real saviour was Yahweh. And Him
they had forsaken! (2 [14-19. 37f.])

Apostasy from Yahweh had been the reason for North Israel's
national ruin. Judah should have learned the lesson, yet she had
not returned to Yahweh "with her whole heart, but feignedly."
As Jeremiah pondered on the fate of Israel, he felt sure that she had
by now repented and would therefore be called back (3 [6-13. 19-25] 4 [1f.]).
His longing for the restoration of his more immediate countrymen
found utterance in some of the most exquisite poems that he
ever wrote. This is saying a good deal, for he was a divinely
appointed poet from whose soul came words that still haunt the
memory by their beauty, and still woo the heart by their grace.

> The people that were left of the sword
>   have found favor in the wilderness,
> Israel goes to his rest.
>   Yahweh appeared to him from afar:
> "Yea, I have loved thee with an everlasting love,
>   therefore with loving-kindness have I drawn thee." (31 [2f.])

These last two lines belong to the most wonderful sayings of the
whole Bible. The glory of the Gospel is in them, proclaiming the

everlasting love of God. Jeremiah's own soul stood forth in these words. He proceeds: Israel shall be restored, Samaria be rebuilt,

> For there shall be a day, that the watchmen shall cry
> upon the hills of Ephraim,
> "Arise ye, and let us go up to Zion
> unto Yahweh our God!" (31 [6])

In another poem Jeremiah starts with a description of how in Ramah, quite near his home, the people had heard for many, many years bitter weeping at the grave of the ancestress of North Israel. Rachel was mourning because her children had gone into exile and had left their mother alone, heartbroken, disconsolate in her grief.

> Hark! in Ramah is heard lamentation
> and bitter weeping,
> Rachel is weeping for her children;
> she refuses to be comforted.

But now Yahweh's answer flows like balm into her wounded heart,

> Refrain thy voice from weeping,
> and thine eyes from tears,
> For thy work shall be rewarded,
> and they shall come again from the land of the enemy. (31 [15f.])

In still another poem Jeremiah represented Yahweh soliloquizing,

> I have surely heard
> Ephraim bemoaning himself thus,
> "Thou hast chastised me and I was chastised,
> as a calf unaccustomed to the yoke:
> Let me come back, that I may return,
> for Thou art my God!
> Surely after I was punished, I repented,
> and after I was instructed, I smote upon my thigh:
> I was ashamed, yea, even confounded,
> because I did bear the reproach of my youth."

This penitent appeal touches Yahweh's heart. He is still musing, but the father's love is aroused,

> Is Ephraim My dear son?
> is he a darling child?
> For as often as I speak of him,
> I do earnestly remember him still,
> Therefore My heart yearns for him:
> I will surely have mercy upon him. (31 [18-20])

Who does not think of the Prodigal Son and his father's longing and yearning? In a separate poem,[1] the prophet calls Israel home.

> Turn again, O virgin of Israel,
>   turn again to these thy cities!
> How long wilt thou go hither and thither,
>   O thou backsliding daughter? (31 21)

This hope was never fulfilled. Later prophets adopted it, but none gave to it such moving and beautiful expression as Jeremiah had done. That was because his heart reached out in these words to his exiled brethren, his whole being longed for their return.

But these prophecies were only an episode. The endeavor of his life belonged to the people of Judah. For them he lived and worked with all his might. When the reformers went through the land in the interest of the Deuteronomic reformation, he gave them his aid and combated the religious perversion of the people, but to him the change of heart was always primary (11 1–17). His vigorous, radical preaching earned him the enmity of many, even among his friends and nearest relatives, for the reformation involved for them the loss of their income and their lifework besides all the rest. They determined to do away with him. Jeremiah was so guileless that it was to him a real providence when Yahweh gave him knowledge of it (11 18–12 6).

He left Anathoth at this time and went to Jerusalem to carry on his prophetic activity in the very heart of the nation. He found an almost incredible corruption there. As he mingled freely among the people in the streets, he failed to discover a single upright man among them.

> Run ye to and fro through the streets of Jerusalem,
>   and see now and know,
> And seek in her broad places,
>   if ye can find a man,
> If there be any that does justly,
>   that seeks truth, —
>   and I will pardon her.
> But though they say, "As Yahweh lives!"
>   surely they swear falsely.

[1] To a witty reader who overlooked this, the sudden change from the son Ephraim to the virgin of Israel seemed so queer that he wrote in the margin, "Verily, Yahweh has created a new thing in the earth: a woman is changed into a man!" A copyist without sense of humor put this into the text.

At first Jeremiah thought that only the poor and uneducated were so degraded.

> And I said, Surely these are the poor,
>   they are foolish;
> For they know not the way of Yahweh
>   nor the law of their God:
> I will go to the great men,
>   and will speak to them;
> For they know the way of Yahweh
>   and the justice of their God.
> But these with one accord have broken the yoke,
>   and burst the bonds! (5 1–5)

How can Yahweh pardon them? He must punish them all for their wickedness. But Jeremiah's conscience was exceedingly sensitive. There might be some righteous persons after all among these sinners. He must investigate again, he felt that Yahweh had made him "a trier among My people, that thou mayest know and try their way." But test as he might, no precious metal was found in the crucible (6 27–30). And when Yahweh said to him once more,

> Thoroughly glean as a vine
>   the remnant of Israel,
> Turn again thy hand as a grape gatherer
>   upon the shoots,

he replied,

> To whom shall I speak and testify,
>   that they may hear?
> Behold, their ear is uncircumcised,
>   and they cannot hearken:
> Behold, the word of Yahweh has become to them a reproach,
>   they have no delight in it. (6 9f.)

As he thinks of these rebuffs, indignation burns in his heart. In vain he tries to hold back, against his will he pours out those scorching words which set free the forces that will sweep the people into ruin.

> I am full of the wrath of Yahweh,
>   I am weary with holding in;
> I will pour it out on the children in the street,
>   and upon the gathering of youths together:
> Yea, even the husband with the wife shall be taken,
>   the aged with him that is full of days.

And their houses shall be turned unto others,
 their fields and their wives together;
For I will stretch out My hand
 upon the inhabitants of the land, — says Yahweh.
For from the least of them even unto the greatest of them
 every one is given to covetousness;
And from the prophet even unto the priest
 every one deals falsely.
They have healed the hurt of My people
 slightly, saying, "Peace,
Peace," when there is no peace! (6 [11—14])

He reiterated his announcement of the Scythians, who will be Yahweh's agents, and depicted them and their advance upon Jerusalem most graphically and dramatically (5 [6.15—17] 6 [1—8.22—26] 8 [14—17]). But the coming catastrophe filled his heart with grief.

Oh that I could comfort myself against sorrow!
 my heart is faint within me.
Behold, the voice of the cry of the daughter of my people
 from the land wide and broad:
"Is not Yahweh in Zion?
 Is not her King in her?" —
"Why have they provoked Me to anger with their graven images,
 and with foreign vanities?" —
"The harvest is past, the summer is ended,
 and we are not saved!" —

For the hurt of my people am I hurt,
 I mourn, dismay has taken hold on me.
Is there no balm in Gilead?
 is there no physician there?
Why then is not recovered
 the health of the daughter of my people?
Oh that my head were waters,
 and mine eyes a fountain of tears,
That I might weep day and night
 for the slain of the daughter of my people! (8 [18]—9 [1])

In this mood he composed those poems which, in the judgment of literary critics, belong to the finest in the literature of the world. First the dirge over the country,

  For the mountains will I take up
  a weeping and wailing,

> And for the pastures of the wilderness
>   a lamentation,
> Because they are burned up,
>   so that none passes through;
> Neither can men hear
>   the voice of the cattle:
> Both the birds of the heavens and the beasts
>   are fled, they are gone.
> And I will make Jerusalem heaps,
>   a dwelling-place of jackals;
> And I will make the cities of Judah a desolation,
>   without inhabitant. (9 [10f.])

Then the lamentation over the people,

> Consider ye, and call
>   for the mourning women,
> And send for the skilful women
>   that they may come!
> And let them make haste and take up
>   a wailing for us,
> That our eyes may run down with tears,
>   and our eyelids gush out with waters.
> For a voice of wailing is heard out of Zion:
>   "How are we ruined!
> We are greatly confounded,
>   because cast down are our dwellings!" (9 [17–19])

And the most moving of all,

> Hear the word of Yahweh, O ye women,
>   and let your ear receive the word of His mouth;
> And teach your daughters wailing,
>   every one her neighbor lamentation:
>
> "Death is come up into our windows,
>   it is entered into our palaces,
> To cut off the children from without,
>   the young men from the streets.
>
> "The dead bodies of men shall fall
>   upon the open field,
> As the sheaves after the harvestman;
>   and none shall gather them." (9 [20–22])

It is a gruesome picture that is painted here of the grim harvester, death, which appears here for the first time in literature to haunt the imagination of men ever after. Whether it impressed Jeremiah's hearers is doubtful. They were too much set in their ways; as a rule they would not hearken, they would not repent. This seemed unnatural to Jeremiah, he saw with sorrow that they would not follow the deepest instincts of their being.

> Yea, the stork in the heavens
> knows her appointed times;
> And the turtle dove and the swallow and the crane
> observe the time of their coming;
> But my people know not
> the law of Yahweh. (8 7)

Of course, they were religious in their way. They brought many sacrifices and were even intent on perfuming the odor of the offerings in order to make them still more acceptable to Yahweh. But Jeremiah was sure that Yahweh had never commanded any sacrifices, but had required from the fathers nothing but obedience to the moral law, and that was His sole requirement now (7 21-26).

> To what purpose comes there to Me
> frankincense from Sheba,
> And sweet cane from a far country?
> Your burnt-offerings are not acceptable,
> nor your sacrifices pleasing to Me. (6 20)

He called the people back to the ways of the good old time, for they alone could lead men to their true goal.

> Stand ye in the ways and see,
> and ask for the old paths,
> Where is the good way, and walk therein,
> *and ye shall find rest for your souls.* (6 16)

Centuries later Jesus used these same words in his immortal appeal (Mt. 11 29) not as a conscious quotation but as something that once heard was unforgettable and had become his own by spiritual appropriation and been deepened by his personal experience. To Jeremiah religion was a matter of the soul. Each man has longings that can find their satisfaction only in God, and the way to God is by repentance and social righteousness. But preach to his people as much and earnestly as he might, he found no response, till finally life among them seemed to him unbearable.

> Oh that I had in the wilderness
>   a lodging-place for wayfaring men;
> That I might leave my people,
>   and go from them!
> For they are all adulterers,
>   an assembly of treacherous men. (9 ²ff.)

The Scythians passed by without doing harm to Judah. They swept through the Philistine plain to the borders of Egypt, where Pharaoh Psamtich turned them back by bribes. On their return they did not go into the hills of Judah either. But they aided, without knowing it, the reform movement in Judah which resulted in the reformation of Josiah in 621, when the entire cult was purified, and centralized in Jerusalem. Jeremiah had always insisted on a change of heart, for religion was not a matter of cult to him so much as a matter of character and life. To him the stress laid on sacrifices had always been obnoxious. Now that the reformation was accomplished, he quickly perceived that it had brought an outward change. External conformity was easier to attain than moral renewal, but it was useless. Soon Jeremiah found himself in sharp opposition to the religious leaders. When they appealed to the lawbook for their justification and applied its test of prophetic authenticity (Deut. 18 ²¹ᶠ·) to Jeremiah whose prediction of doom through the northern foe had not been fulfilled; when they challenged his authority and rejected the living word of God that he had given, Jeremiah attacked them bitterly and charged them with fraud:

> How do ye say, "We are wise,
>   and the law of Yahweh is with us"?
> But, behold, the false pen of the scribes
>   has made of it falsehood.
> The wise men are put to shame,
>   they are dismayed and taken:
> They have rejected the word of Yahweh,
>   and what manner of wisdom is in them? (8 ⁸ᶠ·)

The insinuation that his prophecy had not been fulfilled and had therefore not been a genuine message from Yahweh must have agitated the sensitive prophet greatly. But he found reassurance in the vision of the rod of an almond tree (*shaked*) which flashed into his mind the words of Yahweh, "I will watch (*shoked*) over My

word to perform it" (1 $^{11f.}$).   And it was not many years before it
was fulfilled !

After King Josiah's tragic death in the battle at Megiddo in
607, his son Jehoahaz sat on the throne but three months, when
Pharaoh Necho deposed him and had him brought to Riblah on the
Orontes.   The people were still mourning over Josiah.   But Jeremiah now told them,

> Weep not for the dead,
>   nor bemoan him;
> But weep sore for him that goes away!
>   for he shall return no more,
>   nor see his native country. (22 $^{10-12}$)

Those were days full of national uncertainty and darkness.
Nobody knew what the future might bring.   But the inviolability
of the temple at Jerusalem had become a dogma, and in their perplexity the people knew that this at least was certain, whatever else
might come : Jerusalem could never be taken, because the temple
of Yahweh was in it.   Only Jeremiah did not share this common
faith and felt driven to shatter it in the name of truth.   He appeared
in the temple court at a time when people from all over Judah were
assembled for worship, and with ringing words he denounced their
trust in Yahweh's temple as unwarranted.   "Amend your ways
and your doings, and I will cause you to dwell in this place.   Trust
not in lying words, saying, The temple of Yahweh, the temple of
Yahweh, the temple of Yahweh are these."   Only if you repent and
lead righteous lives, will you be saved.   Else "I will do to the
house which is called by My name, as I did to Shiloh" whose temple
had been destroyed in the Philistine wars.   " And I will cast you
out of My sight, as I have cast out all your brethren, even the whole
seed of Ephraim."   This was a most daring speech, but Jeremiah's
spiritual courage ever rose to the height of the occasion, if he was
sure that Yahweh spoke through him.   It sounded like blasphemy
to his hearers and in their wrath they demanded his death.   Only
the intervention of the princes who recalled Micah's similar prophecy
and Hezekiah's attitude to it, and the powerful aid of his friend
Ahikam, a son of Josiah's chancellor Shaphan, saved him from
certain death.   Another prophet, Uriah, who had also prophesied

very much like Jeremiah, had to flee for his life to Egypt, but was extradited and executed in Jerusalem (ch. 7 and 26).

Jehoiakim, at the beginning of whose reign this happened, had been made king by Pharaoh Necho, probably because of his pro-Egyptian sympathies. He was entirely different from his father Josiah. Jeremiah gives a striking character sketch of him, in which he compares his luxurious building and oppressive treatment of the people with the plain but righteous life of his father Josiah:

> Woe to him that builds his house by unrighteousness,
>   and his chambers by injustice;
> That uses his neighbor's service without wages,
>   and gives him not his hire;
> That says, I will build me a wide house
>   with spacious chambers,
> And cuts him out windows; and it is ceiled with cedar,
>   and painted with vermilion.
> Shalt thou reign, because thou strivest
>   to excel in cedar?
> Did not thy father eat and drink,
>   and do justice and righteousness?
> He judged the cause of the poor and the needy,
>   then it was well with him.
> Was not this to know Me?
>   says Yahweh.
> But thine eyes and thy heart are not
>   but for thy covetousness,
> And for shedding innocent blood,
>   and for oppression and violence, to do it. (22 [13-17])

When Jeremiah wrote this, he had had opportunity to know and to judge him by his deeds, which led to this severe condemnation:

Therefore thus says Yahweh concerning Jehoiakim, the son of Josiah, king of Judah:

> They shall not lament for him,
> "Ah my brother! or Ah sister!"
> They shall not lament for him,
> "Ah lord! or Ah his glory!"
> He shall be buried with the burial of an ass,
>   drawn and cast forth
>   beyond the gates of Jerusalem. (22 [18f.])

Jehoiakim was Necho's vassal till 605, when the Pharaoh was decisively beaten by Nebuchadrezzar at Charchemish. Although

Nebuchadrezzar could not at the time follow up his victory on account of his father's death which called him back to Babylon to ascend the throne, Syria and Palestine came under his sway. The Chaldeans were now the dominant world power and all the great movements among the nations were affected by their control. To Jeremiah it was at once plain that the Chaldeans were the northern enemies whom Yahweh had so long declared He would bring upon his people on account of their sins. Soon he announced that Nebuchadrezzar was the servant of Yahweh who would carry out His purpose of punishing Judah for its disobedience (25^{1-11}). In a grand vision Yahweh gives to Jeremiah the cup of wrath which he must present to Judah, to all the surrounding nations, and to Egypt in order that they should drink, become intoxicated, and fall into a stupor from which they should never rise again (25^{15-29}).[1] It is probable, though by no means certain, that Jeremiah foretold the catastrophe in special oracles to Egypt (46^{1-12}) and Philistia (47^{1-7}). It would involve all of them. Jeremiah knew the temper of these nations and of Judah too well to believe that the clash with Nebuchadrezzar could be averted. He could not hope that his people would heed his warning. Too long and too persistently had they resisted his message. They had lost the very capacity of repentance.

> Can the Ethiopian change his skin,
>> or the leopard his spots?
> Then may ye also do good,
>> that are accustomed to do evil. (13^{23})

This is the classical formulation of the profound psychological and religious truth, which Hosea had seen before Jeremiah. He had no hope of the king either. He knew his pride and vanity. He warned him and the people, to humble themselves and not embark on dangerous adventures.

---

[1] This passage was worked over by interpolators who believed it referred to a universal judgment. They inserted therefore a number of nations which they thought belonged here and made v. 26 to read "and the king of Sheshach (= Babylon) shall drink after them" showing that they misunderstood the historical situation altogether. Some of the additions were not yet in the Hebrew original of the Greek version. The list that remains after they are all removed contains Judah, Egypt, Philistia, Edom, Moab, Ammon, Dedan, Teman, Buz, and the mingled people that dwell in the wilderness.

> Hear ye, and give ear;
>   be not proud;
> Give glory to Yahweh your God,
>   before it grow dark,
> And before your feet stumble
>   upon the mountains of twilight,
> And while ye look for light,
>   He turn it into the shadow of death,
>   and make it gross darkness.

He knows that they will not hear,

> My soul weeps in secret for your pride,
>   and mine eyes weep sore,
> Because Yahweh's flock is taken captive. (13 [15-17])

Jeremiah had judged correctly. But by his plain speech he incurred the king's displeasure, and could no longer appear in public as freely as before. The result was that he dictated the prophecies that he had given so far to his scribe Baruch, and on a fast-day in 603 he sent Baruch to read the scroll to a vast assembly in the temple. It made a great impression, a hearer informed the princes of it, and they sent for Baruch, who read it to them. After telling him that he and Jeremiah should hide themselves, they took it to the king and Jehudi read it to him. But he cut it in pieces with his pen-knife and threw them one by one into the fire, in spite of the protestation of some of the princes. Jeremiah and Baruch he commanded to be apprehended, but they had hidden themselves too well. Jeremiah thereupon dictated his prophecies again to Baruch, "and there were added besides to them many like words" (ch. 36).

Jeremiah had always been a man of prayer; with intense earnestness he interceded again and again for his people. Some of his prayers are preserved; they are of touching simplicity and beauty, as the following shows:

> Though our iniquities testify against us,
>   work Thou for Thy name's sake, O Yahweh;
> For our backslidings are many,
>   we have sinned against Thee.
> O Thou hope of Israel,
>   its Saviour in time of trouble,
> Why shouldst Thou be as a sojourner in the land,
>   and as a wayfaring man that turns aside to tarry for a night?

> Why shouldst Thou be as a man affrighted,
>> as a mighty man that cannot save?
> Yet Thou, O Yahweh, art in the midst of us,
>> and we are called by Thy name,
> Leave us not! (14 [7-9])

But these prayers were in vain, Yahweh could not accept them, for the people's penitence was not sincere.

> Though Moses and Samuel stood before Me,
>> yet My mind would not be toward this people.
> Cast them out of My sight, and let them go forth. (15 [1])

In hours of loneliness the bitter tragedy of his life overwhelmed Jeremiah's soul.   Once he cried out,

> Woe is me, my mother, that thou hast borne me
>> a man of strife and a man of contention to the whole earth!
> I have not lent, neither have men lent to me,
>> yet every one of them does curse me. —
> So be it, Yahweh, if I am guilty,
>> if I did not intercede with Thee
> In the time of evil and in the time of affliction
>> for the good of the enemy.
> Have I an arm of iron,
>> or a bronze coat of mail? [1]
> Thou knowest!
> O Yahweh, remember me, and visit me,
>> avenge me of my persecutors;
> Take me not away in Thy longsuffering:
>> Know that for Thy sake I have suffered reproach.
> Thy words were found and I ate them,
>> and they were to me a joy and the rejoicing of my heart,
> For I am called by Thy name,
>> O Yahweh, God of hosts.
> I sat not in the assembly of them that make merry nor rejoiced;
>> I sat alone because of Thy hand,
>> for Thou hast filled me with indignation.
> Why is my pain perpetual,
>> and my wound incurable,
>> that refuses to be healed?
> *Thou hast been to me as a deceitful brook,*
>> *as waters that fail!*

His grief had carried him too far: he had charged Yahweh with untrustworthiness!   He knew that he had greatly offended and that

---

[1] The reading of this cry of unbearable anguish is not certain.

he was no longer worthy of being Yahweh's prophet. But there came to his soul in that dark hour Yahweh's earnest message, in which He called the prophet himself to repentance:

> If thou return, I will let thee come back,
>   that thou mayest stand before Me;
> And if thou wilt take forth the precious from the vile,
>   thou shalt be as My mouth.
> They shall return to thee,
>   but thou shalt not return to them.
> And I will make thee to this people
>   a brazen fortified wall;
> And they shall fight against thee,
>   but they shall not prevail against thee;
> For I am with thee to save thee
>   and to deliver thee, says Yahweh.
> And I will deliver thee out of the hand of the wicked,
>   and I will redeem thee out of the hand of the terrible. (15 $^{10-12.\ 15-21}$)

What an hour this had been to Jeremiah! Humbly he reports it too in his utter truthfulness. It is as if he wanted to purge his soul by his confession. He had many such times when he came to Yahweh with his plea, driven by his desperate need. The unexpected depths of his heart that were revealed to him in such seasons of despair led him to meditate on the inscrutability of the human heart. And it was a comfort to him that God knows the heart, and that He can heal it.

> The heart is too deep for any man
>   who can know it?
> "I, Yahweh, search the mind,
>   I try the heart,
> To give every man according to his ways,
>   according to the fruit of his doings."
> Heal me, O Yahweh, and I shall be healed,
>   save me, and I shall be saved,
>   for Thou art my hope.
> As for me, I have not hastened
>   after Thee for evil,
> Neither have I desired the woful day,
>   Thou knowest.
> That which came out of my lips
>   was before Thee.
> Be not a terror to me,
>   Thou art my refuge in the day of evil. (17 $^{9f.14.16f.}$)

Jeremiah's life was full of persecution not only by the king but especially by the priests and the professional prophets. After one of his addresses, in which he had attacked them, they said,

> Come, and let us devise devices against Jeremiah,
>   for the law shall not perish from the priest,
> Nor counsel from the wise,
>   nor the word from the prophet.
> Come, and let us smite him with the tongue,
>   and let us give heed to all his words,

in order that they might trap him and bring about his undoing. Earnestly Jeremiah prayed to Yahweh not to recompense evil for good,

> Remember how I stood before Thee
>   to speak good for them,
>   to turn away Thy wrath from them. (18 $^{18-20}$)

Another of these experiences, which now seem to us like so many confessions on the part of Jeremiah, is recorded in ch. 20 $^{7-10}$. It contains the famous confession, which throws much light on the life of Jeremiah's soul,

> As often as I speak, I cry out,
>   I cry, "Violence and destruction!"
> Because the word of Yahweh is made a reproach to me
>   and a derision, all the day.
> And if I say, "I will not make mention of Him,
>   nor speak any more in His name,"
> Then there is in my heart as it were a burning fire
>   shut up in my bones,
> And I am weary with forebearing,
>   and I cannot contain.

The most terrible of all is Jeremiah's curse of his birth, it is full of the blackness of despair:

> Cursed be the day wherein I was born,
>   let not the day wherein my mother bore me be blessed, etc. (20 $^{14-18}$)

Not even the bold author of the Poem of Job dared to take over this desperate curse without modification (Job 3). These "confessions" cannot be dated with certainty, for Jeremiah suffered persecution not only during Jehoiakim's rule. Probably some of them belong to the reign of Zedekiah. The last two stand at present directly after the story of the shameful insult that had been offered to him by

Pashhur the priest who had put him in the stocks after his object-lesson with the potter's earthen bottle, which he had broken before the people as a sign of how they would be broken by Yahweh (19 ¹⁻20 ⁶). It may well be that the burning sense of this public humiliation occasioned Jeremiah's sad complaint and his outbreak of despair.

But he always conquered himself in his intimate communion with God, who came to be his only friend. And he was always ready to go out again and proclaim the unwelcome truth. What he had foreseen came about. For three years Jehoiakim remained quietly Nebuchadrezzar's vassal, but then he rebelled. The war was protracted, because Nebuchadrezzar could not march himself against Jerusalem. But in 597 he came. At his approach a group of Rechabites had sought refuge in Jerusalem. One day Jeremiah took them into one of the chambers of the temple and placed bowls full of wine and cups before them and told them to drink. But they refused. Their ancestor Jonadab had strictly commanded them to live as nomads in tents, to abstain from agriculture and especially vine-culture, and never to drink any wine. It was the protest of fanatic Yahwism against Baalism. These Rechabites had always been true to it; they had entered the city only because they had fled before Nebuchadrezzar. In what striking contrast their loyal obedience to their father's command stood to Judah's shameful disobedience to Yahweh! Let the people take note of it, for they will be punished for their unfaithfulness, while the Rechabites will be rewarded for their fidelity, their family will never be completely extinct (ch. 35).

During the siege of Jerusalem, Jehoiakim died. He was not "buried with the burial of an ass, drawn and cast forth beyond the gates of Jerusalem," as Jeremiah had predicted, but slept honorably "with his fathers" (2 Ki. 24 ⁶). His son Jehoiachin, or Coniah as Jeremiah called him, succeeded as king. The situation in Jerusalem became more critical. Jeremiah tried against hope to bring the people to repentance. He made a special appeal to Jehoiachin and his mother:

> Say thou to the king and the queen mother,
>   Humble yourselves, sit down,
> For your headtires are come down,
>   even the crown of your glory.

> The cities of the South are shut up,
>   and there is none to open them:
> All Judah is carried away captive,
>   it is wholly carried away captive. (13 [18f.])

It was all in vain.   Soon Jeremiah proclaimed,

> As I live, says Yahweh,
>   though Coniah were
> The signet upon My right hand,
>   yet would I pluck thee thence. (22 [24])

The king and his mother shall go into exile never to return.   Jehoiachin had been king only three months when Jerusalem was taken
and he with the *élite* of his people was carried into captivity to
Babylon, where he died long afterwards.   After they had gone
Jeremiah said,

> Is this man Coniah a despised broken vessel?
>   is he a vessel wherein none delights?
> Wherefore are they cast out,
>   he and his seed,
> And are cast into a land
>   which they know not? (22 [28])

After this first band of captives had been carried away, Jeremiah
found his work in Jerusalem still harder.[1]   The people who had
remained appeared to him wholly bad, while the exiles, at least in
comparison with the people in Judah, seemed to him so much better
that he gradually began to conceive a hope of their restoration.   In
a vision both parties were compared to two baskets of figs, the one
very good, the other very bad: Yahweh looks with favor upon the
exiles and will bring them back to their home; the people in Judah,
however, will be exterminated, they are so bad.   Just as in his early
days Jeremiah had believed that the experience of the exile had
turned the heart of Israel to Yahweh, so now he hoped that the Jewish exiles would learn to know Yahweh.   It is true, they had lost
the capacity of repentance, but Yahweh said,

> I will give them a heart to know Me,
>   that I am Yahweh:
> And they shall be My people,
>   and I will be their God,

---

[1] There is an oracle in 49 [34-38] which is alleged to have been given by Jeremiah
against Elam "at the beginning of the reign of King Zedekiah."

For they shall return to Me
with their whole heart. (24 ^{7})

When Zedekiah sent an embassy to Nebuchadrezzar, Jeremiah wrote a letter to the exiles in Babylonia in which he admonished them to give up their hope of an immediate return and to settle down in Babylonia to the ordinary pursuits of life.   Let them not be deceived by any prophets who predict the speedy restoration.   They must first learn the bitter lessons of the exile; not until they seek Yahweh with their whole heart will they be permitted to return. Religion was to Jeremiah a spiritual matter, it was not bound to the temple or the country.   What a wonderful truth this was, the people did not perceive; it was an epoch-making contribution to the development of religion.   Religion could be practised in Babylonia as well as in Judah.   One of the exiles, Shemaiah, wrote back indignantly to the priest Zephaniah in Jerusalem, inquiring why he had not put Jeremiah in the stocks and in shackles.   Zephaniah showed the letter to Jeremiah — with a significant smile, we may presume (ch. 29).

In Jerusalem also Jeremiah aroused much opposition by the stand that he took in national affairs.   To him they were a religious concern.   Yahweh had appointed Nebuchadrezzar as His servant and had given him dominion over the various nations.   Rebellion against him meant rebellion against Yahweh's will and would be punished.   That was Jeremiah's position to the end.   When in 593 ambassadors came from Edom, Moab, Ammon, Tyre, and Sidon to persuade Zedekiah to join their alliance against Babylon, he appeared with bonds and bars upon his neck and told them in unmistakable sentences that any nation that would not put its neck under the yoke of the king of Babylon would be destroyed by Yahweh. To Zedekiah he gave the same warning.   Hananiah, a prophet, vehemently opposed Jeremiah and announced that Yahweh would break the yoke of the king of Babylon within two full years and restore the sacred temple vessels and the exiles to Jerusalem.   In confirmation Hananiah took the bar from Jeremiah's shoulder and broke it.   Jeremiah could only reply at the first moment, "Amen: Yahweh do so!"   But he added, significantly enough, that the former prophets had always prophesied calamity, that the presumption was therefore always in favor of the prophet of doom, and

that a prophet of peace must first be authenticated by the fulfilment of his prediction. With this he left. But soon afterwards
he returned and announced with absolute clearness of conviction,
"Thus says Yahweh: Thou hast broken the bars of wood; but
thou hast procured in their stead bars of iron." The Babylonian
yoke cannot be broken. To Hananiah himself Jeremiah predicted
that he should die within a year, "because thou has spoken rebellion
against Yahweh." And he died the same year in the seventh
month (ch. 27f.). It is possible that Jeremiah gave at this time
special oracles of doom for Edom (49 $^{7f.\ 10f.22}$), Moab (48, now greatly
worked over), and Ammon (49 $^{1-5}$). The alliance was not made;
perhaps Jeremiah had impressed the king with his earnestness and
sincerity. But Zedekiah appears to have had to go to Babylon in
order to clear himself of suspicion. It is said that Jeremiah wrote
on a scroll a prophecy of Babylon's destruction, gave it to one of the
king's companions, Seraiah, a brother of Baruch, in order that he
should read it aloud in Babylonia, then bind a stone to it, cast it into
the Euphrates and say, "Thus shall Babylon sink and shall not rise
again because of the evil that I will bring upon her" (51 $^{59-64}$). It
is difficult to believe that Jeremiah did this, for he was still firmly
convinced that Nebuchadrezzar was Yahweh's servant and that
opposition to him was rebellion against Yahweh. And this remained his firm conviction also when Zedekiah was at length unable
to resist the force of popular sentiment and Egyptian diplomacy,
and joined the anti-Babylonian alliance. Soon a Babylonian army
besieged Jerusalem. Jeremiah knew that his prediction would
wholly be fulfilled and told two messengers of the king that Yahweh
would give the city into the hand of the king of Babylon (21 $^{1-10}$).
But Zedekiah could not act in accordance with this instruction.
So the siege continued and grew severe. Then all Hebrew slaves,
male and female, were freed under a solemn covenant. But as
soon as the enemy turned his main attention to the capture of the
Judæan cities in the South, they were again put in bondage. Jeremiah denounced this treachery and foretold the return of the Chaldeans and the capture and sack of Jerusalem (ch. 34). They had
to raise the siege, however, entirely for a while, because an Egyptian
army advanced in the South.[1] But Jeremiah was sure that they

[1] For Egypt Jeremiah had a threatening oracle too (46 $^{13-26}$).

would soon return. During this interval he wanted to go to his native town Anathoth to receive his share of an inheritance. As he was leaving the city, he was made prisoner by the captain on duty at the gate on the charge that he was falling away to the Chaldeans. He was taken before the princes, flogged, and imprisoned in the house of the pit belonging to Jonathan the scribe. While he was there, King Zedekiah sent for him to ask for an oracle; he gave it, it was always the same, "Thou shalt be delivered into the hand of the king of Babylon." At the same time he implored the king not to send him back to the house of Jonathan lest he die there. He was therefore committed to the court of the guard, where he received a loaf of bread every day until it was all spent (ch. 37). Even here he reiterated his Cassandra messages of the certain fall of the city and counselled the people to fall away to the Chaldeans. Then the princes demanded his death from Zedekiah, who consented against his better judgment. They threw him into a dungeon which was full of mire and where he would have perished miserably, if the Ethiopian eunuch Ebedmelech had not rescued him with the help of three men whom the king had given to him for this purpose. From the court of the guard where he was put again, Zedekiah summoned him once more for a secret council. Jeremiah advised him that his only way of escape was to go out to the king of Babylon and capitulate, and he need not be afraid of the Jews that had fallen away to the Chaldeans. But if he would not heed this advice, he would be carried into captivity and the city would be burnt. The king was well-meaning but weak; he asked Jeremiah not to tell the princes anything of this conversation, but to put them off when they inquired by saying that he had asked the king not to send him back to Jonathan's house. This the prophet did, to save the unhappy king from his own courtiers! (Ch. 38)

While he was in the court of the guard, an event of great importance happened to him. His cousin Hanamel came from the country and asked him to buy his field at Anathoth from him, because he was his nearest kinsman and as such obliged to help. It seemed preposterous. Jeremiah had predicted for many years the ruin and desolation of the land, and now, when the Chaldeans were in the country and the fulfilment of his prophecies was at hand, there came this strange offer. But its very strangeness showed to Jeremiah that Yahweh was behind it. He bought the field, and in his soul the glad hope was born, "Houses and fields shall yet again be bought in this land" (32 $^{6-15}$). And as he looked into the future, he foresaw the time when Yahweh would make a new covenant with Israel, not as the old one that had been written on tables of stone,

> I will put My law in their inward parts,
>   and in their hearts will I write it;
> And I will be their God,
>   and they shall be My people.
> And they shall no more teach
>   every man his neighbor,
> And every man his brother, saying,
>   "Know Yahweh!"
> For they shall all know Me,
>   from the least of them unto the greatest of them:
> For I will forgive their iniquity,
>   and their sin will I remember no more. (31 $^{31-34}$)

By it the ideal relation between God and man will be introduced, true religion will prevail. It consists essentially in the knowledge of God and implies communion with Him and true morality as the result of it. The law will then be, what it ought always to have been, the natural expression of the heart. With what infinite sadness had Jeremiah exclaimed that the birds know the law of their coming and going, "but my people know not the law of Yahweh" (8 ^{7}). In the time to come they will follow the deep, inward law of their being, the instincts of their hearts, they will ever do God's will and thus be in true fellowship with Him. Jeremiah has no wonderful descriptions of the future glory. His outlook is sombre outwardly, because to him the glory was all within: the greatest thing is the knowledge of God and the doing of His will. So he could see the awful destruction of Jerusalem and the captivity of his people without being heartbroken. He had seen all this before, he had suffered anguish for it in his soul, but when the fall came he looked into the future full of hope. The nation had perished, the temple lay in ruins, but true religion had not perished. It would find its home again in a new city whose people would know and obey Yahweh.

Jeremiah was left in the country with Gedaliah, who had been made governor of the province. But when Gedaliah was murdered by the fanatic prince royal Ishmael, Jeremiah was taken by the people, who feared the vengeance of Nebuchadrezzar, to Egypt, against his vigorous protest. In Tahpanhes (Daphne) in Egypt he was seen one day carrying great stones to the plaza before the royal palace and making a base. To the astonished Jews he explained that Yahweh would send His servant Nebuchadrezzar to Egypt and upon these stones would he set up his throne and spread his pavilion, for he would conquer Egypt, destroy its temples, and carry away its idols (ch. 43). Their flight to Egypt had not taken the fugitives out of Nebuchadrezzar's reach! Neither the symbolic object-lesson nor the address made any impression upon them.

To Jeremiah's utter dismay the Jews began their old idolatrous worship again, especially the women, and when Jeremiah rebuked them, they answered that as long as they had served the Queen of Heaven it had been well with them and they would serve her again. He replied by predicting their virtual extermination, and as a sign of the truth of this prediction he announced to them the certain defeat which Pharaoh Hophra would suffer at the hand of his enemies (ch. 44).

This is the last we hear of him who was in many ways Israel's greatest prophet. He grasped with deep insight the fundamental elements of religion and stated them with great clearness. In him all the best of Amos, Hosea, and Isaiah was brought to full fruition. He spiritualized religion by separating it from all outward institutions, even from the nation. They all perish, but religion remains: the soul in fellowship with God. Religion is a matter of the individual heart. Like Hosea, to whom he was so similar, Jeremiah incarnated his message. He must be solitary and alone, he must not marry, nor have children, because all parents and children would soon perish in the terrible catastrophe. He must not go into a house of mourning to express his sympathy, because men would soon die and not be buried and lamented. He must not be glad with happy people, because the voice of gladness and mirth would soon be hushed in the land (16 $^{1-9}$). Despised, forsaken, persecuted, he was a man of sorrows. Yet ever did he do his work bravely and faithfully, although his heart would well-nigh break. Ofttimes he was ready to despair, but ever the strong voice came to him that had come in the great hour when he first knew that he was Yahweh's prophet, "Fear not, for I will be with thee!" And he conquered, and though his people treated him shamefully during his lifetime, he won the homage of their hearts in the end: to them he became "The Prophet," and to the great prophet of the exile he became the type of the true servant of Yahweh, pointing forward to the man on Calvary. Greater honor can hardly be given to any man than was thus given to Jeremiah of Anathoth, the prophet of the heart.

Jeremiah collected his oracles, as we saw, first in 604, when he dictated them to Baruch. After the destruction of this roll he wrote a second enlarged edition. The sentence "and there were added besides to them many like words" (36^{32}) may refer not only to this time but to successive additions, for his book contains now oracles from him as late as 586. There are three elements to be distinguished in our present edition: 1. Jeremiah's own work, 2. Baruch's biography of Jeremiah, 3. Later additions. If we arrange Jeremiah's own work according to chronology, we may group as follows:

During the reign of Josiah 1–6.7 ^{21}–12 ^{6} (except 10 $^{1-16}$) and 31 $^{2-6.15-21}$.
During the reign of Jehoiakim 7 $^{1-20}$ 12 ^{7}–13 ^{17} 13 ^{20}–20 (except 17 $^{19-27}$) 22 $^{1-23}$ 25 $^{1-24}$ (worked over).
During the reign of Jehoiachin 13 $^{18f.}$ 22 $^{24-30}$.
During the reign of Zedekiah 21.23 $^{1f.\ 9ff.}$ 24.
After the fall of Jerusalem 31 $^{31-34}$.

It is quite uncertain whether even a nucleus of the oracles against the nations (46–51) goes back to Jeremiah, but it is not impossible (cf. pp. 155. 161. 163).[1]

Baruch was not only Jeremiah's scribe but also his friend; he was an educated man of a noble family, a man of character and great personal influence. He was Jeremiah's intimate from the reign of Jehoiakim on, he visited him in prison and accompanied him to Egypt. He loved and revered the great prophet with all his heart and set him a monument in a biography. That is the reason why we know so much more of Jeremiah than of the other prophets. We are indebted to this biography for much valuable history. Parts of it were later on connected with Jeremiah's oracles. They

---

[1] These oracles against the nations circulated at first as an independent book. When they were inserted in the Book of Jeremiah, some manuscripts had them at the end (46–51), others, represented by the Greek Version, had them in a different order between Jer. 25 ^{13} and 25 ^{14}.

are now found in 19 ¹–20 ⁶ 26–29.32.34–45. To the time of Jehoiakim refer 19 ¹–20 ⁶ 26.35.36 ; to Zedekiah's 27–29.32.34.37f. ; to
the time after the fall of the city, 39–44. Baruch ended his book
with a prophecy which Jeremiah had given to him personally in 604.
In view of the terrible crisis which was so soon to come upon his
people, Baruch must ask nothing for himself. Yahweh will spare
his life. That must suffice ; it is a great boon. The little oracle
formed, as it were, a seal upon Baruch's book.

Both Jeremiah's and Baruch's books were later on much worked
over. A great many passages appear twice, some even three times.
In the Greek Version a number of these repetitions and other additions do not yet occur, indeed its original Hebrew text had some
2700 words less than our Hebrew text, a clear indication that the
text was worked over by later scribes. Literary criticism has shown
that the diffuseness of style, which is at times wearisome, was not due
to Jeremiah but to copyists and editors. Professor Duhm, one of
the greatest commentators of modern times, believes that Jeremiah
wrote only in poetry and only in the so-called *kinah* or elegiac metre,
so that only about one fifth of the book can be regarded as original.
He overstates the truth, most probably, but we owe to him our appreciation of the exquisite literary quality of Jeremiah's writings ;
he rightly declares that Jeremiah might have become the greatest
lyrical poet of Israel, if he had not been a prophet. The haunt-
ing beauty of his poems quite justifies this estimate.

CHAPTER XII

EZEKIEL AND THE HOLINESS CODE

AMONG the exiles that were carried to Babylonia in 597 was Ezekiel, a priest of Jerusalem who was destined to become one of the most influential prophets. At Tel Abib on the banks of the river Chebar, the grand canal which passed by the city of Nippur, he saw the awe-inspiring vision that made him a prophet. It was an unforgettable day, the fifth of the fourth month, roughly corresponding to our June, in 593. In a trance he saw the throne of Yahweh in a great storm-cloud that came from the north and flashed lightning in all directions. Four mysterious beings, looking like men but each with four heads, that of a man, a lion, an ox, and an eagle, and with four wings, shining in unearthly brilliance, bore aloft the throne which had four glittering wheels whose rims were covered with eyes. As they approached with a deafening roar, Ezekiel saw that

Upon the form that looked like the throne was something like the appearance of a man upon it above. And I saw something like shining metal from what looked like his loins and upward; and from what looked like his loins and downward I saw an appearance like fire, and there was brightness round about it. As the appearance of the bow that is in the cloud in the day of rain, so was the appearance of the brightness round about. This was the appearance of the likeness of the glory of Yahweh. (1 $^{26-28}$)

Ezekiel saw, of course, in a flash, what takes so long to tell. Overwhelmed by the power of the vision, Ezekiel fell down on his face, but heard at once the voice of Yahweh commanding, "Son of man, stand upon thy feet, and I will speak with thee!" The Spirit entered into him so that he could stand up to be commissioned as Yahweh's prophet to his people: he must go and give to them God's messages without fear; whether they will hear in their rebelliousness or not, in any case they will know that a prophet has been among them. What he must say was given him in a scroll written on both sides, containing "lamentations, and mourning, and woe." This he had to eat, "and it was in my mouth as honey for sweetness."

Jeremiah also had "eaten" Yahweh's words and they had been the joy and rejoicing of his heart. Like Isaiah Ezekiel was to have no success, like Jeremiah he would have to face much opposition. But

Behold, I have made thy face hard against their faces, and thy forehead hard against their foreheads. As an adamant harder than flint have I made thy forehead: fear them not, neither be dismayed at their looks, though they are a rebellious house. (3 $^{8f.}$)

As the glory of Yahweh departed with the sound of a great rushing, Ezekiel was lifted up by the Spirit. "And I went in bitterness, in the heat of my spirit; and the hand of Yahweh was strong upon me." It was the natural feeling of resentment against the psychic pressure that held him enthralled. "Then I came to them of the captivity at Tel Abib . . . and I sat there overwhelmed among them seven days," completely stunned by the awful experience of the vision.

How strongly Ezekiel was influenced by his predecessors, especially by Isaiah and Jeremiah, is apparent at once. But he took almost three chapters (1 ^{4}–3 ^{15}) to tell his inaugural vision, while Isaiah told his in thirteen verses, suggesting rather than minutely describing, but arousing in the reader the feeling of deep reverence which had filled him in those moments of awe. Ezekiel was a theologian and his theological interest was prominent even in his inaugural vision, as we shall see.

A week after his call, the prophet was made the pastor of the exiles in a message that reveals his highly developed sense of personal responsibility for each individual soul entrusted to his care.

Son of man, I have made thee a watchman to the house of Israel: when thou hearest a word at My mouth, give them warning from Me. When I say to the wicked, Thou shalt surely die; and thou givest him not warning, nor speakest to warn the wicked from his wicked way, to save his life; the same wicked man shall die for his iniquity; but his blood will I require at thy hand. And if thou warn the wicked, and he turn not from his wickedness, nor from his wicked way, he shall die for his iniquity; but thou hast delivered thy soul. Again, when a righteous man turns from his righteousness, and commits iniquity, and I lay a stumblingblock before him, he shall die: because thou hast not given him warning, he shall die for his sin, and his righteous deeds which he has done shall not be remembered; but his blood will I require at thy hand. But if thou warn the righteous man, that he sin not, and he do not sin, he shall surely live, because he took warning; and thou hast delivered thy soul. (3 $^{17-21}$)

As he went forth to fulfil his mission, he used every means at his disposal to impress the people with the one great truth which he had to deliver: the certainty of the near ruin of Jerusalem and Judah. As a result of the terrible impression the vision of Yahweh had made upon him, leaving him stunned for a week, his nervous system was so severely shaken that he was subject to cataleptic attacks. But he came to see in a vision that they were one of God's ways of speaking through him to the people.

Go, shut thyself within thy house. But thou, son of man, behold, I will lay bands upon thee, and bind thee with them, and thou shalt not go out among them: and I will make thy tongue cleave to the roof of thy mouth, that thou shalt be dumb, and shalt not be to them a reprover; for they are a rebellious house. But when I speak with thee, I will open thy mouth, and thou shalt say to them, Thus says the Lord Yahweh: He that will hear, let him hear; and he that will forbear, let him forbear: for they are a rebellious house. (3 24–27)

In the course of a series of object-lessons which he enacted at the divine command his cataleptic tendency was made an impressive vehicle of prophecy. In the first object-lesson he pictured the impending siege of the city.

Thou, son of man, take thee a tile, and lay it before thee, and portray upon it a city, and lay siege against it, and build forts against it, and cast up a mound against it; set camps also against it, and plant battering rams against it round about. And take thee an iron pan, and set it for a wall of iron between thee and the city: and set thy face toward it, and it shall be besieged, and thou shalt lay siege against it. This shall be a sign to the house of Israel. And thou shalt set thy face toward the siege of Jerusalem, with thine arm uncovered: and thou shalt prophesy against it. (4 1–3.7)

In the second object-lesson Ezekiel portrayed the plight of the besieged and the rationing of foodstuffs and water.

Take thou also unto thee wheat, and barley, and beans, and lentils, and millet, and spelt, and put them in one vessel, and make thee bread thereof. And thy food which thou shalt eat shall be by weight, twenty shekels a day: from time to time shalt thou eat it. And thou shalt drink water by measure, the sixth part of a hin: from time to time shalt thou drink. Moreover he said to me, Son of man, behold, I will break the staff of bread in Jerusalem: and they shall eat bread by weight, and with fearfulness; and they shall drink water by measure, and in dismay: that they may want bread and water, and be dismayed one with another, and pine away in their iniquity. (4 9a.10f.16f.)

Between these two now stands the object-lesson of the length of the exile of Israel and of Judah, which was enacted in two long cataleptic spells.

> Moreover lie thou upon thy left side, and bear the punishment of the house of Israel; according to the number of the days that thou shalt lie upon it, thou shalt bear their punishment. For I have appointed the years of their punishment to be to thee a number of days, one hundred and ninety days: so shalt thou bear the punishment of the house of Israel. And, when thou hast accomplished these, thou shalt lie on thy right side, and shalt bear the punishment of the house of Judah: forty days, each day for a year, have I appointed it to thee. And, behold, I lay bands upon thee, and thou shalt not turn thee from one side to the other, till thou hast accomplished the days of thy straits. (4 $^{4-6.8}$)

To an object-lesson illustrating the suffering in a foreign land belongs the preparation of unclean food, such as the people will have to eat in exile. It is now interwoven with the object-lesson of the scarcity of bread during the siege.

> Take thou also unto thee wheat, and barley, and beans, and lentils, and millet, and spelt, and put them in one vessel, and make thee bread thereof; [according to the number of the days that thou shalt lie upon thy side, even one hundred and ninety days, shalt thou eat thereof.] And thou shalt eat it as barley cakes, and thou shalt bake it in their sight with dung that comes out of man. [And Yahweh said, Even thus shall the children of Israel eat their bread unclean, among the nations whither I will drive them.] Then said I, Ah Lord Yahweh! behold, my soul has not been polluted; for from my youth up even till now have I not eaten of that which dies of itself, or is torn of beasts; neither came there abominable flesh into my mouth. Then He said to me, See, I have given thee cow's dung for man's dung, and thou shalt prepare thy bread thereon. (4 $^{9.\,12-15}$)

With these and similar symbolic actions (compare, *e.g.*, 5 $^{1-12}$ 12 $^{1-20}$ 21 $^{18-23}$), all of them intensely interesting and of deep significance, Ezekiel announced the coming catastrophe of Judah and Jerusalem. The reason for it was the idolatry and moral iniquity of the people. In a vision of great historical value Ezekiel described the idolatry in the temple of Jerusalem. A bright angel took him by a lock of his hair to Jerusalem and showed him the image which provoked Yahweh's jealousy, the cult of the mysteries, the lamentation for Tammuz or Adonis, and the worship of the sun, all of them in the temple (ch. 8)!

But this religious corruption was not all. The moral iniquity of "the bloody city," of kings and princes, priests and prophets and people cried to heaven (7 ^{23} 9 ^{9} 11 $^{6ff.}$ 22. 24 $^{6f.}$ 34 $^{1-10}$). Ezekiel put moral and religious sins on the same basis. The whole history of Israel from the beginning was one of blackest unfaithfulness to Yahweh. Judah was worse than Israel, yea than Sodom (ch. 16. 23). The inevitable result of such wickedness must be fearful punishment. Ezekiel heard in his vision how the destroying angels were summoned, and saw how one of them set a mark upon the foreheads of the pious in Jerusalem before the terrible slaughter of the inhabitants began and before the angel scattered heavenly fire over the city (ch. 9f.). "And the glory of Yahweh went up from the midst of the city, and stood upon the mountain which is upon the east side of the city" (11 [23]). That was a prerequisite, for the city could never be destroyed as long as Yahweh was in it!

The judgment was coming; "that they may know that I am Yahweh" was Ezekiel's constant refrain. It was not to be disciplinary and redemptive but strictly punitive. His holy name had been profaned, Yahweh must vindicate His holiness by justice.

In this connection Ezekiel worked out a severe theory of individual retribution. Religion was to him a matter of the individual. Reward for righteousness or wickedness was strictly individual too. Over against the complaint of the people, which voiced itself in the bitter irony of the proverb, "The fathers have eaten sour grapes, and the children's teeth are set on edge," Ezekiel insisted that each one is rewarded or punished for his own deeds not for those of another, "the soul that sins shall die," "Yahweh is righteous and will judge every one after his own ways,"— every single individual! And only for what he himself has done will he be held responsible. There is no indiscriminate punishment, no suffering for the sins of others, no hereditary guilt. Neither will the goodness of another have any vicarious influence. Nobody will be saved by the righteousness of another.

Though these three righteous men, Noah, Daniel, and Job, were in it (the city), they should deliver but their own souls by their righteousness, says the Lord Yahweh. (14 [14-20])

Every man stands or falls by himself. The solidarity of society, which had hitherto been emphasized so strongly, is here broken up. There is no organic social relation among its individual personalities. They are each independent entities. Ezekiel carried this principle still further by separating the moral life of the individual into single separate acts. Life was to him not an organic whole, but composed of countless single acts. Character was not taken into account. This has been called the atomism of the moral life, for life is divided into atoms in this theory. If a righteous man sins, his whole life of righteousness is not counted. If a wicked man repents and does justly, his whole life of wickedness is not counted.

As I live, says the Lord Yahweh, I have no pleasure in the death of the wicked; but that the wicked turn from his way and live: turn ye, turn ye from your evil ways; for why will ye die, O house of Israel? (33 [11])

This theory is elaborated especially in ch. 18 and 33.

The extremes of Ezekiel's position were due to the practical exigencies of the pastoral appeal. He needed to emphasize the truth that God would accept the sinner, if he sincerely repented, no matter what his past life of sin had been. That he also at times predicted the indiscriminate extermination of the righteous and the wicked in the destruction of the city is seen from 21 [3],

Behold, I am against thee, I will draw forth My sword out of its sheath, and will cut off from thee the righteous and wicked.

As pastor Ezekiel could not merely emphasize the negative side of his doctrine of retribution, but must show to men an ideal of piety which was attainable. And this he did. God had given them a law. To keep it insures life (20 [11–13]). The spirit of Deuteronomy was strong in Ezekiel.

As pastor and spiritual counsellor of the exiles he had to deal also with practical problems which the elders proposed to him. One was in connection with the manner of worship from which all idolatrous elements are to be banished (14 [1–11]). Another had to do with the question of erecting a sanctuary to Yahweh in Babylonia. Ezekiel frowned upon it, in the spirit of Deuteronomy. Learn the lessons of history: it was your idolatry, your worship on the high places, that ruined you. Yahweh wants only one place, Jerusalem, as His sanctuary!

For in My holy mountain, in the mountain of the height of Israel, says the Lord Yahweh, there shall all the house of Israel, all of them, serve Me in the land: there will I accept them, and there will I require your offerings, and the first-fruits of your oblations, with all your holy things. With the sweet savor will I accept you, when I bring you out from the peoples, and gather you out of the countries wherein ye have been scattered; and I will be sanctified in you in the sight of the nations.   And ye shall know that I am Yahweh, when I shall bring you to the land of Israel, to the country which I sware to give to your fathers.   And there shall ye remember your ways, and all your doings, wherein ye have polluted yourselves; and ye shall loathe yourselves in your own sight for all your evils that ye have committed.   And ye shall know that I am Yahweh, when I have dealt with you for My name's sake, not according to your evil ways, nor according to your corrupt doings, O ye house of Israel, says the Lord Yahweh. (20 [40-44])

Underlying all of Ezekiel's teaching was his belief in the awful holiness or physical majesty and absolute power of Yahweh.   This had been wrought into every fibre of his being in the awe-inspiring visions of Yahweh.   Beside Him there was no other god, *i.e.* no real god.   The gods of the nations were to Ezekiel only angels.   In the inaugural vision the four throne bearers and the heavenly throne symbolized the gods of the four corners of the world and the sky with its countless stars (eyes): Yahweh was enthroned above them all, the other gods were but His ministers or parts of His throne!   And again, the seven destroying angels in ch. 9, representing, as they most probably do, the gods of the seven planets,[1] were no longer rivals of the omnipotent Yahweh.   The beginning of the later highly developed Jewish angelology is here made.   As yet Yahweh Himself spoke to Ezekiel, but the angels performed the various deeds, they tended to become intermediaries between the transcendent God and weak, mortal man ("the son of man").   This must not be taken to mean that Ezekiel entertained a more spiritual conception of God by emphasizing His transcendence.   He merely stressed the holiness of God, which Isaiah had proclaimed so strongly. And he emphasized it in such a way that the God of Jeremiah with His tenderness and solicitude, coupled with His great moral earnestness, seems quite different from this God whose passion is His own holiness and who punishes with relentless wrath.   God's interest in the nations, according to Ezekiel, was only to compel the recognition of His holiness by His almighty power: "They shall know that I am Yahweh, when I shall lay My vengeance upon them."   Again and again this idea is expressed.   This acknowledgment of His holiness is all that Ezekiel was interested in.   He never thought of a conversion of the nations or of the establishment of intimate rela-

[1] Compare especially the heavenly writer with the inkhorn with the god Nabu, the scribe of the gods.

tions with them. The universal implications of monotheism he
never understood. To him Yahweh and Israel belonged together;
Jerusalem was the centre of the world, where Yahweh dwelt. He
held this not as a traditional doctrine, but as a vital element of his
faith. We find therefore with him a universal God but not a universal religion.

Up to the fall of Jerusalem in 586 Ezekiel remained the prophet
of doom; in ever varied manner he proclaimed the end of Judah and
Jerusalem. He enacted strange object-lessons, narrated remarkable
visions, delivered searching addresses, allegories, and parables until
the catastrophe came. On the day that Nebuchadrezzar began the
siege,

> The word of Yahweh came to me, saying, Son of man, behold, I take away
> from thee the desire of thine eyes with a stroke: yet thou shalt neither mourn
> nor weep, neither shall thy tears run down. Sigh, but not aloud, make no
> mourning for the dead; bind thy headtire upon thee, and put thy shoes upon
> thy feet, and cover not thy beard, and eat not the bread of mourners. So I
> spoke to the people in the morning; and at even my wife died; and I did in
> the morning as I was commanded. (24 $^{15-18}$)

When the people asked him why he behaved so strangely, he told
them that soon the temple, the desire of their eyes, would be profaned and the children they had left behind in Jerusalem would be
slain. Then they would do as Ezekiel was now doing (24 $^{19ff.}$).
For Tyre and Egypt against whom Nebuchadrezzar also warred, he
had oracles predicting their ruin (ch. 26–30). One night in January,
585, half a year after Jerusalem had fallen, Ezekiel felt the hand of
Yahweh upon him; the terrible presentiment that something awful
had happened struck him dumb with fear. On the morrow the news
came, "The city is smitten." Then his mouth was opened again
so that he could speak. He was no longer dumb. The great tension
under which he had been was over. The crisis had passed. His
predictions of doom had been fulfilled (33 ^{21f}).

A new period began for him. Soon he looked forward into the
future, and became a prophet of restoration. He reasoned as fol-
lows. The fundamental principle that controlled all actions of
Yahweh was His holiness. The profanation of His holy name by
Israel had necessitated their punishment, "that they may know that
I am Yahweh." But now after they had been taken into exile, it

was the nations that profaned it by ridiculing Israel and Yahweh, who had been impotent to save His people: "These are the people of Yahweh! and they are gone forth out of His land!"   To vindicate His holiness before the whole world Yahweh must show His absolute power in order that all should know that it was not due to His impotence but to His judgment that Israel had been carried into captivity.   Thus He will punish the nations that surrounded Judah and restore His people to its own land (ch. 36).   Ammon, Moab, Edom, and Philistia will fearfully suffer, "that they may know that I am Yahweh."

Therefore say to the house of Israel, Thus says the Lord Yahweh: I do it not for your sake, O house of Israel, but for My holy name, which ye have profaned among the nations, whither ye went.   And I will sanctify My great name, which has been profaned among the nations, which ye have profaned in the midst of them; and the nations shall know that I am Yahweh, says the Lord Yahweh, when I shall be sanctified in you before their eyes. (36 $^{22f.}$)

Israel will be restored.   Her political resurrection is foretold in the famous vision of the Dry Bones which are revivified by the Spirit of God (37 $^{1-14}$).   Yahweh, the good shepherd, will gather all His scattered flock from all countries and bring them back to their homeland (34 $^{11ff.}$).   But only the righteous will be permitted to return; in a cleansing judgment in the Syrian desert all rebels and sinners will be removed (20 $^{34-39}$ 34 $^{17-22}$).   To the remnant Yahweh will give a new heart and a new spirit, and His own Spirit will dwell in them as a moral force making them loyal and obedient.

And I will sprinkle clean water upon you, and ye shall be clean: from all your filthiness, and from all your idols, will I cleanse you.   A new heart will I give you, and a new spirit will I put within you; and I will take away the stony heart out of your bosom, and I will give you a heart of flesh.   And I will put My Spirit within you, and cause you to walk in My statutes, and ye shall keep Mine ordinances, and do them.   Then shall ye remember your evil ways, and your doings that were not good; and ye shall loathe yourselves in your own sight for your iniquities and for your abominations. (36 $^{25-27.31}$)

In all this Yahweh takes the initiative.   He cannot wait for Israel's repentance.   But Ezekiel believed that it would inevitably come as a result of Yahweh's wonderful grace.   The prophets before him had maintained that repentance must precede forgiveness and restoration.   Ezekiel believed that "we love God because He first loved us."   This morally renewed people will return to Palestine, both Israel and Judah, and there they will be united under one Davidic king, a strong and numerous nation, blest with fertility and peace.

The word of Yahweh came again to me, saying, And thou, son of man, take thee a stick, and write upon it, " Judah, and the children of Israel attached to him " : then take another stick, and write upon it, " Joseph, the stick of Ephraim, and all the house of Israel attached to him " : and join them for thee one to another into one stick, that they may become one stick in thy hand. And when the children of thy people shall speak to thee, saying, Wilt thou not show us what thou meanest by these ? say to them, Thus says the Lord Yahweh : Behold, I will take the stick of Joseph, which is in the hand of Ephraim, and the tribes of Israel attached to him ; and I will put them with it (with the stick of Judah) and make them one stick, and they shall be one stick in the hand of Judah.   And the sticks on which thou writest shall be in thy hand before their eyes.   And say to them, Thus says the Lord Yahweh : Behold, I will take the children of Israel from among the nations, whither they are gone, and will gather them on every side, and bring them into their own land : and I will make them one nation in the land, upon the mountains of Israel ; and one king shall be king to them all ; and they shall be no more two nations, neither shall they be divided into two kingdoms any more at all ; neither shall they defile themselves any more with their idols, but I will save them from all their backslidings, wherein they have sinned, and will cleanse them : so shall they be My people, and I will be their God.

And My servant David shall be king over them ; and they all shall have one shepherd : they shall also walk in Mine ordinances, and observe My statutes, and do them.   And they shall dwell in the land that I have given to Jacob My servant, wherein their fathers dwelt ; and they shall dwell therein, they, and their children, and their children's children, for ever : and David My servant shall be their prince for ever.   Moreover I will make a covenant of peace with them ; it shall be an everlasting covenant with them ; and I will set My sanctuary in the midst of them for evermore.   My tabernacle also shall be with them ; and I will be their God, and they shall be My people.   And the nations shall know that I am Yahweh that sanctifies Israel, when My sanctuary shall be in the midst of them for evermore. (37 [15-28])

Ezekiel based his hope for the future entirely upon the exiles. The people who had remained in Palestine after the catastrophe of 586 felt themselves the true heirs of the nation. But Ezekiel strongly opposed them, they were idolaters and murderers, and Yahweh would surely exterminate them (33 [23-29]). Similarly, the Edomites, who had occupied Judæan territory, would be driven out, their own country would be devastated or they themselves would be destroyed (ch. 35).

In order to remove any doubt that the new condition of happiness and peace would prevail forever, and in order that Yahweh should be recognized the world over, Ezekiel introduced an entirely new element into the prophetic thought of the future. After the restoration, the northern enemy who had been predicted by former prophets will come. Gog of Magog as the head and representative of united heathendom will attack Israel with a vast army, but Yahweh Himself will fight against him with the forces of nature. The immense multitude of the slain will be a prey to the ravenous birds and beasts, and it will take more than seven months to bury the remains. The mass of weapons will be so great that they will serve as fuel for fire for seven years, for they will not be needed for war any more (ch. 38f.).

To these great hopes of political and moral restoration Ezekiel added the ecclesiastical. The restoration could be perfect and lasting only if Yahweh dwelt in the midst of His people forever. In 586 before the destruction took place, He had left Jerusalem because His holy name had been profaned. He will come again and the very name of the city will be "Yahweh is there." But to insure His perpetual presence every profanation of His holy name must be made impossible. Ezekiel meditated long on this problem. He believed it could be solved by the sharp antithesis between the sacred and profane. This was the basic principle of his plan, which he completed early in 573 and which he had worked out so thoroughly that it stood objectively before him in a vision (ch. 40–48). He was carried in the trance to Jerusalem, where an angel appeared as his guide and instructor and showed him the new order.

The first point of importance was that the new sanctuary should be guarded against every profanation. He saw that this had been done by isolating it on the top of the high temple hill, which was situated in Judah in the middle of a strip of territory comprising 25,000 square cubits. It was walled in and surrounded by two courts. From the open space which surrounded the outer wall Ezekiel ascended a stairway to one of the four gates of the outer court; passing through it, he ascended another stairway to one of the four gates of the inner court, in the middle of which stood the sanctuary on a still higher level, up to which a stairway led, with only one entrance from the east. It was divided into the entrance hall, the holy place, and the holy of holies. Ezekiel was told, "Son of man, this is the place of My throne, and the place of the soles of My feet, where I will dwell in the midst of the children of Israel forever." The isolation of the temple was complete. The royal palace did no longer adjoin nor did the royal graves defile it, and the city was about 1½ miles south of it. Immediately surrounding the temple was an open space. At a distance of 50 cubits, surrounding the temple precincts, was an area of 10,000 by 25,000 cubits where the priests would live. Adjoining them in the north, the Levites had an equally large district. The city was south of the priests, but separated from them by 500 cubits. The sanctuary was thus well protected, at least externally, against defilement. But the principle was carried still further. East and west of the sacred square, extending to the Jordan and Dead Sea and to the Mediterranean, respectively, were the royal domains. To the north the tribe of Judah, to the south the tribe of Benjamin immediately adjoined, for they were the most faithful; the others lived to the north or south of them each in an equally large district. The whole land was sacred, to be inhabited only by Yahweh's people. In their midst, safeguarded on all sides against defilement, Yahweh dwelt in His temple. The people had access only to the outer court. The priests alone could minister in the house. The holy of holies not even the priest Ezekiel entered in his vision: only the angel went in.

The second point of importance in the sharp antithesis between the sacred and profane was the personnel of the temple. The foreign temple slaves were abolished. In the former temple they had performed the menial tasks, "uncircumcised in heart and uncircumcised in flesh." But no longer may any uncircumcised foreigner enter the temple; his presence would defile it. Their places were to be taken by the Levites, who did not belong to the sons of Zadok the Jerusalem priests. They were the priests of the ancient sanctuaries outside of Jerusalem which had been abolished in 621. The Deuteronomic law (18 6-8) had provided that they should participate in the cult at Jerusalem. But the Zadokites did not permit them to share their rich income. Ezekiel ordered therefore that while they should gain their living in the temple at Jerusalem, they might do so only as priests of an inferior class, they should be watchmen and butchers and do all the other menial tasks that the old temple slaves had formerly done.   He justified this degradation as a penalty for their idolatrous service on the high places.

Thus says the Lord Yahweh, No foreigner, uncircumcised in heart and uncircumcised in flesh, shall enter into My sanctuary, of any foreigners that are among the children of Israel.   But those Levites that went far from Me, when Israel went astray, that went astray from Me after their idols, they shall suffer punishment.   They shall be ministers in My sanctuary, having oversight at the gates of the house, and ministering in the house : they shall slay the burnt-offering and the sacrifice for the people, and they shall stand before them to minister to them.   Because they ministered to them before their idols, and became a stumblingblock of iniquity to the house of Israel ; therefore have I lifted up My hand against them, says the Lord Yahweh, and they shall suffer punishment.   And they shall not come near to Me, to execute the office of priest to Me, nor to come near to any of My holy things, to the things that are most holy ; but they shall bear their shame and their abominations which they have committed.   Yet will I make them keepers of the charge of the house, for all the service thereof and for all that be done therein. (44 [9-14])

The Zadokites, the Jerusalem priests, alone may perform the real priestly functions, they alone may officiate in the inner court and the sanctuary.   In order that even they may not defile the temple, strict orders were given : they should wear only linen garments in the temple lest they perspire, and they must put them off when they leave the inner court lest they sanctify the people by their touch. They must not drink wine when they go on duty ; they dare not marry a widow, except the widow of a priest, nor a divorced woman ; nor may they go into the presence of a dead person, unless it be the nearest relative.

The third point on which Ezekiel concentrated his attention was the cult.   It was necessary to devise a cultic system for the continual renewal of the fellowship between Yahweh and Israel by removing any accidental profanations.   Through the cult, especially through the sin-offerings, atonement was made, the sanctuary cleansed, Yahweh pacified.   These sin-offerings were to be brought especially on New Year's Day, on the Passover, and on the fifteenth of the seventh month.   The prince must provide for these sacrifices.   Definite regulations for the daily as well as the Sabbath and New Moon sacrifices are given.   The cult becomes of central importance in the life of the restored community, and imperils again the personal element in religion, the intimate personal com-

munion with God.   Ezekiel did not feel this danger, because he
presupposed a morally regenerated people.

The political side was minimized in this plan of the new constitution of Israel.   The country was only on the west of the Jordan,
from Hamath in the north to Kadesh and the Egyptian frontier
in the south.   No claim was made to any territory east of the
Jordan.   But Palestine shall belong to Israel in its entirety.   No
Philistines or Edomites will be there, for they will be destroyed.
Only Israel shall live there and such foreigners as have been received into full citizenship.   It seems as if the political status of
the Davidic king was also lowered.   He is called not king but prince,
and his main business appears to be to provide for the maintenance
of the cult from the taxes which he receives from the people.   But
Ezekiel may have avoided the term king, because he would not
offend the Babylonian government.   And in 45 $^{8-12}$ 46 ^{18} he refers
to the social and political administration and the duties of a just
government, although, according to his principle, the people in the
restored community would all be holy and righteous.   His sense
of reality here was stronger than the ideal.   It was just the opposite
in the apportionment of the territories of the different tribes, for
each gets an equal strip of land from the Mediterranean to the Jordan or the Dead Sea, irrespective of all demands of history or topog-
raphy.

The programme was essentially particularistic.   Ezekiel never
thought of the conversion of the nations and their participation in
the blessings of the new era.   The wonderful river flowing out of
the sanctuary (ch. 47) is neither literally nor figuratively a blessing
for the whole world.   The desert and the Dead Sea are impossible in
the holy land where Yahweh dwells and where everything is fruitful.
The blessings of the river were material not spiritual.   The trees
were for food and for medicine.   Strikingly enough, the salty
marshes which served the needs of daily life were not transformed
into fertile fields.   Ezekiel's practical sense shines through in this
provision.

Ezekiel stood between the priestly and prophetic movements;
more priestly than Deuteronomy he was still a prophet, who at the
transition of one age to another worked for the transformation
of the older, freer, national ideas into the newer, stricter, ecclesi-

astical ideals and institutions. He therefore has been well called the Father of Judaism. He was extremely influential. His pronounced individualism and particularism; his emphasis on the transcendence of God with its accompanying angelology; his teaching concerning the future, Gog of Magog and the reign of blessedness until his attack,[1] the new Jerusalem and the wonderful river; but especially his subordination of the political state to the religious community and his emphasis on the cult influenced theology and the ecclesiastical constitution profoundly.

Ezekiel was an able writer. His book is very clearly arranged and in the main in strict chronological order with definite dates. The first part contains prophecies of judgment (ch. 1–24), the second prophecies of hope, involving negatively the punishment of the nations (ch. 25–32) and positively the restoration of Israel (ch. 33–48), of which the plan of a new constitution forms the end (ch. 40–48). Ezekiel's clear and logical mind is manifest in the arrangement. Some passages of hope which are now in the first, although they really belong to the second part, may have been put there by Ezekiel himself, for we know that he revised his book. On New Year of 571 he corrected an oracle against Tyre (29 [17–20]) which he had given in 586 and in which he had predicted its capture by Nebuchadrezzar. After the Babylonians had been obliged to raise their 27 years' siege, Ezekiel promised to Nebuchadrezzar the conquest of Egypt as a compensation for Tyre!

Ezekiel's style shows no distinction. He was prosaic even when he wrote poetry. Not that he lacked imagination; he delighted in allegories and symbolic expressions (which sometimes offend our taste) and he could visualize things and situations sharply, but he had no poetic talent. He was a thinker and knew how to write lucidly. But he loved and never wearied of reiteration. Still, not all repetitions come from him, many are due to an ill-edited text, and the occasional obscurities are the work of bad copyists. His book deserves much study not for its literary qualities but for its significant contributions. He may not be so attractive as Jeremiah, but he was more immediately influential.

A writer who was akin to Ezekiel in spirit, thought, and expres-

---

[1] Ezekiel did not specify the length of this period, later writers made it 1000 years, the millennium.

sion compiled shortly after 570 B.C. the little law book in Leviticus
17–26, which is commonly and appropriately called the Holiness
Code, or abbreviated H.   In spite of the great catastrophe that
had broken upon the Jews, he could not let go his belief that
Yahweh would not cast them off forever, that there must be a future
for them, if they repented.   And so he worked in the midst of the
exile for the restoration.   He was not a man of thrilling visions,
but his conviction burnt in his soul like a steady flame and made him
work out the norms of the future community in this law book, which
mediated between Deuteronomy and the later Priest Code, in which
it was afterwards incorporated but where it can still easily be distinguished by its characteristic phraseology and the subscription,

These are the statutes and ordinances and laws, which Yahweh made between Him and the children of Israel in Mount Sinai by Moses. (Lev. 26 46)

His controlling thought was the holiness of Yahweh and the obligation of the people to be holy also.   One of his formulas is, "Ye
shall be holy for I, Yahweh your God, am holy" (Lev. 19 2 20 7.26
21 8), another is the ever repeated "I am Yahweh (your God)," to
which there is added several times "who sanctifies you" (or
"them" or "him").   This holiness was primarily physical, it was
not moral perfection but especially the separation from everything
tabooed by the religion of Yahweh.   Holy to Yahweh meant
separate from any other god and whatever belonged to his cult, it
implied avoidance of everything that defiled, it referred to ritual
sanctity.   Its characteristic meaning is brought out in Lev. 20 26,

You shall be holy unto Me, for I, Yahweh, am holy, and have set you
apart from the peoples that you should be Mine.

The first law of H, at least in the order in which we have the
code now, is a prohibition of secular slaughter.   Deuteronomy had
permitted it, because after the centralization of the cult in Jerusalem
it would have been impossible to compel the people to go to the
temple for every animal that was to be slaughtered.   There had
been no distinction between sacred and secular slaughter before;
every slaughter was a sacrifice.   When now the distinction was
made, the ordinary man did not always remember that there was
such a distinction, his slaughter was to him a sacrifice, and it was
easy enough to regard it as brought to the local demons.   To guard

against this, H forbade the practice of secular slaughter altogether :

> To the end that the children of Israel may bring their sacrifices, which they
> sacrifice in the open field, even that they may bring them to the priest, and sac-
> rifice them for sacrifices of peace-offerings to Yahweh. And the priest shall
> sprinkle the blood upon the altar of Yahweh and burn the fat for a sweet
> savor to Yahweh. And they shall no more sacrifice their sacrifices to the he-
> goats, after which they play the harlot. (Lev. 17 [5-7])

If H thought at all of the practicability of this law in combination
with the centralization of worship in Jerusalem, he must have expected only a small territory about Jerusalem for the restored
community. Closely connected with slaughter was the prohibition
of eating the blood which was sacred to Yahweh, for it is the seat of
life,

> I have given it to you upon the altar to make atonement for your souls,
> for it is the blood that makes atonement by reason of the life. (17 [11])

In ch. 18 laws are given regulating the sexual life, forbidding
marriage among very near relatives and certain sexual abominations
which were practised by the Egyptians and Canaanites. For the
Jews they were all defiling and punishable by death.[1] How seriously concerned H was about these matters appears from his insertion of a parallel list in ch. 20, where the punishment for each crime
is added and an exhortation to holiness concludes the whole.
Moloch worship is condemned in both chapters, witchcraft is
stamped as a moral crime at the end of ch. 20.

A law containing certain food taboos was also found in H, for in
20 [25] we read,

> Ye shall therefore make a distinction between the clean beast and the un-
> clean, and between the unclean fowl and the clean : and ye shall not make your
> souls abominable by beast, or by bird, or by anything wherewith the ground
> teems, which I have separated from you as unclean. (Lev. 20 [25])

A specified list appears in Lev. 11, in which vv. [43-45] are according
to style and thought quite certainly from H.

The whole emphasis in these laws is on cultic purity, and the
same is true of the laws for the priests and high priests, and the right

---

[1] An advance on earlier customs appears in the prohibition of the marriage of
brother and half-sister (contrast Gen. 20 [12] 2 Sam. 13 [13]), of a man and his brother's
wife (contrast the "Levirate" marriage of Deut. 25 [5f.]), and of a husband and his wife's
sister during the lifetime of the wife (contrast Leah and Rachel, Gen. 29).

quality of sacrificial animals (Lev. 21f.) as well as of the laws concerning the holy days and festivals, Sabbath, Unleavened Bread, Feast of Weeks and of Booths (23 $^{1-3.9-12.15-20.39-44}$). The ancient agricultural meaning of the great harvest feasts is still preserved, but the Feast of Booths is already interpreted (in addition to the Feast of Unleavened Bread) as a memorial of the Exodus from Egypt.

How strong H's cultic interest was, may be seen from a comparison of the law of the Sabbath year in Deut. 15 with Lev. 25. In Deut. 15 it is wholly ethical, in Lev. 25 it is cultic. This is quite significant, for the Sabbath year was originally a strictly social and economic institution designed for the amelioration of the lot of the poor. In H,

> The seventh year shall be a sabbath of solemn rest for the land, a sabbath unto Yahweh: thou shalt neither sow thy field, nor prune thy vineyard. (25 ^{4})

H declares that during the Exile the land enjoyed its Sabbaths and "the rest which it had not in your Sabbaths, when ye dwelt in it" (26 $^{34f.}$). The land belongs to Yahweh, He alone is the owner, His people are only His tenants. Part of the time the land is to be left to Him alone, it is to be allowed to rest from its production, to keep a Sabbath unto Yahweh. This is withal a splendid thought.

But H had also the social and moral interests of the people at heart. The holiness in which he was interested is not wholly cultic. In ch. 25 he adds laws against taking unfair advantage of the poor, makes provisions for the buying back of property that had to be sold because of the poverty of the owner, and gives admonitions to aid the impoverished fellow Jews, to charge no interest on loans to them, and not to treat them as slaves with rigor, if they had been compelled to sell themselves, for they are the slaves of none but Yahweh (25 $^{14.17-25.35-40a.42f.47-49.53.55}$). Besides, there is the famous ch. 19 with its great social laws, among which vv. $^{17f.}$ easily take first rank:

> Thou shalt not hate thy brother in thy heart: thou shalt surely warn thy neighbor, and not incur sin because of him. Thou shalt not take vengeance nor bear any grudge against the children of thy people; but thou shalt love thy neighbor as thyself: I am Yahweh.

This is the highest point in the ethics of the Old Testament, where

the inner disposition, the heart, not only the outward deed counts.
Jesus regarded it as the commandment which must be joined directly
to the greatest commandment, love of God and love of the neighbor.
It is true, that "neighbor" meant to H the fellow Jew and therein
his limitation appears.   But he did not confine it wholly to them,
for a little later he says,

> The stranger that sojourns with you shall be to you as the native among
> you, and thou shalt love him as thyself; for ye were strangers in the land of
> Egypt: I am Yahweh your God. (19 34)

The spirit of the finest sections of Deuteronomy is seen in such laws.
D's influence appears also in H's concluding exhortation (ch. 26)
which is modelled on D's.   Here however the phraseology of Ezekiel
is so apparent that Ezekiel has sometimes been regarded as the author
of this chapter, indeed some have proposed him as the author of the
entire Holiness Code.   That is given up at present.   But Ezekiel
was the spiritual kinsman of H.   Both worked for the future restoration, impelled thereto by their unconquerable faith in God, who
would yet save His people.   After describing the experiences of the
exile which have come to Israel because of its disobedience to the
divine laws, H looked forward to the future:

> And they shall confess their iniquity, and the iniquity of their fathers, in
> their trespass which they trespassed against Me, and also that, because they
> walked contrary to Me, I also walked contrary to them, and brought them into
> the land of their enemies: if then their uncircumcised heart be humbled, and
> they then accept of the punishment of their iniquity; then will I remember
> My covenant with Jacob; and also My covenant with Isaac, and also My cov-
> enant with Abraham will I remember; and I will remember the land.   The
> land also shall be left by them, and shall enjoy its Sabbaths, while it lies
> desolate without them: and they shall accept of the punishment of their in-
> iquity; because, even because they rejected Mine ordinances, and their soul
> abhorred My statutes.   And yet for all that, when they are in the land of their
> enemies, I will not reject them, neither will I abhor them, to destroy them ut-
> terly, and to break My covenant with them; for I am Yahweh their God; but
> I will for their sakes remember the covenant of their ancestors, whom I brought
> forth out of the land of Egypt in the sight of the nations, that I might be their
> God: I am Yahweh. (Lev. 26 40–45)

Ezekiel and H were destined to play a large part in the legal
development of religion which culminated in the so-called Priest

Code and in the reign of legalism.[1] Fortunately there were poets and prophets both during the exile and after, to whom the other sides of religion were more important.

[1] We do not have H in its original form. When it was incorporated in the great Priestly Law Code it was worked over and later priestly elements were added, especially the priestly calendar of the festivals (Lev. 23 $^{4-8.13.14.18b.19a.21-38}$), the law of jubilee (Lev. 25 $^{8-12.15f.26-34.41.44.50-52.54}$), the prescriptions regarding the golden candlestick and the shewbread (Lev. 24 $^{1-9}$), and the story of the blasphemer who was stoned to death (Lev. 24 $^{10-15a.16b.22a.23}$). A few sections appear to have been separated from it (Ex. 31 $^{13-14a}$ Lev. 11 $^{43-45}$ Num. 15 $^{37-41}$).

CHAPTER XIII

EXILIC POETS AND PROPHETS

SHORTLY before the capture of Jerusalem when famine was driving the people to despair, King Zedekiah and his soldiers attempted to escape from the city by night. But the Chaldeans overtook him in the plains of Jericho and brought him captive to Nebuchadrezzar at his headquarters at Riblah where he had to witness the execution of his sons and of the other royal princes before he himself was blinded and taken to a Babylonian dungeon for the rest of his life. One of his party who had been with him on that fatal night was a poet who carried the scenes of the siege and the flight fresh in his mind and kept his sorrow deep in his heart till it broke forth into two lamentations which are preserved in the second and fourth chapters of our Book of Lamentations. The terrible scenes of the famine, the pitiful cry of the babies for food and drink, the ghastly sight of faces black and withered from suffering, and the horror of mothers eating the flesh of their own children were unforgettable.

> The tongue of the sucking child cleaves
> to the roof of his mouth for thirst:
> The young children ask bread
> and no man breaks it to them.
> They that are slain with the sword are better
> than they that are slain with hunger;
> For these pine away, stricken through,
> for want of the fruits of the field.
> The hands of the pitiful women
> have boiled their own children;
> They were their food
> in the destruction of the daughter of my people. (Lam. 4 [4.9f.])

The fate of the priests and prophets, the anxious, fruitless waiting for relief from Egypt, and the flight with Zedekiah were before the poet:

> Our pursuers were swifter
>   than the eagles of the heavens:
> They chased us upon the mountains,
>   they laid wait for us in the wilderness.
> The breath of our nostrils, the anointed of Yahweh,
>   was taken in their pits;
> Of whom we said,"Under his shadow
>   we shall live among the nations." (4 19f.)

With a bitter prediction to Edom that her punishment also will come very soon ch. 4 closes.

The second chapter is quite similar and gives us vivid and valuable touches of the siege of Jerusalem. It ends with the moving appeal,

> See, O Yahweh, and behold
>   to whom Thou hast done thus!
> Shall the women eat their fruit,
>   the children that are dandled in the hands?
> Shall the priest and the prophet be slain
>   in the sanctuary of the Lord?
> The youth and the old man lie
>   on the ground in the streets;
> My virgins and my young men
>   are fallen by the sword:
> Thou hast slain them in the day of Thine anger;
>   Thou hast slaughtered, and not pitied.
> Thou hast called, as in the day of a solemn assembly,
>   my terrors on every side;
> And there was none that escaped or remained
>   in the day of Yahweh's anger:
> Those that I have dandled and brought up
>   has mine enemy consumed. (2 20-22)

The author took the characteristic lamentation metre with its longer first and shorter second half lines to express the sorrow of his heart. He also made use of an alphabetic acrostic, beginning each strophe with a new letter in the order of the alphabet, and did it so well that the artificial side is quickly forgotten by the reader.

It was probably another survivor of the great catastrophe who wrote perhaps a little later in the Exile a prayer which is now the fifth chapter of the Book of Lamentations. He put the cruel sufferings of the people before Yahweh and implored Him for mercy and help. He did not write in lamentation metre or in acrostic form, but his poem would be of especial value if we could be sure that he was one of the people that had been left in the land. But this is uncertain, and for all we know he may have been the same as the author of ch. 2 and 4, even though he did not use the acrostic and the lamentation metre.

The writer of ch. 1 did use them, but his mood was different from that of the others; he was full of deep penitence. He painted Zion's sad condition after 586 and let the unhappy one speak herself later on,

> Is it nothing to you, all ye that pass by?
>   behold and see,
> If there be any sorrow like unto my sorrow,
>   which is brought upon me,
> Wherewith Yahweh has afflicted me
>   in the day of His fierce anger. (1 ¹²)

Zion knows that her troubles are due to her sins against Yahweh, she has deserved her punishment, but she prays that her enemies also may soon get their desert.

All four of these lamentations are now grouped around the long acrostic psalm in ch. 3. This is composed in lamentation metre and the acrostic is accentuated, so that not only the first but every line of each strophe begins with the same letter of the alphabet. The artificiality of this is apparent. The poem is less vivid than the others and seems to be further removed from the catastrophe. It begins with,

> I am the man that has seen affliction
>   by the rod of His wrath,

and it was probably responsible for the early but untenable tradition that Jeremiah was the author of the Book of Lamentations. The one who collected the lamentations in this book did not yet ascribe them to Jeremiah, but simply called them "Lamentations." The Greek translation however prefaced the book as follows, "And it came to pass, after Israel was led into captivity and Jerusalem laid waste, that Jeremiah sat weeping, and lamented with this lamentation over Jerusalem, and said." The other versions followed this lead. It was quite natural that these poems should have been ascribed to Jeremiah, for he was the only inspired author of that period whose name was handed down to posterity ; the names of the real authors were unknown.

The feelings of many Jews in their Babylonian exile, their sorrow and homesickness, their love for Jerusalem and their hatred for their enemies, the Babylonians and the shameless Edomites, who had gloated over Judah's fall, found expression in Psalm 137, which attracts us by the beauty and pathos of its beginning and repels us by the savage cruelty of its conclusion.

> By the rivers of Babylon,
> There we sat down, yea, we wept,
> When we remembered Zion.
> Upon the poplars in its midst
> We hanged up our harps.
> For there our captors required of us songs,
> And mirth our tormentors :
> "Sing us one of the songs of Zion."
>
> How shall we sing Yahweh's song
> In a foreign land ?
> If I forget thee, O Jerusalem,
> May my right hand be forgotten.
> May my tongue cleave to the roof of my mouth,
> If I remember thee not ;
> If I set not Jerusalem
> Above my chief joy.
>
> Remember, O Yahweh, against the Edomites
> The day of Jerusalem ;
> Who said, " Rase it, rase it,
> Even to its foundation !"
> O daughter of Babylon, thou destroyer,
> Happy shall he be, that rewards thee
> As thou hast served us.
> Happy shall he be, that takes and dashes
> Thy little ones against the rock.

We shudder at this vindictive imprecation and turn with a feeling of relief to those exquisitely beautiful prayers which are preserved in Isaiah 63^{7-16} $63^{17}-64^{12}$. The author wrote in the early part of the Exile, most probably in Palestine, where he saw not only the ruins of the city and the temple, but also the incredible influence of the Chaldean occupation.

'Tis only a little while that they have possessed Thy holy people,
    that our adversaries trod down Thy sanctuary,
And we have (already) become as they over whom Thou never borest rule,
    as they that were not called by Thy name. (Isa. 63 [18])

The present was hopeless.   So our author turned to God's dealings
in the past in order to revive his hope for the future.

I will recall the loving kindnesses of Yahweh,
        the praises of Yahweh,
According to all that Yahweh has bestowed on us,
        and the great goodness toward the house of Israel. (63 [7])

The great time of the beginnings of the nation came into his mind
with all the romance woven about it by gratitude and love, how
Yahweh had made them His own and placed His trust in them
and had said,

"Surely, they are My people,
        children that will not deal falsely."
So He was their Saviour
        in all their affliction.
Not a messenger and an angel,
        His own presence saved them.[1]
In His love and in His pity
        He redeemed them,
And He bore them and carried them
        all the days of old.
But they rebelled and grieved
        His holy Spirit;
Therefore He was turned to be their enemy,
        and Himself fought against them. (63 [8-10])

Unwittingly the poet has come here to a point from which he
can derive no inspiration.   So he breaks off this line of thought
and decides once more to recall the days of Moses and God's wonderful deeds in that golden age of Israel's past.   This kindles his hope
anew and he breaks forth into the passionate prayer,

Look down from heaven, and behold
        from the habitation of Thy holiness and of Thy glory!
Where are Thy zeal and Thy mighty acts,
        the yearning of Thy heart and Thy compassions?

[1] The translation "in all their afflictions He was afflicted," etc., which carried
with it the profound truth of divine fellowship and sympathy in suffering, if not of
God's own atoning suffering, has to be given up because it does not represent the original but a later text.

Do not restrain Thyself!
   for Thou art our Father,
Though Abraham know us not,
   and Israel do not acknowledge us,
Thou, O Yahweh, art our Father,
"Our Redeemer" from of old is Thy name. (63 [15f.])

The second prayer is altogether similar, but the consciousness of sin is more strongly in the foreground of the poet's thought. He sees the disheartening and demoralizing effects of the fearful calamity. Despair and doubt are twin brothers, and doubt gives way to denial, and denial to indifference.

O Yahweh, why dost Thou make us to err concerning Thy dealings,
   and hardenest our hearts against Thy fear? (63 [17])

The people cannot understand God's dealings, and the result is that though it is but a short time ago that this terrible thing happened they have lost their faith and do not feel that they have anything to do with Yahweh any more. Oh, that Yahweh would only come down and interfere as in the days of old! The poet is conscious of the sins of the people and of the justice of God's punishment.

But now, O Yahweh, Thou art our Father:
   we are the clay, and Thou our potter;
   and we all are the work of Thy hand.
Be not wroth very sore, O Yahweh,
   neither remember iniquity forever:
   behold, look, we beseech Thee, we are all Thy people. (64 [8f.])

A penitent plea for help, not without hope but full of sadness and without certitude!

Quite different in tone is the finely buoyant poem which is now incorporated in the Book of Deuteronomy, ch. 32. It is called the Song of Moses because a deuteronomic editor attributed it to Moses and gave it a corresponding setting. In reality it was composed during the Exile by an unknown author. He lived in Babylonia and had come under the influence of Ezekiel; perhaps he was one of his friends and disciples. He also looked back over the history of Israel, remembered the faithful love and care of Yahweh and the haughtiness and faithlessness of Israel, which provoked Yahweh's anger and His decision to chastise them severely. He would indeed have gone to the utmost limit of punishment.

I said, I would scatter them afar,
  I would make the remembrance of them to cease from among men;
Were it not that I feared the provocation of the enemy,
  lest their adversaries should judge amiss,
Lest they should say, Our hand is exalted,
  and Yahweh has not done all this. (Deut. 32 $^{26f.}$)

This sounds quite like Ezekiel! It is solely Yahweh's regard for His own holy name that restrained Him from annihilating His people, and that now moves Him to interfere on their behalf. His own people shall "know that I am Yahweh," Ezekiel would have phrased it, and the nations also "shall know that I am Yahweh." Our poet expresses it differently, with much poetic power.

For I lift up My hand to heaven,
  and say, As I live for ever,
If I whet My glittering sword,
  and My hand take hold on judgment;
I will render vengeance to Mine adversaries,
  and will recompence them that hate Me.
I will make Mine arrows drunk with blood,
  and My sword shall devour flesh;
With the blood of the slain and the captives,
  from the head of the leaders of the enemy. (Deut. 32 $^{40-42}$)

With a call to His people to rejoice among the heathen because of Yahweh's vengeance on His enemies and His expiation of Israel's sins the poem comes to an end. Ezekiel never predicted disaster to the Chaldeans, but his disciple was sure that it would soon be upon them. He lived in the latter part of the Exile. Prophetic voices presently began to be heard announcing Babylon's fall.

In 562 Nebuchadrezzar had died, his son Amel-Marduk had freed King Jehoiachin from prison and allowed him to live at his court. It was the first ray of hope for the Jews. Soon greater things happened. Cyrus entered upon his brilliant career. At first, king of the little kingdom of Anshan, east of the Persian Gulf, he became in quick succession king of Persia and Media, and in 547–546 attacked and defeated Croesus of Lydia in one campaign. Nabunaid, or Nabonedos as the Greeks called him, the last king of Babylon, was Croesus' ally. Cyrus now turned against him. The details of the war are unknown, only of the final stage are we fully informed by contemporary inscriptions.   In 539 Babylon fell into the hands of the Persians.

At least three prophets watched eagerly these movements and, years before Babylon fell, they predicted its doom.   The first of them wrote the two poems of Isaiah 13 and 14 [4–21]. The former is a prophecy.   Yahweh has stirred up the Medes against Babylon, He is mustering them for battle.   They are His consecrated agents on the Day of Yahweh when He punishes "the world for its evil and the wicked for their iniquity."   Following the pattern of Zephaniah, the prophet pictured the awful day, when the sun shall grow dark in the morning, the moon and the stars shall not shine, the earth and the heavens will shake "by the wrath of Yahweh of hosts."   But few will escape.   "I will make a man more rare than fine gold."

> Every one that is found shall be thrust through;
>   and every one that is taken shall fall by the sword.
> Their infants also shall be dashed in pieces before their eyes;
>   their houses shall be rifled, and their wives ravished. (Isa. 13 [15f.])

Babylon shall be completely overthrown, never to be built again. The ghastly desolation and utter desertion of the once glorious city are graphically described.   The author was a poet of great dramatic power.

In the second poem his art rises still higher.   He sings a song of hate, full of gruesome beauty, describing the descent of the king of Babylon to Sheol.   At last the oppressor has ceased, his staff is broken "that ruled the nations in anger, with a persecution that none restrained.   The whole earth is at rest" and rejoices; even the cedars of Lebanon exult because they will no more be felled.   The fall of the tyrant stirs even Sheol.

> Sheol from beneath is moved for thee
>   to meet thee at thy coming;
> It stirs up the dead for thee,
>   even all the chief ones of the earth;
> It has raised up from their thrones
>   all the kings of the nations.
> All they shall answer
>   and say unto thee,
> "Art thou also become weak as we?
>   art thou become like unto us?

Thy pomp is brought down to Sheol,
  and the noise of thy viols:
The worm is spread under thee,
  and worms cover thee."

How art thou fallen from heaven,
  O day star, son of the morning!
How art thou cut down to the ground,
  that didst lay low the nations!
And thou saidst in thy heart,
  "I will ascend into heaven,
I will exalt my throne
  above the stars of God;
And I will sit upon the mount of congregation,
  in the uttermost parts of the north;
I will ascend above the heights of the clouds;
  I will make myself like the Most High."
Yet thou shalt be brought down to Sheol,
  to the uttermost parts of the pit. (Isa. 14 [9-15])

Full of astonishment all shall look upon the slain tyrant, whose body shall not rest in an honorable grave but will be cast forth and trampled under foot,

Because thou hast destroyed thy land,
  thou hast slain thy people. (Isa. 14 [20])

His sons also shall be slain "that they rise not up and possess the earth and fill the face of the world with cities."

These two poems were later connected by an editor who missed a reference to Israel's restoration and lordship over the nations (14 [1-4a]). He probably added also two verses at the end in which the complete ruin of Babylon is predicted.

These poems, masterly in their poetic diction and full of dramatic power, are not of high religious or moral value, because they are charged with the wild spirit of triumphant hate. The poet was a nationalist prophet like Nahum, in whose class he belongs.

Totally different was the second prophet who foretold Babylon's fall. He was not a great poet but a true seer; he lived in Palestine not in Babylonia; no word of hate or of triumph over the fallen foe fell from his lips. In his day he appears to have been noted, for inquirers came to him even from Edom. His oracles are preserved in Isaiah 21 [1–15]. In the evening twilight, ordinarily his season of refreshment, he had an experience which filled him with anguish and fear. He had seen a terrific storm, such as sweeps through the desert south of Judah, and had heard in an audition the terrible words,

> The robber is robbing, the destroyer destroying!
> Go up, O Elam, besiege, O Media!
> Make all the sighing to cease! (Isa. 21 [2])

Quickly the vision changed. He saw a banquet hall with the (Babylonian) princes at a feast. All of a sudden the cry rang out, "Rise up, ye princes, anoint the shield!" This vision had thrown the prophet into a terrible excitement. He did not know its real significance. Had he been a greater prophet, he would have had no doubt. Now, very much like Habakkuk, he got ready for God's answer. We note a most interesting thing for the psychology of prophecy. He fell into a trance and set up his second self as a watchman, ordering it to see and remember so as to be able to report later on. This reminds one of commands given to a person before he is hypnotized. It was also suggested what he would see, "a troop, horsemen in pairs, a troop of asses, a troop of camels." He had to wait so long that he finally "cried as a lion" ·

> O Lord, I stand upon my watch-tower
>   continually by day,
> And am set in my ward
>   whole nights.

Then suddenly he saw,

> And behold, here comes a troop of men,
>   horsemen in pairs,

and heard the message,

> Fallen, fallen is Babylon;
> And all the graven images of her gods
> Are broken unto the ground! (Isa. 21 [8f.])

Thereupon he turned to his people that had so long been threshed and beaten and gave them the word of relief from Yahweh Himself, but added no word of exultation, no word of sated revenge!

The Edomites heard of this prophet and came to ask his advice. "Watchman, what of the night?" How late is it? What is the present situation in this world crisis? Does this struggle of the Chaldeans with the Medes and Persians mean for us day or night, freedom or merely a change of overlord? The watchman did not know. Now it was like morning, now like the night. Everything is still uncertain. But come again, he tells them, perhaps a definite answer can be given then. We note with surprise the uncertainty of this prophet, but with delight the absence of any trace of hatred for the Edomites, Israel's bitter national foes (Isa. 21 $^{11\,f.}$).

His humane feeling appears also in his last oracle, in which he is solicitous for the welfare of Arabian caravans in their flight from the war zone. The attack of Cyrus had begun. Babylon was doomed! (Isa. 21 $^{13-17}$)

The third of these anonymous prophets who predicted its fall was the greatest of them; some call him the greatest of all the Old Testament prophets. To him a separate chapter must be devoted.

CHAPTER XIV

DEUTERO–ISAIAH

NOBODY had watched the marvellous victories of Cyrus more eagerly than a young Jew, whose name is unknown, but who is now generally called the Second or Deutero-Isaiah, because his book was affixed to Isaiah's.   His heart began to stir with a great hope, which soon grew into a firm conviction.   He had a prophet's insight and interpreted the events of history in the light of the fundamental prophetic conviction that Yahweh was the supreme director of all movements of history.   Yahweh must be behind these glorious triumphs of Cyrus; the great Persian's career was explicable only on this supposition.   What then was Yahweh's plan?   What did He intend to accomplish through this wonderful conqueror?   He could not doubt, he knew it all too well.   From 546 on he proclaimed to his people deliverance and restoration.   He had a poet's wondrous language, and the music of his words stole into their sad hearts almost against their will as he began,

> Comfort ye, comfort ye My people,
>   says your God.
> Speak ye comfortably to Jerusalem,
>   and cry unto her,
> That her warfare is accomplished,
>   that her iniquity is pardoned,
> That she has received of Yahweh's hand
>   double for all her sins. (Isa. 40 $^{1-2}$)

He heard in an audition how the heavenly beings were at work in the desert, preparing a miraculous highway for Yahweh, because He would go straight through the Syrian desert at the head of his exiled people, leading them home to Jerusalem and Judah.

> Hark! one is crying, "In the wilderness
>   prepare ye the way of Yahweh;
> Make level in the desert
>   a highway for our God!

> Every valley shall be exalted,
>> and every mountain and hill shall be made low,
> And the uneven shall be made level,
>> and the rough places a plain:
> And the glory of Yahweh shall be revealed,
>> and all flesh shall see it together." (Isa. 40 $^{3-5}$)

How the vision inspired the prophet! He came back to it again and again, and it was ever more marvellous to him. His thoughts flew to Jerusalem and he called upon the city to watch for the coming of Yahweh.

> O thou that tellest good tidings to Zion,
>> get thee up on a high mountain;
> O thou that tellest good tidings to Jerusalem,
>> lift up thy voice with strength,
>> lift it up, be not afraid;
> Say unto the cities of Judah,
>> "Behold, your God!"
> Behold, Yahweh comes as a victor,
>> and His arm has ruled for Him.
> Behold, His reward is with Him,
>> and His recompense before Him.
> He will feed His flock like a shepherd,
>> He will gather the lambs in His arm,
> And carry them in His bosom,
>> and will gently lead those that have their young. (Isa. 40 $^{9-11}$)

It was all so certain to our prophet that he saw it already accomplished. He knew that Babylon would fall and sang her funeral dirge. Cyrus was Yahweh's agent, he would set the exiles free, send them home and command that Jerusalem and the other cities be rebuilt. What a bright hope this was! Again and again the poet broke forth into song because of the joy that this message brought to his soul. If he could only inspire the people with his faith! But most of them were too weary and had ceased to hope. In the great Babylonian civilization they constantly felt the tremendous power of the Chaldean empire. Its mighty armies, gigantic buildings, and great material wealth had crushed all hope out of their hearts: Babylon was far too mighty, far too powerful to be overthrown. But the prophet had heard a voice in which sounded the power of eternity:

> Hark! one said, "Cry!"
>> and I said, "What shall I cry?"
> "All flesh is grass,
>> and all its goodliness is as the flower of the field.
> The grass withers, the flower fades,
>> when the breath of Yahweh blows upon it;
> The grass withers, the flower fades,
>> but the word of our God shall stand forever." (Isa. 40 [6–8])

All human power is ephemeral, "surely the people is grass." Empires crumble to pieces and fall, but the word of our God is eternal: the fall of Babylon and the deliverance of the exiles are sure.

> For as the rain comes down
>> and the snow from heaven,
> And returns not thither,
>> but waters the earth,
> And makes it bring forth and bud,
>> and gives seed to the sower
>> and bread to the eater;
> So shall My Word be,
>> that goes forth out of My mouth:
> It shall not return unto Me void,
>> but it shall accomplish that which I please,
>> and it shall prosper in the thing whereto I sent it. (Isa. 55 [10f.])

With mighty words the prophet proclaimed the omnipotence of Yahweh. Let the people think of the really tremendous things in the world of nature and ask but the question, who can do them? Can the nations do any of them? Compare them with Yahweh and see how insignificant they are: mortal men that perish in a moment!

> Who has measured the waters in the hollow of his hand,
>> and meted out heaven with the span,
>> and comprehended the dust of the earth in a measure,
>> and weighed the mountains in scales,
>> and the hills in a balance?
> Who has directed the Spirit of Yahweh,
>> or being His counsellor has taught Him?
>> with whom took He counsel, and who instructed Him,
>> and taught Him the right path,
>> and showed Him the way of understanding?
> Behold, the nations are as a drop of a bucket,
>> and are accounted as the small dust of the balance,
>> behold, He takes up the isles as a very little thing,
>> all the nations are as nothing before Him,
>> they are accounted by Him as less than nothing and vanity.

"To whom then will ye liken Me,
    that I should be equal to him?" says the Holy One.
Lift up your eyes on high,
    and see, who has created these,
That brings out their host of number,
    and calls them all by name;
Because of the greatness of His might and the strength of His power
    not one is lacking. (Isa. 40 [12–15.17.25f.])

None can be compared to Yahweh. There is no other God besides Him, He alone is God. Deutero-Isaiah was the protagonist of monotheism. In majestic imagery he summoned the nations with their idols before the tribunal of Yahweh: here let them prove their deity, here let them show their power! Have they ever predicted anything that they were going to do? and have they ever done it? They cannot reply, and the obvious conclusion is,

    Behold, ye are of nothing,
      and your work is of nought;
      an abomination is he that chooses you. (Isa. 41 [24])

Deutero-Isaiah ridiculed the worship of images. He identified the gods with their idols and showed the supreme folly of worshipping a piece of wood overlaid with silver and gold, and fastened with nails lest it fall down. In all the world there is only one God: Yahweh! He alone has shown Himself to be God. He it was that called Cyrus and set him on his victorious career. For who was it that had predicted his victories? Surely not the idols, whose worshippers he has come to overthrow! No one else but Yahweh, who has directed the history of the world from the beginning and will do so to the end, the eternal, omnipotent God, the creator and ruler of the world. The prophet never tired of emphasizing this conviction, he was mastered and inspired by it. One feels that it was something that had come with all the force of an original discovery to him, although he thought that everybody had known it from childhood.

    Have ye not known? have ye not heard?
      has it not been told you from the beginning?
      have ye not understood from the foundations of the earth? (Isa. 40 [21])

He was the first to expound monotheism, the first to reason about the unity of God. How profoundly he had grasped this truth is seen especially in his answer to the objection against Yahweh's use of the foreigner Cyrus as His "anointed one," His Messiah.

> Does one strive with his maker?
>   a potsherd with the potter?
> Does the clay say to him that fashions it,
>   "What makest thou?
>   And thy work has no handle?"
> Does one say to a father, "What begettest thou?"
>   or to a woman, "With what travailest thou?"
> Thus says Yahweh,
>   the Holy One of Israel and his maker:
> "Do you ask Me of the things that are to come; concerning My sons,
>   and concerning the work of My hands will you command Me?
> I have made the earth,
>   and created man upon it:
> I, even My hands, have stretched out the heavens,
>   and all their host have I commanded.
> I have raised him up in righteousness,
>   and I will make straight all his ways:
> He shall build My city,
>   and let My exiles go free,
> Not for price nor reward,
>   says Yahweh of hosts. (Isa. 45 $^{9-13}$)

Yahweh uses as His instrument whom He will. The creature has no right to give orders to the creator; Yahweh is absolutely sovereign; He created the world and orders it according to His plan; He has chosen Cyrus as His instrument, and Cyrus will carry out His plans.

The unity of God was the one pole of Deutero-Isaiah's teaching of God. The other, which he emphasized just as strongly, was Israel's special relation to Him. In gracious, kindly, and endearing words he spoke of Yahweh and His love for His people. Some of the most charming passages are devoted to it. Immediately after his powerful exposition of Yahweh's omnipotence he proceeded,

> Why sayest thou, O Jacob,
>   and speakest, O Israel,
> "My way is hid from Yahweh,
>   and the justice due to me is passed away from my God?"
> Hast thou not known?
>   or hast thou not heard?
> An eternal God is Yahweh,
>   the creator of the ends of the earth;
> He faints not, neither is weary;
>   there is no searching of His understanding.

> He gives power to the faint;
>> and to him that has no might he increases strength.
> Even the youths shall faint and be weary,
>> and the young men shall utterly fall:
> But they that wait for Yahweh shall renew their strength;
>> they shall mount up with wings as eagles:
> They shall run and not be weary;
>> they shall walk and not faint. (Isa. 40 [27-31])

The power of religious hope has seldom been more beautifully expressed. The prophet's own experience, his own optimism and enthusiasm shine through here. His mission was to comfort, and he comforted indeed. With exquisite tenderness he answered Mother Zion's complaint, for he knew so well her doubt and the weariness of heart it brings:

> Zion said, "Yahweh has forsaken me,
>> and the Lord has forgotten me."
> Can a woman forget her sucking child,
>> that she should not have compassion on the son of her womb?
> Yea, these may forget,
>> yet will not I forget thee. (Isa. 49 [14f.])

The pathos and power of these lines are unsurpassed. Mother Zion, who has been bereaved of her children, will suddenly have them again, and many more than she ever had before, when the exiles will return (49 [16-21]). Compare at least one other of these exquisite poems, 51 [17ff.] or 54 [4-8]. In the latter Israel is the wife of Yahweh, now forsaken and grieved in spirit, but really a wife of youth, whom He had loved with all the passion of His first love, and whom He will not cast off forever.

> For a small moment have I forsaken thee;
>> but with great mercies will I gather thee.
> In overflowing wrath I hid My face from thee for a moment,
>> but with everlasting lovingkindness will I have mercy on thee,
>> says Yahweh, thy Redeemer. (Isa. 54 [7f.])

The point that is emphasized in all these passages is the love of Yahweh for Israel, His special relation to her, He can never forget her, for she is peculiarly His own.

The two ideas of Yahweh, the God of the whole world and the God of Israel, may exclude each other, if either is stressed too much. Their relation constituted a real problem. If there is only one

God, who rules the world and guides the affairs of the nations, He must be the God of all and be interested in all. But could the long historic connection between Yahweh and Israel be given up? No, the reconciliation between the two ideas Deutero-Isaiah found in the belief that Yahweh had chosen Israel as His servant in order that through him the knowledge of the one God and of true religion might be mediated to the nations. The salvation of the world is God's purpose, Israel's restoration is only the means to this end. Cyrus is the anointed instrument who prepares the conditions which will make the establishment of the true universal religion of Yahweh possible. That is why it is given to him to overthrow the nations, who are adherents of false religions, and to restore Israel, the possessor of the true religion. Cyrus himself will come to know and worship Yahweh as the only true God, and the nations through him, for Yahweh had girded him,

> That they may know from the rising of the sun
> and from the west,
> That there is none beside Me:
> I am Yahweh, and there is none else. (Isa. 45 [6])

The fall of Babylon and the deliverance of Israel in which the victories of Cyrus culminate, together with the spectacular homeward march of the exiles will attract the attention of the whole world, "and all flesh shall see it together." Yahweh will call "the escaped of the nations," will ask them whether all this is not proof of His sole deity, and will invite them all:

> Look unto Me, and be ye saved,
> all the ends of the earth;
> For I am God, and there is none else.
> By Myself have I sworn,
> The word is gone from My mouth
> in righteousness, and shall not return,
> That unto Me every knee shall bow,
> every tongue shall swear. (Isa. 45 [22f.])

A universal God and a universal religion are the crown of history, the goal of the world! Heaven and earth may perish; in and above this perishing world there is an eternal reality, the salvation of true religion.

> Attend unto Me, O My people,
>> and give ear unto Me, O My nation:
> For a law shall go forth from Me,
>> and My justice for a light of the peoples.
> I will bring near in a moment My righteousness,
>> My salvation is gone forth,
>> and Mine arm shall judge the peoples;
> The isles shall wait for Me,
>> and on Mine arm shall they trust.
> Lift up your eyes to the heavens,
>> and look upon the earth beneath;
> For the heavens shall vanish away like smoke,
>> and the earth shall wax old like a garment,
>> and they that dwell therein shall die like gnats:
> But My salvation shall be forever,
>> and My righteousness shall not be abolished. (Isa. 51 [4-6])

So clearly no prophet had ever expressed the sum of Israel's religion. It is true that at times Deutero-Isaiah laid undue stress on Israel's glory, although this was really only incidental to the attainment of the higher glory of universal religion. It is true that he made fellowship with Yahweh dependent on the individual's becoming a member of Israel (44 [5]), that he foretold that the Davidic king would be "a prince and commander to the peoples" (55 [3-5]), and that the Egyptians, Ethiopians, and Sabeans would go to Israel in chains, fall down and supplicate,

> Surely, God is in thee, and there is none else,
>> there is no God.
> Verily, with thee God hides Himself,
>> the God of Israel, the Saviour. (Isa. 45 [14f.])

It is true he said that Yahweh would give nations as a ransom for Israel (43 [3f.]), that Israel should thresh the peoples and beat them to pieces (41 [15f.]), that kings and queens should attend the returning exiles, and that in abject humiliation

> They shall bow down to thee with their faces to the earth,
>> and lick the dust of thy feet. (Isa. 49 [23])

But all this is so entirely out of harmony with his prophecies of universal religion, that it seems incredible that Deutero-Isaiah should have written it. Yet it is not impossible that even he was carried away to appeal to Israel's pride by his desire to inspire them with new hope at times when the higher truth found no response.

One wishes that he had not yielded to the temptation, or that he had at least not put these words into Yahweh's mouth. He stimulated thereby, quite unwittingly, the national and religious arrogance of the later Jews, and made it easy for them to miss the really great truths which he proclaimed.

But it cannot cloud the glory of his essential message, which is so great that we are still thrilled by it, especially when we read those four poems in which he worked out his own original contribution with singular beauty and magnanimity, the so-called "Poems of the Servant of Yahweh" (Isa. 42 $^{1-4}$ 49 $^{1-6}$ 50 $^{4-9}$ 52 ^{13}–53 ^{12}), which we have not touched upon so far. Here a profound interpretation of Israel's suffering is given in the light of her mission. The problem of innocent suffering is solved by fixing the attention upon its purpose, not upon the reason for it. Israel is the servant of Yahweh. He is now despised and crushed, without national existence, far from his own land, in exile. But he is still Yahweh's servant, through whom true religion is to be established in all the world. It seems impossible. All his work in exile must be vain; it means but suffering and shame. But no, this very suffering is part of Yahweh's plan! Through it His purpose for the world will be accomplished. For He is about to restore Israel to such marvellous glory that the nations and kings of the world will be astounded and come to a true understanding of Israel's suffering. Yahweh Himself calls upon them,

> Behold, My servant shall prosper,
>> he shall be exalted and lifted up and very high!
> Just as many were astonished at him,
>> because his visage was so marred that it was not that of a man,
>> and his form so that it was no longer human;
> So shall many nations wonder,
>> kings shall shut their mouths at him:
> For that which had not been told them shall they see,
>> and that which they had not heard shall they consider.

The heathen themselves now speak:

> Who could have believed that which we have heard?
>> and to whom had the arm of Yahweh been revealed?
> For he grew up before Him as a tender plant,
>> and as a root out of a dry ground:

He had no form nor comeliness, that we should look at him,
nor beauty, that we should desire him.
He was despised and forsaken of men,
a man of sicknesses, and acquainted with disease,
And as one from whom men hide their face
he was despised, and we esteemed him not.

This had been their natural explanation of Israel's suffering and bitter fate. But now in the light of his glorious restoration they see the real meaning of his suffering: Israel had suffered for their sakes. Sorrowfully they confess,

Surely, he has borne our sicknesses,
and carried our sufferings,
While we esteemed him stricken,
smitten of God and afflicted.
But he was wounded for our transgressions,
he was bruised for our iniquities;
The chastisement of our peace was upon him,
and with his bruises we are healed.
All we like sheep have gone astray,
we have turned every one to his own way:
And Yahweh laid upon him
the punishment of us all.

In this confession of Israel's vicarious suffering for them the heathen appropriate inwardly its fruit. The prophet agrees with them and now dwells on the servant's patience in all his affliction.

He was oppressed, yet he humbled himself,
and opened not his mouth,
As a lamb that is led to the slaughter,
and as a sheep that before its shearers is dumb.
By oppressive judgment he was taken away,
and who took note of his fate,
That he was cut off out of the land of the living,
for our transgressions smitten to death?
And they made his grave with the wicked,
and with evil-doers his mound,
Although he had done no violence,
neither was any deceit in his mouth.

But this innocent suffering was in accordance with Yahweh's plan, which the prophet proceeds to reveal. Without it the light of true religion would never have come to the heathen.

But it pleased Yahweh to crush him:
  if he would make his soul an offering for sin,
He would see calamity for length of days,
  but the purpose of Yahweh would succeed through him.
As a result of the travail of his soul he would see light
  and be satisfied with the knowledge of his vindication.

Yahweh Himself takes up the last word "vindication," and holds out to His servant the victor's crown for his willing, vicarious suffering.

The vindication of My servant is for many,
  and it is their punishment that he has been bearing.
Therefore will I divide him a portion with the great,
  and he shall divide the spoil with the strong:
Because he poured out his soul unto death,
  and was numbered with the transgressors,
Yet he bore the sin of many,
  and has been making intercession for the transgressors.[1] (Isa. 52 [13]–53 [12])

The glorification of Israel is not an end in itself but the means to the end. It is incidental to something far greater, far more wonderful: the conversion of the whole world to the one and only God, Yahweh. It was one of the greatest things that Deutero-Isaiah could do that he enunciated this clearly and unmistakably.

And now Yahweh did say,
  He that formed me from the womb for His servant:
That He would bring Jacob again to Him,
  and Israel should be gathered unto Him,
And I should be honored in the eyes of Yahweh,
  and my God had become my strength;
And He said, "The raising up of the tribes of Jacob
  and the restoration of the preserved of Israel
Are less significant than thy being My servant;
  so I will give thee for a light to the Gentiles,
That My salvation may be
  to the end of the earth." (Isa. 49 [5f.])

The servant's mission is to mediate universal salvation. Upheld by Yahweh and empowered by His Spirit, he will enter upon the active part of his work. As he goes forth to bring true religion to

[1] Unfortunately the text of this poem (Isa. 52 [13]–53 [12]), especially of its conclusion, has been ill preserved. The above translation of 53 [11f.] is based on a text whose reconstruction is unfortunately not quite certain.

the heathen, the hearts of the peoples meet him, they know that he has the true knowledge of God, which alone will satisfy their deepest cravings.   Yahweh is not longing alone, they long for Him too.

> Behold, My servant, whom I uphold,
>> My chosen, in whom My soul delights:
> I have put My Spirit upon him,
>> he will bring forth justice to the Gentiles.
> He will not cry, nor lift up his voice,
>> nor cause it to be heard in the street.
> A bruised reed will he not break,
>> and a dimly burning wick will he not quench.
> He will bring forth justice in truth.
>> He will not fail nor be discouraged,
> Till he have set justice in the earth;
>> and the isles shall wait for his instruction. (Isa. 42 $^{1-4}$)

Justice is here equivalent to the true moral religion; its universal establishment is the divinely appointed goal of the history of the world.   Israel as God's missionary servant and prophet is commissioned to win all nations for this end.

Deutero-Isaiah presented here the ideal which he had for his people.   He knew that the reality was totally different, Israel was "a people robbed and plundered, snared in holes, and hid in prison houses," a "deaf" and "blind" servant (42 $^{18-22}$).   They had not taken this suffering upon themselves with willing patience.   The prophet had idealized them in his poems.   He wanted to rouse them by holding up before them this high ideal of their world-wide mission.   He knew how wonderful his message was, and that the people might not believe it.

> For My thoughts are not your thoughts,
>> neither are your ways My ways, says Yahweh.
> For as the heavens are higher than the earth,
>> so are My ways higher than your ways,
>> and My thoughts than your thoughts. (Isa. 55 $^{8f.}$)

The wonder of it filled the poet with such joy that he must sometimes break forth into song, and all through his book there are such lyrical outbursts as this,

> Sing unto Yahweh a new song,
>> and His praise from the end of the earth, etc. (Isa. 42 $^{10-12}$)

He was the most enthusiastic of the prophets.   He had wonderful truths to proclaim, but he never attempted to convince men by the force of his logic alone; he placed himself on the highest level and by the contagious power of his enthusiasm and of his own profound belief he tried to inspire them with new hope and courage, with new loyalty and trust. How well he knew the human heart! How he touched every chord by the music of his words! He carried the people away by his own enthusiasm to see his vision and to hope with him. He had passages of exquisite beauty; as with the touch of a mother's tenderest caress he comforted as seldom a man has comforted, for he was one of the greatest comforters of the race. No preacher could excel him in the moving power of his appeal, "Ho, every one that thirsts, come ye to the waters" (55 $^{1-3}$); no saint could surpass him in his certitude,

> For the mountains may depart,
>   and the hills may be removed;
> But My lovingkindness shall not depart from thee,
>   neither shall My covenant of peace be removed,
>   says Yahweh, that has mercy upon thee. (Isa. 54 ^{10})

Deutero-Isaiah wrote only in poetry. That is why some critics cannot regard 44 $^{9-20}$, in which the folly of idolatry is ridiculed with biting irony, as coming from him, for it is entirely in prose.[1] There are some who believe that the Poems of the Servant of Yahweh were not composed by him either, not because they were not written in poetry, for they were, but because they are unrelated to their context and they are said to differ in their ideas from Deutero-Isaiah's. But the latter reason we have seen not to be true, and the former is not a serious argument, for Isa. 40–55 is not a single poem but a collection of poems, and there is no reason to expect a close connection between them and the adjoining passages. Indeed, the understanding of the book is deepened and its literary attraction is enhanced, if the single poems are separated and read and enjoyed by themselves. Else even Deutero-Isaiah may become monotonous, although his rhythmic language is melody to the ear. He is surpassingly gentle when he comforts, overpowering when he describes Yahweh's omnipotence, clear and forcible when he reasons, compelling when he sets forth his hope or calls to repentance, always

---

[1] This was a favorite theme of later writers. In Jer. 10 $^{1-16}$ one of them inserted an attack upon the worship of idols quite in the manner and style of Deutero-Isaiah.

beautiful, never dull or commonplace.   His style is so finely wrought and so clearly marked that it can never be forgotten when its peculiarities have once been perceived.   Many later poets and prophets show the influence which his style had upon them.   But his finest and deepest thoughts were understood by but few, until He came who embodied the ideal of the Servant of Yahweh in himself : Jesus of Nazareth.   To Christians the Book of Deutero-Isaiah is so dear for that reason, and because it is so evangelical. We still delight in calling him the Evangelist of the Old Testament, although he never spoke of the Christ.[1]

Perhaps Deutero-Isaiah's indefatigable insistence, perhaps a growing insight into the political situation roused other prophets also to predict the fall of Babylon.   A whole anthology of such prophecies is gathered in Jer. 50 [2]–51 [58].   The collection was made at a later time, but the historical background of the single oracles is that of the last few years of the Babylonian exile.

---

[1] The interpretation which sees in the Servant of Yahweh the Messiah is untenable. Deutero-Isaiah himself called Israel the servant of Yahweh.   Compare, *e.g.*, 41 [8], "but thou Israel, My servant, Jacob whom I have chosen," and 49 [3], "Thou art My servant, Israel, in whom I will be glorified."   Deutero-Isaiah did not prophesy of Jesus Christ, but his ideal was fulfilled in him, as far as a single personality could do it.

CHAPTER XV

DEUTERONOMISTIC HISTORIANS

THE prophets had been profoundly interested in history, because to them God was the import of all history and the goal toward which it tended. They saw Him at work behind all events, weaving at the loom of time. His will was all controlling and destined to be carried out with all the terrors of retribution. History thus became more significant than ever, for here God's work was manifest. The prophets viewed it on a wide horizon, for God was working everywhere. He used the Syrians and Assyrians, the Scythians and Babylonians as His instruments, in order to establish righteousness in the world. The petty national limits were cast aside, and at last a prophet had arisen who unfolded the divine purpose for all the nations of the world. This conviction of the victory of righteousness was for the prophets not the result of historical study but of their own inner experience. They did not derive it from history, but found it confirmed there.

The author of Deuteronomy and the men who carried through the reformation of Josiah were disciples of the great prophets and also deeply interested in history. The fall of the Northern Kingdom in 722 and the terrible catastrophe of Judah in 701, followed by the punishment of Assyria and Jerusalem's deliverance, were eloquent demonstrations of the prophetic teaching that defection from Yahweh brought national ruin and that loyalty to Him was the only way of national salvation. To one of the deuteronomists the whole history of Israel and Judah enforced the great lessons of this reformation, and as early as 600 B.C., more probably even before the death of Josiah in 608, he wrote the story of Israel and Judah from the building of the temple to the reformation by which it became the sole legitimate sanctuary of Israel, for his heart was filled with the hope that his people might learn from this history that only whole-hearted allegiance to Yahweh and exclusive worship at Jerusalem would secure salvation and national permanence, while defection from Yahweh and worship at the local sanctuaries would bring ruin to Judah as inevitably as they had done to Israel. His work is contained in the Books of Kings, from 1 Ki. 1 to 2 Ki. 23 [25a], and is naturally divided into three great sections: (1) the story of Solomon (1 Ki. 1–11); (2) the divided kingdom of Israel and Judah till the fall of Israel (1 Ki. 12 to 2 Ki. 18 [12]); (3) the history of Judah alone until Josiah (2 Ki. 18 [13]–23 [25a]). The whole history was presented here from the deuteronomic point of view. Every king was tested by the norm of exclusive loyalty to Yahweh and of worshipping only at the sole legitimate sanctuary in Jerusalem. The history of three centuries was viewed in the light of one great religious principle. This assured a mastery of the entire material, which doubtless was a great achievement. One might see in it a philosophy of history applied to this particular period. But this must not be exaggerated. Our author was not interested in history for its own sake, but only in so far as it afforded to him illustrative material. He was a teacher of religion who used history as his object lesson; it taught the great truths in which he was interested with convincing power. If we judge his work from the side of historiography, our admiration is greatly lessened, for then we can see in it not an advance but rather a catastrophe, since it was the beginning of that development which subordinated history to religion and led to the historical constructions in which facts were made to substantiate dogma.

Our writer used his sources with discretion. He refers to the Book of the Acts of Solomon and to the Chronicles of the Kings of Israel and of Judah as sources for the further study of the various kings. He used in addition also the Annals of the Temple; the three cycles of stories clustering around Elijah, Elisha, and Ahab-Joram-Jehu; and perhaps a biography of Isaiah. It is probable that the Books of the Acts of the Kings of Israel and of Judah, respectively, to which he so often referred, were not the royal annals themselves, but two literary works by earlier historians who had used the official annals as the basis of their comprehensive treatment of the history. These were familiar and accessible to our writer, as well as to his readers. He himself had taken from them the historical material which was based on the official annals themselves. He could not use everything, so he made his selections and arranged them for his purpose. This explains why so many things of the highest historical importance were omitted, *e.g.* why he had almost nothing to say about such great kings as Omri and Jeroboam II. We must also bear in mind that he was a Judæan and therefore especially interested in Judah. But since he was above all a prophetic teacher and as such deeply impressed by the northern stories of Elijah, Elisha, and Ahab-Joram-Jehu, he incorporated a large part of them. If he had not done so, our knowledge of Israel would be scanty indeed. Now it cannot be asserted that in his use of the sources he ever deliberately changed the facts in order to conform them to his dogma, even though he understood and interpreted the entire history in its light. But by selecting his material, omitting the non-usable or non-tractable, skilfully arranging the suitable, and imposing his own point of view upon it, he actually did present a historical construction which was different from the real history itself. Fortunately, however, much that contradicted his own view found its way in, because he excerpted his older sources literally. He furnished them with introductions and conclusions of his own, and frequently added observations in his characteristic deuteronomistic style, but the excerpts themselves he did not change. In one sense this shows that he was not a master of historiography, else he would have told the entire history in his own words and thus have made the whole consistent throughout. We are glad that he wrote as he did, for this enables us to disengage his own material from that of his sources and thus to recover the more original and historical presentation of the older books, which would otherwise have been completely lost.

For the first part of his book, the history of Solomon (1 Ki. 1–11), our author used besides the famous David story (1 Ki. 1f.) the Book of the Acts of Solomon, to which he definitely refers in his conclusion, and most probably the Royal and the Temple Annals, although he does not mention either by name. He grouped the whole story around the building and dedication of the temple. That was to him the natural centre. Before and after it he put the stories which celebrate Solomon's wisdom, might, and wealth. Wherever suitable he inserted his religious observations, *e.g.* at the beginning,

Only the people sacrificed in the high places, because there was no house built for the name of Yahweh until those days. And Solomon loved Yahweh, walking in the statutes of David his father: only he sacrificed and burnt incense in the high places. (1 Ki. 3 2f.)

A slight censure is intended here, for Solomon offered also at Jerusalem "before the ark of the covenant of Yahweh," as the writer informs us (3 15), why then not always and exclusively there? The story of the dedication of the temple offered a fine chance for expansion to the author. He added an address by Solomon to the people and an extraordinarily beautiful prayer of dedication, full of the warm, appealing language and the characteristic thought of Deuteronomy (8 14-43. 52-66). In his first story of Solomon, which told of the king's prayer for wisdom at Gibeon and God's answer, the author added the condition,

And if thou wilt walk in My ways, to keep My statutes and My commandments, as thy father David did walk, then I will lengthen thy days. (1 Ki. 3 14)

He had already put this condition into the mouth of the dying David, as he gave to Solomon his last charge (2 1-12). And now it sounds like an undertone through the story of Solomon's splendor and glory.[1] It was not all glory! How could it be, for Solomon had not fulfilled the condition! Our author found the notices of the rebellions of Hadad of Edom, Rezon of Damascus, and Jeroboam of Ephraim in his sources. Clearly, if Solomon had obeyed God wholeheartedly, they would not have come, for disasters were always, according to the teaching of Deuteronomy, the result of sin. Besides, directly after Solomon's death his kingdom was split in two. What was the reason for this catastrophe? Our author had read in his sources,

King Solomon loved many foreign women, and he had 700 wives, princesses, and 300 concubines. . . . Then Solomon built a high place for Chemosh, the god of Moab, in the mount that is before Jerusalem, and for Milcom, the god of the Ammonites. (1 Ki. 11 1a.3a.7)

This gave him the clew. He elaborated it further and showed how,

---

[1] In 6 12f. it is repeated with slight modifications, and in 9 4f. also. But 6 12f. is probably a later insertion, since it was not in the Greek Version, and 9 4f. is part of the interpolation of the exilic continuator of the Book of Kings, of whom we shall still have to speak.

It came to pass, when Solomon was old, that his wives turned away his heart after other gods; and his heart was not perfect with Yahweh his God, as was the heart of David his father.

And Solomon did that which was evil in the sight of Yahweh, and went not fully after Yahweh, as did David his father.

And Yahweh was angry with Solomon, because his heart was turned away from Yahweh, the God of Israel, who had appeared to him twice, and had commanded him concerning this thing, that he should not go after other gods: but he kept not that which Yahweh commanded. Wherefore Yahweh said to Solomon, Forasmuch as this is done of thee, and thou hast not kept My covenant and My statutes, which I have commanded thee, I will surely rend the kingdom from thee, and will give it to thy servant. Notwithstanding in thy days I will not do it, for David thy father's sake: but I will rend it out of the hand of thy son. Howbeit I will not rend away all the kingdom; but I will give one tribe to thy son, for David My servant's sake, and for Jerusalem's sake which I have chosen. (1 Ki. 11 $^{4. \ 6. \ 9-13}$)

Then the rebellions of Hadad, Rezon, and Jeroboam are told, and the impression is created that they had been sent as a punishment for Solomon's apostasy in his old age, although they really belonged to the beginning of his reign as the excerpts from the sources themselves show (cf. 11 $^{21.25.27}$). This is an illustration of how history may be distorted in the interest of a theory without modifying the facts, by simply rearranging and viewing them from a doctrinal standpoint. In the story of the beginnings of the rebellion of Jeroboam the author expanded the prediction of the prophet Ahijah in his characteristic manner by supplying the reason for the division of the kingdom and inserting, as in Solomon's case, the condition for Jeroboam's permanent success (11 $^{32-39}$), filling thereby the reader's mind with mingled hope and fear, and preparing him for the worst.

The second part contains the history of Israel and of Judah (1 Ki. 12—2 Ki. 17). The order is chronological, but with this restriction that the author told the whole story of the reign of each king by itself, and not until the end was reached did he begin the story of the king or kings who had come to the throne in the other kingdom in the meantime. This is sometimes awkward, *e.g.* since Ahab of Israel came to the throne before Jehoshaphat of Judah, Ahab's whole story, in part of which Jehoshaphat was an important figure, was told before Jehoshaphat's accession to the throne was mentioned. That was reported after the story of Ahab had been completed. The histories of the two kingdoms are thus interlocked.

In order to hold the whole history together a chronological scheme was necessary. The author got his chronological information regarding the length of the reigns and the various years in which certain important things had happened from the Royal Annals. But for the whole there was as yet no era.[1] So our author connected the histories of the two kingdoms by synchronisms, in which he computed in which year of the reigning king of the one kingdom a king came upon the throne in the other. The years of the reigns he had from official sources and they are therefore reliable,[2] the synchronisms however were his own work and are not always correct.

[1] 1 Ki. 6 [1] which counted the years from the Exodus, according to which the 4th year of Solomon was the 480th after the Exodus, is quite isolated and belongs to another, later hand. Compare the Roman chronology beginning with the founding of the city of Rome.

[2] He counted the last year of the predecessor as the first year of the new king. Thus if Jehu came to the throne in 842, as we can compute from the Assyrian data, his predecessor Joram's last year was also 842. Counting 12 years of his reign, we come to 853. His brother Ahaziah reigned 2 years (854-853), both together 14 years, which, by the author's manner of figuring, are contained in 854-842, because 853 is counted twice. If we keep this in mind, we discover that the figures given in the Book of Kings are quite trustworthy. Only two mistakes have crept into the long lists, which may be corrected by assigning to Amaziah of Judah 9 years instead of 29, and to Pekah of Israel 5 years instead of 20. Then the lists are as follows. The last figure 587 corresponds really to our 586. According to the preexilic Israelite year, 587 lasted from Oct. 587 to Oct. 586. According to our reckoning the fall of Jerusalem was in Aug. 586.

ISRAEL		JUDAH	
Jeroboam (22)	932–911	Rehoboam (17)	932–915
		Abijam (3)	915–913
Nadab (2)	911–910	Asa (41)	913–873
Baasha (24)	910–887		
Elah (2)	887–886		
Zimri (7 days)	886		
Omri (12)	886–875		
Ahab (22)	875–854	Jehoshaphat (25)	873–849
Ahaziah (2)	854–853		
Joram (12)	853–842	Joram (8)	849–842
		Ahaziah (1)	842
Jehu (28)	842–815	Athaliah (7)	842–836
Jehoahaz (17)	815–799	Jehoash (40)	836–797
Joash (16)	799–784	*Amaziah (29)	797–789
Jeroboam II (41)	784–744	Azariah (52)	789–738
Zechariah ($\frac{1}{2}$)	744	Jotham coregent (12)	750–738
Shallum ($\frac{1}{12}$)	744		

At the beginning of the reign of each king the author gave an introduction containing the date of his accession, its length, and a comprehensive judgment of the king; in the case of the Judæan kings also the age of the king at his accession and often the name of his mother. Take as an example for the Judæan kings Abijam:

> Now in the eighteenth year of King Jeroboam the son of Nebat began Abijam to reign over Judah. Three years reigned he in Jerusalem: and his mother's name was Maacah the daughter of Abishalom. And he walked in all the sins of his father, which he had done before him; and his heart was not perfect with Yahweh his God, as the heart of David his father. Nevertheless for David's sake Yahweh his God gave him a lamp in Jerusalem, to set up his son after him, and to establish Jerusalem; because David did that which was right in the eyes of Yahweh, and turned not aside from anything that He commanded him all the days of his life, save only in the matter of Uriah the Hittite. (1 Ki. 15 $^{1-5}$)

Or the somewhat longer introduction of the "reformer" Asa:

> And in the twentieth year of Jeroboam king of Israel began Asa to reign over Judah. And forty and one years reigned he in Jerusalem: and his mother's name was Maacah the daughter of Abishalom. And Asa did that which was right in the eyes of Yahweh, as did David his father. And he put away the sodomites out of the land, and removed all the idols that his fathers had made. And also Maacah his mother he removed from being queen, because she had made an abominable image for Asherah; and Asa cut down her image, and burnt it at the brook Kidron. But the high places were not taken away: nevertheless the heart of Asa was perfect with Yahweh all his days. And he brought into the house of Yahweh the things that his father had dedicated, and the things that himself had dedicated, silver, and gold, and vessels. (1 Ki. 15 $^{9-15}$)

For the Israelite kings take as an example Baasha:

ISRAEL		JUDAH	
Menahem (10)	744–735	Jotham (4)	738–735
Pekahiah (2)	735–734	Ahaz (16)	735–720
*Pekah (20)	734–730		
Hosea (9)	730–722		
		Hezekiah (29)	720–692
		Manasseh (55)	692–638
		Amon (2)	638–637
		Josiah (31)	637–607
		Jehoahaz (¼)	607
		Jehoiakim (11)	607–597
		Jehoiachin (¼)	597
		Zedekiah (11)	597–587/6

In the third year of Asa king of Judah began Baasha the son of Ahijah to reign over all Israel in Tirzah, twenty and four years. And he did that which was evil in the sight of Yahweh, and walked in the way of Jeroboam, and in his sin wherewith he made Israel to sin. (1 Ki. 15 [33f.])

Or the longer introduction of the "sinful" Ahab:

And in the thirty and eighth year of Asa king of Judah began Ahab the son of Omri to reign over Israel: and Ahab the son of Omri reigned over Israel in Samaria twenty and two years. And Ahab the son of Omri did that which was evil in the sight of Yahweh above all that were before him. And it came to pass, as if it had been a light thing for him to walk in the sins of Jeroboam the son of Nebat, that he took to wife Jezebel the daughter of Ethbaal king of the Sidonians, and went and served Baal, and worshipped him. And he reared up an altar for Baal in the house of Baal, which he had built in Samaria. And Ahab made the Asherah; and Ahab did yet more to provoke Yahweh, the God of Israel, to anger than all the kings of Israel that were before him. (1 Ki. 16 [29-33])

The standard of the judgment is the deuteronomic law. The verdict is based on the king's fidelity to Yahweh and especially, in the case of an Israelite king, on whether he had worshipped the golden calves introduced by the archsinner Jeroboam I, and in the case of a Judæan king on whether he had worshipped on the high places or not. All the northern kings were condemned, and even such godly Judæan kings as Asa and Jehoshaphat, who were zealous adherents of Yahweh and exterminators of heathen cults, did not altogether escape the author's censure, because they had not removed the high places (15 [14] 22 [43]). These judgments were so stereotyped that they were applied even to a king like Zimri who reigned only 7 days (16 [19]) !

At the conclusion of each reign the author also used a regular formula, in which he referred his readers to other historical works for the study of the secular aspects of the king's reign and then stated as a rule, the place of his burial and the name of his successor, *e.g.*

And the rest of the acts of Abijam, and all that he did, are they not written in the Book of the Chronicles of the Kings of Judah? And there was war between Abijam and Jeroboam. And Abijam slept with his fathers; and they buried him in the city of David: and Asa his son reigned in his stead (1 Ki. 15 [7f.])

The work of the author is easily distinguishable from the excerpts of his sources. The account of the division of the kingdom under Rehoboam (1 Ki. 12 [1-20]) he gave entire. It is of priceless historical value. But of his own accord he added that the prophet Shemaiah sent the army of 180,000 (!) Judæans and Benjamites home, because the schism of the kingdom had been intended by Yahweh (12 [21-24]). He wove around a few facts in his sources a complete story of Jeroboam's apostasy, which is so important to him for the understanding of the whole history of the Northern Kingdom. His own work is printed in italics :

Then Jeroboam fortified Shechem in the hill-country of Ephraim, and dwelt therein ; and he went out from thence, and fortified Penuel. *And Jeroboam said in his heart, Now will the kingdom return to the house of David: if this people go up to offer sacrifices in the house of Yahweh at Jerusalem, then will the heart of this people turn again to their lord, to Rehoboam king of Judah; and they will kill me.*

Whereupon the king took counsel, and made two calves of gold; and he said unto the people, It is too much for you to go up to Jerusalem : behold thy gods, O Israel, which brought thee up out of the land of Egypt. And he set the one in Beth-el, and the other put he in Dan. *And this thing became a sin; for the people went before the one, even unto Dan. And he made houses of high places, and made priests from among all the people, that were not of the sons of Levi. And Jeroboam ordained a feast in the eighth month, on the fifteenth day of the month, like unto the feast that is in Judah, and he went up unto the altar which he had made in Bethel, to sacrifice to the calves that he had made: and he placed in Bethel the priests of the high places that he had made. And he went up to the altar which he had made in Bethel on the fifteenth day in the eighth month, even in the month which he had devised of his own heart: and he ordained a feast for the children of Israel, and went up to the altar, to burn incense.* (1 Ki. 12 [25-33])

In narrating the visit of Jeroboam's wife to the prophet Ahijah for the purpose of asking Yahweh's oracle regarding her sick son (14 [1-18]) the author put into the prophet's mouth the condemnation of Jeroboam and of Israel on account of his defection from Yahweh.[1]

The invasion of Judah by Pharaoh Shishak under Rehoboam (14 [25-28]) was to him a punishment for the religious transgressions of Judah. Here again we must distinguish the facts, derived from his sources, and his religious interpretation of them. This is necessary all the way through. The conspiracy of Baasha against Nadab and the assassination of the king and of the whole house of

---

[1] 1 Ki. 13 is a very late prophetic legend which was inserted after the exile.

Jeroboam were predicted by Ahijah as the inevitable result of
Jeroboam's sin (15 $^{25-32}$). But the new king walked in Jeroboam's
way too! And quite promptly the prophet Jehu announced to him
also that he would not be allowed to found a dynasty. His son Elah
was murdered by Zimri (15 ^{33}–15 ^{14}) who reigned but seven days
when he perished at the capture of Tirzah by Omri, also for no
other reason than that he had worshipped the golden calves! For
this he could hardly have found much time during his brief reign,
as he was besieged by Omri directly after his regicide (16 $^{15-20}$).
Of the reign of Omri, one of the greatest kings of Israel, the author
tells nothing but that he built Samaria, the famous capital of Israel,
a significant accomplishment indeed, but only one. The Moabite
king Mesha has told us in his monument that Omri conquered the
whole East Jordan country; and the Assyrians still called Israel "the
house of Omri" a hundred years after the downfall of his dynasty!
But to our author his reign yielded no illustrative material of any
value, so he passed it with his stereotyped phrases which would
never suggest Omri's importance for the history of the Northern
Kingdom. Of Ahab, his son, we know more, because the author
used here the stories of Elijah and also the prophetic source of Ahab.
He left the excerpts which he made from them practically untouched;
only Elijah's prediction of the complete extermination of his house
he expanded (21 $^{20b-26.27-29}$) and noted its fulfilment (22 ^{38}).
The Elisha stories also contained enough religious material so that
our author did not have to add anything to them. But in the Jehu
story he inserted a repetition of his prophecy to Ahab by Elijah in
the words of the young prophet who anointed Jehu as king (2 Ki.
9 $^{7-10a}$). The story of the revolution in Jerusalem under Athaliah
and the restoration of the temple under Joash (2 Ki. 11 $^{1-20}$ 12 $^{4-16}$)
was taken from the Temple Annals. For the following reigns the
author derived but little narrative material from his sources, the
defeat of Amaziah by Jehoash of Israel whom he had challenged
presumptuously (2 Ki. 14 $^{8-14}$) is the most important of them. For
Jeroboam II of Israel and Azariah of Judah there are only the usual
stereotyped phrases, and nothing of signal importance, and yet
their reigns were the most splendid after Solomon! A single hint
of this is contained in the brief reference to Jeroboam's successful
wars against Hamath and Damascus. But he who wants to know

about them may read the Book of the Acts of the Kings of Israel!
Our author had but little use for them. The story of the last two
decades of Israel, with its revolutions and regicides, was quickly told,
ever with the same punctilious introduction and conclusion and a
few extracts from the annals. In Ahaz's reign the Syro-Ephraimitic
war was described in the words of this source, while Ahaz's setting
up of a brazen altar made after the pattern of an altar in Damascus
was taken from the Temple Annals. Then the end of Israel came.
In 722 Samaria fell into the hands of the Assyrians after a siege
of three years. The people were carried into exile. Naturally
here was the point where the author could show that their sin,
especially the sin of Jeroboam, had caused this terrible disaster
(2 Ki. 17 $^{18.21-23}$).

From now on only Judah was left, and in the third part the
story from Hezekiah to Josiah is told (2 Ki. 18 ^{1}–23 ^{25a}). For
Hezekiah the writer had a longer introduction than usual, for he
regarded him as a great reformer and attributed to him the destruction of the high places, making him thus anticipate Josiah's
great reformation in 621 B.C., whether rightly or not is questionable.

He removed the high places, and broke the pillars, and cut down the Asherah: and he broke in pieces the brazen serpent that Moses had made; for
unto those days the Israelites burned incense to it; and it was called Nehush-
tan. (2 Ki. 18 ^{4})

The great invasion of Sennacherib was told in three accounts: (1)
in 18 $^{13-16}$ which came from the annals, (2) in 18 ^{17}–19 $^{8.9a.36f.}$, (3) in
19 $^{9b-35}$. It is not certain whether the second and third are accounts
of the same campaign in 701 B.C. or whether they refer to a later
campaign of Sennacherib. The stories of Hezekiah's sickness and
of the embassy of Merodachbaladan (2 Ki. 20 $^{1-19}$) were probably
taken from a biography of Isaiah, for he is the central figure in
them. Most of the story contained in 2 Ki. 18 ^{13}–20 ^{19} is also found
in the Book of Isaiah (ch. 36-39). The most valuable historical
information is always that which was derived from the annals.
Of Manasseh, who reigned for 55 long peaceful years, the author has
nothing to say except of his apostasy and his shedding much innocent blood in Jerusalem. After Amon's reign, which was soon cut
short by his assassination, his son Josiah came to the throne, the
reformer after the author's heart. Since the story was written while

Josiah was still living, we need not assume that the writer had here any written source, although it need not be excluded.

The first edition of the Book of Kings extended only to the reign of Josiah, and closed with this high encomium of the king,

And like unto him was there no king before him, that turned to Yahweh with all his heart, and with all his soul, and with all his might, according to all the law of Moses. (2 Ki. 23 [25a])

The book was intended as a piece of prophetic propaganda. By showing in the long history of Israel and Judah how only whole-hearted and exclusive loyalty to Yahweh could save the nation from disaster, the author wanted to rouse the people to a clear under-standing of their duties in order that they might avoid the terrible punishment that would surely come from Yahweh if they were not faithful to him. The reformation of Josiah had filled him with high hopes. But it turned out differently from what he had expected. Josiah's death in battle in 608 was followed by a strong reaction against the deuteronomic reformation. The end of Judah's king-dom was at hand. In 597 the first exiles, headed by King Jehoiachin himself, were carried away. In 586 the city and the temple were destroyed and the great Babylonian exile began for the people.

During the exile, about 560 or a little later, a writer took up the thread of the story where our author had left it and told of the last unhappy kings of Judah and the events connected with the fall of Jerusalem and the captivity (2 Ki. 23 [25b]–25 [30]). It was a sad ending, written in the spirit of the earlier deuteronomistic writer and in the same style which had first been fashioned by the author of the Book of Deuteronomy and then adopted by all his disciples. But this exilic continuator felt that the whole book must be revised in the light of the tragedy that had befallen Judah too. So he inserted at appropriate places references to Judah's fate. In Solomon's prayer of dedication he added a moving paragraph in which the king looked forward to the exile and implored Yahweh to forgive His people, if they repented (1 Ki. 8 [44–51]). In Yahweh's second appear-ance to Solomon he showed how Yahweh had foretold in solemn warning the fearful plight of the exile for His people, if they did not keep his commandments (9 [1–9]). In his review of the reasons which led to the fall of the Northern Kingdom (2 Ki. 17 [7–17]) he added at the end:

Also Judah kept not the commandments of Yahweh their God, but walked in the statutes of Israel which they made. And Yahweh rejected all the seed of Israel, and afflicted them, and delivered them into the hand of spoilers, until He had cast them out of His sight. (2 Ki. 17 19f.)

To the description of the sinfulness of Manasseh he supplied vivid touches and told how the prophets predicted that Jerusalem and Judah also would be completely destroyed, because they had been seduced by Manasseh to commit worse sins than the Amorites.

Therefore thus says Yahweh, the God of Israel, Behold, I bring such evil upon Jerusalem and Judah, that whosoever hears of it, both his ears shall tingle. And I will stretch over Jerusalem the line of Samaria, and the plummet of the house of Ahab; and I will wipe Jerusalem as a man wipes a dish, wiping it and turning it upside down. And I will cast off the remnant of Mine inheritance, and deliver them into the hand of their enemies; and they shall become a prey and a spoil to all their enemies; because they have done that which is evil in My sight, and have provoked Me to anger, since the day their fathers came forth out of Egypt, even unto this day. (2 Ki. 21 12-15)

The same ominous threat he inserted in Huldah's oracle (2 Ki. 22 15-20) and with it he began his continuation of the history : Josiah's reformation had averted the anger of Yahweh but for a brief time (23 25a-27). Surely, Judah as well as Israel had deserved their fearful fate ! The whole book thus became a great confession of sin. And indeed, to this penitent frame of mind the author wished to bring his people by this revised history. If only they would clearly see the spiritual causes of their national disaster and repent ! Then Yahweh might hear in heaven His dwelling place and forgive, as Solomon, according to the continuator, had prayed, and the little ray of light that had pierced the gloom in the liberation of King Jehoiachin from prison by Evil-merodach of Babylon (2 Ki. 25 27-30) might be the herald of the coming dawn, the beginning of salvation.

The history of the kingdom had thus been edited by these deuteronomistic teachers in accordance with their pragmatic view of history. But the deuteronomic theory pointed back to Moses as the first to whom the demand of the centralization of worship in one place had been revealed by Yahweh. Some deuteronomists felt therefore the need of writing the earlier history too, beginning with the time of Moses. Of course, since the temple had not been in existence before Solomon, the principle of the centralization of worship could not be used as the dominating idea in the light of which the whole history could be understood and presented. But it was only one aspect of the larger idea of wholehearted loyalty to Yahweh and exclusive worship of Him. And this larger idea became to them the master key that unlocked the true meaning of history.

For the story of Moses a summary was prepared on the basis of JE, which Moses was made to deliver as an introductory address when he gave to the people the deuteronomic law (Deut. 1–4[44]). Reviewing the events from Horeb on, he showed how the people's quarrelsomeness had been too great a burden for him alone so that he had to appoint judges to help him in his work; how the people's disobedience and lack of faith had prevented them from entering the land long ago; how they had fared with the Edomites, Moabites, and Ammonites; how they had conquered the East Jordan country; and how Yahweh was angry with Moses because of the people and would not allow him to enter the promised land. This historical survey is the basis for the exhortations to keep the law which Moses was to give to them that day.

Behold, I have taught you statutes and ordinances, even as Yahweh my God commanded me, that ye should do so in the midst of the land whither ye go in to possess it. Keep therefore and do them; for this is your wisdom and your understanding in the sight of the peoples, that shall hear all these statutes and say, Surely this great nation is a wise and understanding people. For what great nation is there, that has a god so nigh unto them, as Yahweh our God is whensoever we call upon Him? And what great nation is there, that has statutes and ordinances so righteous as all this law, which I set before you this day? (Deut. 4 [5–8])

Let them remember that Yahweh is a spiritual being, that they saw no form of Him at Mount Horeb, and that they must therefore never make an image of Him nor worship the sun, moon or stars! The nations may serve them, for Yahweh has allotted these to them, but Israel He has made His own people, and He is quite jealous of their affection. If they are not faithful, they will not long remain in the promised land, for

Yahweh will scatter you among the peoples, and ye shall be left few in number among the nations, whither Yahweh will lead you away. (Deut. 4 [27])

The exile is predicted here, and the author now adds with a strong hopefulness the beautiful promise which had such immediate application to his own time,

And there ye shall serve gods, the work of men's hands, wood and stone which neither see, nor hear, nor eat, nor smell. But from thence ye shall seek Yahweh thy God, and thou shalt find Him, when thou searchest after Him with all thy heart and with all thy soul. When thou art in tribulation, and all these things are come upon thee, in the latter days thou shalt return to Yahweh thy God, and hearken to His voice; for Yahweh thy God is a merciful God; He will not fail thee, neither destroy thee, nor forget the covenant of thy fathers which He swore to them. (Deut. 4 28–31)

No other people ever had such wonderful experiences with God as Israel,

Know therefore this day, and lay it to thy heart, that Yahweh is God in heaven above and upon the earth beneath; there is none else. And thou shalt keep His statutes, and His commandments, which I command thee this day, that it may go well with thee, and with thy children after thee, and that thou mayest prolong thy days in the land, which Yahweh thy God gives to thee for ever. (Deut. 4 39f.)

The story of Joshua and the conquest of Canaan was completely rewritten by a deuteronomist on the basis of JE, with a special predilection for E's point of view. E in contrast to J had represented the conquest of Canaan as the work of united Israel under the leadership of Joshua in two victorious campaigns which resulted in the crushing defeat of the Canaanites. This fitted exactly into the deuteronomist's view. He underscored and exaggerated the complete extermination, since it was in harmony with the law of Deuteronomy which commanded the absolute extirpation of the inhabitants of Canaan. As a hearty believer in this theory he told the story of the conquest as he thought it must have happened. Here the facts were made to conform to a preconceived theory. Dogma mastered history.

So Joshua smote all the land, the hill-country, and the South, and the low-land, and the slopes, and all their kings: he left none remaining, but he utterly destroyed all that breathed, as Yahweh, the God of Israel, commanded. And Joshua smote them from Kadeshbarnea even unto Gaza, and all the country of Goshen, even unto Gibeon. And all these kings and their land Joshua took at one time, because Yahweh, the God of Israel, fought for Israel (Josh. 10 40–42).

And all the spoil of these cities, and the cattle, the children of Israel took as a prey for themselves; but every man they smote with the edge of the sword, until they had destroyed them, neither left they any that breathed. As Yahweh commanded Moses His servant, so Moses commanded Joshua, and so did Joshua; he left nothing undone of all that Yahweh commanded Moses (Josh. 11 [14f.])

After the occupation of Canaan (Josh. 21 [43-45]) and Joshua's dismissal of the Reubenites and Gadites to their transjordanic seats with warm words of recognition and of exhortation to love Yahweh and to serve Him with all their heart and with all their soul (22 [1-6]), Joshua delivered his farewell address to the people (Josh. 23) which was patterned after E's (Josh. 24) and in which he demanded of them careful observance of the law (of Deuteronomy) and strict segregation from the heathen whom Yahweh had driven out before them, lest they become a snare to them, and Israel be quickly expelled from the country which Yahweh had given them.

For the story of the Judges the deuteronomist took his material from the older book of hero tales by JE, prefaced it with an introduction, and furnished each story with a framework in which his characteristic point of view was fully expressed. If Israel had remained wholly true to Yahweh, they would have enjoyed the full blessings of His theocratic rule. But after Joshua's death,

The Israelites did that which was evil in the sight of Yahweh, and served the Baalim; and they forsook Yahweh, the God of their fathers, who brought them out of the land of Egypt, and followed other gods, of the gods of the peoples that were round about them, and bowed down to them: and they provoked Yahweh to anger. And the anger of Yahweh was kindled against Israel, and He delivered them into the hands of the spoilers that despoiled them, and He sold them into the hands of their enemies round about, so that they could not any longer stand before their enemies. Whithersoever they went out, the hand of Yahweh was against them for evil, as Yahweh had spoken, and as Yahweh had sworn to them: and they were sore distressed. And Yahweh raised up judges, who saved them out of the hand of those that despoiled them. And when Yahweh raised them up judges, then Yahweh was with the judge, and saved them out of the hand of their enemies all the days of the judge: for it repented Yahweh because of their groaning by reason of them that oppressed and vexed them. But it came to pass, when the judge was dead, that they turned back, and dealt more corruptly than their fathers, in following other gods to serve them, and to bow down to them; they ceased not from their doings, nor from their stubborn way. (Judg. 2 [11f.14–16.18f.])

It was a constant cycle of defection, punishment, and deliverance, ever repeated. According to this principle the stories of the greater judges were retold and by an artificial chronology made to appear in historical sequence. Defection from Yahweh brought Israel so and so many years under foreign oppression, from which they were delivered by a judge, who "judged" Israel so and so many years. After his death the same rhythm of defection, oppression, and deliverance began again until the people finally demanded the monarchy from the last Judge Samuel, for this Deuteronomic Book of Judges extended to the farewell address of Samuel (1 Sam. 12) which expresses so perfectly the deuteronomist's point of view. A special framework consisting of introduction and conclusion was provided for each Judge. The story of Othniel may serve as a sample; it is entirely from the deuteronomist's pen and may contain no historical element at all beyond the name of Othniel.

And the Israelites did that which was evil in the sight of Yahweh, and forgot Yahweh their God, and served the Baalim and the Asheroth. Therefore the anger of Yahweh was kindled against Israel, and he sold them into the hand of Cushan-rishathaim king of Aram Naharaim: and the Israelites served Cushan-rishathaim eight years. And when the Israelites cried unto Yahweh, Yahweh raised up a saviour to the Israelites, who saved them, even Othniel the son of Kenaz, Caleb's younger brother. And the Spirit of Yahweh came upon him, and he judged Israel; and he went out to war, and Yahweh delivered Cushan-rishathaim king of Aram Naharaim into his hand: and his hand prevailed against Cushan-rishathaim. And the land had rest forty years. And Othniel the son of Kenaz died. (Judg. 3 [7-11])

In the following verse the next cycle begins,

And the Israelites did that which was evil in the sight of Yahweh, and Yahweh strengthened Eglon the king of Moab against Israel, because they had done that which was evil in the sight of Yahweh. (Judg. 3 [12])

In this manner the whole period is treated. One may not withhold his admiration for this solemn, impressive, and effective presentation. How grandly the conviction of the righteous and merciful God of Israel is brought out in the history of His people! And yet from an historical point of view how distorted and wrong this presentation is! It has altogether modified the actual significance of the Judges. Dogma rules again. The political and economic forces are entirely subordinated. Secondary causes are neglected. Religion is the sole cause of all: God is jealously watching over the fidelity of His people and punishes or delivers in accordance with Israel's behavior. Moreover, everything is magnified to national proportions. The sufferings affect the entire nation, the Judges are deliverers of the whole people and theocratic rulers of all Israel.

while in reality they had been local and tribal heroes. Their chronology had not been given in the older sources, but now they are brought into the rhythm of defection and punishment, repentance and deliverance in an artificial scheme of chronology which is controlled by the underlying idea that the period from the Exodus to the building of the temple, that central event of history according to the deuteronomist, was 480 years or 12 generations of 40 years each. For the single figures the number 40 and its component parts are important. It shows the striving of the author after a systematic presentation of history, by which the whole could be grasped more easily, and it must be evaluated as such and not simply be condemned.

Some of the stories in the older book the deuteronomist could not use: the summary of the conquest of Canaan with its special references to parts not conquered (Judg. 1 1–2 5), because it differed from his deuteronomistic view; the stories of Micah and the Danites (Judg. 17f.) and of the outrage at Gibeah (Judg. 19–21), because they contained no "Judge," and were therefore unsuitable for his purpose; also the brief references to the minor Judges, and the story of Abimelech whose character unfitted him for a place among the Judges, and perhaps the concluding chapter of the Samson stories (Judg. 16). Fortunately the older book still persisted, and later, after the Babylonian exile, someone reinserted the omitted parts in the book. But the deuteronomistic point of view about this period prevailed and has dominated the ideas of all the centuries down to our own.

The story of Samuel was part of the Book of Judges and traces of the particular framework of the Judges appear in it too. It did not need much redaction, because in the combined story the Ephraimitic source had already pointed out the great lessons of theocratic religion in which the deuteronomist was interested. The one important addition is the modification of the prophecy in 1 Sam. 2 27–36 which originally predicted that Samuel would be chosen in Eli's place. The editor made it into a prediction of Zadok's sole legitimate priesthood (cf. 1 Ki. 2 26f.) and foretold the time after the deuteronomic reformation when the country priests had lost their positions and came as suppliants to Jerusalem:

And I will raise Me a faithful priest, that shall do according to that which is in My heart and in My mind: and I will build him a sure house; and he shall walk before Mine anointed for ever.   And it shall come to pass, that every one that is left in thy house shall come and bow down to him for a piece of silver and a loaf of bread, and shall say, Put me, I pray thee, into one of the priests' offices, that I may eat a morsel of bread. (1 Sam. 2 35f.)

Thus modified the prophecy became of great importance for the deuteronomist view of history.   The superiority of the Zadokite priesthood at Jerusalem had been predicted so long ago!

The story of Saul and of David shows few traces of deuteronomist influence.   But one insertion became of the greatest significance: in the prophecy of Nathan in which David was told, in reply to his intention to build a house for Yahweh, that He had always dwelt in a tent since the days of the Exodus and that He had never commanded that a temple be built for Him, but that he would build a house (a dynasty) for David,

When thy days are fulfilled, and thou shalt sleep with thy fathers, I will set up thy seed after thee, that shall proceed out of thy bowels, and I will establish his kingdom. (2 Sam. 7 12)

Here the deuteronomist interpolated:

He (i.e. this son) shall build a house for My name, and I will establish the throne of his kingdom forever. (2 Sam. 7 13)

With this single sentence, more precisely with the first half of it, the divine sanction of the temple at Jerusalem was expressly given in an oracle by a prophet of Yahweh.   Deuteronomy had never mentioned Jerusalem as the particular place which Yahweh had "chosen to cause His name to dwell there."   But now Yahweh had definitely said, "He shall build a house for My name."   This referred, as every child knew, to Solomon and his temple in Jerusalem.   An irrefragable basis was thus given to the deuteronomic claim of Jerusalem's sole sanctity.   Yahweh Himself had provided it in this oracle.

Several of the older Saul and David stories were not to the taste of the editor, the story of the rejection of Saul containing Samuel's sacrifice of Agag (1 Sam. 15); the story of Saul's visit to the witch at Endor (1 Sam. 28 3-25); and especially the extremely valuable series of court stories in 2 Sam. 9–20 which did not seem to David's credit.   For the first and last he prepared summaries which should take their places (1 Sam. 14 47-51 2 Sam. 8).   The second he simply omitted. But fortunately, they were all later on reinserted; they were far too precious to be lost.

When the deuteronomistic history was complete it spanned the period from the Exodus to the Babylonian exile. Many writers had been working on this new edition of Israel's history, but all wrote from the same point of view, with the same purpose, and in the same style. Their history was pragmatic, dominated by religious convictions. Their interest was not historical but religious. History was to them but the great textbook which illustrated the truths of religion.

Magnificent as the new work was in many ways, it could not dislodge the older books of J and E in the affection of the people, for they had become not only dear to them by long use, but they were invested with a certain authority. Besides, they carried the history back to the patriarchs, yea even to the creation. It was therefore finally decided to combine the deuteronomic work with JE. For the Pentateuch the need was first felt, and the law book was inserted in the place where apparently the older Law Book of the Covenant had stood before. The latter was then placed in the Sinai context where it now is (Ex 20 24–23). It is quite significant that aside from Deuteronomy it is here in the Pentateuch that we find the only important deuteronomistic traces.[1] Only later the combination of the rest of the deuteronomistic work with the older books of Joshua, Judges, and Samuel was regarded as necessary.

[1] Ex. 20 22f. 22 21b. 22. 24. 25b. 31 23 4. 5. 9a. 11b. 12b. 13a. 20–23 34 10–17. 24.

CHAPTER XVI

THE EARLIER POSTEXILIC PROPHETS

WHEN after the fall of Babylon a company of Jewish exiles returned to Judah, nothing but disappointment awaited them. None of the glorious events predicted by Deutero-Isaiah had come true on their homeward march. And in Judah itself a weary struggle for existence resulted. Few in number and poor in means, they found it hard to cope with the difficulties. Drought and failure of the crops aggravated their distress, till finally, disillusioned and disappointed, they were in danger of losing their faith in Yahweh. He had not returned to them, He was still angry with them; there was no hope. Then a man of plain speech but of much practical sense and enthusiasm roused their religious faith by summoning them to work for the Lord. Haggai, the prophet, agreed with the people that Yahweh had not come back to Jerusalem, but maintained that it was their own fault. For how could He dwell among His people, if they provided no home for Him? They had built their own houses, but the house of God was still in ruins. Yahweh had sent the hard seasons in order to bring them to their senses. But so far they had not understood God's purpose. Let them but build the temple and all will be changed. Haggai's appeal, made on the first day of the sixth month of the second year of Darius (520 B.C.) met with instant response. Headed by Zerubbabel the governor and Joshua the high priest, the people began the work at once (1 $^{2-12.14}$). On the twenty-fourth day of the same month (our September) the foundation was laid, and Haggai fired the people again with his speech; let them but mark this day well, it is the turning point in their fate; from this day Yahweh will bless them (1 $^{15.13}$ 2 $^{15-19}$). Four weeks later, when it appeared that the building would be poor in comparison with the splendid temple of Solomon, Haggai met the discouragement with some brave words of hope (2 $^{1-9}$): Yahweh is with us, and that is after all more important than anything else. Never fear, He will provide for the beauty and splendor of the temple Himself.

For thus says Yahweh of hosts: Yet a little while, and I will shake the heavens, and the earth, and the sea, and the dry land; and I will shake all nations; and the precious things of all nations shall come; and I will fill this house with glory, says Yahweh of hosts. The silver is Mine, and the gold is Mine, says Yahweh of hosts. The latter glory of this house shall be greater than the former, says Yahweh of hosts; and in this place will I give peace, says Yahweh of hosts. (Hag. 2 $^{6-9}$)

It may be that the news of the great revolution in the north and east of the Persian empire, which shook its very foundations, had come to Jerusalem and awakened the hope that Yahweh would shake the nations again and compel them to bring immense tribute into His temple.

Thus encouraged, the people worked on and did so well that two months later, on the twenty-fourth day of the ninth month (December, 520) the Samaritans asked permission to join them in building the temple. But Haggai, fearing that this "unclean" element would contaminate the new temple, strongly opposed their request. He insisted that contact with holiness could not sanctify the unclean, but contact with uncleanness infallibly defiled.

So is this people, and so is this nation before Me, says Yahweh; and so is every work of their hands, and where they come near, it is unclean. (Hag. 2 $^{10-14}$)

That Haggai carried his point, we know from Ezra 4 $^{1-4}$. On the same day he prophesied to Zerubbabel, who was of Davidic descent, perhaps out of gratitude for his aid in this matter, which had convinced Haggai that he was worthy of becoming king of Judah.

Speak to Zerubbabel, governor of Judah, saying, I will shake the heavens and the earth; and I will overthrow the throne of kingdoms; and I will destroy the strength of the kingdoms of the nations; and I will overthrow the chariots, and those that ride in them; and the horses and their riders shall come down, every one by the sword of his brother. In that day, says Yahweh of hosts, will I take thee, O Zerubbabel, My servant, the son of Shealtiel, says Yahweh, and will make thee as a signet; for I have chosen thee, says Yahweh of hosts. (Hag. 2 $^{21-23}$)

Haggai was strongly influenced by Ezekiel in his view of the importance of the temple for the new community and his fear of its profanation by foreigners, and like him he combined priestly and prophetic interests. He was no great prophet, but by his practical initiative he rendered a genuine service to his people. His eagerness and enthusiasm are still refreshing.

His book was probably put together by one of his disciples. Like Ezekiel's it is in prose and its sections are carefully dated by the day, month, and year. It is small and simple, without any passage of power and beauty. But for the history of the time it is of the highest value. There is a small dislocation in our present text, for 2 $^{15-19}$ originally followed I $^{15.13}$.

Haggai had begun his work on the first day of the sixth month of the year 520. Two months later, on the first of the eighth month, Zechariah joined him and called the people to repentance. He reiterated the message of the former prophets from whom he had learned and on whom he consciously depended in his thought and speech. We cannot help feeling that the conspicuously frequent repetition of "says Yahweh" (it occurs, *e.g.*, five times in two verses I $^{3f.}$) suggests that he lacked the strong spiritual authentication of his prophethood and the invincible certitude that had dominated the minds of the great prophets before him. And we find it not strange, in view of this, that he encountered much doubt and disbelief regarding his mission. Four times he felt the need of appealing to the fulfilment of his predictions for his vindication, "and ye shall know that Yahweh of hosts has sent me to you" (2 $^{9.11}$ 4 ^{9} 6 ^{15}). And so it would almost seem as if the remarkable series of visions which distinguish him among the prophets, were in reality not visions but allegories in which he tried to make his message more interesting and convincing to the people. But that would probably go too far. We need not doubt that Zechariah actually saw in the night of the twenty-fourth day of the eleventh month of the same year (February, 519, according to our reckoning) eight visions in which the pressing problems of his day were solved in a remarkable manner. In the first vision (I $^{7-17}$) he saw the heavenly patrol guard, who on their swift horses had traversed the earth that day, and heard them report to their superior, the angel of Yahweh,

We have gone to and fro through the earth, and behold, all the earth sits still and is at rest.

The mighty political revolutions that had been stirring the Persian empire and from which Haggai had hoped so much, had all been put down. Another hope was destroyed. And the angel of Yahweh, who had Israel's fate at heart, voiced the great disappointment in his plea,

O Yahweh of hosts, how long will Thou not have mercy on Jerusalem and on the cities of Judah, against which Thou hast had indignation these seventy years?

Yahweh replied with "comforting words" to the angel who acted as Zechariah's guide and interpreter in these visions, and he in turn told him,

Cry thou, saying, Thus says Yahweh of hosts: I am jealous for Jerusalem and for Zion with a great jealousy. And I am very sore displeased with the nations that are at ease; for I was but a little displeased, and they helped forward the affliction. Therefore thus says Yahweh: I am returned to Jerusalem with mercies; My house shall be built in it, says Yahweh of hosts, and a line shall be stretched forth over Jerusalem. Cry yet again, saying, Thus says Yahweh of hosts: My cities shall yet overflow with prosperity; and Yahweh shall yet comfort Zion, and shall yet choose Jerusalem. (Zech. 1 14-17)

In the second vision (1 18-21) he saw four horns and four smiths. The angel interpreted the horns as symbols of the enemy nations and the smiths as their executioners. The prophet was sure that Yahweh's purpose of punishing the nations, which was an indispensable prerequisite of the coming age of glory, would be carried out. As far as he could see, there was no human power that Yahweh was using. But He does not depend on human forces, He sends His heavenly ministers to execute His will. We come here upon a characteristic trait of the apocalyptic seer in contradistinction from the prophet: lacking the great historical agents on earth, he unveils the secrets of heaven and shows the activity of the angelic beings in the great movements on earth. To enhance the mystery and impressiveness of the revelation the apocalyptic writer uses allegory as a favorite means of presentation.

In the third vision (2 1-13) an angelic surveyor went forth to measure the area on which Jerusalem should be rebuilt and to mark the line of the wall. He was young, not initiated into the counsel of God. The interpreting angel told therefore another angel,

Run, speak to this young man, saying, Jerusalem shall be inhabited as villages without walls, by reason of the multitude of men and cattle therein. For I, says Yahweh, will be to her a wall of fire round about, and I will be the glory in her midst. (Zech. 2 4f.)

Any movement of refortifying Jerusalem by building a strong city wall is frowned upon here, but not avowedly for political reasons, although the prophet must have known that the Persians would not have tolerated it. To him Yahweh's own protection was more than enough and besides, he looked forward to a large increase of the population which at present was so small and so poor. He therefore called upon the exiles that were still in the land of the north to flee and come home with the wealth of the nations, for Yahweh had sent His angel "after glory" (*i.e.* riches) "to the nations which plundered you." None will dare to hinder you, "for he that touches you, touches the apple of His eye." Afterward many nations will join themselves to Yahweh, when he dwells among His people in Zion.

In the fourth vision (3 ¹⁻⁸ 4 ⁶ᵇ⁻¹⁰ᵃ 3 ⁹ᶠ·) Joshua the high priest stood before the angel of Yahweh in the soiled garments of an accused person. At his right was his accuser, the Satan, a heavenly being, who, according to the prologue of the Book of Job, went all over the earth to spy on people and make complaint to Yahweh about their sins. Here he accused Joshua and with him the people, whose representative the high priest was. But the angel of Yahweh would not listen to him, for were they not like "a brand plucked out of the fire," had they not but just escaped from captivity? He therefore ordered that Joshua's soiled garments be taken off and fresh ones be put on him as a sign that the sins had been forgiven. Then he had a clean turban put on his head, and told him that if he would faithfully discharge the duties of his office, he would always have access to the heavenly court, as mediator between Yahweh and His people. Moreover, Joshua and his fellow-priests were a sign that the restoration would surely be carried out: they would minister in the new sanctuary. In confirmation of this he placed the beautiful topstone which should crown the temple at its completion before Joshua. Then the sin of the land would be removed by Yahweh and the golden time would break.

In a passage which has accidentally been displaced (4 ⁶ᵇ⁻¹⁰ᵃ) the significance of the "sign" is made clearer. Great difficulties had arisen which threatened to hinder the completion of the temple. From Ezra 4 we know of the enmity of the Samaritans; from Ezra 5 of the interference of the Persian satrap Tattenai. Was the work after all to be frustrated? The Jews already talked of resorting to force. But the prophet, who had opposed the refortification of Jerusalem before, replied,

This is the word of Yahweh to Zerubbabel, saying, Not by might nor by power, but by My Spirit, says Yahweh of hosts. Who art thou, O great mountain? before Zerubbabel a plain; and he shall bring forth the top stone with shoutings of Grace, grace to it. The hands of Zerubbabel have laid the foundation of this house; his hands shall also finish it; and ye shall know that Yahweh of hosts has sent me to you. For he that has despised the day of small things shall rejoice, and shall see the plummet in the hand of Zerubbabel. (Zech. 4 $^{6b-10a}$)

After this vision Zechariah fell asleep. But the angel came again and waked him to show him four other visions. In the fifth vision (4 $^{1-6a.\ 10b-14}$) he saw a golden candlestick with seven lamps and beside it two olive-trees. The angel explained the seven lamps [1] as "the eyes of Yahweh, which run to and fro through the whole earth," and the two olive-trees as "the two anointed ones, that stand by the Lord of the whole earth," the representatives of the political and of the religious government. This meant that the new community was to be a theocracy, with the king and the high priest as the agents of the real Ruler in heaven.

In the sixth vision (5 $^{1-4}$) Zechariah saw how the thieves and perjurers among the people were to be exterminated by a terrible curse which was written on a huge flying roll. Its magic power would destroy them all and, besides, it would enter into the house of every one of them and utterly demolish it. What a queer means, to our minds, of getting rid of criminals! To the ancients it was by no means strange, for they believed in the magic efficacy of the curse.

In the seventh vision (5 $^{5-11}$) the very principle of wickedness was removed from the country. The prophet saw how a woman was thrust into a large container which was then closed by a leaden lid, and how two other women with the wings of a stork carried her through the air to Babylonia, where she belonged and where she could carry on her wickedness. She had no place in the new community in Judah!

In the eighth vision (6 $^{1-8}$) the prophet saw the heavenly patrol-guard riding forth on the work of the new day that had dawned.

---

[1] After omitting the Zerubbabel oracle, which does not belong here, the connection between v. ^{6} and v. ^{10} is as follows, "Then he answered and spoke to me, saying, These seven are the eyes of Yahweh," etc.

After a while the angel interpreter shouted the welcome news to him, "behold, they that go toward the north country have placed My Spirit in the north country." There among the Jewish exiles in Babylonia (cf. 2 ⁶) the Divine Spirit was at work, arousing their love for their homeland.

As a direct evidence of this Zechariah was commanded by Yahweh on the same day to go to the house of a certain Josiah and receive there gold and silver from some Jews who had just come from Babylonia, and to make a crown. This he should place on Zerubbabel's head, for

He shall build the temple of Yahweh and bear the glory and shall sit and rule upon his throne, and Joshua shall be priest at his right hand, and the counsel of peace shall be between them both.

The crown should be preserved in the temple as a memorial of the donors. Others also would come and aid in the building of the temple (6 ⁹⁻¹⁵). Like Haggai, Zechariah was sure that Zerubbabel was ordained to be king. But he believed also that the high priest should be his peer, on the same level of authority, representing the religious side of the theocracy. As far as Zerubbabel was concerned, this dream was never fulfilled. What happened to him personally we do not know. Whether he was removed by the Persians, who had learned of this movement, whether he was executed, we cannot tell. But the Persians never appointed another Davidic governor of Judah. The high priest became the sole native ruler. Somebody, mindful of this, changed the crown of Zerubbabel to crowns for Joshua, and the clause, "and Joshua shall be priest at his right hand" into "and he shall be a priest upon his throne," so that our present Hebrew text is a prophecy of the rule of the high priest! Fortunately, the "correction" was not consistent and left some tell-tale marks, and the Greek translation was made from a manuscript, which had not yet corrected the prophecy in order to make it conform to history.[1]

On the fourth day of the ninth month of the fourth year of Darius (February, 518), an inquiry was made of the priests and the

[1] A similar correction was made in a prophecy of the Messianic King, which comes most probably from this time and is now preserved in Jer. 23 ⁵ᶠ· and 33 ¹⁵⁻¹⁸. It predicted the righteous "Branch," who should reign as king:

Behold, the days come, says Yahweh, that I will raise unto David a righteous Branch, and he shall reign as king and deal wisely, and shall execute justice and prophets whether the fast-day that commemorated the destruction of the temple should still be kept. To this Zechariah replied that the people had not fasted for Yahweh's benefit on that day or on the day that commemorated the murder of Gedaliah either. Yahweh was interested not in fasting but in social justice, as the former prophets had preached. The fathers' refusal to listen to them had brought the judgment upon them. Yahweh was now intensely in earnest about Zion's restoration, and desired that Jerusalem should become "the city of truth" and the temple hill "the holy mountain." He was going to repeople the city with returning exiles so that old men and women and young boys and girls should fill the streets with their gracious presence and their joyful mirth. This would all come when the temple was completed. Let the people work diligently on its reconstruction, and they will experience Yahweh's favor in rich harvests. Let them be truthful and peaceable, and abstain from fraud, theft, and perjury. They may be sure that these fast-days, and the others too that commemorated the beginning of the siege of Jerusalem and the day of its capture, will be turned into festivals of joy. And moreover,

Thus says Yahweh of hosts: It shall yet come to pass, that there shall come peoples, and the inhabitants of great cities; and the inhabitants of one city shall go to another, saying, Let us go speedily to entreat the favor of Yahweh, and to seek Yahweh of hosts: I will go also. Yea, many peoples and strong nations shall come to seek Yahweh of hosts in Jerusalem, and to entreat the favor of Yahweh. Thus says Yahweh of hosts: In those days it shall come to pass, that ten men shall take hold, out of all the languages of the nations, they shall take hold of the skirt of him that is a Jew, saying, We will go with you, for we have heard that God is with you. (Zech. 8 [20-22])

Only the first eight chapters of the Book of Zechariah come from this prophet. The rest is later. That which distinguishes him among the prophets is his series of visions. Here we discover his originality, for they are really a little apocalypse. Zechariah was

righteousness in the land. In his days Judah shall be saved, and Israel shall dwell safely; and this is his name whereby he shall be called: Yahweh our righteousness. (Jer. 23 [5f.] 33 [15f.])

To this was later added in Jer. 33 [17f.],

For thus says Yahweh: David shall never want a man to sit upon the throne of the house of Israel; neither shall the priests the Levites want a man before Me to offer burnt-offerings, and to burn meal-offerings, and to do sacrifice continually.

And this was solemnly elaborated in the next verses 33 [19-22].

one of the first apocalyptic writers, although not the first, foı Ezekiel preceded him in this also. His great dependence on his predecessors, his fusion of priestly and prophetic interests, his love of allegory, his belief in magic, all show that he was not a great prophet, but he is most interesting for all that. His writings are in prose and, the visions excepted, not in remarkable prose. Like Ezekiel and Haggai, he dated the various sections of his book most carefully. The fact that it was put among the canonical books later on shows that the people had actually come to believe "that Yahweh of hosts had sent" him.

Haggai and Zechariah had worked hard for the rebuilding of the temple in order that Yahweh might have a home among His people. But were they right in this? Not everybody believed so. A prophet of deep spiritual insight whose work is preserved in Isaiah 56 ^{9}–58 ^{12} 59 $^{1-15a}$ 65 $^{1-16}$ 66 $^{1-6.15-18a.24}$ declared, quite in the spirit of the greatest of the earlier prophets,

> Thus says Yahweh, "Heaven is My throne,
>   and the earth is My footstool.
> What manner of a house will ye build unto Me?
>   and what place shall be My rest?
> For all these My hand made,
>   and so they all came to be, says Yahweh.
> But to this man will I look, to him that is poor
>   and of a contrite spirit, and that trembles at My word.
> He that kills an ox is as he that slays a man.
>   he that sacrifices a lamb as he that breaks a dog's neck,
> He that offers an oblation as he that offers swine's blood,
>   he that burns incense as he that blesses an idol!" (Isa. 66 $^{1-3a}$)

You must prepare a house for Yahweh indeed, but not a temple made with hands. Prepare your hearts for Him, for He makes His home with people of contrite and humble spirit. The whole sacrificial system is worse than useless. Only obedience to His will can prevent the coming of the calamities you fear. This bold word may have earned the prophet much enmity and hate. For Haggai and Zechariah had persuaded the leaders and the people to their views. But our prophet also had adherents, who "trembled at His word." They were abused, yea even excommunicated! But he encouraged them,

Hear the word of Yahweh, ye that tremble at His word:
Your brethren that hate you have said,
   they that cast you out for My name's sake,
" Let Yahweh be glorified,
   that we may see your joy."
But it is they that shall be put to shame! (Isa. 66 [5])

The prophet could not prevent the building of the temple. But he did not give up his prophetic mission after it was built. Like Micah of old he had heard the divine call,

Cry aloud, spare not,
   lift up thy voice like a trumpet,
And declare unto My people their transgression,
   and to the house of Jacob their sins. (Isa. 58 [1])

And he did. He told them that Yahweh was anxious to come to His people, but they must prepare the way and remove all obstacles,

For thus says the high and lofty One,
   that inhabits eternity, whose name is Holy:
"I dwell in the high and holy place,
   and with him that is of a contrite and humble spirit,
To revive the spirit of the humble,
   and to revive the heart of the contrite." (Isa. 57 [15])

But for the wicked there is no peace (57 [14ff.]). Let the people not say that Yahweh is either unable or unwilling to help them, for it is nothing but their moral corruption that prevents Him.

For your hands are defiled with blood,
   and your fingers with iniquity;
Your lips have spoken lies,
   your tongue mutters wickedness.

Therefore is justice far from us,
   neither does righteousness overtake us:
We look for light, but behold darkness,
   for brightness but we walk in obscurity, etc. (Isa. 59 [1-15])

Their social iniquity went hand in hand with much zeal for worship and external ordinances, especially fasting. On the very fast-days they fought and quarrelled and exacted work from their laborers.

Is such the fast that I have chosen?
   the day for a man to afflict his soul?
Is it to bow down his head as a rush,
   and to spread sackcloth and ashes under him?
Wilt thou call this a fast,
   and an acceptable day to Yahweh?

Is not this the fast that I have chosen:
  to loose the bonds of wickedness,
  to undo the bands of the yoke,
To let the oppressed go free,
  and that ye break every yoke?
Is it not to deal thy bread to the hungry,
  and that thou bring the poor that are cast out to thy house?
When thou seekest the naked, that thou cover him,
  and that thou hide not thyself from thine own flesh?

Then shall thy light go forth as the morning,
  and thy healing shall spring forth speedily;
And thy righteousness shall go before thee,
  the glory of Yahweh shall be thy rearward.
Then shalt thou call and Yahweh will answer;
  thou shalt cry, and He will say, "Here I am!" (Isa. 58 $^{5-9a}$)

The spirit of the old prophets was still living, for this is prophetic religion. If the people will but do away with oppression, perjury, and lying, if they will but show mercy and kindness, the great and wonderful restoration will surely be accomplished. But only then!

The prophet knew that the leaders were largely responsible for the poor condition of the people. They should have been its spiritual guides, but they were so negligent and selfish that they had lost all spiritual discernment and did not see the dangers that invaded the community (56 ^{9}–57 ^{2}). There was a party, against whom these leaders did not take strict measures; they were addicted to rank religious apostasy and practised all the abominable rites of the ancient nature, Moloch, and mystery cults. The prophet had no hope for them. It seemed useless to him to call these people to repentance. They would be exterminated. He heard in his spirit the fearful tumult in the temple, Yahweh was about to destroy them with fire and sword (Isa. 66 $^{6.15-18a.24}$).

This prophet interpreted so clearly the essential spirit of moral religion that we hesitate to attribute to him two sections which are now closely connected with his work (Isa. 56 $^{1-8}$ 58 $^{13f.}$). Of course, after the temple had been built, he may have accepted the inevitable and may have laid his principal emphasis on the ethicizing and spiritualizing of the religious system; and it is true that the spirit of catholicity which pervades Isaiah 56 $^{1-8}$ is akin to his. We saw in Haggai the tendency of exclusiveness toward any persons who

might profane the sanctuary.   It was the spirit of Ezekiel that
grew stronger all the time.   The holiness of the people, which was
an imperative condition for Yahweh's return, could be maintained
only by excluding all foreigners and all eunuchs from the temple.
The prophet who wrote Isaiah 56 [1-8] protested strongly against
this narrow attitude.   There is no reason whatever to exclude
these eunuchs and these foreigners, if they fulfil the fundamental
obligations of the religion of Yahweh, for fellowship with God is
not a matter of blood or of bodily perfection.   If the eunuchs keep
the moral law, observe the Sabbath, and hold fast the covenant,

> I will give to them in My house
>   and within My walls a memorial and a name
> Better than of sons and of daughters,
>   I will give to them an everlasting name,
>   that shall not be cut off.

And "the foreigners that join themselves to Yahweh, to minister to
Him, and to love the name of Yahweh to be His servants" and that
observe those three basic requirements,

> I will bring them to My holy mountain,
>   and make them joyful in My house of prayer :
> Their burnt-offerings and their sacrifices
>   shall be accepted upon Mine altar ;
> For My house shall be called
>   a house of prayer for all peoples. (Isa. 56 [1-8])

The strong emphasis on the Sabbath is striking.   During the exile
it had become one of the distinguishing signs of Judaism.   Ezekiel
already had said, "Moreover also I gave them My Sabbaths, to be
a sign between Me and them, that they might know that I am
Yahweh that sanctifies them" (Ezek. 20 [12]).   In Isaiah 58 [13f.] keeping
the Sabbath by cessation from work and pleasure and idle talk, in
hearty conformity with the spirit of the sacred day, is declared to be
one of the conditions of the future greatness of Israel.   A believer
in the blessings of true Sabbath observance for the nation inserted
a long passage in the Book of Jeremiah (17 [19-27]).   All of these
authors were living in the period when the priestly writer celebrated
the Sabbath as the crown of creation in Gen. 2 [1-3] (cf. ch. XVII).

Now all of a sudden we seem to hear Deutero-Isaiah's voice
again, sweet and melodious, full of joy and comfort, charming the

hearer by its beauty. But it was not himself but one of his disciples who had caught the master's style and melody, though not his highest ideas. We may call him the Third or Trito-Isaiah, although this name has usually been applied to the whole of Isaiah 56–66, and not only to Isaiah 59 [15b]–63 [6] 65 [17–25] 66 [7–14.18b–23], because it was thought that only one prophet was responsible for all those chapters. He felt that he was sent on the same mission as his master, to comfort the people and to inspire them with faith in the coming of the glorious restoration. In a passage that Jesus later on could use with reference to himself he expressed the consciousness of his prophetic mission.

> The Spirit of the Lord Yahweh is upon me,
>   because Yahweh has anointed me;
> To preach good tidings to the meek, He has sent me,
>   to bind up the broken-hearted,
> To proclaim liberty to the captives,
>   and the opening of the prison to them that are bound;
> To proclaim the year of Yahweh's favor,
>   and the day of vengeance of our God;
> To comfort all that mourn,
>   to appoint to them that mourn in Zion,
>   to give to them a garland for ashes,
> The oil of joy for mourning,
>   the garment of praise for the spirit of heaviness;
> That they may be called trees of righteousness,
>   the planting of Yahweh, that He may be glorified. (Isa. 61 [1–3])

He was sent to a disheartened people, who felt still forsaken by Yahweh (62 [4]), for though the temple had been erected, it was a poor house without splendor and glory, and Yahweh had not taken up His abode in it. Jerusalem and the cities of Judah were not yet built up, the walls were still in ruins, and only a few people lived there. Trito-Isaiah faced this condition and voiced the wonderful hope of Deutero-Isaiah in words almost as beautiful as those of his master.

> Arise, shine, for thy light is come,
>   and the glory of Yahweh is risen upon thee.
> For, behold, darkness shall cover the earth,
>   and gross darkness the peoples;

> But Yahweh will arise upon thee,
>   and His glory shall be seen over thee.
> And the nations shall come to thy light,
>   and kings to the brightness of thy rising. (Isa. 60 [1-3])

Let Jerusalem but look up, great caravans are coming, bringing back her exiled children and untold treasures, the wealth of the nations. From everywhere they come with silver and gold, frank-incense and flocks for the temple of Yahweh, which will be glorified thereby. Full of ecstasy Trito-Isaiah foresees the time when foreigners shall build up Jerusalem's walls and kings shall minister to her.

> Thy gates also shall be open continually,
>   they shall not be shut day or night,
> That men may bring unto thee the wealth of the nations,
>   and their kings led captive. (60 [11])

> And the sons of them that afflicted thee
>   shall come bending unto thee,
> And all they that despised thee
>   shall bow themselves down at the soles of thy feet. (Isa. 60 [14])

Jerusalem will be the mistress of the peoples. Any nation that will not obey her will be destroyed (60 [12]). Not only will foreigners build up the ruined cities, but

> Strangers shall stand and feed your flocks,
>   and foreigners shall be your ploughmen and your vine-dressers.
> But ye shall be named the priests of Yahweh;
>   men shall call you the ministers of our God. (Isa. 61 [5f.])

How the thought of lordship fills this prophet's mind! There is never a thought of Israel's servantship as with Deutero-Isaiah, nor does the idea of the priesthood of Israel imply spiritual mediatorship; it is only another way of expressing the lordship of these gentlemen priests. Trito-Isaiah missed the highest glory of his ideal. Nevertheless not only this external splendor, wealth, fertility, and lordship, but also moral and spiritual glory will crown the golden age of Zion.

> I will also make thy officers peace,
>   and thine exactors righteousness.
> Violence shall no more be heard in thy land,
>   desolation nor destruction within thy borders;

> But thou shalt call thy walls Salvation,
>> and thy gates Praise.
> The sun shall be no more thy light by day,
>> neither for brightness shall the moon give light to thee,
> But Yahweh will be to thee an everlasting light,
>> and thy God thy glory.
> The sun shall no more go down,
>> neither shall the moon withdraw itself,
> For Yahweh will be thine everlasting light,
>> and the days of thy mourning shall be ended.
> Thy people also shall all be righteous,
>> they shall inherit the land forever,
> The branch of My planting,
>> the work of My hands, that I may be glorified.
> The little one shall become a thousand,
>> and the small one a strong nation,
> I, Yahweh, will hasten it in its time. (Isa. 60 $^{17-22}$)

The prophet was full of eager anticipation. He was constantly interceding with Yahweh in passionate prayer to perform His act of restoration.

> For Zion's sake will I not hold my peace,
>> and for Jerusalem's sake I will not rest. (Isa. 62 ^{1})

> I have set watchmen
>> upon thy walls, O Jerusalem,
> They shall never hold their peace
>> day and night.
> Ye that are Yahweh's remembrancers,
>> take ye no rest,
> And give Him no rest,
>> until He establish,
> And till He make Jerusalem
>> a praise in the earth. (Isa. 62 $^{6f.}$)

But he knew that the prerequisite for the political restoration and glorification of Jerusalem was the collapse of the heathen powers. And thus he announced that Yahweh Himself would intervene against His enemies. The great upheavals in the Persian empire had passed. There was no one like Cyrus who could be Yahweh's agent in His final judgment of the nations. So Trito-Isaiah showed in splendid imagery, how Yahweh Himself put on His armor for the battle with His foes (Isa. 59 $^{15b-21}$), and in a dramatic poem of great splendor and power he described Yahweh's return from the judgment.

> Who is this that comes stained red,
>   with garments dyed redder than a grape-gatherer's?
> Who is this that is glorious in his apparel,
>   marching in the greatness of his strength?
> "I that speak in righteousness,
>   mighty to save."
> Wherefore art Thou red in Thine apparel,
>   and Thy garments like his that treads in the vinevat?
> "I have trodden the winepress alone;
>   and of the peoples there was no man with Me:
> Yea, I trod them in Mine anger,
>   and trampled them in My wrath,
> And their lifeblood is sprinkled upon My garments,
>   and I have stained all My raiment.
> For the day of vengeance was in My heart,
>   and the year of My redeemed is come.
> And I looked, and there was none to help,
>   and I wondered that there was none to uphold.
> Therefore Mine own arm brought salvation to Me.
>   and My wrath, it upheld Me.
> And I trod down the peoples in Mine anger,
>   and made them drunk in My wrath,
> And poured out their lifeblood on the earth." (Isa. 63 [1-6])

Yahweh's terrible judgment on the nations now forms the prelude and the postlude of Trito-Isaiah's poems. Two other poems of his describing the glory of the future are now placed in Isa. 65 [17-25] 66 [7-14. 18-23], while the beautiful exilic prayers of Isa. 63 [7]-64 [12] are appended to the main stock of poems, most appropriately indeed, for they still had their profound meaning for this later time. In Isa. 65 [17ff.] the creation of a new earth and a new heaven is foretold. The significant point in it is the undisturbed joy and peace of the people.

> I will rejoice in Jerusalem
>   and joy in My people;
> And there shall be heard in her no more
>   the voice of weeping and the voice of crying.
> There shall be no more thence an infant of days
>   nor an old man that has not filled his days,
> For the child shall die a hundred years old,
>   and the sinner shall be accursed. (Isa. 65 [19f.])

Men will grow old as in primeval days in order that they may taste to the full the happiness of the new age. It is not yet immortality that is hoped for, but it is a stage on the way to it. Universal peace will prevail even in nature. Quoting the First Isaiah our prophet concludes,

> The wolf and the lamb shall lie down together
> and the lion shall eat straw like the ox;
> and dust shall be the serpent's food.
> They shall not hurt nor destroy
> in all My holy mountain, says Yahweh. (Isa. 65 [25])

In the last section (Isa. 66 [7–14. 18–23]) the only new thought is that Yahweh will miraculously repeople the country and choose from the returning exiles Levitical Priests. The small number of the inhabitants had troubled Zechariah too. For the new temple many more priests were needed. But they will come!

These great hopes Trito-Isaiah never tired of putting before the people. True enough, he fell short of Deutero-Isaiah's highest vision, but who will maintain that his activity was not of utmost importance? Did he not put new hope into the hearts of his people? Did he not ever impel them to look beyond the sordid cares of the present and the disheartening pettiness of the day, forward to the golden future where life would be glorified, sorrow and care forgotten, joy and peace never ending? Surely, to fill men's hearts with a divine discontent with the present, an ardent hope for the future, and a firm belief in God and the certain fulfilment of His purpose is a task worthy of a true prophet.

The feeling that Yahweh had not yet taken up His abode in the temple distressed many minds, and while spiritual leaders sought the explanation in the moral condition of the community, others believed that there might be some external reason for it. Some were troubled by the loss of the ark which had been Yahweh's throne in the holy of holies of the former temple. It had perished in 586, and it had not been restored in 516. Was it not likely that this was the cause of Yahweh's delay in returning to His people? A nameless prophet answered this question in an oracle which has been inserted in the Book of Jeremiah (3 [14–18]):

And it shall come to pass, when ye are multiplied and increased in the land, in those days, says Yahweh, they shall say no more, The ark of the covenant of Yahweh; neither shall it come to mind; neither shall they remember it; neither shall they miss it; neither shall it be made any more. At that time they shall call Jerusalem the throne of Yahweh; and all the nations shall be gathered unto it, to the name of Yahweh, to Jerusalem: neither shall they walk any more after the stubbornness of their evil heart. (Jer. 3 [16f.])

In Isaiah 34f. we have two prophecies which sound as if they had been written by Trito-Isaiah or, if not by him, by another disciple of Deutero-Isaiah. The miraculous transformation of the desert and the wonderful highway through it are portrayed in Deutero-Isaiah's phrases. It is a glowing picture whose brilliance is enhanced by the dark background upon which it is painted, for the first of the two prophecies deals with Edom's punishment (Isa. 34). Impressively the prophet begins with the judgment of Yahweh on the nations and on heaven and earth. The heathen armies will be slaughtered,

> And the mountains shall be melted with their blood,
>   and all the host of heaven shall be dissolved,
> And the heavens shall be rolled together as a scroll;
>   and all their host shall fade away,
> As the leaf fades from off the vine
>   and as a fading leaf from the figtree. (Isa. 34 [4])

But all this is but the beginning. To our prophet the world-judgment was of far less importance than the fate of Edom, for he hated Edom with a terrible hatred and attributed his own vindictiveness to Yahweh, who would avenge Jerusalem by destroying Edom so fearfully that it would become a veritable hell, peopled only by all manner of unclean animals. That he degraded God to the level of his own cruelty, never entered this prophet's mind.

It is true, the Edomites had given the Jews just cause for revenge. In 586 when Jerusalem fell, they had taken the enemies' part, had entered and plundered the holy city with them, had jeered at the Jews, had cut off the fugitives at the crossroads and delivered them to the Chaldeans. Is it any wonder that the Jews exulted when the news came that Edom was hard pressed by the Arabians and that they were driven out of their country? Obadiah, a man of passionate spirit and an ardent patriot, exultantly issued a terrible poem of hate. He used an older oracle of Edom's fall as text (vv. [1-4.8f.]) and showed most vividly, partly in the words of the older oracle (vv. [5-7]), how it had been fulfilled (Ob. [1-14.15b]),

> As thou hast done,
>   it shall be done to thee,
> Thy dealing shall return
>   upon thine own head.[1]

Another writer, whose prophecy was incorporated later in the Book of Jeremiah (49 [7-22]), also used the older oracle for his own prediction of Edom's punishment. But there was at least a redeeming touch of pity for the helpless Edomite widows and children in his words,

> Leave thy fatherless children,
>   I will preserve them alive;
> And let thy widows trust in Me.

This note of sympathy is still more pronounced in the fine prophecy of Isaiah 15f. against Moab, which was also threatened by the Nabatean invasion. Not only is Judah here called upon to give refuge and protection to the fugitive Moabites, but the prophet himself weeps bitterly,

> My heart sounds like a harp for Moab,
>   and mine inward parts for Kir-heres. (Isa. 16 [11])

One feels that bonds of sympathy and friendship knit the author to Moab, perhaps even marital ties. Rarely did a prophet exhibit such feeling of compassion for an enemy country in time of distress.

In this same period a prophetic editor added the conclusion to the Book of Amos (9 [8b-15]) which made that dark book of judgment end in a golden vision of hope and light. After the exiles, thoroughly sifted of all their wicked elements, have returned to their homes, the Davidic dynasty will be reëstablished; Edom and all territories that at any time had belonged to Israel will be reconquered; and wonderful fertility will prevail.

> Behold the days come, says Yahweh,
> That the ploughman shall overtake the reaper,
>   and the treader of grapes him that sows seed;
> And the mountains shall drop sweet wine,
>   and all the hills shall melt. (Am. 9 [13])

---

[1] The rest of the little book vv. [15a. 16-21] comes from a later time.

The exiles will all participate in the work and the fruits of the restoration, and never again will they be deported from their home. It is quite possible that this writer added the oracle against Edom in the famous address which opens the Book of Amos ($1^{11f.}$).

Edom had not been the only guilty one in the fateful year of 586. Moab and Ammon also had mocked and reviled the unhappy Jews. Ezekiel had already pronounced terrible judgment upon them. An editor of the Book of Zephaniah inserted a prophecy against them in 2^{8-11}, predicting perpetual desolation to their lands because of their scornful behavior toward the Jews who will become their lords.

> The residue of My people shall make a prey of them,
>   and the remnant of My nation shall inherit them. (Zeph. 2^{9b})

In the prophecy against Philistia (Zeph. 2^{4-7}) the editor interpolated the lines,

> And the coast shall be for the remnant of the house of Judah (2^{7a})
> For Yahweh their God will visit them, and bring back their captivity. (2^{7c})

National vengeance and national aggrandizement are the keynotes of these hopes. But joined with them is a high note:

> Yahweh will be terrible to them,
>   for He will famish all the gods of the earth;
> And men shall worship Him, every one from his place,
>   even all the isles of the nations. (Zeph. 2^{11})

Unfortunately, this note is absent from the other prediction which is now inserted in Isaiah 11^{11-16}, where the return of the exiles from all quarters of the earth and their conquest of Philistia, Edom, Moab, and Ammon are foretold. It is a pity that so much space was given to these purely national hopes.

After the dedication of the temple the people had been zealous in the performance of their cultic duties. But it was not long before difficulties arose, which the early enthusiasm had easily overcome. The maintenance of the temple and its cult was expensive, the people were poor, and no king or government paid for the cost of the temple and its clergy. Bad seasons and heavy taxes made it still harder for the people, so that they sometimes delayed or withheld their tithes or substituted inferior animals for the perfect ones that they had vowed. The priests either did not have the heart or the authority to compel them to stricter observance of their religious duties, and their own position and influence suffered inevitably thereby. Sorcerers, on the other hand, reaped a good harvest, for as always in bad times simple-minded people were easily led astray into trying to better their fortunes by magic or to revive their hopes by clairvoyance. For religious purity and devotion the growing custom of intermarriage with foreigners constituted another serious problem. Living among the descendants of the people who had occupied the land after 586, the Jews had mingled and intermarried with them. Their children sometimes spoke the dialect of their mothers rather than Hebrew. The purity of Jewish blood was vitiated, and the devotion to Yahweh undermined. It happened that Jews became enamoured with young and beautiful foreign girls and divorced their old Jewish wives without mercy in order to marry the foreigners, if they did not simply commit adultery. Unfortunately, all sorts of social wrongs were rampant. The rich oppressed the laborers and the poor defenceless classes, the widows, orphans, and strangers. There was much lying and stealing, blasphemy and perjury. And as so often the wicked prospered, while the righteous suffered hardship of every kind. It is no wonder that many began to doubt God's love and justice, and ask whether religion was after all worth while. Such were the conditions that Malachi faced.

His real name we do not know, for "Malachi" which means "my messenger" was due to a wrong interpretation of his prophecy, "Behold, I send My messenger" (3 [1]), which was taken to refer to the prophet himself. About 460 he arose and argued with the people, presumably in the temple, in earnest debate about these problems, taking them up point by point, stating the people's position and then giving his answer. First, at least in the arrangement of his book, he insisted on Yahweh's love for Israel and proved it to the people, who had challenged him to point out an evidence of His love, by calling their attention to the terrible catastrophe that had befallen Edom.

Was not Esau (the ancestor of Edom) Jacob's brother? says Yahweh: yet I loved Jacob, but Esau I hated, and made his mountains a desolation. (Mal. 1 [2f.])

Malachi knew his hearers. They hated Edom bitterly. Her punishment filled them with joy and satisfaction and was indeed to them a sign of Yahweh's love for Israel. It was a telling argument, especially as it was followed by the prediction that all attempts at recovery by Edom would be frustrated by Yahweh's eternal wrath against them. To us the joy over Edom's fall is quite intelligible, but to attribute it to God's hatred is repugnant. Excessive anthropomorphism was responsible for this.

Malachi next took up the question of inferior sacrifices, and charged the priests with treating the obligation of perfect offerings with contempt.

When ye offer the blind for a sacrifice, (ye say) it is no evil! and when ye offer the lame and the sick, it is no evil! Present it now to thy governor; will he be pleased with thee? or will he accept thy person? says Yahweh of hosts. (Mal. 1⁸)

How much less than a mere governor can Yahweh be pleased with it,

For I am a great King, says Yahweh of hosts, and My name is feared among the Gentiles! (Mal. 1¹⁴)

Full of indignation the prophet exclaimed,

Oh, that there were one among you that would shut the doors (of the temple), that ye might not kindle fire on Mine altar in vain! I have no pleasure in you, neither will I accept an offering at your hand. (Mal. 1¹⁰)

Yahweh has no need of the Jerusalem temple.

For from the rising of the sun even to its setting My name is great (honored and feared) among the Gentiles, and in every place incense and a pure offering are offered to My name, for My name is great among the Gentiles, says Yahweh of hosts. (Mal. 1¹¹)

According to this the heathen bring all their sacrifices to Yahweh, since He is the sole reality behind all the gods that are worshipped and their sacrifices are purer and more acceptable than those of the Jews. After Deutero-Isaiah it is not surprising that a prophet should draw this conclusion.[1] Its significance must however not be

[1] But could he then say, "in every place incense is offered to *My name*"? That is just what was not done, surely not to Yahweh's name! Or was this merely a slip of the pen? No, it was due to Malachi's insistence on the honor that was bestowed on Yahweh's name among the heathen "for My name is great among the Gentiles." From v. ¹⁴ it is quite clear that this means that it is the heathen that fear His name, for He is a great King. The Jews, *i.e.* the priests whom Malachi addressed, despised Yahweh's name, the heathen honored it. Now that we have come to know from the papyri that the Jews had a temple at Elephantine in southern Egypt, many think Malachi meant the Jews in the dispersion, who in every place offered incense to Yahweh's name and a pure offering. But then Malachi exaggerated very much, for they did not have temples or altars "in every place" where they could offer.

exaggerated, for Malachi never thought of the conversion or redemption of the heathen and according to him Yahweh "hates" Edom. He was intent on bringing out the truth that Yahweh has no need of the unclean sacrifices in the Jerusalem temple, He receives offerings enough, and pure ones too, all over the world! It is noteworthy that to Malachi the cult is so important. The preëxilic prophets had rejected the whole sacrificial system, Malachi believed in its efficacy and value. He insisted, however, on true sacrifices and pressed back of the unfit offerings to the spirit that prompted them, irreverence, deceit, avarice. Rather than this kind he will have none at all and close the temple altogether.

It almost seems as if Malachi was himself a priest, for when he now turned upon the priests, none could be sharper in his judgment, but was it not only because none had a higher ideal of the priesthood?

My covenant was with him: life and peace I gave to him, with (true) fear he feared Me, and stood in awe of My name. The direction of truth was in his mouth, and unrighteousness was not found in his lips: he walked with Me in peace and uprightness, and turned many away from iniquity. For the priest's lips keep knowledge, and men seek direction at his mouth; for he is the messenger of Yahweh of hosts. (Mal. 2 [5-7])

Because the priests do not come up to his ideal, they have become "contemptible and base in the sight of all the people."

The problem of the marriages with foreign women is opened by the prophet with the question,

Have we not all one father? has not one God created us?

We expect that he will proceed with this brotherhood of all to sanction the custom of intermarriage with the nations. But far from it, Malachi continued,

Why do we deal treacherously every man against his brother, profaning the covenant of our fathers? (Mal. 2 [10])

It is the brotherhood of all Jews not of all men that he had in mind and the obligation of mutual fidelity among the Jews is deduced from it. Some Jews had violated the holiness of Yahweh by marrying "the daughter of a foreign god" and treacherously divorcing the wives of their youth. They had not cared to get "godly seed," children from wives of their own race and religion. True enough, of some it could be said,

Not one has done so who had a residue of the spirit.   And what is it with the one?   He sought a godly seed.   Therefore take heed to your spirit, and let none deal treacherously with the wife of his youth.   For I hate putting away (divorce), says Yahweh, the God of Israel. (Mal. 2 ^{15f.})

Next came the question of God's justice. The people said, "Every one that does evil is good in the sight of Yahweh, and He delights in them"; or "where is the God of justice?" The answer to this was the prediction of the impending judgment of Israel, in which the priesthood will be purged of all its base elements and restored to its true ideal, and the wicked will be punished.

Behold, I send My messenger, and he shall prepare the way before Me and the Lord, whom ye seek, will suddenly come to His temple; and the messenger of the covenant, whom ye desire, behold, he comes, says Yahweh of hosts. But who can abide the day of His coming? and who shall stand when He appears? for He is like a refiner's fire, and like fullers' soap: and He will sit as a refiner and purifier of silver, and He will purify the sons of Levi, and refine them as gold and silver; and they shall offer to Yahweh offerings in righteousness. Then shall the offering of Judah and Jerusalem be pleasant to Yahweh, as in the days of old, and as in ancient years.

And I will come near to you to judgment; and I will be a swift witness against the sorcerers, and against the adulterers, and against the false swearers, and against those that oppress the hireling, the widow, and the fatherless, and that turn aside the sojourner from the right and fear not Me, says Yahweh of hosts. (Mal. 3 ¹⁻⁵)

This is not the judgment on the nations but on His own people, and a sharp distinction is made between the individual righteous and wicked. Yahweh is tired of the complaint that He makes no such distinctions.

After dealing once more with the question of the withheld tithes and promising great fertility and divine protection of the harvest, if they bring the tithes into the temple, Malachi came back again to the complaint of the people that religion is not worth while.

Ye have said, It is vain to serve God; and what profit is it that we have kept His charge, and that we have walked mournfully before Yahweh of hosts? and now we call the proud happy; yea, they that work wickedness are built up; yea, they tempt God, and escape. (Mal. 3 ^{14f.})

Malachi noted that "they that feared Yahweh" talked the matter over among themselves, and Yahweh listened and had "a book of remembrance" written for them and promised to spare them on the day when all the wicked will be burnt up root and branch:

To you that fear My name shall the sun of righteousness arise with healing in its wings; and ye shall go forth and gambol as calves of the stall.   And ye shall tread down the wicked; for they shall be ashes under the soles of your feet in the day that I do this, says Yahweh of hosts. (Mal. 4 $^{2f.}$)

Then they will know that God makes a distinction between the righteous and the wicked, and that it is worth while to serve Him!

There is a freshness in the lively debates of the little book that makes it interesting reading.   It is written in prose which sometimes has the rhythmic swing of poetry.   How much impression the intense earnestness of this priestly prophet made on the people we do not know.   The economic forces that he opposed were too strong. More than the preaching of a prophet was needed to change these conditions.   Outside help was necessary.   It came with Nehemiah and Ezra and the large body of earnest Jews who came with them from Babylonia.   But Malachi had prepared the way for them.

CHAPTER XVII

THE PRIEST CODE AND THE PRIESTLY EDITORS

THE changed estimate of the temple and its worship on the part of the early postexilic prophets was due to the spirit of the age. Ezekiel had seen that the restoration of Israel and its religion must centre around the temple. When the Jews came back from captivity, they found that this was true: the temple was the rallying ground of the new community. Prophets and priests alike believed that zeal for the temple and its worship would kindle enthusiasm for Yahweh, that the spirit of true moral religion could best be quickened and nurtured by ritual religion. Moreover, now that Judah was no longer a nation but a Persian province, its only hope of independent and effective organization lay in religion, with which the Persian government as a rule did not interfere. Judah must therefore be organized as a theocracy, which was to be symbolized and realized in a hierocracy. The priests must be the leaders, the high priest, as God's direct representative, the visible head of the people.

Ezekiel and the compiler of the Holiness Code had already begun to preserve the temple ritual. Others followed them, compiling, systematizing, and reforming laws and usages in accordance with Judah's changed conditions. The result was the Priestly Law or the Priest Code, abbreviated P, in which a priestly author about 500 B.C. gathered the fruits of this work and presented it to the people. It forms now one of the four great documents of the Hexateuch and is easily recognized by its style, its manner of presentation, and its point of view. Its style is formal, precise, dry, full of phraseological mannerisms which distinguish it sharply from the other documents. Lists and genealogies, exact measures and chronological dates abound. Its presentation and point of view are controlled by priestly and legal interests. The name "Priest Code," appropriate as it is, may yet be misleading, for it was not merely a law book, but it combined history with law, and the author wrote for the people not for the priests, desiring to teach them the authority and the importance of the religious institutions of Israel, in order to move them to repentance and to a wholehearted acceptance of the entire cultic apparatus through which alone, to his mind, salvation could be achieved. History was entirely subordinated to this end.

P began with the creation of the world in a wonderfully impressive and majestic story. His priestly interest at once appears, for the climax of the whole creation is the Sabbath. God "rested on the seventh day from all His work which He had made, and God blessed the seventh day and hallowed it." The Sabbath was embedded in the very constitution of the world; it is one of its foundations! In the summary form of a genealogy P carried the history of the world quickly down to Noah, where he tarried to tell the story of the deluge, because it culminated in the so-called Noachian laws which prohibited murder and the eating of blood for all mankind. In the table of the nations he summarized the period from the deluge to Abram [1] and then gave a brief history of Abram [2] which is fuller only in the stories of the origin of circumcision (Gen. 17) and of the acquisition of the burial place at Hebron (Gen. 23). Circumcision, like the Sabbath, was one of the most significant religious institutions of Israel for P, because during the exile and in the dispersion both were distinguishing signs of the covenant, by which the Jew could be recognized. The buying of the burial ground was so important to P, because thereby Israel was bound to Canaan; here was its home, for here its ancestors were buried. For Isaac P had only a genealogy ($25^{19f.\ 26b}$). In the story of Jacob he emphasized the imperative duty of the purity of the blood and voiced his opposition to intermarriage with the Canaanites. Jacob was sent to his kinsmen in Syria to marry among his own people (28^{1-9}). By contrast Esau's marriages with foreign women are mentioned ($26^{34f.}$); aside from these only his settlement on Mount Seir and his genealogy are given of Esau ($36^{6-8.\ 40-43}$). Jacob's further

[1] Gen. $1^{1}-2^{4a}$ 5 (except v. ^{29}) 6^{9-22} $7^{6.\ 11.\ 13-16a.\ 17a\ 18-21.\ 24}$ $8^{1.\ 2a.\ 3b-5.\ 13a.\ 14-19}$ $9^{1-17.\ 28f.}$ $10^{1-7.\ 20.\ 22f.\ 31f.}$

[2] Gen. $11^{10-27.\ 31f.}$ $12^{4b.\ 5}$ $13^{6a.\ 11b.\ 12a}$ $16^{1a.\ 3.\ 15f.}$ $17.$ 19^{29} $21^{1b.\ 2b.\ 3-5}$ $23.$ $25^{7-11a\ 12-17}$.

history, his death in Egypt, and his burial at Machpelah were told in a few verses. It is woven into the Joseph story.[1]

The succeeding events were treated in the same manner. After a brief account of Israel's oppression in Egypt, P told of the call of Moses, to whom was revealed for the first time the name of Yahweh and with it the complete and the final revelation of His will; he continued this with Moses' commission to Pharaoh and the story of the plagues.[2] At the exodus from Egypt P's interest centred in the institution of the Passover (Ex. 12 [1-14. 28]). A rapid sketch of the exodus, in which only the passage through the Sea of Reeds and the giving of the Manna are elaborated,[3] brings us to Mount Sinai in less than a dozen additional sentences.[4] Here Moses ascended the mountain (24 [15-18a]) and the great law sections begin.

The laws of the sanctuary with all its paraphernalia, and of the institution of the priesthood are given first (Ex. 25-29) and their execution is narrated in the groundwork of Ex. 35-40 and in Lev. 8f. Yahweh had sanctioned only one sanctuary. P believed therefore that it must have existed even at the time of Moses in the tabernacle. Again, Yahweh had consecrated as His legitimate priests only Aaron and his sons, more specially Eleazar and Ithamar. In the story of the sons of Aaron, Nadab and Abihu, P told how these priests were exterminated for their unauthorized offering of incense (Lev. 10 [1-5]). The portion of the meal-offering which belonged to the priests was definitely determined (Lev. 10 [12-15]), and a calendar of sacred days and festivals was fixed by the days of the month (Lev. 23 [4-8. 13f. 21. 23-38. 39aβ]).

Then the narrative is resumed. The people were numbered, their places in the camp and on the march were assigned, the Levites also were numbered and given their various duties.[5] After the departure from Sinai the stories of the spies with the refusal of the people to invade the country; of Korah's and his company's rebellion; and of the divine approval of Aaron's priesthood as shown in

---

[1] Gen. 29 [24. 28b. 29] 30 [22a] 31 [18b] 33 [18b] 35 [6a. 9-13. 15. 22b-29] 37 [1.2ac] 41 [46a] 46 [6f.] 47 [6ac. 7-11. 27b. 28] 48 [3-6] 49 [1a. 28b-33] 50 [12f.]

[2] Ex. 1 [1-5. 7. 13. 14b] 2 [23b-25] 6 [2-12] 7 [1-13. 19. 20a. 21b. 22] 8 [1-3. 12-15] 9 [8-12.]

[3] Ex. 14 [1. 2. 4. 5a. 8. 9. 10c. 15ac. 16b. 17f. 21ac. 22f. 26. 27a. 28a.] 16 [1-3. 9-14. 15b-17. 21a. 31a. 32. 34. 35a.]

[4] Ex. 12 [37a. 40f. 51] 13 [20] 17 [1a] 19 [1. 2a.]

[5] Num. 1 [1-47] 2 [1-16. 18-31. 34] 3 [14-39.]

the budding of his staff were told at length.[1]   Laws concerning the
duties and rights of priests and Levites were appropriately inserted
at this point.[2]   After the miraculous issuing of the water from the
rock, the death of Aaron, and the investiture of Eleazar, the people
reached in three stages the steppes of Moab.[3]   Here Moses assigned
to Reuben and Gad their territories, defined the limits of the territory of all Israel, named the chiefs who were to distribute the land,
and set apart the cities of refuge.[4]   Then at Yahweh's command
he ascended Mount Nebo to view the land, and died.   Joshua became his successor.[5]

The story of the conquest of Canaan P told very briefly.   Besides the crossing of the Jordan and the Passover at Gilgal we have
from P only the designation of the Gibeonites as wood-cutters and
water-carriers for Israel and a summary of the defeated Canaanitish
kings.[6]   The distribution of the land among the tribes however he
gave in detail,[7] so that the whole extent of Israel's territory might
be before the reader.   This was of much importance for P, because
he believed that the whole country belonged to Israel as an inalien-
able possession and that it would be restored to them again by God
in the future.   Israel and the land belonged together.

It is apparent even from this sketch that P used history merely
for the purpose of teaching the origin and the sanctity of the various
rites and institutions.   He had learned from the Babylonians about
the four world-epochs but he viewed them from his priestly angle:
at the creation the Sabbath was instituted; after the deluge the
prohibition of eating blood was imposed; in Abram's time circumcision; in Moses' time the Passover.   These four periods were four
stages in the revelation of God's will; the last marked the climax, for
to Moses was revealed the final revelation, the perfect law of God.

The Priest Code in its original form was complete about 500 B.C.,
or a little later.   When it was adopted by the solemn assembly of

[1] Num. 10 [11f.] 13 [1–17a. 21. 25. 32a] 14 [1aα. 2. 5–7. 10. 26. 29. 34–38] 16 [1a. 2b–7a. 18. 19b–24a. 35] 17 [6–28].

[2] Num. 18 [1–15. 17–21. 24–32].

[3] Num. 20 [1a. 2. 3b. 4. 6.7b. 10. 12. 22–29] 21 [10. 11a] 22 [1].

[4] Num. 32 [1a. 2b. 4a. 18f. 28–32] 34 [1–12 16–29] 35 [9–29].

[5] Deut. 32 [48–52] 34 [1a. 7–9].

[6] Josh. 4 [10. 16. 18f.] 5 [10–12] (in part) 9 [15b. 17–21] 12 [9–24].

[7] Josh. 13 [15–21a. 23–27aα. 28. 32] 14 [1f.] 15 [1–12. 20–45. 48–62] 16 [4–8] 17 [1a] 18 [1. 11a. 12–28] 19 [1–7. 8b. 10–48. 51].

the people under the leadership of Ezra (Neh. 8–10) as a part of the fundamental law of the church-state of Judah, the Holiness Code had already been incorporated in it (Lev. 17–26), with characteristic modifications, of course, and additions to bring it altogether into harmony with P. Whether Ezra himself was responsible for its insertion, or for any part of the composition of P, we do not know. A beginning had been made and soon after Ezra a great many additions were introduced. It was a time of great interest in such matters. The temple with its worship stood in the centre of the people's life, and with it the care for the ritual holiness of the people. A collection of laws concerning sacrifices had been prepared (Lev. 1–7) and another on ritual cleanness (Lev. 11–15). In course of time these were incorporated in P, for they were part of the priestly law. Similarly, the laws for the Nazirite (Num. 6), concerning a suspected adulteress (Num. 5 [11–31]), and the purification by the ashes of a red heifer (Num. 19). When the day of atonement became the climax of the great system of expiation, the ritual concerning it was introduced too (Lev. 16). The late institution of the year of jubilee was connected with the Sabbath year, at the end of a cycle of seven Sabbath years, as the fiftieth year.[1] There were moreover a number of points which were in need of additional legislation. Thus the law on sacrifice in Num. 15 [1–31] was added as a supplement to Lev. 1–3 ; the law on trespass in Num. 5 [5–10] to Lev. 5 [20–26] ; and the law in Num. 28f. containing directions for the sacrifices on the feasts, to the calendar of feasts in Lev. 23. A detailed treatment of vows and tithes was supplied in Lev. 27 and Num. 30. Certain cases not foreseen in the law had to be decided by additional legislation : e.g. what was to be done, if one happened to be unclean or on a journey at the time of the Passover festival (Num. 9 [1–14]) ? or what course was to be pursued with the inheritance, if there was no male heir in the family? could daughters inherit? (Num. 27 [1–11]). The interest in the sanctuary was responsible for many other additions and elaborations, both in the laws of the sanctuary (Ex. 25–29)[2] and in the description of their execution (Ex. 35–40).[3] The interest

[1] Lev. 25 [8–13. 15. 16. 26–34. 40b. 41. 44–46. 50–52. 54].

[2] Ex. 27 [20f.] 28 [42f.] 29 [9b. 21. 26–30. 33. 35b–42] 30 [1]–31 [17].

[3] P had treated this quite summarily in Ex. 35 [4–8. 1ff. 20–27.] 29 36 [8] 39 [32. 33a. 43] 40 [1f. 16f. 33b. 34].

in the priesthood led to the incorporation of the prohibition for the priests of drinking wine or other intoxicants before the services in the temple (Lev. 10 $^{6-11}$), and of several regulations concerning the Levites.[1] They were introduced at various times and by various priestly writers. The tendency of the time was towards heightening the ritual, which necessitated all this supplementary legislation that modified the older law, applied it to new conditions, or harmonized the differences. It is quite natural that the narrative sections were not greatly augmented. A few genealogies and lists; the stories of the stoning of a man for blasphemy and of another for Sabbath breaking;[2] the order of the march; additions to the Korah story; the stories of the zeal of Phineas and of the raid against Midian; the record of Israel's journeyings; the assignment of territory to the sons of Machir by Moses; and the story of the altar beyond Jordan[3] — these are the main additions to P's narrative.

The work of supplementing lasted a long time. It was not complete even at the time of the translation of the Pentateuch into Greek, about 250 B.C. There was, unfortunately, no intelligent scheme in the process of incorporating all these additional elements. In a number of cases it is quite manifest why a particular section was inserted just where it now is. Thus, e.g., the sacrificial code in Lev. 1-7 was introduced before Lev. 8, because in the consecration of Aaron and his sons certain sacrifices were mentioned which made prior information about their character appropriate. But nevertheless Lev. 1-7 breaks the original connection between Ex. 40 and Lev. 8. In many cases we do not understand the reason why an insertion was made just at a particular point. The result is that the clear arrangement of the original P has given way to a conglomerate, and the incorporation of so much priestly matter has also tended to obscure the fact that P intended his book not for the priests but for the people as a popular manual of religious rites and institutions.

The style of all this priestly literature is quite uniform and stere-

---

[1] Num. 1 $^{48-54}$ 3 $^{5ff.}$ 4. 8 $^{5-26}$ 16 $^{1a\beta.\ 7c.\ 8-11}$ 17 $^{1-5}$.

[2] These are precedents for the judges, and therefore really legal passages too.

[3] Gen. 36 $^{1-5.\ 9-30}$ 46 $^{8-27}$ Ex. 6 $^{14-25}$ Num. 10 $^{13-28}$ 16 $^{1a\beta.\ 7c.\ 8-11}$ 17 $^{1-5}$ 25 $^{6-18}$ 31. 33 Josh. 13 $^{29-31}$ 22 $^{9-34}$.

otyped like that of a school. It is dry and prosaic, as a rule, given
to specific formulæ and precise systematic statement. In the story
of creation this very quality enhances the dignity of the narrative so
that it rises to majestic grandeur, but this is an exception. The
style is so well marked that it is quite easy even for a beginner to
single out the priestly work. P's desire for preciseness and accuracy
is well illustrated in the exact dates and figures which he gives. But
however accurate they may seem to be, they turn out to be altogether unreliable. The whole chronology of the Pentateuch is due
to a definite artificial system. The exact age of the antediluvians
was, of course, not handed down by any reliable tradition but was
an adaptation of an early Babylonian chronological scheme, which
P used in such a way that the constantly decreasing number of the
years of their lives served as an indication of the constantly increas-
ing sinfulness of mankind. For long life was always connected with
piety ; the more pious a man was, the older he was likely to become.
Again, it can hardly be assumed that Noah kept a log-book in which
he noted on certain definite days the measurements of the log.
Quite cleverly these dates are used to show that the flood lasted an
entire solar year ! Still further, it can be shown that P arrived at
the exact number of 603,550 for all Israel in Num. 1 [46] by the artificial, favorite scheme of figuring called gematria : the numerical
value of the consonants of *rōsh kol benê Yisra'el* = "the sum of all
the children of Israel" was added up, *rosh kol* = 551, *benê Yisra'el*
= 603; the latter was then multiplied by 1000 = 603,000, and 551
(= *rosh kol*) was added = 603,551; in a round figure 603,550.

The spirit pervading P is no less marked than the style. The
whole of life is viewed from a religious, or rather priestly, standpoint. The writers were priests, and their ideal was the theocracy
with the implied hierocracy. Their theological ideas were far in
advance of JE. One has but to compare the two creation stories
(Gen. 1–2 [4a] P, Gen. 2 [4b–24] J) to see this. The naïve representations
of God's appearances so marked in J were no longer possible. God
was too highly exalted. The long process of purging the ancient
tales of all heathen and inferior ideas was brought by P to a successful completion. Many things had to be rejected as incompatible
with P's theology and ethics. But it is noteworthy that the victory
over the lower and foreign religious practices was not won by radical

rejection, but by thorough reinterpretation.   In this P followed JE's lead, rather than D's.

P was especially interested in instruction in the law.   But though the law was both moral and ritual, P did not work out the moral side, because his primary concern was ritual.   Not that he regarded the moral as non-essential; he presupposed it.   The incorporation of the moral and social laws of Lev. 19 (H) and the institution of the year of jubilee (Lev. 25) show that social values were by no means neglected by P.   That most difficult problem of the concentration of the landed property in the hands of a few, against which the prophets had fought with all their might, albeit without success, the priestly writers tried to solve by the legal establishment of the year of jubilee, at the end of seven Sabbath years, that is, in every fiftieth year, in which all landed property had to be returned to the original owner and all Hebrew slaves had to be set free.   The magnificent conception that Yahweh alone is the owner of the land and of its produce and the inhabitants are only His tenants, who are to share equally in the blessings of the land and to whom their particular portion is to be restored in the fiftieth year, if for some reason a family has had to part with it, is combined with the similar idea that Yahweh alone is the lord and master of the Israelites, that they can therefore never be the real slaves of another, and that they and their children must be given their liberty in the fiftieth year, if they had been compelled to sell themselves into servitude.   This is a heightening of the Sabbath year, which H had already included.   The priestly interest is apparent in the figuring out of the year; it comes at the end of seven Sabbath years.   But the social interest must not be denied, although the year of jubilee remained a priestly utopia.   In spite of this solemn law, it was never carried out in practice.

The priests had ultimately the same aim as the prophets.   They wanted to make the people acceptable to God.   But while the prophets insisted that this could be done only by morality, the priests believed it could best be accomplished by ritual holiness.   In and through the cult they sought to educate the people in obedience to Yahweh; by regulating their whole life through many ceremonial precepts they hoped to discipline them to constant remembrance of Yahweh.   Obedience was to them, as to the prophets, the all important concern, but it was not obedience to the voice of conscience, the inner law of which Jeremiah had spoken, but obedience to all these outward regulations, which they imposed on the people as the direct command of Yahweh. "Ye shall be holy, for I Yahweh, your God, am holy" was their underlying principle. This holiness was mainly cultic, external; it was gained by avoidance of all idolatrous and superstitious practices and by observance of all the laws concerning ritual cleanness, food, sacrifices, and festivals. Religion was a matter of the cult. The earlier prophets had violently protested against such a conception of religion and rejected the entire cultic apparatus as contrary to the will of God. But they had not succeeded in the long run. When the question of the organization of religion in the light of the prophetic ideals was attempted, it was seen that a purely moral and spiritual religion was too high and exacting for the mass of the people. External forms were necessary, worship had to be carried on. How could this be done so as to be acceptable to Yahweh? Above all else by removing every heathen element from the cult! Deuteronomy had seen this, and in Josiah's reformation all heathen paraphernalia were relentlessly put away; the many local high places, the breeding spots of impure cults, were destroyed and all legitimate worship was centralized in Jerusalem. Although a reaction against this reform set in after Josiah's death, the principle of the one legitimate sanctuary was so firmly established that P could take it for granted.

According to P there had always been only one legitimate place of worship, even in the days of the wilderness wanderings, for at God's command Moses had prepared the tabernacle, the tent of revelation, where all worship was carried on. P carried therefore his ideal back into the past, and what had been accomplished only after a long historical development he presented as existing from Moses' time on. The tabernacle was the pattern of the later temple at Jerusalem, and all cultic worship was possible only there. That is why the patriarchs in P's own story never sacrificed, and why the altar in the East Jordan country was only a memorial, never intended for sacrificial purposes (Josh. 22). P was altogether unconcerned about the historical possibility of such an elaborate tabernacle in the wilderness, as he described in Ex. 25–30. The ideal, to him, was actually realized in the past.

This involved also the establishment of the hierocracy by Moses. The whole, long development of the priesthood was simply ignored. The differentiation of the Levites from the Aaronite or Zadokite priests and their degradation, which Ezekiel still had to justify, were for P facts from the beginning. The struggle of the Levites for priestly rights he placed in the wilderness period, where Korah and his company reached out for them with such tragic results (Num. 16).[1] The office of the high priest too, which took so long to evolve, was instituted already by Moses according to P. He alone may enter the holy of holies; at his installation he is anointed with the sacred oil and is really the visible head of the theocracy. He wears the purple and the tiara. For a king there is no place. The ideal, we see, was intended for the postexilic people, whom P would win by his fictitious presentation of its origin in ancient history and the divine commands through which it was established.

The whole cult too had been instituted by Moses, P taught. It was the means of securing and insuring the ritual holiness of the people, by which alone Yahweh's continued dwelling among His people could be guaranteed. By the cult any sin which might be upon the people or any individual could be removed; wilful sins, real crimes were however not included, because they could only be removed by the death or the excommunication of the sinner. Only ordinary offenses were removed by ritual atonement. The whole cult, according to P, was designed for the expiation of sin. The object of every sacrifice was atonement; the mysterious, atoning efficacy of the blood was experienced in every one. Animal sacrifices with their blood were therefore specially valuable and numerous. The expiatory character of the cult dominated also the festivals. In P they had lost their character of gratitude and joy to a large extent. They were now freed from all connection with nature and its seasons, in order that nothing might remind one of their original connection with the Canaanite land and its religion. They were now fixed definitely by the days of the month. The great festivals were now framed by two

---

[1] The story of Nadab and Abihu, who offered a sacrifice of incense which Yahweh had not commanded and who were therefore punished by lightning (Lev. 10) is another instance of P's method of placing the later struggle of certain priestly families (from the local sanctuaries?) for priestly rank and office among the Zadokites in Jerusalem in the wilderness period.

solemn days of holy convocation at the beginning and the end. They were no longer occasions of joy, but feasts of reconciliation. The old joyous cult, with its harvest festivals and sacrificial meals and dinner parties, had become a serious solemn affair.   The cult was no longer the spontaneous expression of the religious mind, but the definite form in which one must approach Yahweh in order to gain atonement.[1]   The ancient meal-offering with its rejoicing in the sanctuary had no real place among the sacrifices ; secular slaughtering and eating had supplanted it.   The diminution of the personal participation of laymen in the sacrifices is striking ; not only was the killing and offering all done by the Levites and the priests, to whom the laymen had only to supply the material, but the presence of the community at the sacrifices was not necessary.   They were efficacious also without them; they bound in a mysterious yet real manner the deity together with the people.   Here an external, mechanical, magic conception of the sacrifices threatened to drive out the importance of personal, moral, spiritual participation in them.   The burnt-offering which was given to the deity entire became more and more prominent; it was the great offering.   Also the sin-offering, which before the exile was virtually unknown, assumed remarkable importance.   It was really a private, penitential act and, like the related trespass-offering, it was brought in order to gain forgiveness from Yahweh.   Transgressions, whether ritual or moral, could be expiated only if a sin offering was brought, for Yahweh had connected forgiveness with the cult !   God's sovereign and free pardon of the sinner, if he only repented, the glory of the prophetic message, was not denied, but it was bound up with the bringing of sacrifices by the penitent sinner.   That the stress laid on the outward offering might easily obscure the need of inward repentance is apparent. Even a careful observer of the ritual might, for one reason or another, forget or neglect to perform the rite prescribed for the various situations in life, and thus bring uncleanness upon himself and by contact upon others, and Yahweh might leave His people.   In order to avoid this a sin-offering was added to the other offerings on every holy day, from New Moon upwards, and a special day, the climax of the whole system, was finally instituted.   Once a year, on the tenth day of the seventh month (Tishri = Sept.–Oct.), on the great Day

---

[1] Fortunately, the practice varied considerably from this sombre theory, cf. pp. 347 ff.

of Atonement the high priest entered the holy of holies and removed the uncleanness of the priests, the sanctuary, and the people by the special ceremonies of the day. Here the private cult was connected with the public cult: the sin-offering of the Day of Atonement atoned for the omissions of sin-offerings on the part of individuals (Lev. 16. 23 [26-32]).[1]

The ritual of the Day of Atonement is instructive.

And Yahweh spoke to Moses, after the death of the two sons of Aaron, when they drew near before Yahweh, and died; and Yahweh said to Moses, Speak to Aaron thy brother, that he come not at any time into the holy place within the veil, before the mercy-seat which is upon the ark that he die not: for I will appear in the cloud upon the mercy-seat. With this shall Aaron come into the holy place: with a young bullock for a sin-offering, and a ram for a burnt-offering. He shall put on the holy linen coat, and he shall have the linen breeches upon his flesh, and shall be girded with the linen girdle, and with the linen turban shall he be attired: they are the holy garments; and he shall bathe his flesh in water, and put them on. And he shall take of the congregation of the children of Israel two he-goats for a sin-offering, and one ram for a burnt-offering.

And Aaron shall present the bullock of the sin-offering, which is for himself, and make atonement for himself, and for his house. And he shall take the two goats, and set them before Yahweh at the door of the tent of meeting. And Aaron shall cast lots upon the two goats; one lot for Yahweh, and the other lot for Azazel. And Aaron shall present the goat upon which the lot fell for Yahweh, and offer him for a sin-offering. But the goat, on which the lot fell for Azazel, shall be set alive before Yahweh, to send him away for Azazel into the wilderness.

And Aaron shall present the bullock of the sin-offering, which is for himself, and shall make atonement for himself, and for his house, and shall kill the bullock of the sin-offering which is for himself. And he shall take a censer full of coals of fire from off the altar before Yahweh, and his hands full of sweet incense beaten small, and bring it within the veil: and he shall put the incense upon the fire before Yahweh, that the cloud of the incense may cover the mercy-seat that is upon the testimony, that he die not: and he shall take of the blood of the bullock, and sprinkle it with his finger upon the mercy-seat on the east; and before the mercy-seat shall he sprinkle of the blood with his finger seven times.

Then shall he kill the goat of the sin-offering, that is for the people, and bring his blood within the veil, and do with his blood as he did with the blood of the bullock, and sprinkle it upon the mercy-seat, and before the mercy-

---

[1] The Day of Atonement was not yet in the law book of Ezra, else it would have been mentioned in Neh. 8f.

seat : and he shall make atonement for the holy place, because of the uncleannesses of the children of Israel, and because of their transgressions, even all
their sins : and so shall he do for the tent of meeting, that dwells with them in
the midst of their uncleannesses. And there shall be no man in the tent of
meeting when he goes in to make atonement in the holy place, until he come
out, and have made atonement for himself, and for his household, and for all
the assembly of Israel. And he shall go out to the altar that is before Yahweh,
and make atonement for it, and shall take of the blood of the bullock, and of
the blood of the goat, and put it upon the horns of the altar round about. And
he shall sprinkle of the blood upon it with his finger seven times, and cleanse
it, and hallow it from the uncleannesses of the children of Israel.

And when he has made an end of atoning for the holy place, and the tent
of meeting, and the altar, he shall present the live goat : and Aaron shall lay
both his hands upon the head of the live goat, and confess over him all the
iniquities of the children of Israel, and all their transgressions, even all their sins ;
and he shall put them upon the head of the goat, and shall send him away by
the hand of a man that is in readiness into the wilderness : and the goat shall
bear upon him all their iniquities into a solitary land : and he shall let go the
goat in the wilderness.

And Aaron shall come into the tent of meeting, and shall put off the linen
garments, which he put on when he went into the holy place, and shall leave
them there : and he shall bathe his flesh in water in a holy place, and put on
his ordinary garments, and come forth, and offer his burnt-offering and the
burnt-offering of the people, and make atonement for himself and for the people.
And the fat of the sin-offering shall he burn upon the altar. And he that lets
go the goat for Azazel shall wash his clothes, and bathe his flesh in water, and
afterward he shall come into the camp. And the bullock of the sin-offering,
and the goat of the sin-offering, whose blood was brought in to make atonement in the holy place, shall be carried forth without the camp ; and they shall
burn in the fire their skins, and their flesh, and their dung. And he that burns
them shall wash his clothes, and bathe his flesh in water, and afterward he shall
come into the camp. (Lev. 16 $^{1-28}$)

The removal of sin by placing it upon the goat that was sent to the
demon Azazel in the wilderness was a survival of ancient polydemonism, which even the late priests could not remove, so they left
it beside the sin-offering. Also in other cases these otherwise so
exclusive priests, who ordinarily rejected all heathen elements, got
rid of them by assimilation and reinterpretation. Thus in the law
of the purification of the unclean with the ashes of a red heifer (Num.
19) an original sacrifice to the dead was reinterpreted and incorporated. In the ordeal by which a woman was tested when she was
suspected of adultery (Num. 5) ancient magic ideas and practices

were sanctioned. The tassels, which every Israelite was to wear and which had formerly been nothing but amulets, were to serve as reminders of the law of Yahweh and as safeguards against sinning (Num. 15 [37ff.]). The golden bells of the high priest's garment had also originally been amulets which protected against demons, and even in P they still served to shield him when he went in and out of the presence of Yahweh in the holy place "that he die not" (Ex. 28[34f.]).

There is much primitive heathenism in the cult, for the cult was not the distinguishing element of Yahweh's religion, indeed Israel had that in common with the other nations who rendered such worship also to their gods. Exclusiveness and rejection of everything that belonged to a foreign religion characterized many priestly laws on ritual purity. The laws concerning clean and unclean animals (Lev. 11) are not to be explained as due to hygienic reasons or to natural aversion but mostly to the fact that these animals were sacred to other gods. The various laws of ritual cleanness were worked out very methodically by the priests. Sexual relations, diseases, death, or other defiling matters were carefully noted and directions for purification were given. The degree of the defilement varied, and so did the degree of purity. For the priests its requirements were more stringent than for the laymen. The closer one is to God, the purer he must be. But everybody must be clean.

The disciplining of the whole life by all these cultic regulations was not an easy task. It was a heavy yoke for many. The economic burden which the cult involved was not light either. The cost of the entire establishment of the temple with its sacrifices and the clergy had to be borne by the people. The public sacrifices alone consumed a large number of animals and other materials.[1] A tax of half a shekel yearly was imposed upon every one "for the service of the tent of meeting" (Ex. 30 [11 ff.]). The support of priests and Levites was costly too; they received not only their definite portions

---

[1] It has been figured out that the daily and other public sacrifices alone required every year 1093 lambs, 113 bullocks, 37 rams, 32 goats; 150.6 ephahs of fine flour (= 5487.86 liters), 342.08 hins of wine, and also of oil (= 2076.43 liters). Besides these, oil for the light, spices for the anointing oil and for the sweet incense, and fine flour for the shew bread had to be furnished.

of the sacrifices, but all the first-fruits and the first-born (for which in the case of men and unclean animals a sum of redemption had to be paid), and the tithes (Num. 18, Lev. 27 [30-33]), and part of the booty (Num. 31 [28 ff.]). The expenses for the people grew larger as the system developed and all sorts of extra requirements were demanded. Trespass-offerings are an illustration. While formerly trespass was purely a matter of civil law (Ex. 22 [7-15]), it was now taken into the cultic system and the offender must not only restore in full plus one fifth of the value to the owner, but he must also bring a ram without blemish as a trespass-offering to the temple, for the offence was not only against the neighbor but also against Yahweh and He forgives only if an offering is brought to Him (Lev. 6 [1-7]). Trespass-offerings were required for a number of things, especially also "if any one sin, and do any of the things which Yahweh has prohibited, though he knew not, yet he is guilty, and shall bear his punishment," and bring a trespass-offering, for "he is certainly guilty before Yahweh" (Lev. 5 [17 ff.]). If we consider in addition the free-will offerings and especially the vows, whose payment was rigidly enforced (Num. 6. 30, Lev. 27), we shall get an idea of the heavy economic burden which the maintenance of the cultic system entailed and shall find it not surprising that the priests felt it necessary to stimulate the people's willingness and joy of giving by telling them of the glad and enthusiastic giving of the fathers for the construction of the sanctuary in the wilderness, for which they were so eager to give that soon more than enough was brought and Moses had to command that they cease giving more (Ex. 35 and esp. 36 [2-7]). Thus did the fathers; could the children do less? Should they not willingly take upon themselves this burden?

To many the law was no burden at all, either economically or religiously. They found in the fulfilment of its commands the way to God and, as we shall see later on in the Psalter, to many it was a joy, a means of mystic fellowship with God. There was no speculation about the reason for the various commands and how they could effect reconciliation; God had commanded them and connected salvation with them. That was enough, obedience was all that was needed for forgiveness.

The ideal of holiness which P had for Israel was inherently exclusive. It necessitated the removal and avoidance of everything that was defiling. This meant not only all sorts of impurities and heathen elements but also heathen people. In the patriarchal story intermarriage with foreigners was deprecated: only defilement could come from this practice. This may be seen in the story of the son of an Egyptian father and an Israelite mother who in a strife with an Israelite blasphemed Yahweh, for which he had to pay with his life (Lev. 24 10–14). It appears still better in the story of the Israelite who had married a Midianite woman and brought her into the camp, for Phinehas who in his zeal killed both of them was greatly rewarded (Num. 25 6–13), and the extermination of the Midianites was ordered and executed as a result of this defilement (Num. 31). Contact and intercourse with heathen are defiling,[1] and Israel must be clean. Strictly speaking, they should have nothing to do with foreigners. That was however impossible in real life. Foreigners lived among them in Palestine, and they could not be driven out. But certain obligations could be imposed upon them, which they must fulfil. There were certain laws that God had given to all mankind. The Sabbath had been written into the very foundation of the world, it should, therefore, really be observed by all men, although this is not definitely stated. At the time of Noah all men were prohibited to murder and to eat blood; that was definitely meant for all. Now of foreigners who resided among them Israel had required even before the exile that they obey these universal laws, but had not seen fit to impose any special religious duties upon them besides the keeping of the Sabbath. For P this was not enough, for he was intent on removing all impurity from Israel; if therefore one of these resident foreigners had become unclean, he must purify himself, for the impurity was contagious. The comparison of a preëxilic law with its exilic formulation illustrates this different point of view:

Ye shall not eat of anything that dies of itself: thou mayest give it to the sojourner that is within thy	And every soul that eats that which dies of itself, or that which is torn of beasts, whether he be a native

[1] It is interesting to note in this connection how strongly P himself was influenced by foreign ideas and practices. He used Babylonian cosmology in the story of creation, Babylonian history with its four ages of the world, Babylonian chronology and geography, yes even Babylonian cultic elements in his ceremonial law. But it must be observed too that they were all so completely assimilated that they were not felt as foreign elements at all.

gates, that he may eat it; or thou mayest sell it to a foreigner: for thou art a holy people to Yahweh thy God. (Deut. 14 [21]) (Israelite) or a resident stranger, he shall wash his clothes, and bathe himself in water, and be unclean until the evening, then shall he be clean. But if he wash them not, nor bathe his body, then he shall bear his punishment. (Lev. 17 [15f.])

The general law in P is this: "Ye shall have one manner of law, as well for the sojourner as for the native," *i.e.* Israelite (Lev. 24 [22]; Num. 15 [15f. 29]). But this has reference only to "the stranger that sojourns among them," the resident foreigner, the client, not to others. Here was the basis for the later, less exclusive, view, that religion and not birth was the real characteristic of the true Jew, that membership in Yahweh's congregation depended on the fulfilment of the law, not on Jewish parentage. But P did not draw this conclusion, his attitude was narrow and exclusive. He did believe in monotheism but not in its universal applications; his conception of God was in many ways exalted and spiritual, but in others limited and particularistic. He had no missionary zeal, no love for the heathen. The precious prophetic heritage of the world was lost in P, for to him the Jews were the people of the law, separate from the nations, without any sense of obligation to bring the true religion to the peoples of the world.

In one direction P led to an altogether unintended liberal result. Although he emphasized the cult at the one legitimate place (Jerusalem) most strongly, he nevertheless showed how Jewish religion could be practised without sacrifices. Certain laws could be kept anywhere, especially the Sabbath and circumcision, which were "signs of the covenant" also in foreign lands. The Jews in the dispersion could not sacrifice, but they could observe many laws of ritual cleanness. On the face of it, it would seem impossible for them to celebrate their festivals anywhere else but in Jerusalem. But P paved the way for the later development by making the Passover once more a family festival, which need not be celebrated at Jerusalem, as D had insisted. The killing of the lamb was not a sacrifice but a secular act, and thus it was possible anywhere. P said nothing of this kind about other festivals, but the tendency had been introduced and it led ultimately to the belief in and to the practice of a religion without sacrificial cult. The only kind of religion left to the Jews after the final destruction of the temple was not the spiritual religion of the prophets but the religion of the law without the sacrificial cult: orthodox Judaism. It is one of the paradoxes of history that the one who insisted more strongly that any other on the absolute importance of the sacrificial cult through which the direct connection between God and His people was maintained should be the one who showed that Jewish religion could exist without it.

Although the Priest Code was adopted under the leadership of Ezra as the fundamental law of Israel, it was not the only sacred book of the Jewish church. The law of Deuteronomy, especially in the edition which had combined JED, was of fundamental authority too, and could not be superseded by P, however earnestly the priestly writers might have wished it. In a sense they felt that they were continuators of this same work. They had laid more stress on the priestly and ritual elements, it is true, but Deuteronomy claimed to go back to Moses, and they themselves believed that they did so too, for they were merely elaborating the Mosaic religion. Whether they were right or not in this conviction makes no difference at this point. In any case, they came to the conclusion that P must be joined together with JED in one composite work. In this compilation, which they promptly undertook, they showed great skill. They felt that they had to exercise wide tolerance for the divergent traditions in JE. They could not agree with them, and yet they could not remove them altogether, because they were sacred to the people. The task was difficult, but they accomplished it; and when it was finished, they had stamped the entire book with their own spirit. The priestly document gave to the whole its own distinctive tone; it was the basis of the compilation, the ground work (*"Grundschrift"*), and supplied the frame and order. In its clearly marked divisions the appropriate parts of JE were inserted. Only rarely did the redactors (= R ^{p}) deviate from P's order in favor of JE's. Usually they gave both P's and the other stories side by side, *e.g.* the story of creation (Gen. 1–2 ^{4a} P; 2 ^{4b} $^{ff.}$ J) or the story of Abraham's covenant (Gen. 15 JE; Gen. 17 P) or the story of Moses's call (Ex. 3 JE; Ex. 6 P). Sometimes they wove both together into a single story, as, *e.g.*, in the stories of the deluge (Gen. 6–8), of Israel's flight from Egypt and the passage of the Sea of Reeds (Ex. 14), of the Manna and the quails (Ex. 16), the genealogy of Noah's sons (Gen. 10). In this interwoven work P predominated. When the redactors gave only one story, they took P's and omitted JE's. Thus they left out JE's accounts of the birth of Ishmael and the death of Abram, and retained only a few fragments of J's genealogies of Seth (Gen. 4 $^{25f.}$ 5 ^{29}). Sometimes the combination of the sources necessitated editorial additions and changes, in order to connect or harmonize the various sections. Thus, e.g., in Gen. 27 ^{46} the editors connected most cleverly JE's story of Jacob's flight to Haran with P's. In Gen. 32 ^{29}–35 ^{10} they changed Israel to Jacob on account of Gen. 35 ^{10} (P).

In Deuteronomy there was very little to do for R ^{p}. Excepting a very few editorial traces (Deut. 1 ^{3} 4 $^{41-43}$ 9 $^{22-24}$ (?) 10 $^{6f.}$ (?)) and the combination of P's story of Moses' survey of the land, and of his death (Deut. 32 $^{48-52}$ 34 $^{1a.}$ $^{7-9}$), they are probably responsible for inserting the interesting dodecalogue (the twelve laws) which in the form of a liturgical office contained twelve curses upon various crimes (Deut. 27 $^{14-26}$). Its original may be quite old, but its present formulation is hardly earlier than the exile.

The result of the combination was a great success. Here was a great historico-legal work, compiled from various sources but held together in a remarkable unity by a grand purposeful plan. It was essentially the plan of J. Only, in the combined work it was more developed. All history is directed by God and illuminated by a great plan which runs through all its phases: the purpose of God to bring all the nations to a true knowledge of Himself. To be sure, this universal conception has its limitation in that it involved for the heathen the individual's incorporation in Israel and the nations' subjection to it. It is true, not the history but the law was the essential element, the revelation of God which regulated the ideal state; and *torah* or law became the official name of the book. But its real significance and greatness lie in its universal aspect, not in its limitations. Long before any Greek or Roman historian applied the universal idea to history it was current in Israel: the history of the world was controlled by a great purpose.

The book was completed by 330 B.C., for the Samaritans who seceded from the Jews and built their own temple on Mount Gerizim had the Pentateuch in substantially the same form as the Jews. That minor changes were still made even after this time, we know from a comparison with the Greek Bible which was translated about 250 B.C. It is in this final form that the Pentateuch exerted an influence upon Judaism, Christianity, and Islam which is unparalleled in history. Here the sum of the development of ages, embodying religion and cosmology, ethics and jurisprudence, was combined in an imposing form. The whole was attributed to Moses, the founder of Israel and of its religion. It was the great Book, the Bible, for the people.

The Book of Joshua had not been included in the great compilation that became authoritative. It was the *law* of Deuteronomy that had first been adopted as canonical, and it was the priestly *law* that was adopted under Ezra. The death of the great lawgiver Moses marked therefore quite naturally the end of the Book of the Law. Both P and the older sources, JE and D, had contained the story of the invasion, the conquest, and distribution of Canaan, and all of them existed still in separate editions and were held in high esteem. These also were now joined together with P. A priestly editor, not the editor of the Pentateuch, combined D and P in the Book of Joshua. For the first part (Josh. 1–12) he took the deuteronomic book of Joshua as his basis, and utilized but a few P sections. For the second part (Josh. 13–24) P supplied most of the material; although D furnished also here the framework. Into this combined work some sections from J and E were inserted later on.

In the older sources, JE and D, the story of Israel had been continued to the time of the Judges and of Samuel. There had been no independent priestly treatment of these times. But now a priestly writer combined the old JE book of Judges with the later deuteronomistic edition. He reintroduced the important Yahwistic summary of Israel's conquest at the beginning (Judg. 1 1–2 5); and the stories of Micah and the Danites (Judg. 17f.), and of the outrage at Gibeah at the end (Judg. 19–21), with some elements of his own. The last story he retouched (Judg. 20, *passim*) and added to it a very late, homiletic story (Judg. 21 1–14. 24f.); the summary of the conquest he worked over (Judg. 1 1a. 4. 8f. 18 2 1b–5a) so that it corresponded more to his own point of view and appeared to treat events "after Joshua's death." It is probable enough that we owe to him also the rein-sertion of the Minor Judges (Judg. 3 [31] 10 [1–5] 12 [8–15]), of the story of Abimelech (Judg. 9), and perhaps of the last Samson story (16). In the deuteronomistic Book of Judges all of these had been omitted as not fitting into the deuteronomistic view of the history of the period. We are all the more grateful to this editor for their preservation, because most of them belong to the historically most valuable material. The deuteronomistic book had already made a new beginning after Joshua's death. The priestly editor separated the book definitely from Joshua on the one hand, and from Samuel on the other, for D's edition of Judges had included Samuel as the last judge.

The Book of Samuel underwent a similar process of redaction. The important sections which had been omitted by the deuteronomistic editor, the story of Saul's rejection and Agag's sacrifice (1 Sam. 15), of the witch of Endor (1 Sam. 28), and the famous series of David stories in 2 Sam. 9–20 were reinserted. Only a few priestly additions, such as the insertion of the Levites in the story of the ark (1 Sam. 6 [15. 17f.]) were made by the editor. Perhaps only one story of the kind which is so characteristic of the postexilic times was introduced: Samuel's victory over the Philistines (1 Sam. 7 [7–14]).

In the Books of Kings more such stories were inserted; most important of all are the stories of the disobedient prophet at Bethel (1 Ki. 13 with the reference to it in 2 Ki. 23 [16–18]), and of Elijah sending fire from heaven upon the captains and soldiers (2 Ki. 1 [9–16]). Aside from these complete stories, the priestly redaction of the Books of Kings is slight, the interpolated clauses and sentences in 1 Ki. 7 [47ff.] 8 [3ff.] in the temple story and especially the additions to the story of the origin of the Samaritan religion (2 Ki. 17 [29–40]) are the most significant.

This long process of writing and editing came to an end sometime in the Greek period. The result justified the arduous labor. The entire history from the creation to the Babylonian exile, from Genesis to 2 Kings, was complete, essentially as we now have it. It was in this form that the books were to gain their great historical importance. But the development of the religion of Israel can be understood only after the literary process which led to this composite form has been unravelled, and the constituent elements have been viewed in their historical development.

CHAPTER XVIII

POSTEXILIC HISTORIANS

AFTER the Jews had returned from captivity, the times were not such as to incite one to write a history of them. Any historical interest that existed was directed to the past. The only contemporary, authoritative sources for the period directly following the exile are the prophetic books (cf. chap. XVI). /The priests kept, of course, the temple journal and genealogical lists, but these were preserved in the temple archives and not given to the public. Not till the latter half of the fifth century do we come upon historical narratives. They were written by the two leading men of the day, Nehemiah and Ezra, who composed memoirs of the great work that had been entrusted to them.

Nehemiah wrote his story after he had returned to the royal court of Artaxerxes in 432 B.C. from his governorship in Jerusalem. In a simple, straightforward, vivid manner he told how in the year 445 B.C., when he was the king's cupbearer, at the Persian court, he learned to his utter dismay of the ruined condition of the walls of Jerusalem; how he gained the king's permission to rebuild them; how he accomplished the work in an incredibly short time in spite of determined opposition within and without Jerusalem; how he enlarged the population of the city; and how he celebrated the dedication of the walls by a solemn festival. Twelve years later, in 433 B.C., he came again to Jerusalem and corrected certain abuses in connection with the temple, the payment of the Levites, the observance of the Sabbath, and the intermarriage with foreigners. These memoirs are now preserved in the Book of Nehemiah.[1] Lucidity of thought and expression characterize them throughout. Here was again a master of description whose keen insight and literary ability make the reader see the various characters and scenes which he had painted with such accuracy and life-likeness. Nehe-

[1] Neh. 1 ¹—7 ⁵· ⁶⁻⁷³ᵃ (= Ezra 2) 11 ¹ᶠ· 12 ³¹ᶠ· ³⁷⁻⁴⁰ 13 ⁴⁻³¹.

miah's own personality stands forth quite clearly. His ability and fearlessness, his devotion and unselfishness, all shine through his story. He wrought for his people and his God. All through his book his prayer goes up like a refrain, "Remember this, O God, for good," as though he had consciously spread the record of his work before his Maker. It is self-evident that such autobiographical material, written by the great leader himself, is of priceless historical value, especially when its inherent trustworthiness is so great as in this case. For historical certainty we should, of course, need other sources from the same period, preferably by one of Nehemiah's opponents or at least by one who held different views. The recently discovered contemporaneous Jewish papyri from Syene and Elephantine throw welcome light on the times of Nehemiah and mention even the high priest Johanan and Nehemiah's archenemy Sanballat "the governor of Samaria," and probably also Nehemiah's brother Hanani who may have been the bearer of a letter concerning the Massoth festival to the Jews of Elephantine, but to Nehemiah himself they do not refer. Neither do we learn anything about him from Ezra, the other leader in Jerusalem.

According to tradition Ezra came to Jerusalem in the seventh year of Artaxerxes = 458 B.C. (Ezr. 7 [8]), but for various reasons it is more probable that he did not come before, but after Nehemiah, perhaps in the thirty-seventh year of Artaxerxes, 428 B.C. While Nehemiah was a man of affairs, Ezra was a man of religion. A priest by birth and training, he had studied the law in Babylonia and become filled with the burning desire to go to the Holy City in order to establish it there. He tells us in his memoirs which he wrote about this undertaking that King Artaxerxes was favorable to his enterprise and permitted him to go with any others who would join him. Among his company there were at first only priests and laymen, but no Levites, as was natural enough in view of their degradation which Ezekiel had justified and which had been embodied in the Priestly Law. But Ezra took quick measures to remedy this, and soon they set out with 38 Levites and 220 Nethinim to go to Jerusalem without military escort, depending solely on the protection of Almighty God.

For I was ashamed to ask of the king a band of soldiers and horsemen to help us against the enemy in the way, because we had spoken to the king,

saying, "The hand of our God is upon all them that seek Him, for good."
(Ezr. 8 ^{22})

They arrived safely in Jerusalem and turned the silver, gold, and
vessels which they had brought from Babylonia over to the temple
(Ezr. 7f.). Shortly afterwards, at a great convocation of the people
in Jerusalem on the first day of the seventh month, Ezra read and
expounded the law. On the second day of this reading he came
upon the law of the feast of tabernacles, and since it was just the
time for it, it was promptly celebrated in strict accordance with this
law (Neh. 8, which is the sequel of Ezr. 8). Not long after, Ezra
learned to his utter astonishment and dismay of the marriages of
many Jews with heathen women, which the law of Deuteronomy
had still permitted (Deut. 21 $^{10ff.}$) but upon which the Priest Code
frowned as defiling. By his contagious enthusiasm for the holiness
of Israel and by the power of his fanatical personality he carried the
people, with few exceptions, with him in his demand that such marriages be dissolved and no more such be entered upon. In a covenant the people solemnly pledged themselves to do thus and to
observe the whole law. Besides this they guaranteed the maintenance of the sacrificial cult at Jerusalem and of the clergy (Ezr. 9f.;
Neh. 9f.). Thus the Priest Code was made the fundamental law of
the community. This is usually dated in the year 444 B.C., because
Neh. 8–10, which are part of the Ezra story, are now woven into the
Nehemiah story and placed in Nehemiah's time. But this was not
the original sequence. In the earliest Greek translation of Ezra,
the so-called First Book of Esdras, Neh. 7 ^{72} 8 $^{1–13}$ follow Ezr. 8.
Originally the order seems to have been Ezr. 7f., Neh. 8, Ezr. 9f.
Aside from this displacement the memoirs of Ezra have suffered by
the work of the editor who changed the autobiographical form into
the biographical (Ezr. 10; Neh. 8–10). This editor was the Chronicler. His point of view is so much like Ezra's that he has in all
seriousness been regarded as the author of these memoirs, but without real justification.

In the fight against the mixed marriages the nativists, led by
Nehemiah and Ezra, won out. But there were also men of broader
sympathies. To one of them we owe most probably the charming
little idyl which has always roused the admiration of literary men

by its exquisite beauty and which Goethe declared to be "the loveliest little whole, that has been preserved to us among the epics and idyls": the Book of Ruth. It tells of the loyalty of Ruth, the daughter-in-law of Naomi, her diligence and prudence and her great reward. After the death of her husband and her two sons in Moab, where the sons had married the Moabite wives Orpah and Ruth, Naomi decided to go back to her native town of Bethlehem in Judah. In spite of her remonstrances Ruth insisted on going with her, declaring in those beautiful words that have since been repeated by thousands of women in the solemn hour of marriage:

> Entreat me not to leave thee, and to return from following after thee; for whither thou goest, I will go; and where thou lodgest, I will lodge; thy people shall be my people, and thy God my God; where thou diest, will I die, and there will I be buried: Yahweh do so to me, and more also, if aught but death part thee and me. (Ruth 1 [16f.])

They arrived in Bethlehem at the beginning of barley harvest and Ruth at once went into the fields to glean after the reapers. She happened on the field of Boaz, who saw her later and invited her to glean only in his field, and gave orders to treat her kindly. To her astonished question, why he should show such favor to a foreigner, he replied,

> It has fully been showed me, all that thou hast done to thy mother-in-law since the death of thy husband; and how thou hast left thy father and thy mother, and thy native land, and art come to a people that thou knewest not heretofore. Yahweh recompense thy work, and a full reward be given thee of Yahweh, the God of Israel, under whose wings thou art come to take refuge. (Ruth 2 [11f.])

When Naomi learned of Ruth's good fortune and in whose field she had been gleaning she rejoiced, for Boaz was one of her near kinsmen. And when the harvest came to an end, she had her plan ready, and Ruth obediently carried it out, although it involved no ordinary risk. But Naomi had estimated Boaz's character rightly. When he started up that night from his sleep on the threshing-floor after the joyful harvest meal and discovered Ruth lying at his feet, he treated her with honor and promised to fulfil his kinsman's duty by marrying her, if a still closer relative did not claim her. Richly laden with gifts Ruth returned home to Naomi. On the morrow Boaz offered the kinsman's privilege of buying Naomi's field to the other relative, but when he refused after learning that he must also marry Ruth in addition, Boaz took her as his wife amidst the loud and hearty felicitations of all the people. In due course, Ruth bore a son, and the happy Naomi became his nurse. And this son Obed became later Jesse's father, and Jesse's son was none other than King David![1]

No lesson is appended, no moral is affixed. The author was far too great an artist for this. Was it not plain to everybody that God is no respecter of race and nationality, that He looks at the heart and rewards such goodness as Ruth's most richly? Even a hated Moabite whom the law would never allow to become a Jew (Deut. 23 [3]; Neh. 13 [1-3]) may be certain of His blessing, if he is only righteous in his life. And surely, God does not look with indiscriminate disfavor upon all mixed marriages, since He blessed Boaz's marriage with the lovely Moabitess Ruth in such signal fashion that they became the ancestors of Israel's greatest king! True religion alone counts with Him and that is a matter of the heart and life, not of race and nationality.

This large-hearted view did not prevail. The opponents were too strong. Nehemiah expelled one of the sons of the high priest, who had married a daughter of the Samaritan noble Sanballat and who refused to give her up. He disdained even to mention the culprit's name in his memoirs. But we know it from Josephus (Antiquities xi, 7 [2] 8 [2]) who tells us that it was Manasseh, whose wife was Nicaso, the daughter of Sanballat the governor. But Josephus placed him (wrongly) in the time of Alexander the Great, a century later. His brother, he tells us, was the high priest Jaddua who in full accord with the people requested him either to divorce his wife or to resign his priestly office. In his perplexity he turned to Sanballat, who promised him the erection of a temple on Mount Gerizim and persuaded him and many Jerusalemites, among them a number of priests who were in similar difficulties, to settle at Shechem and to found the Samaritan church. So it came about that on Mount Gerizim a priesthood officiated with a high priest of pure highpriestly blood as its head. A bitter controversy arose between

[1] A later writer added the longer genealogy of Boaz carrying it back to Perez, because he had been mentioned in 4 [12].

the two factions at Jerusalem and Gerizim. The one party claimed that the law sanctioned Jerusalem, the other Gerizim, as the sole legitimate place of worship (cf. John 4 [20]). The "Samaritans" had taken the law with them; it was as sacred to them as to the Jews, and thus they appealed to it in justification of their claim. Deut. 27 [4] was distinctly in their favor, for here Mount Gerizim was mentioned as the place where Yahweh had commanded an altar to be built, whereas nowhere in the whole book of the law was Jerusalem named as the sole place of worship. This was most uncomfortable to the Jews, and so in time they changed the reading in Deut. 27 [4] from "Gerizim" to "Ebal" in order to get rid of this argument. This was however not enough for the Jews. They tried to worst their opponents by casting contempt upon their origin. They told that the Samaritans were a mongrel race which had been transplanted to the province of Samaria by the Assyrians after all the Israelites had been taken into exile. They knew nothing of Yahweh, and only a plague of lions compelled them to send to their government in Assyria for a priest who should instruct them in "the law of the god of the land." But even after this priest had come and taught them, they retained their own religion in combination with their newly learnt fear of Yahweh. Their religion was therefore nothing but heathenism mixed with some ingredients of Yahweh cult. This story got eventually into the Book of Kings (2 Ki. 17 [24ff.]). The Chronicler held the same view.

There may be an anti-samaritan bias also in the Aramaic story of the restoration of the temple which is now preserved in Ezra 5 [1]–6 [18], for here the legitimacy of the Jerusalem temple, not the religious but the political legitimacy, is proved by documents which show the official sanction of its erection by the Persian kings Cyrus and Darius. When the Persian governor Tattenai found on a tour of inspection that the Jews were busily engaged in rebuilding the temple, he asked for their authorization and was referred by them to a decree of Cyrus which had permitted it. Upon his report to Darius, search was made in the archives and the decree was found. The king renewed and amplified it, and the temple was completed on the third day of the month Adar in the sixth year of the reign of Darius (March, 515). The author of this story gave also the correspondence between King Artaxerxes and his officials in Syria about the rebuilding of the walls of Jerusalem (Ezr. 4 8–24). He can hardly have stopped with this, for it resulted in the cessation of the building for a time. He must have told how the fortifications were later on completed by royal permission. But this sequel is not preserved ; the story of Nehemiah now takes its place. The author wrote his story in Aramaic, perhaps because he wanted it to be read by friend and foe alike. The people spoke Aramaic and not Hebrew in his time. Possibly he thought, since the Aramaic was the diplomatic language of the Western Persian empire, that the Persian officials would also take cognizance of his tract. Too little is preserved however to allow us more than to query whether he intended to influence them to oppose the building of the Samaritan temple. We are not sure when he wrote, presumably before the fall of the Persian empire (331 B.C.) because he appealed so strongly to the Persian sanction of the Jerusalem temple. The trustworthiness of his story has been much debated. If the order in which the Aramaic story at present appears in Ezr. 4 8–6 18 were original, we should place very little reliance on its historical accuracy, for the temple would have been rebuilt according to it under Darius II (424–405) instead of Darius I (522–485), which would be a glaring historical mistake. But the present order is due to the editor, who overlooked that the correspondence of Artaxerxes concerned the rebuilding of the city walls and who placed it here, because it seemed to him to give a documentary explanation of the problem, why the temple was not rebuilt by the exiles directly after their return from Babylonia under Cyrus. Apart from this, the story makes the impression of being well informed historically. The official documents too appear to be copies of genuine letters and edicts. It is much to be regretted that not more of this Aramaic history has been handed down.

The interest of the age was not primarily in history but in religion, and in history only as a means of religious education. Religious truths alone were important. History enforced and illustrated them. The Books of Samuel and Kings offered a great store of illustrative material. But the truth had not always been brought out in them and many facts needed explanation. Accepting the dogma of retribution without reserve, priest and lay scholars asked, e.g., why the pious King Uzziah had been punished by leprosy, and why the great reformer Josiah had fallen in battle, if piety was always rewarded with long life and happiness; or why so wicked a king as Manasseh was permitted to reign 55 years, longer than any other king, if wickedness was always punished by disaster and premature death? Such matters constituted problems for investigation and research (*midrash* as the Hebrew would say). Answers in the form of stories were given by scholars and scribes, and all these various tales and explanations were collected in the large book of "the Midrash of the Book of the Kings." It is no longer in existence, but it was utilized by the Chronicler, who refers to it in 2 Chr. 24 [27]. Most probably he meant this book also when he referred to "the Book of the Kings of Judah and Israel"; or when he spoke of "the words of Samuel the seer, of Nathan the prophet, of Gad the seer, of Shemaiah the prophet, of Iddo the seer, of the Seers; or of the Prophecy of Ahijah the Shilonite, the Vision of Iddo the seer, of the history of Uzziah by Isaiah the prophet; or of the words of Jehu, son of Hanani, *which are inserted in the Book of the Kings of Israel*, and the vision of Isaiah the prophet the son of Amoz *in the Book of the Kings of Judah and Israel.*" He thought that the prophets were the authors of the history of their time and he referred therefore to the particular sections in the Midrash of the Book of the Kings in this manner.

The Chronicler followed in the footsteps of the deuteronomists who had been pragmatic historians. He believed most heartily in their doctrine of retribution, and applied it even more thoroughly than they had done. But while they had viewed history and judged the individual kings from the point of view of the deuteronomic law, the Chronicler viewed, arranged, and modified history in the light of the Priest Code. His interests were primarily ecclesiastical; in the centre of his interest stood Jerusalem and the temple, and his history was really an "Ecclesiastical Chronicle of Jerusalem." He wrote not earlier than 300 B.C., more probably in the third century. He began his story with Adam and ended it with Ezra and Nehemiah, for these books formed originally a part of his work.

His introduction consisted of a history from Adam to David, in the form of genealogical lists with frequent historical notices inserted (I Chr. 1–9). This reminds us at once of P. The material for this he took mainly from the Hexateuch and the Books of Samuel, some additional lists perhaps from the temple archives. It is significant that he also felt impelled to begin his history with Adam; he indicated thereby that the whole history of the world culminated in the temple at Jerusalem. He was so greatly interested in the priests and Levites, the only legitimate ministers of Yahweh, and still more in the Levitical singers and musicians and their liturgy, that one cannot escape the conclusion that he himself was one of them.

The real story began for him with David. A comparison of his treatment of the history of David with that of the Books of Samuel which forms the basis of his work is most instructive. The struggle for the kingship was omitted; directly after the death of Saul,

> Yahweh turned the kingdom to David the son of Jesse. Then all Israel gathered themselves to David unto Hebron . . . and anointed David king over Israel according to the word of Yahweh by Samuel. (1 Chr. 10 ^{14}–11 ^{3})

The kingship of Saul's son Eshbaal was also completely ignored; David was Saul's immediate successor! After "all Israel" had helped David capture the stronghold of Zion, three lists of the adherents of David are given, the first (11 $^{10-47}$) was taken from 2 Sam. 23, the second and third (12 $^{1-22.\ 23-40}$) are characterized by immense numbers, "a great host, like the host of God" in the second, more than 300,000 in the third, among them 4600 Levites and 3722 priests, — wholly incredible!

> All these, being men of war, that could order the battle array [including the priests and the Levites!] came with a perfect heart to Hebron to make David king over all Israel: and all the rest also of Israel were of one heart to make David king.

How different all this is from the story in the Book of Samuel! David's first act after his conquest of Zion, according to the Chronicler, was the bringing of the ark thither, but the tragic death of Uzzah who had tried to steady the falling ark with his hand was interpreted as a sign of Yahweh's anger and the ark was left at Obededom's house for the next three months (1 Chr. 13). This time was filled out with the building of David's palace and his war against the Philistines, for secular matters were only episodes to the Chronicler (1 Chr. 14). Then David prepared to bring the ark to its appointed place. Here the Chronicler revels in priests and Levites. David had discovered that

None ought to carry the ark of God but the Levites, for them has Yahweh chosen to carry the ark of God, and to minister into Him forever. . . . Because ye (the Levites) bore it not at the first, Yahweh our God made a breach upon us, because we sought Him not according to the ordinance.

It makes no difference to the Chronicler that this is in direct contradiction to 2 Sam. 6, which he himself had excerpted in ch. 13 (see vv. [11f.]). This was his view of the matter: David appointed Levitical singers and musicians for the festal procession and then the Levites carried the ark to the city into the tent that David had pitched for it. After the offerings had been brought,

He appointed certain of the Levites to minister before the ark of Yahweh, and to celebrate and to thank and praise Yahweh, the God of Israel,

and a festal psalm, prepared for the occasion by David, was sung by Asaph and his brethren. The ministers of the religious services were then definitely assigned (15f.). The plan of David to build a temple and Yahweh's opposition through Nathan (ch. 17) as well as David's wars are reproduced in the words of the Book of Samuel, but it is noteworthy that everything that reflects badly on David was omitted, the stories of Meribaal and Zibah, of Bathsheba and Uriah, of Tamar and Amnon, of Absalom's rebellion, and of the offering of the sons of Saul. Similarly David's almost disastrous encounter with the Philistine giant Ishbibenob was omitted, and the report of 2 Sam. 21 [19] that "Elhanan the son of Jaareoregim the Bethlehemite slew Goliath the Gittite, the staff of whose spear was like a weaver's beam" was characteristically harmonized with 1 Sam. 17 by making Elhanan slay "the brother of Goliath"! In the story of David's census the Chronicler made also certain characteristic corrections of the older report. It was not Yahweh who moved David to number Israel, but "Satan," for God tempts no man to evil. Joab did not count Levi, evidently because the law (Num. 1 [49]) had forbidden the numbering of Levites, nor Benjamin apparently because the holy city was located in Benjamin. David paid not 50 shekels for Araunah's threshing floor, but the more royal sum of 600 shekels. The sacredness of this place was not only revealed by the appearance of the angel there, but the divine acceptance of the altar which David built there was accentuated by the Chronicler in the addition,

> And he called upon Yahweh, and He answered him from heaven by fire upon the altar of burnt offering. (21 ^{28})

And yet the Chronicler was too much under the sway of the Priest Code's conception, that the tabernacle was the only legitimate place of worship until the temple had been built, not to feel the need of adding the explanation:

> At that time, when David saw that Yahweh had answered him in the threshing-floor of Ornan the Jebusite, then he sacrificed there. For the tabernacle of Yahweh, which Moses made in the wilderness, and the altar of burnt-offering, were at that time in the high place at Gibeon. But David could not go before it to inquire of God; for he was afraid because of the sword of the angel of Yahweh. Then David said, This is the house of Yahweh God, and this is the altar of burnt-offering for Israel. (1 Chr. 21 ^{28}–22 ^{1})

Then the Chronicler told how David prepared the temple. He followed here no source, but gave his own ideas of what must have occurred. Everything so far had been leading up to this. David arranged for the workmen and for all the materials that were needed for the building of the temple, for

> David said, Solomon my son is young and tender, and the house that is to be built for Yahweh must be exceeding magnificent, of fame and of glory throughout all countries: I will therefore make preparation for it. So David prepared abundantly before his death.
>
> Then he called for Solomon his son, and charged him to build a house for Yahweh, the God of Israel. And David said to Solomon his son, As for me, it was in my heart to build a house to the name of Yahweh my God. But the word of Yahweh came to me, saying, Thou hast shed blood abundantly, and hast made great wars: thou shalt not build a house to My name, because thou hast shed much blood upon the earth in My sight. Behold, a son shall be born to thee, who shall be a man of rest; and I will give him rest from all his enemies round about; for his name shall be Solomon, and I will give peace and quietness unto Israel in his days. He shall build a house for My name; and he shall be My son, and I will be his father; and I will establish the throne of his kingdom over Israel for ever. (1 Chr. 22 $^{5-10}$)

Quite differently 2 Sam. 7 (cf. 1 Chr. 17) had explained why David did not build the temple. After all the preparations were completed, including the appointment of the priests, Levites, doorkeepers, and singers, who were all carefully divided into classes and assigned their offices by lot, and among whom the musicians were treated with special consideration (David himself invented their instruments for them and assumed the final direction), — after all this had been arranged, a great convocation of the leaders of Israel was called together, to whom Yahweh's oracle that Solomon should be the next king and the builder of the temple was unfolded; whereupon the plan of the temple in all its details, sketched by Yahweh Himself, was given to Solomon, accompanied by warm exhortations to carry out the plan which had been so carefully prepared in every way.   After an appeal to the assembled nobles, who contributed liberally for the work, David prayed, and all blessed Yahweh and rejoiced with sacrifices before Him.   Then they made Solomon king, "the second time" the Chronicler says (29 ²²), for David had already made him king in 23 ¹.   The palace intrigue as a result of which Solomon had actually gained the throne was of course omitted.   Nothing must mar the picture of the great saint who had built the temple.   How much at variance the David of the Chronicler is from the David of the Books of Samuel and Kings! There he is a king and hero, a warrior and statesman, the real founder of the kingdom; here he is the sweet singer of Israel, the founder of the temple, and the author of its liturgy.   There he is surrounded by warriors and men of affairs, here by priests and Levites.   There we have secular, here ecclesiastical history.   The hero has become a saint, the king a liturgist.   Which picture is historical and which is not, is manifest at once.

In the first story of Solomon, that of his worship at Gibeon, the difference between the deuteronomistic and the priestly points of view appears quite characteristically.   1 Ki. 3 ²⁻⁴ had said, in justification of his offering on "the great high place,"

Only the people sacrificed in the high places, because there was no house built for the name of Yahweh until those days.   And Solomon loved Yahweh, walking in the statutes of David his father: only he sacrificed and burnt incense in the high places.   And the king went to Gibeon to sacrifice there; for that was the great high place: a thousand burnt-offerings did Solomon offer upon that altar. (1 Ki. 3 ²⁻⁴)

The Chronicler, to whom the tabernacle at Gibeon was the sole legitimate sanctuary, needed no justification for this.   He wrote therefore,

So Solomon, and all the assembly with him, went to the high place that was at Gibeon; for there was the tent of meeting of God, which Moses the servant of Yahweh had made in the wilderness.   But the ark of God had David brought up from Kiriath-jearim to the place that David had prepared for it; for he had pitched a tent for it at Jerusalem.   Moreover the brazen altar, that Bezalel the son of Uri, the son of Hur, had made, was there before the tabernacle of Yahweh and Solomon and the assembly resorted to it.   And Solomon went up thither to the brazen altar before Yahweh, which was at the tent of meeting, and offered a thousand burnt-offerings upon it. (2 Chr. 1 $^{3-6}$)

But the conclusion of the story in 1 Ki. 3 ^{15} he could not use, so he wrote for

He came to Jerusalem, and stood before the ark of the covenant of Yahweh, and offered up burnt-offerings, and made a feast to all his servants. (1 Ki. 3 ^{15})	So Solomon came from the high place that was at Gibeon, from before the tent of meeting, to Jerusalem. (2 Chr. 1 ^{14})

Solomon, according to the Chronicler's view, could not have sacrificed in Jerusalem before the temple was built.   So he omitted the reference to it.   At the beginning he had added that the king was accompanied by an assembly of the notables of Israel in order to enhance the splendor and glory of the scene, and now he followed it by a description of Solomon's immense wealth.   Then the story of the building of the temple was begun.   The preparations, including the contract with King Hiram of Tyre, and the description of the temple differ comparatively little from the Book of Kings, but in the dedication the Chronicler elaborated in characteristic fashion the part of the priests and Levites and especially of the singers and musicians. 1 Ki. 8 $^{10f.}$ had only mentioned,

And it came to pass, when the priests were come out of the holy place, that the cloud filled the house of Yahweh so that the priests could not stand to minister by reason of the cloud, for the glory of Yahweh filled the house of Yahweh.

After " the holy place " the Chronicler inserted,

For all the priests that were present had sanctified themselves, and did not keep their courses; also the Levites who were the singers, all of them, even Asaph, Heman, Jeduthun, and their sons and their brethren, arrayed in fine linen, with cymbals and psalteries and harps, stood at the east end of the altar and with them a hundred and twenty priests sounding with trumpets; it came to pass, when the trumpeters and singers were as one to make one sound to be heard in praising and thanking Yahweh; and when they lifted up their voice with the trumpets and cymbals and instruments of music, and praised Yahweh, saying, For He is good; for His lovingkindness endures for ever. (2 Chr. 5 $^{11b-13a}$)

The statement that Solomon "stood before the altar of Yahweh" was annotated by the explanation that he had made for himself "a brazen pulpit" on which he stood and prayed, for the Chronicler could not believe that the saintly Solomon had arrogated to himself priestly rights. Instead of the blessing of Solomon (1 Ki. 8 $^{54-61}$), which was again a priestly function, the Chronicler told of fire descending from heaven and consuming the sacrifices, and of the glory of Yahweh filling the whole temple (2 Chr. 7 $^{1-3}$). The priests' and especially the musicians' part had not been brought out in the old story, so the Chronicler added,

And the priests stood, according to their offices; the Levites also with instruments of music of Yahweh which David the king had made to give thanks to Yahweh (for His lovingkindness endures for ever), when David praised by their ministry: and the priests sounded trumpets before them; and all Israel stood. (2 Chr. 7 ^{6})

Instead of sending the people away on the eighth day, as 1 Ki. 8 ^{66} had done, the Chronicler had them celebrate this day in Jerusalem in accordance with the priestly law of Num. 29 ^{35}. In the remaining part of the story of Solomon the Chronicler changed the statement that Solomon had ceded twenty Galilean cities to Hiram into the directly opposite assertion that Hiram had given them to Solomon, who settled Israelites in them; and asserted that Solomon did not subject any Israelite to forced labor in his building operations but only the Hittites, Amorites, Perrizites, Hivites, and Jebusites. The moving of Solomon's queen, the Pharaoh's daughter, from the city of David into Solomon's palace, after it had been completed, was commented upon in this wholly unhistorical but characteristically priestly manner,

For he said, My wife shall not dwell in the house of David king of Israel, because the places are holy whereunto the ark of Yahweh has come. (2 Chr. 8 ^{11})

The presence of the foreign woman would have a defiling effect! That the Chronicler omitted the darker sides of Solomon's brilliant picture, his polygamy and his building of shrines for the gods of his wives, as well as the rebellions against him, is only what we should have expected from his previous treatment of this saint and prince of peace.

In the succeeding history the Chronicler's two fundamental principles are worked out again and again: the conviction that the Priestly Law had been in force in Israel from the time of Moses on, and the prophetic-deuteronomic principle of retribution. In the light of them the history is not only judged but modified. The Chronicler believed that Judah was the people of the law, Israel had fallen away from Yahweh under Jeroboam I and had lost its position as the people of Yahweh.

> And the priests and the Levites that were in all Israel resorted to him [Rehoboam] out of all their border. For the Levites left their suburbs and their possession, and came to Judah and Jerusalem: for Jeroboam and his sons cast them off, that they should not execute the priest's office to Yahweh; and he appointed him priests for the high places, and for the he-goats, and for the calves which he had made. And after them, out of all the tribes of Israel, such as set their hearts to seek Yahweh, the God of Israel, came to Jerusalem to sacrifice unto Yahweh, the God of their fathers.
>
> So they strengthened the kingdom of Judah, and made Rehoboam the son of Solomon strong, three years; for they walked three years in the way of David and Solomon. (2 Chr. 11 $^{13-17}$)

Abijah made this plain in an address to the Israelites before he began the battle with them:

> And now ye think to withstand the kingdom of Yahweh in the hand of the sons of David; and ye are a great multitude, and there are with you the golden calves which Jeroboam made you for gods. Have ye not driven out the priests of Yahweh, the sons of Aaron, and the Levites, and made you priests after the manner of the peoples of other lands? so that whosoever comes to consecrate himself with a young bullock and seven rams, the same may be a priest of them that are no gods. But as for us, Yahweh is our God, and we have not forsaken Him; and we have priests ministering to Yahweh, the sons of Aaron, and the Levites in their work: and they burn to Yahweh every morning and every evening burnt-offerings and sweet incense: the showbread also set they in order upon the pure table; and the candlestick of gold with its lamps, to burn every evening: for we keep the charge of Yahweh our God; but ye have forsaken Him. And, behold, God is with us at our head, and His priests with the trumpets of alarm to sound an alarm against you. O children of Israel, fight ye not against Yahweh, the God of your fathers; for ye shall not prosper. (2 Chr. 13 $^{8-12}$)

The Israelites were no better than the heathen! Judah alone was Yahweh's people. Continuity of the legitimate cult of Yahweh was found only in Jerusalem. The history of Israel was therefore omitted, and only when Israel came into contact with Judah and had to be mentioned, was it referred to. This totally unhistorical point of view was due to the Chronicler's belief in the existence of the Priestly Law and of the organized hierocracy from the beginning. The reverse side of this condemnation of Israel was the idealization of Judah at the cost of historical veracity. Thus the Chronicler omitted the characteristic verses of 1 Ki. 14 [22-24], which told of Judah's apostasy and contradicted his theory, also the unfavorable judgment of the author of the Books of Kings upon Rehoboam's successor Abijah (1 Ki. 15 [3-5]), for the first kings of Judah could only have been upholders of the true religion from which the Israelitish kings had fallen away! In his address to the Israelites, quoted above in part, Abijah showed his loyalty to Yahweh. Just why Asa should then have had need of removing all the foreign altars and high places, the pillars and the Asherim (2 Chr. 14 [2-5]), is not easily understood. But the Chronicler had found part of this in the Book of Kings, and he thought it worth while to magnify the reform of Asa. In 2 Chr. 15 [17] he had almost overlooked this, for he said there, just as 1 Ki. 15 [14], "but the high places were *not* taken away," but he added, lamely enough, "out of Israel," so that the reader might think of the Northern Kingdom! And yet he meant "out of Judah," for the next king Jehoshaphat again "took away the high places and the Asherim out of Judah" (2 Chr. 17 [6]). Nevertheless, the Chronicler said in 20 [33], "howbeit the places were not taken away" (= 1 Ki. 22 [43])! The influence of the Chronicler's source makes itself felt in these contradictions. Besides, the idealization of Judah could not be carried through with absolute consistence, because the Chronicler wanted to represent the good kings as reformers and that necessitated, of course, a previous defection. In order to get this prerequisite, he painted the bad kings as lapsing into heathenism. Thus he wrote of Joram,

He slew all his brethren with the sword and divers also of the princes of Israel . . . he made high places in the mountains of Judah, and made the inhabitants of Jerusalem to play the harlot and led Judah astray. (2 Chr. 21 [4. 11])

And of "the sons of Athaliah, that wicked woman," he said they "had broken up the house of God, and all the dedicated things of the house of Yahweh they bestowed upon the Baalim" (24 [7]), in spite of the fact that, even according to the Chronicler, the true cult was carried on in the temple all the time by the priest Jehoiada! Of Ahaz he made an absolute idolater, by interpreting the story of the setting up of a new altar of Damascene pattern in 2 Ki. 16 [10ff.] in this astonishing manner:

And in the time of his distress he trespassed yet more against Yahweh, the same king Ahaz.   For he sacrificed to the gods of Damascus, which smote him; and he said, Because the gods of the kings of Syria helped them, therefore will I sacrifice to them, that they may help me.   But they were the ruin of him, and of all Israel.   And Ahaz gathered together the vessels of the house of God, and cut in pieces the vessels of the house of God, and shut up the doors of the house of Yahweh; and he made him altars in every corner of Jerusalem.   And in every city of Judah he made high places to burn incense unto other gods, and provoked to anger Yahweh, the God of his fathers. (2 Chr. 28 [22-25])

Not even Manasseh could be painted worse in his idolatry.

The reformations were restitutions of the old pure Yahweh worship.   They did not indicate progress, for the perfect law had already existed from the time of Moses, and the hierocracy, its executing organ, also.   The greatest reformers were Hezekiah and Josiah.   Hezekiah's first act was the reopening and purification of the temple, which his predecessor Ahaz had closed and defiled.   This restoration of the cult, the celebration of the Passover at Jerusalem, the destruction of the high places, the pillars and the Asherim, and the organization of the income of the priests and Levites by insisting that the people bring to them their tithes were by far the most important acts of the reign of Hezekiah according to the Chronicler. The priests and the Levites had a large place in all these.   That Hezekiah destroyed the brazen serpent, the Chronicler omitted, for it seemed incredible to him that such an idol should have been in the temple so long.   "The Asherah," which had also been there at the Jerusalem altar, the Chronicler changed into the plural "the Asherim," so that the reader must think of these as connected with the heathen altars in Judah (31 [1]).   Similarly in the reformation of Josiah the detailed description of the reformation 2 Ki. 23 [4-20] was omitted and the general statement substituted, "and Josiah took away all the abominations out of all the countries that pertained to the children of Israel" (2 Chr. 34 [33]).   But the Passover that was celebrated thereupon in Jerusalem was described most elaborately and especially the part that the priests and the Levites played in it (35 [1-19]).   In the story of the finding of the law book which led to the reformation the Chronicler omitted in 34 [15] "and he read it" after "and Hilkiah delivered the book to Shaphan," and in 34 [18] he wrote "and Shaphan read *therein* before the king" instead of "and Shaphan read *it* before the king."   In the Book of Kings

(22 [8. 10]) the book was not large, but for the Chronicler this torah was the entire Pentateuch, which could not be read so quickly!

The priests and Levites had a large place in the Chronicler's descriptions of the great festivals, but they were of great importance also elsewhere. Thus the sounding of the trumpets by the priests contributed materially to Abijah's victory over Jeroboam (2 Chr. 13 [12. 14]), and the singing of the Levites won for Jehoshaphat his battle against the Moabites and Ammonites! After fasting and praying and receiving through the Levite Jahaziel the divine oracle:

The battle is not yours but God's . . . ye shall not need to fight in this battle, set yourselves, stand ye still and see the salvation of Yahweh with you,

Jehoshaphat marched with his army on the following morning against the enemy. Before proceeding to the attack he exhorted his people briefly,

Hear me, O Judah, and ye inhabitants of Jerusalem: believe in Yahweh your God, so shall ye be established; believe His prophets, so shall ye prosper. And when he had taken counsel with the people, he appointed them that should sing to Yahweh, and give praise in holy array, as they went out before the army, and say, Give thanks to Yahweh, for His lovingkindness endures for ever. And when they began to sing and to praise, Yahweh set liers-in-wait against the children of Ammon, Moab, and Mount Seir, that were come against Judah; and they were smitten. (2 Chr. 20 [22ff.])

The Judæans had literally nothing to do but to take the spoil, which they did for three days.

And on the fourth day they assembled themselves in the valley of Beracah[1]; for there they blessed Yahweh: therefore the name of that place was called The valley of Beracah unto this day. Then they returned, every man of Judah and Jerusalem, and Jehoshaphat in the forefront of them, to go again to Jerusalem with joy; for Yahweh had made them to rejoice over their enemies. And they came to Jerusalem with psalteries and harps and trumpets to the house of Yahweh. (2 Chr. 20 [26-28])

That this is not history must be clear to any one. It is a pious tale. One of the most instructive examples of the Chronicler's method of modifying history in accordance with his priestly theory is his story of the temple revolution by which Joash became king in 2 Chr. 23 [1-11] as compared with that of 2 Ki. 11 [4-12]. It seemed incredible to the Chronicler that the pious priest Jehoiada should have conspired

[1] Beracah means blessing.

with the captains of the royal body-guard in the temple to make Joash king. He could never have ordered that these Carites and the guard should enter the temple, for that would have been sacrilegious. No, he used the Levites for that! Besides, Jehoiada never entered into a secret plot; he arranged everything openly! The historical improbabilities of this the Chronicler did not consider, it was enough for him that the story now agreed with his dogma.

Alongside of this priestly theory the Chronicler was profoundly interested in the prophetic-deuteronomic theory of retribution and showed how all through history piety and goodness were rewarded, idolatry and wickedness were punished. And just as he let the kings in their addresses to the people enunciate the priestly principles, so he let prophets all through history predict good or bad to the kings according to their piety or wickedness. These prophecies were of course always fulfilled so that together with the history they formed a remarkable series of illustrations of the doctrine of retribution. Good fortune was an evidence of piety, calamity a proof of wickedness. This works as follows: 1 Ki. 14 [25] told of Pharaoh Shishak's invasion and his plundering of Judah and Jerusalem in the fifth year of Rehoboam. The Chronicler promptly concluded that Rehoboam had been faithful for three years, but that in his fourth year "he forsook the law of Yahweh and all Israel with him," whereupon in the fifth year Shishak marched against him. The prophet Shemaiah explained to him and his princes the connection between the two things, "Thus says Yahweh, Ye have forsaken Me, therefore have I also left you in the hand of Shishak." They humbled themselves and Yahweh's wrath was mitigated, as the Chronicler concluded from the fact that Rehoboam reigned twelve years more (2 Chr. 12 [1-12]). If he had not repented, Yahweh would have cut him off at once. — Asa was a pious king, and as such blest by Yahweh, but in his old age he suffered from the gout and later died from it. What could have been the reason for this? The Chronicler knows. Asa had been unsuccessful in his war against Baasha and had called the Syrians to his aid. A prophet denounced him for this, "because thou hast relied on the king of Syria, and hast not relied on Yahweh thy God." Asa threw him into prison, and "at the same time oppressed some of the people." No wonder that he was visited by the painful disease! But even "in his disease he sought not to Yahweh but to the physicians!" So he died. The chronology of the Book of Kings did not quite suit the Chronicler for this pragmatism, for according to it Baasha lived only till the 26th year of Asa, and Asa did not get the disease until his old age. But the Chronicler knew how to get around this difficulty; he placed the war with Baasha in his 36th, his disease in his 39th, and his death in his 41st year! Facts had to yield to theory, dogma modified history. — The good king Jehoshaphat had bad luck with his fleet on the Red Sea, "for the ships were broken at Eziongeber" (1 Ki. 22 ^{48}). How could this happen to so pious a king? The Chronicler supplied the reason: Jehoshaphat had allied himself with Ahaziah, the wicked king of Israel, and the prophet Eliezer predicted, "because thou hast joined thyself with Ahaziah, Yahweh has destroyed thy works" (2 Chr. 20 ^{37}). This is directly opposed to 1 Ki. 22, for there Jehoshaphat refused to go into partnership with Ahaziah!

Although Joash was a pious king, his war against Hazael ended in defeat, and ultimately he was assassinated. How could this be explained? The Chronicler declared, slightly modifying the statement of Kings, "and Jehoash did that which was right in the eyes of Yahweh all his days wherein Jehoiada the priest instructed him" (2 Ki. 12 ^{3}) to "all the days of Jehoiada the priest" (24 ^{2}). After Jehoiada's death the king became wicked, forsook the house of Yahweh, and served the Asherim and idols, in spite of the earnest solicitations of the prophets and especially of Zechariah the son of Jehoiada, who was stoned at the king's command for his warning! The victory of the Syrians was Joash's punishment for this. He became very ill too, and during this illness he was murdered in his bed by two foreign servants of his (2 Chr. 24 $^{15-26}$). — Amaziah also was a good king, but he was badly defeated by Jehoash of Israel. Why? Because after his victorious war against Edom "he brought the gods of the children of Seir, and set them up to be his gods, and bowed down himself before them and burned incense unto them." To us this may seem incredible, because he had just defeated the Edomites by the help of Yahweh, but the Chronicler thought it must have happened so. He could explain his defeat by Jehoash only as the well-deserved punishment for such shameful behavior. And moreover,

> From the time that Amaziah turned away from following Yahweh they made a conspiracy against him in Jerusalem; and he fled to Lachish: but they sent after him to Lachish, and slew him there. (2 Chr. 25 [27])

And yet according to 25 [25] "Amaziah lived after the death of Joash . . . 15 years"! The Chronicler overlooked the inconsistency here. — The great King Uzziah became leprous. What had he done to merit this terrible punishment? The Chronicler gave the reason,

> But when he was strong, his heart was lifted up, so that he did corruptly, and he trespassed against Yahweh his God; for he went into the temple of Yahweh to burn incense upon the altar of incense. And Azariah the priest went in after him, and with him fourscore priests of Yahweh, that were valiant men: and they withstood Uzziah the king, and said to him, It pertains not to thee, Uzziah, to burn incense to Yahweh, but to the priests the sons of Aaron, that are consecrated to burn incense: go out of the sanctuary; for thou hast trespassed; neither shall it be for thine honor from Yahweh God. Then Uzziah was wroth; and he had a censer in his hand to burn incense; and while he was wroth with the priests, the leprosy broke forth in his forehead before the priests in the house of Yahweh, beside the altar of incense. And Azariah the chief priest, and all the priests, looked upon him, and, behold, he was leprous in his forehead, and they thrust him out quickly from thence; yea, himself hasted also to go out, because Yahweh had smitten him. (2 Chr. 26 [16–20])

Ahaz was a wicked king and had deserved severe punishment, but according to 2 Ki. 16 he got out of the Syro-Ephraimitic war by becoming an Assyrian vassal. To the Chronicler it was inconceivable that such a man should have escaped punishment. So he told that the Israelites defeated him fearfully, killing 120,000 Judæan soldiers and taking 200,000 captives with much booty to Samaria; that the Edomites and Philistines also attacked and defeated Ahaz; and that the Assyrian king Tiglathpileser, whom he had called to his aid, marched against him and harassed him, "although he had taken a portion out of the house of Yahweh and out of the house of the king and of the princes, and had given it to the king of Assyria." For "Yahweh brought Judah low because of Ahaz" (2 Chr. 28 [19]). History here is completely rewritten in the interest of dogma.

Even more wicked than Ahaz was Manasseh, and yet he reigned peacefully for 55 years. How was this possible? Was not the wicked punished and cut off in the midst of his years? The Chronicler said, he was actually punished, and that quickly enough. The

Assyrians attacked him, put him in chains, and carried him to Babylonia. But there he implored Yahweh, who mercifully restored him to his kingdom in Jerusalem, whereupon he became a reformer, removing " foreign gods, and the idol out of the house of Yahweh " etc. (2 Chr. 33 10–17). This is in direct opposition to historical facts (cf. Jer. 15 4). — The great reformer Josiah's unfortunate death in the battle at Megiddo, so incredible to his own contemporaries, so great a problem to the prophetic mind, was explained by the Chronicler as due to his disobedience to the word of God which he spoke to him *through Pharaoh Necho* (35 21f.) ! He had no difficulty in inventing reasons. — Wicked Jehoiakim was punished for his wickedness by Nebuchadrezzar, who bound him in fetters and carried him to Babylon (36 6). But unfortunately the Chronicler had overlooked that Jehoiakim had died before Nebuchadrezzar could take the city !

In view of such palpable modifications and inventions of facts in the interest of doctrine, we cannot trust the Chronicler's historical accuracy where we cannot control him by older sources. The wealth and power of the pious kings, together with their great armies and their strong fortifications, were no less the result of his theory than some of the stories above mentioned. He was no real historian, but a religious teacher, who used history as the illustration and proof of his doctrines. That he was only a representative of his time is certain; the Priest Code shows that. In his own time the Priestly Law was in full force and the Chronicler pictured how things must have happened under the rule of this law in the past, for to him there was no past without it. How the law worked in his own time, we may learn from him, and here his book is very valuable, but for past history we must turn to the older sources. We may grant that in a few cases some brief notes of his may have been derived from more ancient manuscripts of the Books of Samuel and Kings than we have, inasmuch as the Greek translation of those books also contains a number of genuine passages which have dropped out of our received Hebrew text.

The Books of Ezra and Nehemiah were originally part of the Chronicler's work, for his interest in the temple led him to write the story of the second temple also, beginning with the edict of Cyrus and ending with the work of Nehemiah and Ezra, through whom the temple was protected and the law introduced and enforced. He used here as his sources the Second Isaiah, Haggai, and Zechariah, the Aramaic history and the memoirs of Ezra and Nehemiah, besides some genealogical lists extending to the time of Alexander the Great. His own part is easily recognizable by the characteristic traits which we have considered and is to be judged accordingly. The story is at present somewhat confused by a displacement in the narrative of the building of the temple and of the walls, for Ezra 4⁷⁻²³ belongs to the time of Artaxerxes and refers to the building of the walls, not of the temple. This displacement was apparently made intentionally, but the change of the original order of the Ezra story (Ezr. 7f.; Neh. 8; Ezr. 9f.; Neh. 9f.) was probably accidental. Since this part of the Chronicler's book had no parallel in the Book of Kings, it was at once recognized as important and separated into an independent book. As such it found its way into the sacred canon much earlier than the other part which constitutes our present Books of Chronicles. Fortunately, the latter were not able to take the place of the Books of Samuel and Kings, else we should have suffered an irreparable loss.

Some stories that might have stood in the Midrash found their way into other books, *e.g.* the story of Abraham's victory over Chedorlaomer and his allies (Gen. 14), which is a glorification of Israel's ancestor.[1] Also the story of the disobedient prophet who had predicted the ruin of the altar at Bethel (1 Ki. 13). These tales partake of the same characteristics as Chronicles; not history but dogma is their main concern. The historical sense of the people seems to have perished. History gives way to romance.

We have an interesting historical romance in the Book of Esther, which comes from the same period. The historical conditions out of which it arose and which form its background can easily be described. In the Persian period the Jews in Babylonia and the eastern parts of the empire had become prosperous and influential. The Book of Nehemiah and the discoveries at Nippur illustrate how some Jews like Nehemiah rose to positions of power and how others like the Murashu Sons at Nippur founded great business

---

[1] A priestly writer added vv.¹⁸⁻²⁰, in which he told of Abraham's giving the tithe to Melchizedek, in order to show that the giving of the tithe to the priesthood at Jerusalem was already practised by Abraham.

houses which carried on vast commercial and financial undertakings. This engendered economic rivalry, envy, and opposition among the other races in the empire, who accused the Jews of avarice and unfair dealings.   Their clannishness and religious arrogance, which had found expression in the insistence on the exclusive character of the Jewish race and its destiny as ruler of the world, with the heathen as its abject slaves, intensified the feelings of opposition to bitter hate.   Their aloofness and their strange customs were apparent to all, their claim to world-conquest could be learned in the synagogues, if not in private intercourse.   Here the non-Jews could hear how their gods were reviled as nonentities and their images as "the work of man's hands," how their religious usages were ridiculed as abominations, how their food was abhorred as unclean, and marital union with them as defiling.   All this was offensive and insulting and only increased their hate.   Everything was ready for an outburst which would lead to massacres and the government could easily be won either to active participation or to passive tolerance.   For it was simple enough to bring the Jews, against their will, into conflict with the state, for certain obligations they could not fulfil, since they were opposed to their religion.   They could not worship the king as divine, nor could they fall down before an image.   It was therefore not hard to charge them with disobedience to the commands of the king and to enlist the forces of the government against them. Whether any pogroms had taken place in Persia we do not know, but Joel 3 [19] shows that some had occurred in Egypt and Edom.

It would seem that not long after the fall of the Persian empire a Jewish author in the East, either in Persia or in Babylonia, wrote a story which takes us right into these situations that led to hate of the Jews and to pogroms, the Book of Esther.   He knew Persian life and conditions well, was familiar with the royal court and palace, with the Persian government and the people, and painted the local color of his story with the sure touch of real knowledge.   He wrote a historical novel which he placed in the reign of Ahasuerus = Xerxes (486–465).   As a work of fiction it lays no claim to historical exactness; on the contrary, a number of historical blunders and impossibilities are deliberately introduced for the greater effectiveness of the plot.   The story is a historical novel and not strict history.

The tale is told with great artistic skill and its plot is unfolded with remarkable literary ability. The beautiful young Jewess Esther is chosen by Xerxes as his queen, after Vashti had been deposed because of her disobedience to the king's command. The king knew nothing of her Jewish origin, for Esther's uncle and foster father Mordecai had forbidden her to speak of it. Now, one day, when he was on duty in the gate of the palace, Mordecai overheard two courtiers plotting the king's death. Through Esther Xerxes was informed, the plot was foiled, and Mordecai's deed was entered in the royal journal, but went unrewarded at that time. Somewhat later Haman was raised to the position of vizier by the king, and everybody was commanded to bow down and do reverence to him. Only Mordecai refused to do so and incurred thereby Haman's deadly enmity. Discovering that Mordecai was a Jew, Haman determined to wreak his vengeance not only on him but on all his people. He said therefore to the king,

There is a certain people scattered abroad and dispersed among the peoples in all the provinces of thy kingdom; and their laws are diverse from those of every people; neither keep they the king's laws: therefore it is not for the king's profit to suffer them. If it please the king, let it be written that they be destroyed: and I will pay ten thousand talents of silver into the hands of those that have the charge of the king's business, to bring it into the king's treasuries. (Esth. 3 $^{8f.}$)

The king gave him at once authority to do with the Jews as he pleased. Haman issued a royal decree whereby the 13th day of Adar was set apart all through the empire for the massacre and spoiling of the Jews. In deep distress Mordecai asked Esther to go to the king and intercede for her people. But Esther replied,

All the king's servants, and the people of the king's provinces, do know, that whosoever, whether man or woman, shall come unto the king into the inner court, who is not called, there is one law for him, that he be put to death, except those to whom the king shall hold out the golden sceptre, that he may live: but I have not been called to come in unto the king these thirty days. And they told to Mordecai Esther's words. Then Mordecai bade them return answer to Esther, Think not thyself that thou shalt escape in the king's house, more than all the Jews. For if thou altogether holdest thy peace at this time, then will relief and deliverance arise to the Jews from another place, but thou and thy father's house will perish: and who knows whether thou art not come to the kingdom for such a time as this? Then Esther bade them return answer to Mordecai, Go, gather together all the Jews that are present in Shushan, and fast

ye for me, and neither eat nor drink three days, night or day: I also and my
maidens will fast in like manner; and so will I go in to the king, which is not according to the law: and if I perish, I perish. (Esth. 4 $^{11-16}$)

On the third day, Esther's perilous undertaking succeeded, the king
received her graciously and offered at once to fulfil her wish, but
she evaded and invited him and Haman to a dinner that day, when
the king asked again, but she could not muster enough courage, and
again put off her petition and invited him and Haman for the following day. Haman, highly elated over this signal honor, met on his
way home Mordecai, who again omitted to pay his reverence to him.
Overcoming his anger, he told his wife and friends of all his honor in
which there was only one flaw: the impudence of the Jew Mordecai.
They counselled him to have high gallows prepared and to ask the
king for permission to hang Mordecai thereon. That night the king
could not sleep and had the royal journal read to him. They
happened upon Mordecai's discovery of the plot of the assassins.
When the king learned that he had not been rewarded for this, he
asked Haman, who had just appeared at the court, "What shall be
done to the man whom the king delights to honor?" Thinking himself to be the object of such grace, he named the most extravagant
honors, and was commanded to show them in person to Mordecai!
Mortified he went home, where his friends warned him that Mordecai
would encompass his fall. At the dinner that day, Esther at last
told the king, who did not know that she was a Jewess, that her own
life and that of her people were in peril, and at his angry question
"Who is he, and where is he, that durst presume in his heart to do
so?" she replied, "This wicked Haman!" This was too much for
the king, who went out into the garden to calm himself. Meanwhile Haman implored Esther for his life and in his fright had fallen
upon the queen's couch. When the king returned and saw him
lying there, he misinterpreted the situation. A courtier suggested
Haman's high gallows which he had prepared for Mordecai.
Thereon he was hanged. His house was given to Esther who made
her uncle her manager. The king made him vizier in Haman's place.
To undo the wicked plan of Haman, Esther once more interceded
with the king to revoke his decree of the Jewish massacre. But
that was impossible, so he gave authority to Mordecai and Esther to
remedy the matter as best they could. They sent out a royal decree

whereby the Jews were given authority not only to defend themselves on the 13th Adar but "to destroy, to slay, and to cause to perish, all the power of the people and province that would assault them, their little ones and their women, and to take the spoil of them for prey" (8 ¹¹). And on that day the Jews massacred 500 men in Susa alone besides Haman's ten sons, but — they did not take their spoil! The Jews were not avaricious! Upon Esther's request (!) the king set apart the next day for another slaughter and 300 more were killed in Susa. In the province 75,000 people lost their lives at the hands of the Jews! In commemoration of this the Jews in Susa celebrated a festival called Purim on the 13th and 14th Adar, in the villages only on the 14th, which they spent in feasting and sending presents to one another. Mordecai wrote a letter to all the Jews in all the provinces of the Persian empire enjoining them to keep this festival. Esther also wrote a second letter "confirming these days of Purim in their appointed times."

The spirit of hate and revenge pervades the book. One feels like characterizing it as a godless book, but its author would probably protest against this. Nevertheless, his studied avoidance of any reference to religion and even of the name of God, where it was naturally called for, is striking. When Mordecai refused to fall down before Haman, we are not told that it was for religious reasons. When he admonished Esther to rescue her people, else help would come "from another source," he meant of course from God, but he did not say so. When Esther fasted three days before her perilous undertaking, prayer is not mentioned, although fasting and prayer inevitably go together in such cases. When the people celebrated their deliverance, they rejoiced and feasted, but did not thank God! This purely secular character of the story finds its explanation probably not in the author's lack of religion or opposition to it but in the non-religious character of the festival of Purim whose origin it describes and for whose introduction and celebration among all Jews everywhere it was written. Purim was not one of the ancient yearly festivals. It had originated in the East, probably in Persia, where the story is placed. It may have been a Persian festival which the Jews adopted and reinterpreted, and which they celebrated on the same day that the Persians did theirs, just as in some places modern Jews have adopted the non-religious features of Christmas, its lighted tree, and presents, but without the Christmas story and the Christian meaning of Christ's birthday. Which particular festival Purim was, we do not know, for none of the suggestions thus far made are satisfactory.

The book was intended to make propaganda for Purim. In Palestine it seems to have met at first with little favor, if not with active opposition. That is probably why Esther and Mordecai are not mentioned by Jesus ben Sira in his list of worthies. It may even be that Nicanor's day, which was celebrated on the 13th of Adar one day before Purim in commemoration of the victory of Judas Maccabæus over the Syrian general Nicanor in 162 B.C., was instituted as a rival festival in Palestine. However that may be, during the Maccabæan wars for religion and national independence the Book of Esther was bound to become more and more popular, for it expressed the spirit of the people during the latter half of the second century. A strong national self-consciousness and pride had been created in those wars. The sufferings inflicted by the hated heathen were not forgotten. The jingo spirit became prevalent, and Esther was one of its most popular expressions. By 114 B.C. the story had been carried to Egypt in a Greek translation, and at the end of the century Purim was a recognized festival in Palestine.

Of course, even then the purely secular character of the Book of Esther was to many an evidence that it was not inspired by God, and orthodox scholars fought for a long time against placing it among the sacred writings. The Greek version tried to obviate their objections by inserting a number of religious interpolations, such as prayers of Mordecai and Esther, which breathe the same exclusive, nationalist spirit. Though they were not introduced into the Hebrew text, the book nevertheless overcame all scruples by its great popularity and its intense patriotism, and has ever since been read as the lesson at the yearly festival of Purim.

CHAPTER XIX

THE WISDOM LITERATURE

ONE of the most interesting and important elements in the development of Judaism is the work of the wise men or sages. They take their place beside the priests as teachers of youth in ethics and religion. In a sense they were the successors of the prophets, for they coined their teaching into current change. Neither rising to the lofty conceptions of the greatest prophets nor partaking of their glorious enthusiasm, they yet kept the true balance between form and spirit in an age of growing legalism by their insistence on wisdom as the true norm and guide of life. As pronounced individualists they addressed themselves to individuals, not to the nation. Indeed national interests were not treated by them, not even the Messianic hope, because it was so largely national, while they themselves were cosmopolitan. Thus Job never called God by His Jewish proper name Yahweh, neither did Ecclesiastes, and if we substitute "God" for "Yahweh" in the Book of Proverbs, the whole book is of universal application. The interest of these wise men was not in Jewish but in human life, and they have therefore been called humanists. This was more unconscious with some than with others, but the fact remains that they addressed their hearers as men, not as Jews, and on common human, not on Jewish, questions. Some of their finest literature is definitely referred to non-Jews: Job and his friends, Lemuel king of Massa (Prov. 31) and Agur son of Yakeh of Massa (Prov. 30) were not Jews, but Arabians. Nothing could show more clearly that they recognized that wisdom is universal. There are indeed striking parallels to our biblical Proverbs and Job and Ecclesiastes among the ancient Egyptians and Babylonians as well as among other nations. This does not mean that Jewish wisdom was dependent upon any of these, but that wisdom is international; everywhere the fruit of life's experience is expressed in this manner, which is of universal application. We have in our Old Testament three wisdom books, Proverbs, Job, and Ecclesiastes. Others, like the Story of Ahikar, the Book of Jesus ben Sira or Ecclesiasticus, and the Wisdom of Solomon, are still extant but do not form part of the Hebrew canon.

In the Book of Proverbs we have a number of collections by various writers dating from different times:

1. 1–9 "The Proverbs of Solomon the son of David, king of Israel," a series of connected addresses containing warnings against wickedness and especially against carnal lust, and exhortations to seek wisdom, the most wonderful of all possessions.
2. 10–22 16 "The Proverbs of Solomon," consisting of wise maxims usually in couplet form, entirely different from the first collection.
3. 22 17–24 22 "Words of the Wise," beginning with the exhortation, "Incline thine ear, and hear the words of the wise," mostly in quatrains.
4. 24 23–34 "These also are (sayings) of the Wise," an appendix to the third collection, also in quatrains and longer groups.
5. 25–29 "These also are Proverbs of Solomon, which the men of Hezekiah king of Judah copied." They are mostly in couplets, but also in tristichs, quatrains, or in larger units.
6. 30 "The words of Agur the son of Yakeh of Massa." The first part is tinged by a mild scepticism, the second part contains a number of numerical proverbs.
7. 31 1–9 "The words of King Lemuel of Massa, which his mother taught him," consisting of warnings against women and wine, and of exhortations to righteous administration of justice.
8. 31 10–31 An alphabetical poem in praise of a worthy wife.

The heart of the book is the second collection, "the Proverbs of Solomon," to which were added first "the Words of the Wise" and their appendix (Nos. 3 and 4) and later the other collection of Proverbs of Solomon (No. 5). The last three sections (Nos. 6–8) are appendices. To the whole book the first section was prefixed as an introduction; it is the latest in point of time and dates not earlier than the Greek period, while the others appear to come from the Persian age. At the beginning the purpose of the teaching of the sages as well as of this book in particular is stated:

The Proverbs of Solomon the son of David, king of Israel, (are designed)
that one know wisdom and instruction,
discern the words of understanding,
receive instruction in wise dealing,
in righteousness and justice and equity;
to give prudence to the simple,

> to the young man knowledge and discretion;
> that the wise man hear and increase in learning,
> and the man of understanding attain unto sound counsels;
> that one understand a proverb and a figure,
> the words of the wise and their riddles. (Prov. 1 [1-6])[1]

By wisdom the sages meant that sagacity and common sense which enables men to live a happy and a prosperous life. And they taught the young the art of life in brief maxims or long exhortations, by shrewd observations and warm personal appeals.   Much of this wisdom is very old and many of the proverbs gathered in these collections had been current among the people a long time.   Their particular form may have been given to them by these sages who were not only collectors but authors.   Tradition regarded Solomon as the wisest of the sages and attributed to him 3000 proverbs in which "he spoke of trees, from the cedar that is in Lebanon even unto the hyssop that springs out of the wall: he spoke also of beasts, and of birds, and of creeping things, and of fishes" (1 Ki. 4 [32 f.]).   But none of these are preserved.   Nevertheless a later age attributed to Solomon at first the second and fifth collections in the Book of Proverbs, and a still later time even the whole book, although four out of the eight sections are definitely assigned to other authors in their superscriptions.   While it cannot be denied that some of the proverbs of the second and fifth collections may indeed come from Solomon, a number of them that praise monogamy and warn against carnal lust, or praise contentment and deprecate wealth, or speak of the king as arbitrary and tyrannical, would sound so strange from his lips that we cannot regard the tradition as reliable.   The superscription of the fifth collection (Prov. 25 [1]) seems at first to embody a historical tradition, "these also are Proverbs of Solomon, which the men of Hezekiah king of Judah copied out."   But it is rather due to the interpretation of the word *yaskîl* in 2 Ki. 18 [7] as meaning *"he showed himself wise,"* instead of "he prospered"; it may indeed be translated thus, although "he prospered" fits the context better.   Quite in the manner of the Chronicler somebody built on this the conjecture that

---

[1] If Prov. 1–9 form the introduction to the whole book, then 1 [1] does not constitute the title for 1–9 only, but is the beginning of the exposition of the purpose of the proverbs which are given in 10 [1ff.].

Hezekiah was interested in conserving the wise sayings of Solomon, and added this to the title of the collection.

The commonest form of the proverb was the couplet, a verse with two parallel members, in which two things were compared to bring out the likeness, the contrast, or the comparative difference. For instance,

> As vinegar to the teeth and as smoke to the eyes,
> so is the sluggard to them that send him. (10 26)

> A glad heart makes a cheerful countenance,
> but by sorrow of heart the spirit is broken. (15 13)

> It is better to dwell in the corner of the housetop,
> than with a contentious woman in a wide house. (21 9)

The tristich is rare:

> As the cold of snow in the time of harvest,
> so is a faithful messenger to them that send him,
> for he refreshes the soul of his masters. (25 13)

But the tetrastichs or quatrains are frequent:

> A continual dropping in a very rainy day
> and a contentious woman are alike:
> He that would restrain her restrains the wind,
> and his right hand encounters oil. (27 15f.)

An example of a pentastich is:

> To have respect of persons in judgment is not good.
> He that says to the wicked, "Thou art righteous,"
> peoples shall curse him, nations shall abhor him;
> But to them that rebuke them shall be delight,
> and a good blessing shall come upon them. (24 23-25)

There are also longer units, hexastichs, etc.; the famous description of the drunkard may serve as an illustration:

> Who has woe? who has sorrow?
> who has contentions? who has complaining?
> Who has wounds without cause?
> who has redness of eyes?
> They that tarry long at the wine,
> they that go to try mixed wine.
> Look not upon the wine when it is red,
> when it sparkles in the cup,

> when it goes down smoothly:
> At the last it bites like a serpent,
>   and stings like an adder.
> Thine eyes shall behold strange things,
>   and thy heart shall utter perverse things.
> Yea, thou shalt be as he that lies down in the midst of the sea,
>   or as he that lies upon the top of a mast.
> "They have stricken me, (shalt thou say,) and I was not hurt,
>   they have beaten me, and I felt it not:
> When shall I awake?
>   I will seek it yet again." (23 [29-35])

A special form of maxim is represented by the numerical proverbs which originated from riddles:

> For three things the earth trembles,
>   and for four, which it cannot bear:
> For a servant when he is king,
>   and for a fool when he is filled with food;
> For an odious woman when she is married,
>   and a handmaid that is heir to her mistress. (30 [21-23])

The teaching of the wise men dealt with the whole range of life; with personal affairs, including good manners as well as good morals; with family relations, including parents, children, and servants; with social intercourse between friends and enemies, between rich and poor; with professional and business matters; and with public life and its interests.   There is a wealth of wisdom, of sober and realistic observation, of sharp epigrammatic characterization, of kindly humor and biting sarcasm, of warm personal exhortation and urgent appeal that makes the Book of Proverbs a veritable mine of good counsel for the art of right living.   It is a pity only that the sages felt so little the need of grouping their sayings in logical order.

The ideal of the wise man is not high.   It is the life of a shrewd, upright man, who knows how to conduct himself wisely so that he may be successful, honored, and happy.   The great motive to wise living is always personal happiness.   There is no concern about making others happy.   Even when the welfare of others is considered, it is always with reference to oneself, as, *e.g.*, in the otherwise so exquisite words:

> Rejoice not when thine enemy falls,
> and let not thy heart be glad when he is overthrown,
> Lest Yahweh see it, and it displease Him,
> and He turn away His wrath from him (24 [17f.])

or in the famous exhortation :

> If thine enemy be hungry, give him bread to eat;
> and if he be thirsty, give him water to drink:
> For thou wilt heap coals of fire upon his head,
> and Yahweh will reward thee. (25 [21f.])

Self-interest dominates even these thoughts, as indeed all the counsels of the sages. They never advise goodness for its own sake. Everything is controlled by the idea of selfish gain, whether a good deed is to be done or a virtue to be inculcated, or whether wickedness is to be refrained from. The fundamental principle of morals and religion is that goodness is rewarded, wickedness is punished. The wise will therefore follow the great moral and religious principles in order that he may be happy. The fool will refuse to do so and perish.

The wise men were profoundly religious, for they were sure that only thus could they be truly successful and prosperous, honored and happy. But it is significant that they attached little importance in their teaching to the ceremonial law. It is not impossible that it is included in such sayings as,

> He that turns away his ear from hearing the law,
> even his prayer is an abomination (28 [9]),

but it is far more probable that the moral law is meant here. The influence of the prophets is strong in the sages. How truly they reflected prophetic thoughts is clear from such maxims as,

> The sacrifice of the wicked is an abomination to Yahweh,
> but the prayer of the upright is His delight. (15 [8])

> By mercy and truth iniquity is atoned for,
> and by the fear of Yahweh men depart from evil. (16 [6])

> To do righteousness and justice
> is more acceptable to Yahweh than sacrifice. (21 [3])

> The sacrifice of the wicked is an abomination,
> how much more when he brings it to atone for wickedness! (21 [27])

> He that covers his transgressions shall not prosper,
> but whoso confesses and forsakes them shall obtain mercy. (28 [13])

Prophetic influence is apparent also in the insistence on the inner man, the character which is to be striven for; the sages emphasized moral self-discipline and the training of the disposition and will.

> The spirit of man is the lamp of Yahweh,
> searching all his innermost parts. (20 [27])

> Who can say, I have made my heart clean,
> I am pure from my sin? (20 [9])

> All the ways of a man are clean in his own eyes,
> but Yahweh weighs the spirits. (16 [2] 21 [2])

The wise men tried to inculcate the principles of a worthy life by glorifying wisdom as its secret and source. This is especially done in the first part (1–9), where in beautiful paragraphs wisdom is personified and shown to be the supreme principle in creation as well as in the life of man. True living consists therefore in harmony with this principle which pervades the universe and reveals itself to the mind of man. God alone knows the way of wisdom, man could never find out its source by his own investigation and endeavor.

> When He made a decree for the rain
> and a way for the lightning of the thunder,
> Then did He see it, and declare it;
> He established it, yea, and searched it out.
> And unto man He said,
> Behold, the fear of the Lord, that is wisdom,
> and to depart from evil is understanding. (Job 28 [26–28]) [1]

Religion and wisdom are here identified. Also Prov. 1 [7] 9 [10] declare that "the fear of the Lord is the beginning (or the chief part) of wisdom."

Agur had tried to understand the secrets of the world only to come to this conclusion,

> I have wearied myself, O God, I have wearied myself, O God,
> and I am consumed.
> Surely I am more brutish than any man,
> and have not the understanding of a man;
> And have not learned wisdom,
> neither have I the knowledge of the Holy One.

---

[1] The beautiful 28th chapter of Job appears to be a later insertion in the poem; it shows that men can find all the treasures of the earth, but the source of the richest treasure, wisdom, only God can make known.

> Who has ascended up into heaven, and descended?
> Who has gathered the wind in his fists?
> Who has bound the waters in his garment?
> Who has established all the ends of the earth?
> What is his name, and what is his son's name?
> If thou knowest? (Prov. 30 [1-4])

No man knows.   But God has revealed it in His word,

> Every word of God is tried,
>   a shield for them that take refuge in Him.
> Add thou not to His words,
>   lest He reprove thee, and thou be found a liar. (30 [5f.])

To Agur the Holy Scriptures are the source of revelation, but ordinarily the wise men think of God Himself directly revealing wisdom.

It was not enough for them to emphasize the divine source of wisdom.   They speculated about wisdom itself, its origin and its relation to man.   They thought of wisdom as a divinely created personality which existed before the creation of the world.   In an exquisite passage wisdom says,

> Yahweh formed me first of His ways,
>   before His works of old.
> I was set up from everlasting,
>   from the beginning, before the earth was.
> When there were no depths, I was brought forth,
>   when there were no fountains, abounding with water.
> Before the mountains were settled,
>   before the hills was I brought forth:
> While as yet He had not made the earth, nor the fields,
>   nor the beginning of the dust of the world.
> When He established the heavens, I was there:
>   when He set a circle upon the face of the deep,
> When He made firm the skies above,
>   when He fastened the fountains of the deep,
> When He gave to the sea its bound,
>   that the waters should not transgress His commandment,
> When He marked out the foundations of the earth;
>   then I was by Him, as a master workman;
> And I was daily His delight,
>   rejoicing always before Him,
> Rejoicing in His habitable earth;
>   and my delight was with the sons of men. (8 [22-31])

Before the creation wisdom existed, and at the creation she was with God as a master workman, the pervading principle of the world.

From God she comes down to plead with men, to win the simple and foolish for the true life, to woo them and tempt them by her own beauty and charm that they may love her and thus find life. For wisdom is personified as a wondrously beautiful woman who allures and tempts young men.

> Wisdom cries aloud in the street,
>> she utters her voice in the broad places.
> She cries in the chief place of concourse,
>> at the entering in of the gates,
> In the city she utters her words. (1 20f.)

She has wonderful gifts to bestow, the glory of life is in her.

> Unto you, O men, I call,
>> and my voice is to the sons of men.
> O ye simple, understand wisdom,
>> and ye fools, be of an understanding heart. . . .
> For whoso finds me finds life,
>> and shall obtain favor of Yahweh.
> But he that misses me wrongs himself,
>> all they that hate me love death. (8 4f. 35f.)

What are the blandishments of sin, which is also personified as a beautiful woman, Madam Folly, and all her temptations to one who has seen the glory of the ideal in the wondrous beauty of Wisdom, which draws him with irresistible attraction to righteousness and life! Here the sages presented a conception closely connected with and perhaps suggested by Greek thought, although the root of this idea of wisdom is to be traced in ancient Hebrew and Semitic religion in general.[1] With the personification of the "word" and of the "spirit" of God it was one of the antecedents of the Logos doctrine of the Gospel according to John, "in the beginning was the Word," *i.e.* Wisdom or Universal Reason.

The Book of Proverbs was the work of orthodox men, who assumed that the righteous and wicked are rewarded according to their deserts. But the validity of this doctrine was challenged and denied by the authors of the Poem of Job and of Ecclesiastes, who could not reconcile it with the facts of life. What heart-burnings it caused to many men and women who had tried their best to fulfil the

---

[1] In the later Wisdom literature, *e.g.* in the Wisdom of Solomon, Greek influence is clear and pronounced.

commandments of God, when suddenly disaster, misfortune, disease came upon them! The righteous is favored by God, he dies in good old age, only the wicked is overtaken by calamity and cut off in the midst of the years. So they reasoned, and then they would search, and pray to God to help them search, their secret hearts to see if there were any hidden sins, for which He was punishing them. And if they were not restored to health and prosperity, their friends would declare that they had after all been sinners, although they seemed to be righteous, for God who tries the heart knew their wickedness and punished them for it. There was only one cause of suffering: sin![1]

But now there arose a man who had felt in his spirit the suffering of these righteous souls, had tasted the bitterness of death that is in this dogma, and his hot heart revolted and protested. He wrote (*ca.* 400 B.C.) his immortal poem and every word that he wrote had "been fiercely furnaced in the blast of a soul that has struggled in earnest," for he wrote the history of a soul that had suffered and battled, despaired and hoped until it finally gained peace. He took as the subject of his work the old well-known story of Job who though righteous had to suffer so terribly. He made it very clear that Job was absolutely blameless. Yahweh Himself gave him this testimony, "there is none like him on earth, a blameless and upright man, one that fears God and turns from evil." But Satan questioned the unselfishness of his piety, "does Job fear God for nought?" Is there any disinterested religion on earth? Would Job be so profoundly religious, if his devotion were not rewarded by prosperity? Would he still be true to his religion, if he lost everything he possessed, his children included, yea, even his health? If he were afflicted with such a horrible disease as leprosy or elephantiasis, which brands him in the eyes of the world as a wicked sinner? The old story told how Job stood the terrible test. He did not renounce God, and was therefore doubly rewarded for his loyalty in the end.[2] The author of the poem however was not satisfied with Job's absolute submission. When his three friends, Eliphaz, Bildad, and Zophar, came to comfort Job, but found no words to express their sympathy, the strain proved too hard for him. He interpreted their

[1] The tenacity of this doctrine is seen in the Gospels, where Jesus still has to fight against it.

[2] The old prose story is contained in Job 1f. 42 $^{7ff.}$

silence in the light of the popular doctrine as an indication that they doubted his righteousness. He had not yet learned to do without the approval of his friends, and so he gave way to despair and cursed the day of his birth (3 $^{1ff.}$).

This opens the debate between Job and his friends on the reason of his suffering. Three times the friends take up Job's arguments, each in his turn; to each Job answers until finally the friends have nothing left to say, and Job takes up his complaint afresh, to be answered by God Himself. The three cycles are contained in ch. 3–14, 15–21, 22–27. Parts of the last speech of Bildad and of Zophar are now wrongly attributed to Job in 26 $^{5–14}$ 27 $^{7–10.13–23}$.

The friends represent the accepted teaching that all suffering is ultimately due to sin. But they had known Job too well to believe that his terrible suffering could be the result of fearful sins, it could not be punitive. So they did not question his piety, but tried to comfort him by pointing out the good intentions that God had with him in this discipline. He need not despair,

> Is not thy fear (of God) thy confidence,
>   the integrity of thy ways thy hope?
> Remember, I pray thee, who (ever) perished, being innocent?
>   or where were the upright cut off?
> According as I have seen, they that plough iniquity,
>   and sow mischief, reap the same.
> By the breath of God they perish,
>   and by the blast of His anger are they consumed. (4 $^{6–9}$)

No man is sinless, no mortal is just before God (4 ^{17}). Let Job remember that, and understand God's gracious plan with him.

> Behold, happy is the man whom God corrects:
>   Therefore despise not the chastening of the Almighty.
> For He makes sore, and binds up,
>   He wounds, and His hands make whole.
> He will deliver thee in six troubles,
>   Yea, in seven no harm shall touch thee. (5 $^{17–19}$)

This suffering is merely a disciplinary, pedagogical means of God, intended to refine Job and to make him all the happier afterwards. So they gave him this advice:

> But as for me, I would seek unto God,
>   and to God would I commit my cause. (5 ^{8})

If thou seek diligently unto God,
  and make thy supplication to the Almighty;
If thou art pure and upright,
  surely, then will He answer thy prayer,
  and compensate thee with the portion due to thy righteousness,
And though thy beginning is small,
  thy latter end He will greatly increase. (8 5-7)

But when Job, stung to the quick by the words of his friends from whom he had expected a different kind of comfort, hotly resents the implications, they charge him with wickedness. His desperate, blasphemous words have revealed to them his true character. And Zophar says to him,

For thou sayest, "My walk is pure,
  and I am clean in Thine eyes."
But oh that God would speak,
  and open His lips against thee,
And that He would show thee the secrets of wisdom!
  for He is manifold in understanding.
Then thou wouldst know that God exacts of thee
  less than thine iniquity deserves. (11 4-6)

And similarly Eliphaz,

When thine iniquity teaches thy mouth,
  and thou choosest the tongue of the crafty,
Thine own mouth condemns thee, and not I,
  yea, thine own lips testify against thee. (15 5f.)

Only in repentance can Job find God's grace returning, let him acknowledge his guilt and he will be saved.

If thou purge thy heart,
  and stretch out thy hands towards Him;
If thou put the iniquity which is in thy hand far away,
  and let not unrighteousness dwell in thy tents:
Surely then shalt thou lift up thy face without spot,
  yea, thou shalt be steadfast and not fear.
For then shalt thou forget thy misery,
  thou shalt remember it as by-gone days. (11 13-16)

At first the friends emphasized the disciplinary, corrective character of suffering, later they insisted on its punitive quality. There is no further development of this theory.

Job shared, of course, at the outset the belief of the friends. While he was still well and happy, it was easy for him to believe that

piety and prosperity, sin and suffering go together. But now that
he himself has been afflicted, he has in his conscience such a strong
opponent of this theory that he denies its truth absolutely. He
does suffer, but he knows that he is innocent. To regard his suffering as merely disciplinary and purifying is absurd, it is far too horrible for that, soon he will die the death of ignominy. He does not
assert that he is sinless, for no mortal is without sin. But to make
man so frail and then punish him for his mortal frailty is unjust.

> If I have sinned, what can I do
>   to Thee, O Thou watcher of men?
> Why hast Thou set me as a mark for Thee,
>   so that I am a burden to Thee?
> And why dost Thou not pardon my transgression
>   and take away my guilt? (7 [20f.])

He agrees that no man can be just before God. But the reason for
this is that God sets the standard of righteousness: what He declares to be right is right. And if He declares that a man is wrong,
as He does with Job, who can hinder Him? He is altogether arbitrary, and He is so wise that no man can prove Him to be wrong, for
He can easily entangle a man by His questions into an admission of
guilt, even if he is innocent.

> Of a truth, I know that it is so:
>   but how can a man be just (in an argument) with God?
> If he should desire to contend with Him,
>   he cannot answer Him one of a thousand.
> However wise in heart, and mighty in strength,
>   who has (ever) hardened himself against Him with impunity? (9 [1-4])

> If it is a matter of strength, lo, He is mighty!
>   and if it is a matter of justice, who will arraign Him?
> Though I am righteous, my own mouth shall condemn me,
>   though I am blameless, it shall prove me perverse. (9 [19f.])

Job readily admits that God is omnipotent and omniscient, as his
friends had declared again and again, but he maintains that His
omnipotence and omniscience are not controlled by morality, for He
destroys the righteous and wicked alike and makes no moral distinctions.

> It is all one, therefore I say,
>   He destroys the blameless and the wicked.

> If a scourge slay suddenly,
>> He mocks at the calamity of the innocent.
> The earth is given into the hand of the wicked,
>> He covers the faces of its judges.
> If it is not He, who then is it? (9 22–24)

God has become Job's enemy, He wants to put him in the wrong.

> I know that Thou wilt not hold me innocent.
> I have to be guilty,
>> why then do I labor in vain?
> If I wash myself white as snow,
>> and make my hands never so clean,
> Yet wilt Thou plunge me into the mire,
>> that my own clothes abhor me. (9 28–31)

And yet Job longs to argue his case with God, but that is out of the question.

> For He is not a man as I am, that I should answer Him,
>> that we should come together in judgment.
> Oh, that there were an umpire betwixt us,
>> who might lay his hand upon us both!
> Let Him take His rod away from me,
>> and let not His terror make me afraid:
> Then would I speak without fearing
>> that He is not honest toward me. (9 32–35)

He would ask God why He is persecuting him so terribly, why it is

> That Thou inquirest after mine iniquity,
>> and searchest after my sin,
> Although Thou knowest that I am not wicked. (10 6f.)

Once uttered, this desire to argue his case in open debate with God grows stronger. Job would gladly die, if he only had that chance. And though God should slay him when he dared to argue so fearlessly with Him, the conviction "that a godless man shall not come before Him" (13 16) would be his salvation. But he makes this reservation,

> Only do not two things to me,
>> then will I not hide myself from Thy face:
> Withdraw Thy hand far from me,
>> and let not Thy terror make me afraid.
> Then call Thou, and I will answer,
>> or let me speak, and answer Thou me. (13 20–22)

The friends seek the reason of the suffering in Job. Job seeks it in

God. The friends declare that Job is a sinner. Job declares that God is arbitrary, unjust, immoral. The root of the matter is not in him but in God. His language does not stop short of blasphemy.

This is the God of his present experience, unjust and cruel. But there comes into his reasoning a new element: he remembers the God of his past experience and thinks of the wonderful, intimate communion he had with God who showed Himself full of justice and love. A strange conflict of indescribable pathos arises in his soul between the God of the past and the God of the present. Already once before, when he spoke of the brief span of life allotted to him before he should go to the land of darkness and death, a little thought had slipped in, as if God would come to long and look for him, but then it would be too late.

> For now shall I lie down in the dust,
>   and Thou wilt seek me diligently, but I shall not be. (7 21)

True enough, Job in the bitterness of his soul interprets his past experience, which is very real to him, in the light of his present experience: God has taken such infinite pains to fashion him and has showed such gracious kindness and love only in order to hide His sinister design, so that He might strike an all the more deadly blow, when at last he had lulled Job into a sense of security.

> Thou hast granted me life and lovingkindness,
>   and Thy care has preserved my spirit.
> yet these things Thou didst hide in Thy heart,
>   I know that this was in Thy mind:
> If I sin Thou wouldst mark me
>   and not acquit me from mine iniquity.
> If I were wicked, woe unto me,
>   and if I were righteous, yet should I not lift up my head. (10 12–15)

He had been mistaken in the past, when he thought God was just and loving, for God was all the time cherishing a bitter hatred against him and His kindness to him was only a mask for His malicious purpose. But Job never refers to this interpretation again, the memory of the blessed time of communion had kindled afresh his old conviction of God's righteousness and it reasserts itself most strongly. There is an instance of this, although he himself is not aware of it, in his contention that God cannot be pleased with unjust defences:

> Will ye speak unrighteously for God,
>> and talk deceitfully for Him?
> Will ye show partiality to Him?
>> will ye be special pleaders for God?
> Would it be well, if He should search you out?
>> or will ye deceive Him as one deceives a man?
> He will surely reprove you,
>> if ye show secretly partiality. (13 7-9)

Here is the old God of truth and righteousness again, although Job does not realize it.   But as the struggle goes on in his soul, he comes to feel dimly that God's present attitude toward him does not express His true character.   His anger must be a passing mood and so he prays,

> Oh that Thou wouldst hide me in Sheol,
>> that Thou wouldst keep me secret, until Thy wrath is past,
>> that Thou wouldst appoint me a set time, and remember me!
> If a man might die, and live again,
>> all the days of my warfare would I wait,
>> till my release should come.
> Thou wouldst call, and I would answer Thee:
>> Thou wouldst have a desire to the work of Thy hands. (14 13-15)

But when Job is overwhelmed again by his unbearable pain, he sees in God once more his cruel foe.   The conflict in his soul is most moving to behold.   He feels very strongly that he will soon die: die innocently, for his death is really a brutal murder committed by God.   But as he thinks of his blood so innocently shed, the old, ingrained belief in the righteous heavenly avenger of innocent blood asserts itself so strongly that he appeals to God — against God!

> O earth, cover not my blood,
>> and let my cry have no resting place.
> Even now, behold, my witness is in heaven,
>> and He that vouches for me is on high.
> My friends scoff at me:
>> but mine eye pours out tears unto God,
> That He would maintain the right of a man with God,
>> and of a son of man with his neighbor! (16 18-21)

A strange dualism appears here in Job's thought of God, the God of righteousness over against the God of arbitrary cruelty.   One who knows Job will vindicate him.   This vindicator must be God Himself, for He is the author of his sufferings and knows therefore that he is innocent. God is arbitrary and cruel indeed, but this very fact shows that the reason of his suffering is in God and not in Job. He can find no refuge with his friends; they will not believe in his innocence, so he is driven in his despair to God, for he cannot get away from the conviction that God is after all truthful. Thus he confidently expects that God will bear witness to him because of His truthfulness. He comes to hope in his vindication; it cannot be far off. Soon he will die, but no matter, God will vindicate him at his grave. How it will be done, he does not say; perhaps he does not know, but he is certain that it will be done. And he is certain also that he himself will see this vindication. The very thought of the vision of God consumes his heart with longing.

> I know that my vindicator lives,
>   and at last He will stand up upon the dust:
> And after (?) my skin is thus destroyed,
>   then without (?) my flesh shall I see God;
> Whom I, even I, shall see on my side,
>   and mine eyes shall behold, and not a stranger.
> My heart is consumed within me. (19 $^{25-27}$)[1]

Job is convinced that God must be righteous in the end! With this the problem, as far as it pertains to Job personally, has received its answer, for Job now knows that God is righteous in spite of His seeming arbitrariness and that He will acknowledge Job's integrity. But the problem concerns not only Job but righteous men everywhere, and now the more general question of the problem of the righteous is discussed. Over against the insistence of the friends that the fate of the wicked is fearful, Job proves conclusively that the facts contradict this theory and shows that the wicked prosper and that God does not do anything at all to indicate that He is truly moral in His dealings with men.

> Wherefore do the wicked live,
>   become old, yea, wax mighty in power?
> Their seed is established with them in their sight,
>   and their offspring before their eyes.
> Their houses are safe from fear,
>   neither is the rod of God upon them. (21 $^{7-9}$)

---

[1] The text and the interpretation of this famous passage are uncertain. But that Job did not assert his belief in his resurrection or his immortality may be pretty safely assumed, for in that case he would have worked this out more fully.

They are prosperous, lead a life of happiness, and do not care for God.

> They say to God, "Depart from us,
>> for we desire not the knowledge of Thy ways.
> What is the Almighty, that we should serve Him?
>> and what profit should we have, if we pray to Him?" (21 14f·)

The argument that the punishment of the wicked is visited upon their children Job tosses impatiently aside, for to him it does not meet the real question.

> How oft is it that the lamp of the wicked is put out?
>> that their calamity comes upon them?
>> that He distributes sorrows in His anger? . . .
> Let Him not reserve his punishment for his children,
>> let Him recompense it to himself, that he may know it,
> Let his own eyes see his destruction,
>> and let himself drink of the wrath of the Almighty!
> For what cares he for his house after him,
>> when the number of his months is cut off? (21 17. 19–21)

As Job thinks of God's injustice in His dealings with men, his high hope fades, his confidence vanishes. Again he cries out,

> Oh that I knew where I might find Him!
>> that I might come even to His seat!
> I would set my cause in order before Him,
>> and fill my mouth with arguments.
> I would know the words which He would answer me,
>> and understand what He would say to me.
> Would He contend with me in the greatness of His power?
>> if only He would give heed to me,
> He would establish justice and would reason with me,
>> so that I should be delivered forever from judgment.
> Behold, I go forward, but He is not there,
>> and backward, but I cannot perceive Him,
> On the left hand I seek Him, but I cannot behold Him,
>> I turn to the right hand, but I cannot see Him. (23 3–9)

Finally, after stating his innocence fully in a very beautiful passage which belongs to the finest that Old Testament ethics has produced,[1] he flings this bold challenge at God:

[1] At least part of this great chapter must be quoted:
> If I have despised the cause of my man-servant
>> or of my maid-servant, when they contended with me;
> What then shall I do when God takes vengeance,
>> and when He visits, what shall I answer Him?

Oh that I had one to hear me! —
　　Lo, here is my signature, let the Almighty answer me! —
　　And that I had the indictment which mine adversary has written!
Surely I would carry it upon my shoulder,
　　I would bind it unto me as a crown:
I would declare unto Him the number of my steps,
　　as a prince would I go near unto Him! (31 $^{35-37}$) [1]

There is the defiance of a titan in this challenge. And God appears! and answers out of a whirlwind. He overawes Job with His terrible majesty and flings question after question at him, not one of which he can answer:

Who is this that darkens counsel
　　by words without knowledge?
Gird up now thy loins like a man,
　　for I will demand of thee and declare thou unto Me.
Where wast thou when I laid the foundations of the earth?
　　Declare, if thou hast understanding!
Who determined its measures? if thou knowest!
　　or who stretched the line upon it?

Did not He that made me in the womb make him?
　　and did not One fashion us in the womb?
If I have withheld aught that the poor desired,
　　or have caused the eyes of the widow to fail,
Or have eaten my morsel alone,
　　and the fatherless has not eaten of it . . .
If I have seen any perish for want of clothing,
　　or that the needy had no covering,
If his loins have not blessed me,
　　and if he has not been warmed with the fleece of my sheep;
If I have lifted up my hand against the fatherless,
　　because I saw my help in the gate:
Then let my shoulder fall from the shoulder-blade,
　　and mine arm be broken from the bone. . . .
If I have rejoiced at the destruction of him that hated me,
　　or was triumphant when evil met him:
Yea, I have not suffered my mouth to sin
　　by asking his life with a curse. . . .
If after the manner of men I have covered my transgressions,
　　by hiding mine iniquity in my bosom,
Because I feared the great multitude,
　　and the contempt of families terrified me,
　　so that I kept silence and went not out of the door —
　　　　　　　　　(31 $^{13-17.\ 19-22.\ 29f.\ 38f.}$)

[1] This section belongs at the end of ch. 31.

> Upon what were its foundations fastened?
> > or who laid its cornerstone?
> When the morning stars sang together,
> > and all the sons of God shouted for joy? (38 2-7)

What does Job know about the mighty work of creation and the marvellous wonders of the world of nature?

> Who shut up the sea with doors,
> > when it broke forth and issued out of the womb? (38 8)

> Hast thou commanded the morning since thy days began,
> > and caused the dayspring to know its place? (38 12)

> Hast thou entered into the springs of the sea?
> > or hast thou walked in the recesses of the deep? (38 16)

What does he know of the realm of death, of the home of light and of darkness, of the treasuries of the snow and the hail, or the mysterious coming of the fog and of the rain and the lightning and thunder? Does he control the forces of the sky, or regulate the constellations' ordered march, or give commands to all the clouds of rain (38 17-38)?

Again, what does Job know of the wonders of God's animal creation? Does he care for the lions? And

> Who provides for the raven his prey,
> > when his young ones cry unto God
> > and grow faint for lack of food? (38 39-41)

What does Job know of the secrets of the mountain-goat, the wild ass, the wild-ox, the horse, the hawk, and the eagle?

> Is it by thy wisdom that the hawk soars,
> > and stretches her wings to the south?
> Is it at thy command that the eagle mounts up,
> > and makes her nest on high? (39 1-12. 26-30)

How can Job dare to criticize God's government of the world and declare it to be immoral, when he knows so little about it? when he understands not even one of the mighty riddles of the world? He thinks that God has nothing else to do but to plague and attack him; as if he were God's only care! In his self-centred view he thinks that the whole world revolves around man and everything is created only for him. But God causes it

> To rain on a land *where no man is*,
>   and on the steppe *where no mortal dwells*,
> To satisfy the waste and desolate ground,
>   and to cause the tender grass to spring forth. (38 [26f.])

Likewise many wild animals will never be tamed and be useful to man.

> Will the wild-ox be content to serve thee?
>   or will he abide by thy crib?
> Canst thou bind with thongs his neck?
>   or will he harrow thy furrows after thee? (39 [9f.])

How insignificant is man in view of the vast complexity of the world, and how ignorant is he about its mysteries! But if God's dealings with the world of nature are so mysterious, it is presumptuous to charge Him with immorality in view of the mysteries of the world of men! If the fault-finder thinks that he can rule the world better, more wisely and righteously than God, let him but try it!

> Deck thyself now with excellency and dignity,
>   and array thyself with honor and majesty,
> Pour forth the overflowings of thine anger,
>   and look upon every one that is proud and abase him,
> And look upon every one that is proud and bring him low,
>   and tread down the wicked where they stand.
> Hide them in the dust together,
>   bind their faces in the hidden place,
> Then will I also confess of thee
>   that thine own arm can save thee. (40 [10-14])

The great problem of human suffering grows small when it is seen in relation to the whole, when man understands that he is not the centre of the universe around whom everything revolves. Before the mighty work of creation and God's wonderful rule of the world of nature, Job is made to feel his own insignificance, becomes conscious of the arrogance of his selfish claims, and confesses,

> I know that Thou canst do all things,
>   and that no purpose of Thine can be restrained.
> Therefore have I uttered that which I understood not,
>   things too wonderful for me, which I knew not.
> I had heard of Thee by the hearing of the ear,
>   but now mine eye sees Thee,
> Wherefore I loathe (my words)
>   and repent in dust and ashes. (40 [4f.] 42 [2. 3b. 5f.])

God had not answered Job's question as to the reason of his suffering at all.   The problem of suffering is as dark as before.   And yet in spite of this Job gains peace.   He does not know and does not need to know why he suffers, for he has been accorded a vision of God. The very fact that God has appeared to him, the vision itself is the solution for him.   In the course of the debate Job had declared that God does not appear to a wicked man.   God's appearance to him implies therefore his vindication.   And indeed God did not charge Job with sin; He only pointed out to him his error and presumption, but in appearing to him He showed that Job was still in favor with Him.   Job learns that a man may suffer from the most horrible disease, and yet be in favor with God !   True piety needs no outward attestation of health, happiness, and prosperity; it does not even need the approval of the righteous, it should rest solely on the witness of conscience.   And if problems come that would drive man to despair, let him but trust his own inner voice in the full confidence that, appearances and feelings notwithstanding, God is on his side as his friend.   For God is righteous and governs the world righteously, however mysterious His rule may be.

After this the epilogue containing the conclusion of the folk tale seems to us superfluous, for we do not need to learn now that Job's prosperity was restored and " Yahweh blessed the latter end of Job more than his beginning."   The poet himself had transcended this solution, but it could not well be missed as the conclusion of the work because the prologue demanded it as the completion of the story.

Later generations did not grasp the power of Job's thought nor could they understand his courage; they thought he was presumptuous and considered himself righteous before God.   This gave offence; so also did the inability of the friends to answer him convincingly.   It seemed incredible to a later poet that Job should have won the debate.   So he added the long Elihu speeches (32–37). But in spite of all his self-importance Elihu says nothing new, virtually all of it had been said before, he only formulated it at times more effectively.   But by his long-winded speeches he interrupts the connection between Job's final challenge (31 $^{35-37}$) and God's appearance (38 $^{1ff.}$).   In order to get the original impression and feel the power of the poem we must omit Elihu's speeches, and give ourselves directly to the grandeur of the appearance and answer of God to Job (38 2–39 12.19–30 40 2.8–14).

Another orthodox writer inserted a beautiful poem on wisdom (28) in which the question is discussed, whence does wisdom come and where is its home? Only God knows the way to it, only He knows its place. Man does not know. How then can he hope to understand the mysteries of God's rule?

The splendid pictures of nature in God's answer incited a poet to add poetic descriptions of the ostrich, hippopotamus, and crocodile (39 13–18 40 15–41 34).

Perhaps two hundred years had passed, when (*ca.* 200 B.C.) another wise man looked on life and its ceaseless round of tasks and inquired into the meaning of it all. It was not only the problem of the suffering of the righteous but of the whole of life that baffled him as he tried to find out its real significance; all his thinking brought to him no answer to his question. He has left a record of his search in the book called by the Jews "Koheleth," by the Greek translators " Ecclesiastes," by ours, " The Preacher." Since "Koheleth" was intended as a proper name, there is no reason for translating it. The book may be entitled "On the Meaning of Life." It contains a number of discourses, which are not arranged in order nor connected with one another; they contain observations, reflections, and wise sayings by a keen observer and brilliant speaker, who was neither a profound nor a systematic philosopher but merely an old man of much experience and common sense.

He had observed the occurrences in nature and in human life. They were ever the same. One generation of men comes and goes, another comes only to go again. The sun rises and sets, only to rise and set again. The wind blows and circles around, coming back again to its starting point. The rivers run into the sea, day after day, year after year, yet the sea is never full, and the rivers well up again from the subterranean ocean to flow again into the sea.

> All things are toiling, no man can speak (of them all),
> The eye is not satisfied with seeing,
> The ear is not filled with hearing. (1 8)

And yet it is ever the same: a ceaseless round of toil and labor with no progress or aim.

That which has been is that which shall be,
And that which has been done is that which shall be done,
And there is no new thing under the sun. (1 [9])

If any one thinks that there is something new, it is only because no record of it was made in former days so that it has been forgotten. There is really nothing new, it is always the same. But what then can be the meaning of this never ending circling, circling, circling? None whatever. Life has no goal and no meaning!

Vanity of vanities, says Koheleth, all is vanity!

It is not the assertion of a young man in a pessimistic mood, but the result of long thought and investigation on the part of a man who had made as wide an induction as possible. It is with profound resignation that the result is given: "All is vanity and a chasing after wind!" Koheleth had had unusual opportunities for observing life, and being gifted with a high degree of intelligence he had probed life in all directions. In order to make his teaching more effective he impersonated Solomon, for nobody could make the test more complete than this wisest of all sages, this richest of all kings. He tried to solve the problem of life, driven thereto by an irrepressible impulse which God had implanted in his heart as in that of all men, the desire to know, which is but " a sorry business," for it worries and wearies them, as Koheleth had found out. He observed and learned, but the more he learned, the sadder he grew, for he

Perceived that this also was a chasing after wind. For in much wisdom is much vexation, and increase of knowledge increases pain. (1 [18])

He tested the pleasures of the world and all the sources of man's happiness, he undertook great works, built houses and vineyards and parks with all that belonged to them, kept a large retinue of servants, had many herds and flocks, got male and female singers and the delights of the sons of men.

And whatsoever mine eyes desired I kept not from them: I withheld not my heart from any joy, for my heart rejoiced because of all my labor; and this was my portion from all my labor. (2 [10])

And then?

Then I looked on all the works that my hands had wrought, and on the labor that I had labored to do; and behold, all was vanity and a chasing after wind, and there was no profit under the sun! (2 [11])

The one thought that takes for him the meaning out of life, that makes wisdom of little value, robs work of its joy, and strips wealth of its power is the thought of death:

I perceived that one event happens to them all, and I said in my heart, As it happens to the fool so will it happen also to me; and why was I then more wise? How the wise man dies even as the fool! So I hated life, because the work that is wrought under the sun was grievous to me; for all is vanity and a chasing after wind. (2 14 ff.)

Nevertheless Koheleth did not throw away life and advise suicide, for to him too, "light is sweet and it is pleasant for the eyes to see the sun" (11 7) and "a living dog is better than a dead lion" (9 4); nor did he scorn wisdom, for he saw that it had an advantage over folly (2 13), and he never maintained that it made no practical difference whether one was a fool or a sage; nor did he despise work, for he had felt too keenly the joy and satisfaction it brings (2 10); nor did he refuse to enjoy wealth and all the pleasures and comfort it bestows. But neither wisdom nor work nor wealth are real ends, the meaning of life is in none of them. For the wise man has the same fate as the fool; the fruit of one's work one must leave to one who has not worked for it and who is perhaps a fool (2 18ff.); one's wealth one may lose by an unlucky adventure (5 13 ff.) or one may not have the capacity to enjoy his riches and honor (6 1ff.).

This is a topsy-turvy world, in which

The race is not to the swift, nor the battle to the strong, neither yet bread to the wise, nor yet riches to the men of understanding, nor yet favor to men of skill; but time and chance overtake them all. (9 11)

Men are not rewarded according to their deserts. Morality does not control the course of the world.

I saw under the sun, in the place of justice: wickedness; and in the place where the righteous should have been: the wicked (3 16). And again I saw all the oppressions that were done under the sun: and, behold, the tears of such as were oppressed, and they had no comforter, and on the side of their oppressors there was power. (4 1)

There was no just government in the land, the king was capricious and tyrannical and the various officials were corrupt (5 8f.). Righteous men perished and wicked men prospered (7 15). Righteousness did not insure happiness and wickedness did not bring punishment:

There are righteous men to whom it happens according to the work of the wicked; again there are wicked men to whom it happens according to the work of the righteous. (8 14)

There is no moral government in this world. God's rule is not according to righteousness, it is so full of mystery that no man will ever understand it, "although he see no sleep with his eyes day or night." From his fate man can never tell whether God loves or hates him (8 16–9 1). Koheleth did not protest and rebel against this lack of morality in the world. He simply accepted the facts of life as they were, and tried to understand them again and again but all in vain. The greatest riddle to him was death, the common fate of all.

To all there is one event, to the righteous and to the wicked, to the good (and to the bad), to the clean and to the unclean, to him that sacrifices and to him that does not sacrifice; as is the good, so is the sinner, he that swears, as he that fears an oath. This is an evil in all that is done under the sun, that there is one event to all. (9 2f.)

Koheleth knew of the hope that was entertained by some that man would rise again, but he could not believe it.

The misery of man is great upon him, for he knows not that which shall be; for who can tell him how it shall be? (8 7)
That which befalls the sons of men befalls the beasts; the same fate befalls them: as the one dies, so dies the other; yea, they all have one breath; and man has no preëminence above the beasts: for all is vanity. All go to the same place, all are of the dust, and all turn to dust again. Who knows of the spirit of man whether it goes upward, and of the spirit of the beast whether it goes downward to the earth? (3 19f.)

Life to him was bounded by the grave. He had no hope of the future either for the individual or for the nation or for the world. The Messianic hope with its splendid dream of future national glory was not for him for he was not a narrow Jew but a cosmopolitan sage. The vision of the regeneration of the world never came to him, for his outlook was individualistic and self-centred. The hope of a resurrection or of immortality he could not make his own, partly from intellectual sincerity, partly from a lack of that deep spiritual passion which made men in his day conquer death in the victorious assurance that their communion with God must be endless no matter what happened. He had no warm, personal faith in God, for God was to him not the living and loving personal-

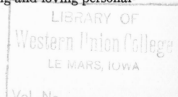

ity, instinct with righteousness and passion that He had been to the prophets and to the author of Job. He was not a God with whom man could enter into intimate relation and communion. He had grown distant, He was the ruler of the world and of men, but His government of the world was not that of a righteous God. Koheleth did not deny His existence, but he did deny His moral character: He was inscrutable and His ways were past finding out. No man could understand Him, although man must ever try to do so.

I have seen the travail which God has given to the sons of men to be exercised therewith. He has made everything appropriate in its time: also He has put ignorance in their heart, so that man cannot find out the work that God has done from the beginning even to the end. (3 ¹⁰ᶠ·)

As thou knowest not what is the way of the spirit into the bones in the womb of her that is with child, even so thou knowest not the work of God who makes everything. (11 ⁵)

God has fixed the world order, He has predetermined all events, and no matter what man may do he cannot change them.

For everything there is a fixed season, and an appointed time for every occurrence under heaven. There is a time to be born, and a time to die; a time to plant, and a time to uproot. (3 ¹ᶠ·)

I know that, whatsoever God does, it shall be forever: nothing can be put to it, nor anything taken from it. (3 ¹⁴)

Consider the work of God: for who can make that straight, which He has made crooked? (7 ¹³)

It is of no use to worry over this and to toil in order to change the unchangeable.

What profit has the worker in that wherein he toils? (3 ⁹)

In the day of prosperity be joyful, and in the day of adversity consider that God has made the one as well as the other, to the end that man should not find out anything that shall be after him. (7 ¹⁴)

Therefore a man should take life as it is and make the most of it as long as he lives:

There is nothing better for a man than that he should eat and drink and make his soul enjoy good in his labor. (2 ²⁴)

> Go thy way, eat thy bread with joy,
> And drink thy wine with a merry heart,
> For God has already accepted thy works.
> Let thy garments be always white,

And let not thy head lack oil.
Enjoy life with the wife whom thou lovest
All the days of thy life of vanity
Which He has given thee under the sun,[1]

for that is thy portion in life, and in thy labor wherein thou laborest under the sun.   Whatsoever thou canst afford with thy substance do, for there is no work, nor planning, nor knowledge, nor wisdom in Sheol, whither thou goest. (9 [7-10])

Koheleth advises therefore the young men of his time in the famous passage:

Rejoice, O young man, in thy youth,
    and let thy heart cheer thee in the days of thy youth,
And walk in the ways of thy heart,
    and in the sight of thine eyes.
And remove vexation from thy heart,
    and put away evil from thy flesh,
Before the evil days come,
    and the years draw nigh of which thou shalt say,
"I have no pleasure in them";
Before the sun is darkened,
    and the light of the moon and the stars,
    and the clouds return after the rain;
In the day when the keepers of the house shall tremble,
    and the strong men shall bow themselves,
And the grinders cease, because they are few,
    and those that look out of the windows be darkened,
    and the doors shall be shut in the street;
When the sound of the grinding is low,
    and one rises at the voice of the birds
    and all the daughters of music are brought low:

[1] Cf. also 3 [12f. 22] 5 [17] 8 [15] 11 [7-10]. There is a striking parallel to this advice in the old Babylonian Gilgamesh epic (cf. footnote on p. 70).

Why, O Gilgamesh, dost thou wander about?
The life that thou seekest, thou wilt not find.
When the gods created man,
Death they ordained for man,
Life they kept in their hands.
Thou, O Gilgamesh, fill thy belly,
Day and night be joyful!
Daily be glad!
Day and night make merry!
Let thy garments be white,
Anoint thy head, and purify thyself!
With the children at thy side,
Enjoy the wife of thy bosom!

> Yea, one is afraid of a height,
> and terrors are in the way;
> And the almond-tree shall blossom,
> and the grasshopper shall be a burden,
> and the caperberry shall burst,
> Because man goes to his everlasting home,
> and the mourners go about the streets:
> Before the silver cord is snapped,
> or the golden bowl is broken,
> Or the pitcher is broken at the fountain,
> or the wheel is broken at the cistern,
> And the dust returns to the earth as it was.
> Vanity of vanities, all is vanity. (11 9–12 8)

This must not be understood as a counsel to make happiness the whole aim of life. Koheleth insisted very strongly on the value of work. But not on work by itself, but on work and joy; work without joy is unbearable:

> What profit has he that labors for the wind? Especially when all his days he is in gloom and in mourning and much vexation and sickness and wrath? (5 16f.)

Live and enjoy, work and play, not alone but in good fellowship. Fulfil life's duties while it lasts, before it is too late. But do not take things too seriously, neither your work nor your play; be not too conscientious, for it does not pay:

> Be not righteous overmuch; neither make thyself overwise: why shouldest thou destroy thyself? Be not overmuch wicked, neither be thou foolish: why shouldest thou die before thy time? It is good that thou shouldest take hold of this, and not withdraw thy hand from that either. (7 16–18)

Koheleth advocated a golden mean! But he never advised licentiousness nor riotous living, for he was not immoral.

Neither was he irreligious. It seemed to him that his advice was in accord with God's plan for man, it was "from the hand of God" (2 24). "That every man should eat and drink, and enjoy good in all his labor is a gift of God" (3 13), it is "his portion" (3 22 5 19). However little warm personal religion he possessed, however little it influenced his life and thought, he did not deny God's reality or His control of the world, nor did he ridicule religious practices; on the contrary he insisted that they must be performed with true reverence and sincerity (5 1–6).

And yet the whole impression of the book was sceptical. Its heterodoxy and pessimism offended the pious and it would never have found its way into the canon of sacred writings, if it had not been edited and revised in the interest of orthodox religion. By a series of interpolations the offensive passages were reinterpreted and the sceptical implications modified. Thus, *e.g.*, the statement that wickedness was enthroned in the land (3 16) was softened by the addition,

I said in my heart, God will judge the righteous and the wicked, for there is an appointed time for every purpose and for every work. (3 17)

Similarly the observation of Koheleth that the wicked who assembled in the sanctuary far from being scorned for their hypocrisy were praised in the city, was toned down by the reflection:

Because the sentence for an evil deed is not executed speedily, therefore the heart of the sons of men is fully set in them to do evil. But though a sinner do evil a hundred times, and prolong his days, yet surely I know that it shall be well with them that fear God, but it shall not be well with the wicked, neither shall he prolong his days which are as a shadow, because he fears not before God. (8 11–13)

That this was directly opposed to Koheleth's own teaching was not felt by the readers of the revised edition of his book. Neither was the insertion in the famous concluding section (cf. p. 335), where the keen edge of Koheleth's advice to the young man to enjoy life before it is too late, was blunted by the interpolations:

But know thou, that for all these things God will bring thee into judgment. (11 9)

Remember also thy Creator in the days of thy youth. (12 1a)

And the conclusion of the whole book now reads in the words of the pious editor:

This is the end of the matter, all has been heard.

Fear God, and keep His commandments, for this is the duty of every man. For God will bring every work into judgment, with every hidden thing, whether it be good or evil. (12 13f.)

This class of additions to Koheleth's teaching is easily recognized (cf. also 7 18b. 26b. 29 12 7b). There is also another class of additions which seek to counteract the heterodox tendency of the original more indirectly. They elaborate the wisdom of "Solomon." Koheleth had impersonated the wise king. A disciple inserted at those points where proverbs and maxims seemed appropriate a number of wise additions, which were in line with the ordinary wisdom of the time and strengthened therefore the reliability of this book of wisdom, and facilitated its eventual recognition as a sacred writing.[1] They are usually recognized by their interruption of the context. Thus in 4 [4] Koheleth had observed that competition and rivalry in work are "vanity and a chasing after wind," and had therefore counselled,

A handful with quietness is better than two handfuls with toil and chasing after wind. (4 [6])

Between these two observations the editor inserted,

The fool holds his hands together and eats his own flesh. (4 [5])

These wise additions contain a great deal of shrewd observation and common sense. Only rarely do they change the thought of Koheleth, as for instance in 3 [1–9]. Koheleth had said,

For everything there is a (fixed) season,
   and an (appointed) time for every occurrence under the sun.
There is a time (appointed) to be born, and a time to die.
There is a time (appointed) for planting, and a time for uprooting. (3 [1f.])

That is, in this world everything is predetermined, it occurs at the time that is appointed for it. And the conclusion is drawn,

What profit then has the worker in that wherein he toils? (3 [9])

What is the use of all his work, since everything that happens is bound to happen, and to happen at the time that is fixed for it? The editor inserted here a number of other illustrations,

There is a time to kill, and a time to heal;
A time to break down, and a time to build up;
A time to weep, and a time to laugh;
A time to mourn, and a time to dance; etc. (3 [3–8])

His intention was evidently to elaborate Koheleth's thought. But he missed the point of it, and the reader now gets the impression that Koheleth meant only that there is an appropriate time for everything.

These additions of the wisdom editor strengthened the impression that Solomon was the author of the book, and the conviction that the saintly and wise king wrote only fit words for edification had

[1] Cf. 4 [5] 5 [3. 7a] 7 [19] 10 [1–3. 8–15. 18f.] etc.

much to do in overcoming the objections to its canonization. But it does not seem that this was the direct intention of the editor, else he would hardly have added at the end this description,

It remains to say that Koheleth was a sage; besides, he taught the people knowledge; yea, he tested and examined and arranged many proverbs. Koheleth sought to find out pleasant words, and he wrote uprightness, words of truth. (12 $^{9f.}$)

Koheleth had been a wise man and a popular teacher, and besides, an author who wrote with fine discrimination and acumen many aphorisms and proverbs, whose style he polished most carefully and whose content was truth. Perhaps we may assume that at least some of the maxims scattered through the book were taken from a collection of Koheleth. In regard to his style, the poem on the ceaseless repetition in the life of nature and of man (1 $^{2-9}$) and the poetic description of old age and death (12 $^{1-8}$) give evidence of Koheleth's literary ability. And yet this Omar Khayyám of the Old Testament would never have received universal recognition, had it not been for his friends and admirers who revised and edited his book, so that now alongside of its pessimism it affirmed the truth of the moral government of the world, the certainty of righteous judgment, and the supreme duty of the fear of God and of obedience to His Law. But withal there is added the warning not to take even this book too seriously:

Furthermore, my son, be admonished:
Of making many books there is no end;
And much study is a weariness of the flesh. (12 ^{12})

One might imagine the old sage, Koheleth himself, commenting on this with his tired smile of resignation,

This also is vanity. Vanity of vanities, all is vanity.

The belief in the future life, with resurrection and immortality, which Koheleth could not make his own, gained more and more ground in the following generations [1] and in its light the riddles of human existence could be solved: the apparent injustice of the present life will be righted in the future. The belief in the moral character of God was preserved in this way.

[1] Compare among others also the two Wisdom books, "The Wisdom of Solomon" and "The Fourth Book of Maccabees," which were written too late to get into the Old Testament Canon. They are now classed among the Apocrypha and Pseudepigrapha.

CHAPTER XX

THE PSALMS AND THE SONG OF SONGS

POETRY and religion go together. In moments of religious experience when the soul is at one with the eternal harmony of God its utterances often become rhythmic and burst into song; common prose is not adequate to express its joy or its longing; in rhythmic rise and cadence flow forth praise and prayer revealing the deepest feelings and desires. That is why the Psalms are so important, for we have here a singularly profound revelation of the inner life of the Jewish people. Here we "can look into the hearts of all the saints," as Martin Luther said in his Second Preface to the Psalter.

Here the hopes and fears of many ages are collected, the longings and yearnings of countless hearts. Here the penitence and grief over sin, the sorrow and anguish over individual and national calamity, the joyful gratitude for forgiveness and restoration, find voice and utterance. Here the passionate plea for revenge on the enemies individual or national, the despair over the apparent injustice of this world order, and the hope of the coming of God's Kingdom, stand side by side. The whole range of human life, its joy and its woe, its light and its shadow, and its daily routine, is treated in the Psalter. There are psalms of common worship, pilgrim songs and processional hymns, calls to worship, hymns of praise and thanksgiving for individual or national deliverance, for the harvest and the joys of nature. There are national psalms, prayers for deliverance from external or internal foes, for national restoration, prayers of trust in national peril and of praise for past deliverance, battle songs, and odes of victory. There are royal psalms, coronation and wedding odes, prayers for the king's just and ideal rule, for God's help in battle or thanksgiving for victory. There are psalms of individual piety with its longings for communion with God and its joy in the experience of it; with its prayers for help and healing, for forgiveness and purification; with its songs of faith and trust and its hymns of thanksgiving and praise.   There are didactic psalms, with the warm, insistent teaching of the fear of God, the divine government in the world, retribution for pious and wicked alike; with their warnings against trust in riches, and concerning the vanity and brevity of life; with their teachings of true worship and true sacrifice, of the blessedness of forgiveness, and of charitableness toward others, of the joys of home and of nature and law; and with their lessons from Israel's great history in the past.   Out of the heart of life they sprang, and to the heart they speak.   Many poets have contributed; some of them were original geniuses of poetic power, others were common versifiers.   They are not grouped according to any chronological, topical, or other principle.   Varied as life itself, they are also tossed together in the same kaleidoscopic manner as life's experiences themselves.

If we knew more confidently the time and conditions, when each psalm was composed, we should often understand much better its true meaning.   The collections that we now have in our Psalter date from the period of the second temple.   But a number of individual psalms are older, some perhaps as old as David, to whom tradition attributes about half of all.   It is almost always difficult to tell from what time they come, for they were frequently worked over and adapted to the needs of new times.   Lines that had reference to particular situations were omitted, as a comparison of the two recensions of the same psalm (14 and 53) shows.   The psalm thus becomes timeless and better fitted to appeal to all times and to voice the needs of all generations.   If Psalm 24 $^{7-10}$ should go back to David, as some recent critics still believe, combined as it now is with Psalm 24 $^{1-6}$ it is a later psalm which presupposes the teaching of the great prophets.   From the time of the monarchy appear to come the royal Psalms 20 and 21; while Psalm 46 reproduces the teaching of Isaiah—one might even be inclined to ascribe it to him, so strong is the power of its faith.   The teaching of the prophets regarding sacrifice is seen in others (Ps. 40. 50. 51); and Deutero-Isaiah's influence is felt in many.   Not only do we hear the echo of the music of his speech, but also his universal ideas of religion, and his view of nature.   Other psalms celebrate the law (Ps. 1. 19 $^{7ff.}$ 119) and show the influence of the legalistic age after the exile, and in their joy over the law they help us to correct our views concern-

ing its unrelieved burdensomeness. The humanism and individualism of the sages are reflected in still others, in which the human problems of retribution are discussed (Ps. 49. 73). Some of the so-
called Messianic psalms show decidedly their late age. Thus Psalm
110 was most probably composed by a poet for Simon the Hasmonean's triumphal day on which he combined the regal and highpriestly offices in his person "after the manner of Melchizedek."
Very few psalms bear the stamp of their origin on their face, as
does Psalm 137 with its sad memory of the Babylonian exile and
its fierce cry of hate. Such psalms as 74. 79. 83 seem almost certainly
to come from the Maccabæan period, for no other historical situations
that we know fit so well the conditions outlined in them. But we
can rarely be entirely certain of the dates of the psalms.

It has always been fascinating to connect the various psalms with
the circumstances in history out of which they appear to come.
They gain much in vividness and interest from such endeavors.
Already in late postexilic times such attempts were made and a good
many psalms were attributed to certain situations, mostly in the
life of David, in which they seemed to have been composed. If a
psalmist described his longing for God by "My soul thirsts for
Thee . . . in a dry and weary land" (Ps. 63 [1]), it was set down as
"A Psalm of David, when he was in the wilderness of Judah." If
a psalmist cried for forgiveness of sin (Ps. 51), it was referred to
David's adultery, "A Psalm of David, when Nathan the prophet
came to him, after he had gone in to Bathsheba." But these
guesses [1] are without value, there is not one of them that can be
accepted as correct. This tradition of Davidic authorship of the
Psalms was established as early as the time of the Chronicler. He
believed that David had planned the temple and arranged for the
singing and the music in the temple services. To the Chronicler
David was not a mighty warrior so much as a writer and singer of
psalms, and to him and to his chief musicians was therefore attributed the authorship of many of them. How this belief arose is
difficult to trace. That David was a musician and poet is certain
(Am. 6 [5]; 1 Sam. 16 [16 ff.]). That he may have written psalms as well as
secular poetry (2 Sam. 1 [19 ff.] 3 [33f.]) we may easily grant. If he did,
some of them may be preserved in our Psalter. But if so, they are

[1] On 14 psalms, 3. 7. 18. 30. 34. 51. 52. 54. 56. 57. 59. 60. 63. 142.

so much worked over that not a single one can be pointed out which every one would recognize as David's.

When after the rebuilding of the temple the services were resumed, the old forms and ritual were doubtless in many cases adhered to, although modifications and adaptations were made. A collection of hymns, old and new, was made, and it was called "the Psalms of David." It was only the first of a number. We can still point out the various collections which are now parts of our Psalter:

1. The first David Psalter [1] in Ps. 2–41.
2. The second David Psalter [2] in Ps. 51–72.
3. The Korah Psalter in Ps. 42–49.
4. The Asaph Psalter in Ps. 50. 73–83.
5. An appendix to the Korah Psalter [3] in Ps. 84–89.
6. The Hallelujah Psalter in Ps. 105–107. 111–118. 146–150.
7. The Pilgrim Psalter in Ps. 120–134.
8. Another David Psalter [4] in Ps. 138–145.
9. The hymns in Ps. 93. 95–100 appear to have formed a special collection also.

In the final edition of the Psalter these collections were put together and the whole was divided into five books,[5] each closing with a special doxology. Psalm 150 serves as a doxology for the whole Psalter. This division coincides with the earlier collections in Books I–III, but it is artificial in the last two books. It appears to have been made in imitation of the Pentateuch in order that the five Books of the Law might find their response in the five Books of Praises.[6] Psalm 1 was prefixed to the whole Psalter to

[1] Ps. 2. 10. 33 have no superscription in the Hebrew Bible, but Greek manuscripts attribute Ps. 2. 33 to David, and Ps. 10 is really a part of Ps. 9.

[2] Ps. 66. 67 are not attributed to David in the Hebrew Bible, but Ps. 67 is in the Greek Version. Ps. 72 is attributed to Solomon; it was joined to the David Psalter because it was probably taken as a prayer of David *for* Solomon.

[3] Ps. 84. 85. 87. 88 are assigned to the Korahites. Ps. 88 is in addition also assigned to Heman the Ezrahite. Ps. 89 is attributed to Ethan the Ezrahite; Ps. 86 to David. Asaph, Heman, and Ethan were David's chief musicians (1 Chr. 15 [17. 19]), while Korah was an ancestor of Heman.

[4] Also Ps. 101. 103. 108–110. 122. 124. 131. 133 are assigned to David.

[5] I. Ps. 1–41; II. Ps. 42–72; III. Ps. 73–89; IV. Ps. 90–106; V. Ps. 107–150.

[6] The total number of psalms (150) is also gotten artificially. Originally some psalms, now counted as two, were one, *e.g.* Ps. 9 and 10 as the alphabetical acrostic

emphasize its legal character, and Psalm 2 to emphasize its Messianic character.

The poetic form of the Psalms is worked out carefully, and it greatly enhances their beauty.

The fundamental principle of Hebrew poetry, the so-called parallelism of the members, — the balancing of the lines that belong together, — makes it possible to perceive much of the poetic beauty of the psalms even in a translation which pays no attention to the rhythm of the original. The important types of this parallelism may be illustrated as follows.

The simplest and most common form is the couplet or distich. In it we find the synonymous parallelism, in which the same thought is expressed in parallel lines,

> The desire of his heart Thou didst grant him,
> and the request of his lips Thou didst not deny (21 [2]) ;

the tautological parallelism, in which the same words are exactly or almost exactly repeated,

> Yahweh, how long shall the wicked,
> how long shall the wicked triumph (94 [3]) ;

the antithetical parallelism, in which the thought of one line is contrasted with that of the other,

> Weeping may tarry for the night,
> but joy comes in the morning (30 [5]) ;

the synthetical parallelism, in which the second line supplements the thought of the first,

> I cry unto Yahweh with my voice
> and He answers me out of His holy hill. (3 [4])

The triplet or tristich is not so common,

> The floods have lifted up, Yahweh,
> the floods have lifted up their voice,
>   the floods lift up their roaring. (93 [3])

---

shows, Ps. 42 and 43 as the refrain in both proves. In other psalms two or more originally unrelated poems are combined, *e.g.* in Ps. 19. 24. 27. 144. Ps. 108 is a combination of Ps. 57 [7-11] and 60 [5-12]. Ps. 40 [13-17] appears as a separate poem in Ps. 70.

The Greek Version counts Ps. 9 and 10 as one, also Ps. 114 and 115, but it divides Ps. 116 and 147 each into two psalms. It has an additional (apocryphal) psalm at the end of the Psalter, Ps. 151.

The tetrastich (four lines) is usually a combination of distichs,

> His mouth was smooth as butter,
>> but war his heart;
> Softer than oil his words,
>> yet were they drawn swords. (55 21)

The pentastich (five lines) is a combination of a distich and a tristich,

> I am wearied with my groaning,
>> every night make I my bed to swim
>> and my couch I flood with tears.
> Languid is my eye from grief,
>> it has grown weak from all oppressors. (6 6f.)

The hexastich (six lines) is a combination of distichs or tristichs,

> Yahweh is King; let the peoples tremble:
>> He sits above the cherubim; let the earth be moved.
> Yahweh is great in Zion:
>> and He is high above all the peoples.
> Let them praise Thy great and terrible name:
>> Holy is He! (99 1-3)

Here the refrain, "Holy is He," proves that we have a stanza of six lines. Also larger units occur, as, for instance, in Psalm 42f., whose three stanzas of eight or nine lines are clearly marked by the refrain which is not counted in these eight or nine lines. The refrain is of high poetic effect. In Psalm 107 a double refrain is used most artistically, the first is in the middle of the stanzas, where it marks the turning point of the people's experience,

> Then they cried unto Yahweh in their trouble
>> and He delivered them out of their distresses (vv.6. 13. 19. 28),

while the second at the end of the stanzas,

> Oh, that men would praise Yahweh for His kindness,
>> and for His wonderful works to the children of men (vv.8. 15. 21. 31),

is always followed by two lines which vary in accordance with the subject of the stanza, e.g. the first described the hunger and thirst of the people in the desert, and thus ends,

> Oh, that men would praise Yahweh for His kindness,
>> and for His wonderful works to the children of men,
>
> For He satisfies the longing soul,
>> and the hungry soul He fills with good. (v.9)

Far less attractive is the use of the alphabet for binding the lines together either into a single whole of 22 lines, in which successive lines begin with successive letters of the alphabet (Ps. 111f.), or into stanzas in which the first word of each couplet (Ps. 25. 34. 145) or of each tetrastich (Ps. 9. 10. 37) is treated thus. Psalm 119 is the most elaborate and artificial of these, each of its 22 stanzas consists of eight lines which begin with the same letter.

The rhythmic movement of the psalms which gives to them their poetic quality in combination with the parallelism of the lines (cf. p. 19f.) is not easily reproduced in a translation. Unfortunately the great English Versions have laid no stress on it. The frequent alliterations and assonances have not been brought out either.

The psalms that were used in the temple services were sung by the temple choir, accompanied by the temple music, and the responses were chanted by the people. In Psalm 150 a list of the musical instruments is given. There are also a number of musical notes in the superscriptions, in the middle, or at the end of many psalms. But their meaning is no longer known, not even of *selah*, which seems to have indicated the place where the music was to set in, or a doxology was to be sung, or a prostration to be made. Sometimes the character of the psalm is indicated by "a song," or "a psalm" (with musical accompaniment), or both; or *miktam;* or *maskîl*, which may mean either a meditation or an artistic song; or *shiggayon*. Sometimes the direction is given that the psalm is to be sung to the accompaniment of stringed or of wind instruments. Fifty-five psalms have the note *lamenasseah* which is usually translated "for the chief musician," but which originally appears to have meant "for musical rendering." Sometimes the melody according to which the psalm was to be sung is given (*e.g.* Ps. 22 is to be sung after the tune of the song "the hind of the morning," Ps. 45. 69 according to *shoshanim* = lilies). Not one of these songs nor any of their tunes is preserved; all tradition of the ancient temple music has perished. But this is perhaps not a serious loss to our appreciation of the psalms, because our sense of tonal harmony is so different from that of the ancient Jews. It would be difficult for us, even if we still had the old music and understood all the directions, to get the same impression from it that the ancient worshippers did when they sang and danced before the Lord.   But it is the contents, not the form, that is the most significant element in them.

To grasp the variety of the religious life which finds its expression in the psalms it is necessary to group those that belong together. Since many were not used in the temple we may divide them into psalms for the public worship either of the whole community or of the individual, and psalms of private devotion, edification, and instruction.

1. PUBLIC WORSHIP IN THE TEMPLE

One cannot easily overestimate the importance of temple worship for Judaism.   The temple stood in the centre of its national and its religious life.   The Jews believed that Yahweh dwelt in the innermost part, the holy of holies; here was His home and His throne.   The worshippers entered, therefore, literally the presence of God when they went into the temple.   There they prayed to Him and thither they turned their faces in their devotions when they were away from it.

Three times a year they were expected to go thither to attend the great annual festivals.   Those were seasons of great joy and festivity.   On the given day the cry of the watchmen rang out, "Arise ye, and let us go up to Zion unto Yahweh our God!" (Jer. 31 [6]), and the bands of pilgrims came from all directions.   They were happy throngs, marching to the sound of the pipe (Isa. 30 [29]) and often singing as they went.   We still have in our Psalter a charming collection of Pilgrim songs (Ps. 120–134), which had originally not been written for pilgrimages but which were used by the pilgrims on their march.   They are on a variety of subjects. Songs dealing with the history of the nation were favorites, *e.g.* Psalm 124.   A solo voice begins, clear and strong,

> If it had not been for Yahweh who was on our side.

This is taken up and repeated by the whole chorus ("Let Israel now say"),

> If it had been for Yahweh who was on our side,
>   when men rose up against us;
> Then they had swallowed us up alive,
>   when their wrath was kindled against us:

> Then the waters had overwhelmed us,
> the stream had gone over our soul;
> Then had gone over our soul
> the proud waters.

It may be that the precentor sang first every distich, as he had done with the first line, and the people sang it after him. But now the mighty chorus bursts forth in unison into praise,

> Blessed be Yahweh, who has not given us
> as a prey to their teeth.
> Our soul is escaped as a bird
> out of the snare of the fowlers:
> The snare is broken,
> and we are escaped.
> Our help is in the name of Yahweh
> who made heaven and earth. (Ps. 124)

The memory of dire national peril lives in this song, but also the joy over God's help.

One of the most beautiful pilgrim songs is Psalm 126 which describes the condition of the returned exiles who had been fired by Deutero-Isaiah's predictions and were disappointed by the different reality; Israel's fate had not really been turned. The glad thanks for the home coming are followed by the humble plea for full deliverance and the confidence that out of the present seed of tears there will yet sprout the harvest of joy:

> When Yahweh turned Zion's fate,
> we were like them that dream.
> Then was our mouth filled with laughter,
> and our tongue with singing:
> Then said they among the nations,
> "Yahweh has done great things for them."
> Yahweh has done great things for us,
> whereof we are glad.
>
> Turn our fate, O Yahweh,
> as the streams in the South land.
> They that sow with tears
> shall reap in joy.
> He that goes forth and weeps,
> when he carries seed for sowing,
> Shall doubtless come home with joy,
> when he brings his (harvest) sheaves. (Ps. 126)

Sometimes the pilgrims sang *de profundis*, the penitential psalm, which is ageless with its cry of the sinful human soul and its longing for the forgiveness of God:

> Out of the depths have I cried unto Thee, Yahweh,
>   O Lord, hear my voice.
> Let Thine ears be attentive
>   to the voice of my supplications.
>
> If Thou, Yahweh, shouldst mark iniquities,
>   O Lord, who could stand?
> But there is forgiveness with Thee,
>   that Thou mayest be feared.
>
> I wait for Yahweh, my soul
>   does wait for His word.
> My soul hopes for the Lord
>   more than watchmen (hope) for the morning.
>
> Yea, more than watchmen for the morning,
>   O Israel, hope for Yahweh;
> For with Yahweh is kindness,
>   and with Him is plenteous redemption.
> And He will redeem Israel
>   from all his iniquities. (Ps. 130)

Songs of homely counsel and wisdom like Psalms 127. 128. 133 or songs of trust like Psalms 125. 131 made the way seem shorter to the pilgrims.   Perhaps when they approached the holy city they sang Psalm 121, which is still one of humanity's exquisite treasures:

> I will lift up mine eyes unto the mountains:
>   from whence shall my help come?

The answer is given not by a priest, but by the singing chorus itself:

> My help comes from Yahweh,
>   who made heaven and earth.
>
> He will not suffer thy foot to be moved:
>   He that keeps thee will not sleep.
> Behold, nor sleeps nor slumbers
>   Israel's keeper.
>
> Yahweh is thy keeper, Yahweh is thy shade
>   upon thy right hand.
> The sun shall not smite thee by day,
>   nor the moon by night.

> Yahweh will keep thee from all evil,
>   He will keep thy soul.
> Yahweh will keep thy going out and thy coming in
>   from this time forth and for evermore. (Ps. 121)

At last the pilgrims arrived at Jerusalem. Many of them saw for the first time the beautiful city that was sanctified by the temple in which Yahweh dwelt, and glorified by the events of history, of which they had heard so much and whose scenes they now could see with their own eyes. With mingled joy and awe they entered the temple, meditated on the kindness of God, and determined to publish His praise and His righteousness to the ends of the earth. Aye, the joy of all the worshippers! and especially of the pilgrims who had come from distant lands as they now walked about Zion and marked each tower and gate, each bulwark and palace; for each had a story of its own, which they must tell to their friends and especially to their children at home (Ps. 48). Compare also the pilgrim song, Psalm 84, with its ardent longing for the temple and its description of the stations of the procession.

When they set out on their homeward march, they sang Psalm 122, that simple song which tells of the joy with which they received the summons to go up to the temple. They now had been to the holy city which binds all the members of the Jewish people together, by the law which requires all to attend the yearly festivals there, and their hearts were full of good wishes and intentions for her welfare and peace.

We can hardly get an adequate conception of the love that the Jews had for Jerusalem.[1] Here they experienced the power of common worship that bound them together with one another and with God. The great festivals with their processional songs and their hymns, their music and public sacrifices, made a deep and

---

[1] In passionate devotion a psalmist cries,

> If I forget thee, O Jerusalem,
>   let my right hand be palsied;
> Let my tongue cleave to the roof of my mouth,
>   if I remember thee not;
> If I prefer not Jerusalem
>   above my chief joy! (Ps. 137 [6])

So deeply rooted was the love for Jerusalem, the centre of the national and religious life of the people.

lasting impression on many hearts.   With profound devotion they joined in the worship.

The services on the great festivals began with processional hymns at the foot of the temple hill.   As the festal procession marched to the temple the choir called upon the whole earth to sing:

> Make a joyful noise unto Yahweh, all ye lands,
>> serve Yahweh with gladness,
>>> come before His presence with singing!
> Know that Yahweh is God,
>> it is He that made us, and we are His,
>>> we are His people and the sheep of His pasture.
>
> Enter His gates with thanksgiving,
>> and His courts with praise:
>>> give thanks unto Him and bless His name!
> For He is good, His kindness is for ever
>> and His faithfulness to all generations. (Ps. 100)

The last two lines were taken up as a refrain and sung by all the people.   Sometimes the festal procession itself sang the call to worship as it approached the temple:

> Oh come, let us sing unto Yahweh,
>> let us make a joyful noise to the rock of our salvation.
> Let us come before His presence with thanksgiving,
>> let us make a joyful noise unto Him with psalms. . . .
>
> Oh come, let us worship and bow down,
>> let us kneel before Yahweh our Maker:
> For He is our God,
>> and we are the people of His pasture.

With this the procession entered the temple, and a priest now addressed the people, in the name of Yahweh, and earnestly exhorted them to obey His commands with all their hearts, that thus their worship might be truly acceptable to Him.

> To-day, oh that ye would hear His voice!
> "Harden not your heart, as at Meribah,
>> as in the day of Massah in the wilderness;
> When your fathers tempted Me,
>> proved Me, and saw My work.
> Forty years long was I grieved
>> with that generation, and said,

> They are people that err in their heart
> and know not My ways:
> Wherefore I swore in My wrath,
> that they should not enter into My place of rest. (Ps. 95)

There were many processional hymns, suitable for different occasions. It is significant that the priests endeavored by means of hymn and sermon to ethicize the public cult and make it a worship in spirit and truth. This is apparent also in the famous processional hymn, Psalm 24, which was used for the celebration of a victory. Most probably the ark was carried back from the battle field into the temple.[1]   A brief but mighty hymn opened the ceremony:

> The earth is Yahweh's, and its fulness,
> the world, and they that dwell therein.
> For He has founded it upon the seas,
> and established it upon the floods.[2]

As the procession ascended the temple hill, the question was asked in solemn appeal,

> Who may ascend the hill of Yahweh?
> and who may stand in His holy place?

To which the priest or priests responded,

> He that has clean hands and a pure heart,
> who has not lifted up his soul to falsehood,
> and has not sworn deceitfully.
> He shall receive a blessing from Yahweh,
> and vindication from the God of his salvation.
> Such is the generation that inquires for Him,
> that seeks the God of Jacob's face.

No ceremonial requirement is mentioned, the entire stress lies on social morality; not on cultic cleanness but on moral purity! In Psalm 15 we have a striking and somewhat fuller parallel to this: the true worshipper of Yahweh is the righteous citizen! The influence of the prophets is distinctly felt here; in Psalm 15 it stands out in bolder relief, because Psalm 15 is not, like Psalm 24, part of a liturgy.   But the endeavor to

---

[1] In Ps. 68 [24f.] such a procession is described,
> They have seen Thy goings, O God,
> even the goings of my God, my King, into the sanctuary.
> The singers went before, the minstrels followed after,
> in the midst of the damsels playing with timbrels.

[2] The earth was believed to rest on a subterranean ocean.

place the temple services on a moral basis is of the greatest importance for all: without morality they are valueless. Only men with clean hands and pure and honest hearts may stand in God's sanctuary. The procession now moves on. At the temple gate they break forth into singing,

> Lift up your heads, O ye gates,
>   and be ye lifted up, ye ancient doors,
>   that the King of Glory may come in!

But from the temple comes the challenge,

> Who is the King of Glory?

At once the answer comes back, clear and strong,

> Yahweh, strong and mighty,
> Yahweh, mighty in battle!

accompanied again by the demand,

> Lift up your heads, O ye gates,
>   yea, lift them up, ye ancient doors,
>   that the King of Glory may come in!

Once more the challenging question,

> Who is the King of Glory?

and once more the enthusiastic reply,

> Yahweh, the God of hosts,
> He is the King of Glory!

and the procession enters the temple (Ps. 24). Then the sacrifices began.

In Psalm 118 we have a more elaborate processional with a festal liturgy. As the procession starts at the foot of the temple hill the leader (cf. Ps. 42 [4]) sings,

> Oh give thanks to Yahweh, for He is good,
>   and His kindness endures for ever.

The refrain "for His kindness endures for ever" is taken up by "Israel," by "the house of Aaron," and by "them that fear Yahweh," in turn. As the procession marches up the hill, they recount in their song the serious trouble out of which their great and only helper Yahweh had saved them; how they had been attacked by all surrounding nations but how Yahweh had helped them to win the victory over them all; and how therefore

> The voice of rejoicing and victory
>> is in the homes of the righteous.

Their suffering had been severe, but full of gratitude and joy the leader declares,

> I shall not die but live,
>> and declare the works of Yahweh.
> Yahweh has chastened me sore,
>> but He has not given me over to death.

By this time the procession has arrived at the temple and the leader of the procession calls to the Levites who keep the gates,

> Open to me the gates of righteousness,
>> that I may enter them and give thanks to Yahweh.

To this demand the Levites respond, stressing the "righteousness" of the gate,

> This is the gate of Yahweh,
>> the righteous may enter it.

The procession now enters singing,

> I thank Thee for Thou hast answered me,
>> and art become my salvation.
> The stone which the builders rejected
>> is become the head of the corner.
> This comes from Yahweh,
>> it is wonderful in our eyes.
> This is the day which Yahweh has made,
>> we will rejoice and be glad in it.

The whole chorus then joins in the plea,

> Save now, we beseech Thee, O Yahweh!
> O Yahweh, we beseech Thee, send now prosperity!

In the temple court the priests welcome the worshipping throng,

> Blessed be he that enters, in the name of Yahweh:
>> we bless you from the house of Yahweh.

The procession responds,

> Yahweh is God, and has given us light.

Whereupon they are exhorted to perform the sacred dance around the altar (cf. Ps. 26 [6]), touching the horns of the altar with the branches which they are carrying, for that was from ancient times the most significant function of the ceremony, the formal act of paying reverence to God, by which the immediate contact with the deity was attained,

> Perform the (sacred) dance with branches,
> even to the horns of the altar.

The procession marched around the altar in the rhythmic steps of the sacred dance, touching with their branches the horns of the altar and singing,

> Thou art my God, and I will thank Thee,
> Thou art my God, I will exalt Thee.[1]

Whereupon the whole chorus joined in with the refrain with which the psalm had begun,

> Oh give thanks to Yahweh, for He is good,
> for His kindness endures for ever.

Special festal hymns were sung at the various yearly feasts. Unfortunately the tradition about this matter is meagre [2] and apparently not always dependable. According to Jewish tradition Psalm 81 was the New Year's hymn, but it seems more likely that it was originally intended for the Passover. The congregation is gathered in the temple. The choir begins,

> Sing aloud unto God our strength,
> make a joyful noise to the God of Jacob.
> Raise a song, and strike the timbrel,
> the pleasant harp with the psaltery.

[1] The use of the first person singular instead of plural in this psalm apparently indicates that the national leader sang those passages, in a representative capacity. It was not he alone that was surrounded by all the nations, nor he alone that was delivered. Although v. 19 says, "I will enter," the priests say in v. 26 "we bless you" (plural).

[2] In the Hebrew Bible Ps. 30 is "a song at the dedication of the House," Ps. 100 "a psalm for the thank-offering," Ps. 38 and 70 are "for (public) confession," Ps. 120–134 pilgrim songs, Ps. 92 is "a song for the Sabbath day." The ancient Greek Version supplements this: Ps. 24 was for the first day of the week (Sunday), Ps. 48 for the second (Monday), Ps. 94 for the third (Tuesday), Ps. 93 for the day before the Sabbath (Friday). A later Greek translation assigns Ps. 81 to Thursday and the Mishna has in addition Ps. 82 for Tuesday. According to the Greek Bible Ps. 29 was for the last day of the feast of tabernacles.

The Talmud mentions also certain psalms that were sung in connection with the extra offerings on the Sabbath and feast days. More important is its tradition that the Great Hallel, Ps. 113–118, was sung on the great festivals. At the Passover Ps. 113f. were sung before the meal, Ps. 115–118 after the meal. Compare Matt. 26 [30] "and when they had sung a hymn, they went out into the Mount of Olives."

> Blow the trumpet at the new moon,
>> at the full moon, on our feast-day.
> For it is a statute for Israel,
>> an ordinance of the God of Jacob.
> He appointed it in Joseph for a testimony,
>> when He went out against the land of Egypt. (Ps. 81 [1-5])

Here the choir stops, and a single voice takes up the song: a priest speaks in the name of Yahweh, like a prophet. He reminds the people of the deliverance from Egypt, which they are celebrating in this festival, of the miraculous gift of water at Meribah and of the legislation at Sinai, and then pleads with them to obey Yahweh wholeheartedly henceforth,

> Oh that My people would hearken unto Me,
>> that Israel would walk in My ways!

Then they would soon experience His wonderful blessing in their victory over their enemies and in plentiful harvests (Ps. 81 [6-16]). We have here again a genuine prophetic sermon in connection with the ceremonies in the temple. Surely, the great prophets had not worked in vain, if priestly men attempted so earnestly to deepen the piety of the temple worshippers and to make religion not only a matter of outward form but of the inner disposition, the moral will.

On the great harvest festivals special prayers of thanksgiving for the harvest were offered. Psalm 67 was one of these. Its scope was not narrow, for a universal element entered almost inevitably into the contemplation of the gift of the harvest. Its blessings were not confined to Israel. The God who has provided so plentifully the fruits of the earth must become manifest to all nations of the world. In His marvellous blessing of Israel the heathen must see what a wonderful God He is. Let them rejoice in Him and fear Him, for He will be their guide too. The congregation looks beyond the material gift of the harvest to the spiritual blessing which Israel is destined to be for the world, and calls on the nations to join them in praise and thanksgiving. The prayer begins with the priestly blessing (cf. Num. 6 [25]):

> God be gracious unto us and bless us,
>> and make His face to shine toward us;
> That Thy way may be known upon earth,
>> Thy salvation among all nations.

> Let the peoples give Thee thanks, O God,
>> let all the peoples give Thee thanks.
> Let the nations be glad and sing for joy;
>> for Thou wilt judge the peoples with equity,
>>> and lead the nations upon earth.
> Let the peoples give Thee thanks,
>> let all the peoples give Thee thanks.
>
> The earth has yielded its increase:
>> may God, even our God, bless us!
> May God bless us;
>> and let all the ends of the earth fear Him. (Ps. 67)

This universal outlook characterizes also the other harvest song, Psalm 65, which is a further proof that the temple cult of the post-exilic times was actuated by the high thoughts of prophetic teaching. The ideals of the great prophets, especially of Deutero-Isaiah, were taken over by the psalmists and presented in the public services to the people.   The temple worship itself is of course regarded as important and as a means of spiritual satisfaction, yet the God worshipped there is not only the God of the Jews but "the confidence of all the earth and the isles afar off"; to Him "shall all flesh come," and He makes "the outgoings of the morning and the evening to rejoice."

Most hymns were not composed for special occasions, but were suitable for any service of praise.   They celebrate God's work in creation and in the processes of nature, or they extol His deliverance of Israel and His righteous rule over them, or they anticipate with great enthusiasm His final judgment of the nations and the establishment of His Kingdom on earth.[1]   One of the most enthusiastic of

---

[1] The hymns or songs of praise have a characteristic form.   They usually, though not always, begin with "Praise Yahweh," or "Sing unto Yahweh," or "Bless Yahweh," or a similar form.   The assembled people, or the priests, Levites and proselytes, or Zion, or the peoples of the earth, or all creation, are addressed to praise Yahweh, and their response is assumed; even that of the heavens, for
> The heavens declare the glory of God,
>> and the firmament shows His handiwork. (Ps. 19 [1])
Then follows the reason for this praise, which differs in accordance with the character of the hymn.   It is interesting to note that the shortest song of praise contains these two elements, the hymnal introduction and the reason for the praise.
> Oh praise Yahweh, all ye nations,
>> laud Him, all ye peoples.
> For His kindness is great toward us,
>> and Yahweh's faithfulness is for ever. (Ps. 117)
There are, however, variations from this regular form.

all the hymns or songs of praise, Psalm 148, is taken up almost entirely with the call to the whole creation to praise Yahweh.   Heaven with its host, the angels, the sun, moon, and stars, and the heavenly ocean, all must praise Yahweh; the earth and the sea with its sea-monsters, fire and hail, snow and fog and storm, mountains and trees, beasts and birds and creeping things, all must praise Him; all mankind, kings and nations, old people and young, all must praise the name of Yahweh,

> For His name alone is exalted,
>   His glory is above the earth and the heavens.
> And He has lifted up the horn of His people,
>   a praise for all His saints,
>   for the Israelites, the people that is near Him. (Ps. 148)

Here is no narrow view.   The psalmist's devotion is not satisfied until the whole wide world resounds with the praise of Yahweh, for His name alone is exalted.   It is true, the reason for this praise is the restoration of the national glory of Israel.   But this is to the poet the beginning of the salvation of the whole world, which shall come through Israel to all nations, and therefore he may well call on them all to rejoice and to praise Yahweh for this deed, for it redounds to their own redemption.   The universal ideas of Deutero-Isaiah are alive in this hymn.

Pure nature hymns are rare, but the few we have are beautiful. It is characteristic that often in the contemplation of nature all narrow, nationalistic thoughts disappear; it is God and man, not God and Jew, that meet in the vast realm of creation.   Psalm 8 is an illustration of this.   The chorus sings the refrain at the beginning and the end; it is not an exhortation to praise but a praise-song itself. The body of the psalm is sung by a solo voice.

> *O Yahweh, our Lord, how glorious*
>   *is Thy name in all the earth!*
>
> Let me sing of Thy glory in the heavens!
>   out of the mouth of babes and sucklings
> Hast Thou founded strength because of Thine adversaries,
>   to still the enemy and the rebellious.
>
> When I consider Thy heavens, the work of Thy fingers,
>   the moon and the stars which Thou hast established;
> What is man that Thou art mindful of him?
>   and the son of man that Thou visitest him?

Thou hast made him but a little lower than God,
and crownest him with glory and honor:
Thou makest him to rule over the works of Thy hands,
Thou hast put all things under his feet.

Sheep and oxen, all of them,
yea, and the beasts of the field,
The birds of the heavens and the fish of the sea,
Whatsoever passes through the paths of the seas.

O Yahweh, our Lord, how glorious
is Thy name in all the earth!

Psalm 29 celebrates God's glory in the thunderstorm.   In high enthusiasm the poet calls not upon the congregation in the earthly temple but upon the heavenly beings to adore and glorify Yahweh in the heavenly temple.

Ascribe unto Yahweh, O ye sons of God,
ascribe unto Yahweh glory and strength.
Ascribe unto Yahweh the glory due to His name;
worship Yahweh in holy array.

The voice[1] of Yahweh is upon the waters,
the God of glory thunders,
even Yahweh upon great waters.
The voice of Yahweh is powerful,
the voice of Yahweh is full of majesty.
The voice of Yahweh breaks the cedars,
yea, Yahweh breaks Lebanon's cedars,
And makes Lebanon to skip like a calf,
and Sirion like a young wild-ox.
The voice of Yahweh cleaves rocks,
cleaves them with flames of fire.
The voice of Yahweh shakes the wilderness,
Yahweh shakes the wilderness of Kadesh.
The voice of Yahweh makes the hinds to calve,
and strips the forests bare,
and in His temple every one says, "Glory."

Yahweh sat enthroned at the Flood,
yea, Yahweh sits enthroned as King forever.
May Yahweh give strength to His people,
may Yahweh bless His people with peace!   (Ps. 29)

These are pure nature psalms.   Psalm 19[1-6] is another.   But usually

---

[1] The thunder was regarded as the primary, the lightning merely as an accompanying element of the thunderstorm.

the praise of God's work in creation is combined with that of His great deeds in history (compare *e.g.* Ps. 33. 135. 136). History was always of great importance for the Hebrews, and the great deliverances of Israel formed the theme of many a psalm. Psalm 99 is a hymn of victory in which the hymnal form differs from the usual pattern in that the call to praise comes at the end of the stanzas and the reason at the beginning. It is a very artistic hymn, celebrating Yahweh as the victorious king of the world, the righteous ruler of His people, and their gracious and forgiving God.

> Yahweh reigns; the peoples tremble,
>   He is enthroned above the cherubim; the earth totters.
> Yahweh is great in Zion,
>   and high above all peoples.
> *Let them praise Thy great and terrible name:*
>   HOLY IS HE!
>
> A Strong One is King, who loves justice,
>   Thou hast established the right,
>   Thou hast executed justice and righteousness in Jacob.
> *Exalt ye Yahweh our God,*
>   *and worship at His footstool:*
>   HOLY IS HE!
>
> Moses and Aaron among His priests,
>   and Samuel among them that call on His name,
>   they called upon Yahweh and He answered them.
> He spoke to them in the pillar of cloud:
>   they kept His testimonies, and the statute that He gave them.
> Thou answeredst them, O Yahweh our God,
>   Thou wast a God that forgave them,
>   and that cleared them of their misdeeds.
> *Exalt ye Yahweh our God,*
>   *and worship at His holy hill:*
>   HOLY IS HE! (Ps. 99)

The response HOLY IS HE! was sung by the people. Other victory hymns are Psalms 68 and 149.

The experience of God's wonderful deliverance from a terrible national danger stirred a poet to write the great hymn of faith, Psalm 46, which gave to Martin Luther the material for his Reformation hymn, "A mighty fortress is our God." There is no exhortation to praise in the psalm, the praise itself is sung directly, three times it reaches its climax in the refrain, in which the whole congregation joined.

> God is our refuge and strength,
>   a very present help in trouble.
> Therefore will we not fear, though the earth change,
>   and though the mountains be moved into the heart of the seas;
> Though its waters roar and foam,
>   though the mountains shake at the swelling of its river.
> *Yahweh of hosts is with us;*
>   *the God of Jacob is our high fortress.*
>
> Let the city of God exult and be glad,
>   the holy dwelling place of the Most High.
> God is in her midst, she shall not be moved;
>   God will help her, and that right early.
> Nations were in tumult, kingdoms were moved:
>   He uttered His voice, the earth melted.
> *Yahweh of hosts is with us;*
>   *the God of Jacob is our high fortress.*
>
> Come, behold the works of Yahweh,
>   who has set wonders in the earth:
> Who makes wars to cease unto the end of the earth;
>   He breaks the bow, and cuts the spear in sunder,
>   He burns the war-chariots in the fire.
> "Be still, and know that I am God;
>   I will be exalted among the nations,
>   I will be exalted in the earth."
> *Yahweh of hosts is with us;*
>   *the God of Jacob is our high fortress.* (Ps. 46)

This is one of the most powerful hymns of faith that ever were sung, but Martin Luther's Christian adaptation is still mightier and greater.

Yahweh's righteous rule was the theme of other hymns. A noble illustration is Psalm 113, where Yahweh, who is exalted above the heavens, is praised for graciously humbling Himself in order to raise the lowest on earth.

> Praise, O ye servants of Yahweh,
>   praise the name of Yahweh.
> Blessed be the name of Yahweh
>   from this time forth and for evermore.
> From the rising of the sun to its setting
>   Yahweh's name is to be praised.

> Yahweh is high above all nations,
>   and His glory above the heavens.
> Who is like Yahweh our God,
>   that has His throne on high,
> That humbles Himself to behold
>   the things in heaven and on earth?
>
> He raises up the poor out of the dust,
>   and lifts up the needy from the dunghill,
> That He may set him with princes,
>   even with the princes of His people.
> He makes the barren woman to keep house,
>   and to be a joyful mother of children. (Ps. 113)

When the Jews sang this hymn on the three great yearly festivals, and on the New Moon day and the festival of the dedication of the temple, they thought of Israel as the humble poor who was to be raised to dignity, and the hymn voiced their faith in the certain exaltation of Israel by the omnipotence of Yahweh, the righteous ruler of the world.

But the whole effect of Yahweh's righteous rule is not seen in the present. He is not exercising His Kingship as yet to the full, the nations do not yet acknowledge Him as the only God and King of the whole world. But the time will come, and perhaps quite soon, for had not the prophets foretold the glorious time, when the Kingdom of God would be established on earth? A number of psalmists, under the direct influence of these prophetic convictions, celebrated in their eschatological hymns the enthronement of Yahweh. In their eager anticipation they saw Him already going up to His heavenly throne, and broke forth into the jubilant cry: Yahweh is King! and called upon all mankind, some even on all nature, to acclaim Him King of all the earth.

> Oh clap your hands, all ye peoples,
>   shout unto God with a ringing cry.
> For Yahweh is most high and terrible,
>   a great King over all the earth.
>
> He subdued peoples under us,
>   and nations under our feet.
> He chose our inheritance for us,
>   the glory of Jacob whom He loved.

God is gone up with a shout,
  Yahweh with the sound of a horn.
Sing praises to God, sing praises,
  sing praises to our King, sing praises.

For God is King of all the earth:
  sing praises with a skilful strain.
God has become King over the nations,
  God has seated Himself upon His holy throne.

The nobles of the peoples are gathered together
  with the people of the God of Abraham:
For to God belong the shields of the earth;
  He is become greatly exalted. (Ps. 47)

The last stanza shows that the subjection of the nations under Israel which was mentioned as the first effect of Yahweh's assumption of the government of all nations is not merely thought of as a political triumph of the Jews but as a means of establishing the spiritual reign of God in the earth.   Together with Israel the representatives of all mankind are gathered to pay homage to the one and only God, who had come down to subject the nations but who now has gone up, accompanied by shouts of acclaim, to sit on His heavenly throne as King of the earth.

In Psalm 96 the universal teaching of Deutero-Isaiah receives its finest expression in the Psalter, for this poet's interest centres in Israel's missionary calling and the salvation of the nations by their recognition of Yahweh, the creator of the heavens, as the only true God.   There is no word of the national exaltation of Israel or the national humiliation of the heathen.   On the contrary, all are to come and worship Yahweh in His temple on Zion.

Oh sing to Yahweh a new song,
  sing to Yahweh, all the earth.
Sing to Yahweh, bless His name,
  proclaim His salvation from day to day.
Declare His glory among the nations,
  His marvellous works among all the peoples.

For great is Yahweh, and greatly to be praised:
  He is terrible above all gods.
For all gods of the peoples are things of naught,
  but Yahweh made the heavens.
Honor and majesty are before Him:
  strength and beauty are in His sanctuary.

> Ascribe to Yahweh, ye families of the peoples,
>   ascribe to Yahweh glory and strength.
> Ascribe to Yahweh the glory of His name:
>   bring presents and come into His courts.
> Oh worship Yahweh in holy adornment,
>   tremble before Him, all the earth.
> Say among the nations "Yahweh has become King!"
>   yea, the world He established that it cannot be moved:
> He will judge the peoples with equity.
>
> Let the heavens be glad, and let the earth rejoice,
>   let the sea roar and its fulness,
> Let the field exult, and all that is in it,
>   then shall all the trees of the wood sing for joy
> Before Yahweh, for He comes,
>   He comes to judge the earth:
> He will judge the world with righteousness,
>   and the peoples with His faithfulness. (Ps. 96)

It is no wonder that the psalmist calls for a new song, the glory is all too great to be expressed by a familiar hymn. Psalm 98 is a companion of Psalm 96 and may have been composed by the same author. Psalms 93 and 97 as well as Psalms 75 and 76 belong to this class of eschatological hymns, as we may call them, since they deal with the last times. Their noble poetic form matches their great prophetic content.

From the poetical point of view the hymns or songs of praise are the finest in the Psalter. Their power of arousing religious enthusiasm, when they were sung in the temple by the choir to the accompaniment of the temple music, was so great that Jer. 33[11], in predicting the return of joy and happiness to the then forsaken and ruined city, joins to the happy voices of the bridegroom and the bride "the voice of them that say, Give thanks to Yahweh, for He is good, for His kindness endures forever."

Not always did the temple resound with joy. Many were the occasions when some national calamity, failure of the harvest, epidemics of disease, defeat in battle, or humiliation by foreign oppressors brought the people to the temple to plead with Yahweh for help and deliverance. Instead of music and song there went up lamentations and prayers, as the people, led by the priests, implored Yahweh. Sometimes the calamity lasted for years in spite of all

prayers.   We may single out in illustration two periods from which
we may date some of these prayers with reasonable assurance, the
time shortly after the return from exile and the time of the Maccabæan sufferings.

Among the pilgrim songs which we quoted (p. 348), there is one
prayer, Psalm 126, which reveals the disappointment and suffering of the exiles in the homeland after their return from Babylon.
The glad joy over the grace of Yahweh in bringing them back
gave way to sorrow and grief when they found out that He had after
all not yet granted them complete restoration.   In sad and plaintive
tones they sang this prayer for the turn of their fate.   Compare
also the other pilgrim psalm from this period, Psalm 123, in which the
plea for deliverance from humiliation is voiced in simple but appealing words.

Psalm 85 was sung in the temple service.   The choir began by
recalling God's grace in restoring Israel from captivity:

> Yahweh, Thou hadst become favorable to Thy land,
>   Thou hadst brought back the captivity of Jacob.
> Thou hadst forgiven the iniquity of Thy people,
>   Thou hadst covered all their sin.
> Thou hadst taken away all Thy wrath,
>   Thou hadst turned back the heat of Thine anger.

But this favor did not last long.   Conditions set in which seemed to
show that Yahweh was still angry, for the people were suffering want
and privation.   Earnestly the congregation therefore pleads,

> Restore us, O God of our salvation,
>   and cause Thine indignation toward us to cease.
> Wilt Thou be angry with us for ever,
>   wilt Thou continue Thine anger to all generations?
> Wilt Thou not quicken us again,
>   that Thy people may rejoice in Thee?
> Show us Thy kindness, O Yahweh,
>   and grant us Thy salvation.

A solo singer now takes up the song, and declares like one of the
prophets that he had listened to Yahweh in this calamity and that
he had distinctly heard the divine answer which spoke "peace to
His people."

> I will hear what Yahweh will speak:
>   Yea, He speaks peace to His people,
>   and to His godly ones, that they turn not again to folly.
> Surely His salvation is nigh them that fear Him,
>   that glory may dwell in our land.
> Kindness and truth are met together;
>   righteousness and love have kissed each other.
> Truth springs out of the earth;
>   and righteousness has looked down from heaven.
> Yea, Yahweh will give that which is good;
>   and our land shall yield its increase,
> Righteousness shall go before Him,
>   and peace in the way of His steps. (Ps. 85)

It is the message of the great comforter Deutero-Isaiah (cf. Is. 45 [8]) that the poet had heard in his soul and that he now gives in lines which are quite worthy of his master.

Psalm 90 also comes in all probability from this early postexilic time. It is not so impassioned, but it moves us by its profound sadness. The deep tones of eternity are sounding through its words. God's eternity is contrasted with man's ephemeral existence, and the cause of the latter is laid bare in man's sinfulness. If only man would learn the lesson! Then he would spend his brief life in harmony with God. Life is so short, and without God's grace so unhappy. Oh that God would again have compassion on His servants, remove the years of misfortune, and bless the work of their hands!

> Lord, Thou hast been a refuge
>   to us in all generations.
> Before the mountains were brought forth,
>   or the earth and the world were born,
>   from everlasting to everlasting Thou art God.
> For a thousand years in Thy sight
>   are but as yesterday when it is past
>   and as a watch in the night.
> Thou turnest man back to dust,
>   and sayest, "Return, ye children of men."
> Thou sowest them year by year,
>   they are like grass which shoots up in the morning:
> In the morning it blossoms and shoots up,
>   in the evening it fades and withers.

For we are consumed in Thine anger,
   and are dismayed in Thy wrath.
Thou hast set our iniquities before Thee,
   our secret sins in the light of Thy countenance.
Thus all our days vanish away in Thy wrath,
   we bring our years to an end as a sigh.
The days of our years are threescore years and ten,
   or if we are in full strength fourscore years.
Yet is their pride but labor and sorrow,
   for it is soon gone and we fly away.
Who knows the power of Thine anger,
   and who fears Thy wrath?
So teach us to number our days,
   that we may get us a heart of wisdom.

Return, O Yahweh, how long?
   and let it repent Thee concerning Thy servants.
Oh satisfy us in the morning with Thy kindness,
   that we may rejoice and be glad all our days.
Make us glad according to the days wherein Thou hast afflicted us,
   and the years wherein we have seen adversity.
Let Thy work appear unto Thy servants,
   and Thy glory upon their children.
And let the gracious kindliness of the Lord our God be upon us;
   and establish Thou the work of our hands upon us;
     yea, the work of our hands establish Thou it. (Ps. 90)

This psalmist has no hope of immortality. This deepens the sadness of his song. But there is a brave manliness in his view of life; and his hope is in God.

In the time of the persecution of the Jews by Antiochus Epiphanes, when the temple had been desecrated, and many devotedly religious people had been killed, a number of psalms were written which were taken over into the public worship, because they voiced so well the suffering of the people and their ardent prayer for help (Ps. 44. 60. 74. 79. 83). They are all in the same strain. Psalm 79 may serve as an illustration.

O God, the nations are come into Thine inheritance,
   they have defiled Thy holy temple,
     they have laid Jerusalem in ruins.
They have given the dead bodies of Thy servants
   to be food to the birds of the heavens,
     the flesh of Thy devoted ones to the beasts of the earth.

> They have shed their blood like water
>   round about Jerusalem, there was none to bury them.
> We are become a reproach to our neighbors,
>   a mockery and derision to them that are round about us.
> How long, O Yahweh, wilt Thou be angry for ever?
>   (how long) shall Thy jealousy burn like fire?
> Pour out Thy fury upon the nations that know Thee not,
>   and upon the kingdoms that call not on Thy name:
> For they have devoured Jacob,
>   and laid waste his homestead.
> Remember not against us our forefathers' iniquities,
>   let Thy compassions speedily come to meet us,
>   for we are brought very low.
>
> Help us, O God of our salvation, for the glory of Thy name,
>   and deliver us and forgive our sins for Thy name's sake.
> Wherefore should the nations say, "Where is their God?"
>   let the vengeance of Thy servants' blood which is shed
>   be made known among the nations in our sight.
> Let the groaning of the prisoner come before Thee:
>   according to the greatness of Thine arm reprieve Thou those that
>   are appointed to die;
> And recompense to our neighbors sevenfold into their bosom
>   their reproach wherewith they have reproached Thee, O Lord.
> So we, Thy people and sheep of Thy pasture,
>   will give thanks to Thee for ever,
>   we will tell of Thy praise to all generations. (Ps. 79)

A passionate desire for vengeance and a profound conviction of Israel's innocence are characteristic of these prayers, and they are intelligible enough in the situation out of which they came. In Psalm 44 [17-22] the innocence of the people is brought out most strongly:

> All this is come upon us; yet have we not forgotten Thee,
>   neither have we been false to Thy covenant.
> Our heart is not turned back,
>   neither have our steps declined from Thy way;
> That Thou shouldst have crushed us into a place of jackals,
>   and covered us with deathly gloom.
> If we had forgotten the name of our God,
>   or spread forth our hands to a strange god;
> Would not God search this out?
>   for He knows the secrets of the heart.
> Nay, but for Thy sake are we killed all the day long;
>   we are accounted as sheep for the slaughter. (Ps. 44 [17-22])

With an excessive anthropomorphism the prayer continues,

> Arouse Thyself!   Why sleepest Thou, O Lord,
>   awake, cast (us) not off for ever!

From a historical point of view these Maccabæan psalms are quite valuable, but religiously they are distinctly inferior.

The royal psalms form a special group.   They were used at great royal functions in the temple, and may be considered together here, although they vary in form;   some of them are prophetic oracles, others are prayers for the king.   At the coronation festival of the king in the temple a psalm was sung which was fitted to the occasion.   Thus Psalm 110 was probably composed expressly for the coronation ceremonies of Simon the Hasmonean in 142 B.C.   It is in the form of a prophecy.   At a given moment the officiating priest announced,

> An oracle of Yahweh unto my lord:
> "Sit down at My right hand,
>   until I make thine enemies
>   a stool for thy feet." . . .
>
> Yahweh has sworn
>   and will not repent:
> "Thou art a priest for ever
>   after the manner of Melchizedek." (Ps. 110)

He is to be a priest-king, high priest and ruler, as Simon at that time actually became.   Later this psalm was interpreted as referring to the Messiah, who was to combine religious and secular lordship in his person (cf. Matt. 22 [41ff.]).

This was also done with Psalm 2, which originally referred to a definite king at the time of his accession.   It is a psalm of great dramatic power.   The king himself speaks, wondering at the rebellion of his subject nations,

> Why do the nations tumultuously assemble,
>   and the peoples devise vain plans?
> The kings of the earth consult with each other,
>   and the rulers take counsel together,
>   against Yahweh and against His anointed:
> "Let us break their bonds asunder,
>   and fling away their cords from us."

> He that sits in the heavens will laugh,
>   the Lord will mock at them.
> Then will He speak to them in His wrath,
>   and dismay them in His fiery anger,
> While I am established as His king
>   upon His holy hill of Zion.

The king proceeds to give the oracle of Yahweh,

> Let me tell concerning the decree:

> Yahweh said to me, "Thou art My son,
>   this day have I begotten thee:[1]
> Ask of Me, and I will give the nations for thy heritage,
>   and the ends of the earth for thy possession.
> Thou shalt break them with a sceptre of iron,
>   thou shalt dash them in pieces like a potter's vessel."

So he warns the rebels,

> Now therefore be wise, O ye kings;
>   be admonished ye judges of the earth.
> Serve Yahweh with fear,
>   submit to Him[2] with trembling,
> Lest He be angry and ye perish in the way,
>   for His wrath is quickly kindled.

To this a liturgical addition is appended,

> Blessed are all they that take refuge in Him. (Ps. 2)

The claim of world dominion which is here made by the king of Zion sounds so extravagant that it is no wonder that the psalm was interpreted as messianic already before the time of Jesus (in the Psalms of Solomon, ch. 17). In the days to come heathendom will determine to overthrow the lordship of the Messiah, but it will be in vain. Originally the psalm referred to a historic king.

Psalm 72 shows how far-reaching the hopes and wishes were for the reigning king. It is the most beautiful of these royal psalms. In it the prayers of the people for the new king are voiced. They pray, most probably during the coronation ceremonies in the temple, for righteous government and eternal life, for prosperity and world dominion.

---

[1] On the day of accession the king was formally adopted by Yahweh as His son. We have here the official formula of adoption.

[2] The literal rendering of the idiomatic phrase is, *Kiss His feet.*

Give the king Thy judgment, O God,
    and Thy righteousness to the king's son.
May he judge Thy people with righteousness,
    and Thy poor with justice.
May the mountains bear peace for the people,
    and the hills righteousness.
May he judge the poor of the people,
    save the children of the needy,
        and crush the oppressor.

May he endure as long as the sun,
    and as the moon, through all generations.
May he come down like rain upon the mown grass,
    as showers that water the earth.
May righteousness flourish in his days,
    and abundance of peace, till the moon be no more.

May he have dominion from sea to sea,
    and from the River to the ends of the earth.
Let his adversaries bow before him,
    and his enemies lick the dust.
Let the kings of Tarshish and of the isles render tribute,
    the kings of Sheba and Saba offer gifts.
Yea, let all kings fall down before him,
    all nations serve him. . . .

So may he live, and may men give him of the gold of Sheba,
    and pray for him continually,
        and bless him all the day long. . . . (Ps. 72)

Here again it was easy to interpret the psalm of the great ideal world ruler, the Messiah who was to come.   But that was not its original meaning.

We have also a prayer for success in battle before the king went forth to war (Ps. 20), and a thanksgiving for victory after his return (Ps. 21), besides other prayers for him in Psalms 61. 89. 132. 144.

2. PRIVATE WORSHIP IN THE TEMPLE

Alongside of the public worship for the whole community there were certain occasions for the individual worshipper when he poured forth his thanksgiving or his petition in the temple.   Under the stress of danger or severe illness or other calamities men prayed to Yahweh

and vowed to bring offerings of thanksgiving, if He would hear them.[1]
If then God granted deliverance, the worshipper came to the temple
with his family and friends to offer the sacrifice which he had vowed
in accordance with his need and his ability, ordinarily a blameless
bullock, sheep, or goat (Lev. 22 [17ff.]) and unleavened cakes with oil
(Lev. 7 [11ff.]). Any one that happened to be in the temple, especially
the poor, joined the party, for the sacrificial animal had to be eaten
that same day [2] and nothing must be left.

Songs of thanksgiving were sung on such occasions. Psalm 66
is one of these. The temple choir began with a hymn,

> Make a joyful noise to God, all the earth:
>   sing forth the glory of His name;
> Make His praise glorious,
>   say unto God, How terrible are Thy works!
> Through the greatness of Thy strength shall Thy enemies
>   come cringing to Thee,
> All the earth shall worship Thee,
>   and shall sing to Thee, shall sing to Thy name.

This hymnal praise continued, one part of the choir singing the
second stanza (vv. [5-7]), another part taking up the third (vv. [8-12]).
Then the worshipper himself who brought the sacrifice stepped forth
and sang,[3]

> I come into Thy house with burnt-offerings,
>   I will pay Thee my vows,
> Which my lips uttered,
>   and my mouth spoke when I was in distress.
> I will offer unto Thee burnt-offerings of fatlings,
>   with the sweet smoke of rams;
> I will offer bullocks with he-goats.

With this he turned to the assembled party and told what God had
done for him:

> Come, and hear, all ye that fear God,
>   and I will declare what He has done for my soul.

---

[1] This was done in early as well as in later times. Hannah, the mother of
Samuel, was not the only one even in early times who prayed in the temple alone and
vowed a vow, if God would grant her petition (1 Sam. 1 [9ff.]). It was her silent prayer
that astonished Eli the priest, for ordinarily people prayed aloud.

[2] The later law (Lev.7 [16ff.]) permitted the eating of special and freewill offerings
also on the second day to meet the exigencies of the occasions.

[3] Cf. Job 33 [27f.]

The sentences that follow lack the concrete description of the individual distress and deliverance, because the psalm was to be used by any one bringing a votive offering.

> I cried unto Him with my mouth,
>   and high praise was under my tongue.
> If I had had iniquity in view in my heart,
>   the Lord would not hear.
> But verily God has heard,
>   He has attended to the voice of my prayer.
> Blessed be God, who has not turned away my prayer,
>   nor (withheld) His kindness from me. (Ps. 66)

The insistence on the absence of any secret evil intention in connection with the prayer must not be overlooked. It shows again the endeavor to ethicize the cultic functions in the temple.

Sometimes men took refuge in the sanctuary, where God dwelt and where their prayers for help seemed so much more effective. This seems to have been so especially in cases of accusation, in persecutions by enemies, and in sickness. Psalm 26 was probably used in connection with clearing oneself of an accusation. Just of what the psalmist was accused is not said. The early law demanded that in certain cases the defendant had to clear himself in the temple by an oath (Ex. 22 [8. 11]) and the later law still has an ancient rite by which a woman suspected of adultery was either vindicated or found out and punished (Num. 5 [11ff.]). This is the underlying idea also in the ceremony for which Psalm 26 is intended. The psalmist had gone to the temple with his accusers, and began by calling upon God, loudly protesting his innocence:

> Judge me, Yahweh, for I have walked in mine integrity,
>   and in Yahweh have I trusted without wavering.
> Try me, Yahweh, and prove me,
>   test my heart and my mind.
> For Thy kindness is before mine eyes,
>   and I have walked in Thy truth.
> I have not sat with insincere persons,
>   neither do I go with dissemblers.

After this prayer followed the symbolic ceremony of the washing of his hands, which was accompanied (we may assume, although it is not stated) with a solemn oath by Yahweh who tests the heart and mind,

> I wash my hands in innocency.

The priest thereupon pronounced him free of the accusation, and the man began the cultic dance around the altar, on which a sacrifice had been brought, and thanked and praised Yahweh,

> I will go around Thine altar, Yahweh,
> That I may make loud thanksgiving to be heard,
>   and tell of all Thy wondrous works:
> Yahweh, I love the habitation of Thy house,
>   and the place where Thy glory dwells.

With a look upon his accusers, the psalmist then prays to God,

> Take not away my soul with sinners,
>   nor my lip with men of blood;
> In whose hands are wicked devices,
>   and their right hand is full of bribes.

He himself will maintain his upright life with God's help,

> But as for me, I will walk in mine integrity,
>   redeem me, and be merciful unto me.
> My foot stands in an even place:
>   in full assemblies will I bless Yahweh. (Ps. 26)

Then "this man went down to his house justified" (cf. Luke 18 [14]), cleared of the accusation, able to take his part afresh in the life of the people.

It is amazing how much distress was caused by the animosity of personal enemies, how bitter were the complaints, and how terrible the calls for vengeance upon them. Most of the prayers for protection from the enemies and for their punishment were originally intended for private use and they could be prayed anywhere. But some of them accompanied the sacrifices in the temple. For instance, Psalm 5 was the morning prayer of a devoted worshipper in the sanctuary.

> Give ear to my words, Yahweh,
>   consider my meditation.
> Hearken unto the voice of my cry,
>   my King and my God,
> For unto Thee I pray in the morning,
>   mayest Thou hear my voice.
> In the morning I arrange (my sacrifice) and look out.

He knows that wicked people are not permitted in Yahweh's temple (cf. Ps. 15),

> But I, through the abundance of Thy kindness
>   may come into Thy house:
> I may worship toward Thy holy temple
>   in the fear of Thee, Yahweh.

Now comes his prayer,

> Lead me, Yahweh, in Thy righteousness,
>   because of mine enemies,
>   make Thy way even before my face.
> For there is no steadfastness in their mouth,
>   their inward part is a yawning gulf,
> Their throat is an open sepulchre,
>   while they flatter with their tongue.
> Declare them guilty, O God,
>   let them fall by their own counsels;
> Thrust them out for the multitude of their transgressions,
>   because they have been defiant against Thee. (Ps. 5)

But let the righteous rejoice over the effective protection of God from their enemies, who are also God's enemies in the psalmist's estimation. There is no pity, much less love for them, but only a relentless spirit of vengeance. It is true enough that when this psalm and similar ones were taken into the public cult of the temple, it was not the personal enemies but the opposing party of the worldly-minded and ungodly Jews for whom the pious party had these "pious" wishes. But originally they were meant for the personal enemies of the individual worshipper. In either case these imprecatory psalms are vitiated for us by the spirit of vengeance. One of the worst of them is Psalm 109 with its fearful curses upon the enemies, which was used in the public worship as a "sacred" song!

In most of the prayers of the sick there is also a complaint over heartless people who had been friends before, but who have turned against the sick, strikingly enough just because of his sickness. It seems incredible to us that one should deny sympathy and help to the sick. But this was due to the doctrine that health and prosperity are the reward of piety, but disease and misfortune the result of wickedness. Disease was therefore an indication of sinfulness. The old man who prays for deliverance from his extraordinary sufferings in Psalm 71 complains,

> Mine enemies speak concerning me,
> and they that watch for my life take counsel together,
> Saying, "God has forsaken him:
> pursue and take him, for there is none to deliver." (Ps. 71 [10f.])

In Psalm 41 the psalmist laments,

> Mine enemies speak evil of me,
> "When will he die, and his name perish?"
> And if one come to see me, he speaks insincerity:
> his heart gathers malice to itself;
> when he goes abroad, he speaks of it.
>
> All they that hate me whisper together against me,
> they imagine evil for me:
> "Some deadly thing has fast hold of him,
> and now that he lies, he will rise up no more."
> Yea, mine own intimate friend in whom I trusted,
> who ate my bread has lifted up his heel against me. (Ps. 41 [5-9])

The suffering from the disease may have been terrible, especially when the sick was covered with loathsome and festering wounds, when his body was racked with fever, and his strength was fast ebbing away, but the bitterness of being forsaken even by his close relatives was more terrible still.

> My lovers and friends stand aloof from my plague;
> and my kinsmen stand afar off. (Ps. 38 [11])

It is easy to understand that some of these sufferers long for an opportunity to pay them back for their cruel behavior.

> But Thou, Yahweh, be gracious to me and raise me up,
> that I may requite them. (Ps. 41 [10])

Nevertheless these psalmists themselves also had the belief that their suffering was the result of their sin, and often confessed it with penitent sorrow:

> O Yahweh, reprove me not in Thy wrath,
> neither chasten me in Thy displeasure. . . .
> For mine iniquities are gone over my head,
> as a heavy burden they are too heavy for me. . . .
> I declare mine iniquity,
> I am sorry for my sin. (Ps. 38 [1. 4. 18])

But occasionally a psalmist was not conscious of any deliberate sin that should deserve such punishment as his serious sickness constituted. Then he pleaded for light on the reason of his suffering,

> Yahweh, why castest Thou off my soul?
> why hidest Thou Thy face from me?   (Ps. 88 [14])

Or like the sufferer of Psalm 22, who had been so brutally wounded by his enemies, he cried out,

My God, my God, why hast Thou forsaken me?
> why art Thou so far from helping me and from the words of my groaning? (Ps. 22 [1])

3. PRIVATE WORSHIP OUTSIDE OF THE TEMPLE

Many of these prayers had originally nothing to do with the temple service; they were prayed at home.   There is no trace of the sacrificial cult in them, they express the deep, personal piety of the psalmist quite independently; the soul is alone with its God.   Here the heart speaks out of its depths, here it prays for help and forgiveness, thanks for God's grace and sings His praise, altogether untrammelled by any system.   In some of them there is even a distinct reaction against the sacrificial system, as *e.g.* in that greatest of all the penitential psalms, that still moves men's hearts to repentance and voices for them their deep need of forgiveness and purification, and the renewing and steadying of their will.

Have mercy upon me, O God, according to Thy kindness:
> according to the multitude of Thy tender mercies blot out my transgressions.
Wash me thoroughly from mine iniquity,
> and cleanse me from my sin.

For I know my transgressions;
> and my sin is ever before me.
Against Thee, Thee only, have I sinned,
> and done that which is evil in Thy sight;
That Thou mayest be justified when Thou speakest,
> and be clear when Thou judgest.
Behold, I was brought forth in iniquity·
> and in sin my mother conceived me.
Behold, Thou desirest truth in the inward parts (?);
> and in the hidden part make me to know wisdom.

Purify me with hyssop, that I may be clean:
> wash me, that I may be whiter than snow.
Make me to hear joy and gladness,
> that the bones which Thou hast crushed may rejoice.

Hide Thy face from my sins,
  and blot out all mine iniquities.
Create in me a clean heart, O God;
  and renew a steadfast spirit within me.
Cast me not away from Thy presence;
  and take not Thy holy Spirit from me.
Restore to me the joy of Thy salvation;
  and uphold me with a willing spirit.
Then will I teach transgressors Thy ways;
  and sinners shall be converted to Thee.

Deliver me from (the land of) silence, O God, Thou God of my salvation;
  and my tongue shall sing aloud of Thy righteousness.
O Lord, open Thou my lips;
  and my mouth shall show forth Thy praise.
For Thou delightest not in sacrifice; else would I give it:
  Thou hast no pleasure in burnt-offering.
My sacrifice, O God, is a broken spirit:
  a broken and a contrite heart, O God, Thou wilt not despise. (Ps. 51 [1-17])

The influence of the great prophets is so unmistakable here, that we read with surprise the incongruous, later addition in v. [18f.] which prays for the restoration of Zion and tells of the sacrifices that will then be offered again in the temple.   To our psalmist animal and cereal sacrifices were of as little value as to Psalm 40, which says,

Sacrifice and offering Thou hast no delight in;
  mine ears hast Thou opened:
Burnt-offering and sin-offering Thou hast not required. (Ps. 40 [6])

Psalm 50, where God is introduced as appearing in a theophany and as addressing the people Himself, makes it plain that their zeal for sacrifices is mistaken.

Hear, O My people, and I will speak,
  O Israel, and I will protest unto thee:
I am Yahweh, thy God,
  [who brought thee out of the land of Egypt].

I will not reprove thee for thy sacrifices;
  thy burnt-offerings are continually before Me.
I will take no bullock out of thy house,
  nor he-goats out of thy folds.
For every beast of the forest is Mine,
  and the cattle on the hills of God.
I know all the birds of the mountains
  and that which moves in the field is Mine.

If I were hungry, I would not tell thee:
  for the world is Mine, and its fulness.
Do I eat the flesh of bulls,
  or drink the blood of goats?

Offer to God the sacrifice of thanksgiving,
  so wilt thou pay thy vows to the Most High;
And call upon Me in the day of trouble:
  I will deliver thee, and thou shalt glorify Me. (Ps. 50 [7–15])

Genuine thanksgiving and heartfelt prayer are the real offerings that please God, and their sincerity must be attested by a righteous life.

Whoso offers the sacrifice of thanksgiving glorifies Me,
  and to him that keeps My way
    will I show the salvation of God. (Ps. 50 [23])

The spiritualization of sacrifice has begun.   Psalm 141 prays,

Let my prayer be set forth as incense before Thee,
  the lifting up of my hands as the evening sacrifice. (Ps. 141 [2])

A psalmist who can say of himself, "the zeal of Thy house has eaten me up," nevertheless declares,

I will praise the name of God with a song,
  and magnify Him with thanksgiving;
And it will please Yahweh better than an ox
  or a bullock that has horns and hoofs. (Ps. 69 [30f.])

And so we find in the Psalter a number of hymns in which the religion of the heart pours itself forth in praise and thanksgiving without any ceremonial trace whatsoever.[1]   The most famous of these personal hymns or songs of praise is Psalm 103.

Bless Yahweh, O my soul;
  and all that is within me, bless His holy name.
Bless Yahweh, O my soul,
  and forget not all His benefits:

---

[1] The form of these songs of the individual is similar to that of the communal hymns.   In the call to praise the psalmist addresses himself, "Bless Yahweh, *O my soul*."   The reason for the praise is also in these hymns the glory and power as well as the love and grace of God, in nature and in history.   But the history is that of the individual.   This passes, however, into that of the people, because the psalmists felt so much at one with them that they could not separate themselves altogether from them even in their personal songs and prayers.

Who forgives all thine iniquities;
  who heals all thy diseases;
Who redeems thy life from the pit;
  who crowns thee with kindness and **compassion**;
Who satisfies thy desire with good things,
  so that thy youth is renewed like the vulture's.

Yahweh executes righteous acts,
  and judgments for all that are oppressed.
He made known His ways to Moses,
  His doings to the children of Israel.
Yahweh is merciful and gracious,
  slow to anger, and abundant in kindness.
He will not always contend;
  neither will He keep His anger for ever.
He has not dealt with us after our sins,
  nor rewarded us after our iniquities.
For as the heavens are high above the earth,
  so great is His kindness toward them that fear **Him**.
As far as the east is from the west,
  so far has He removed our transgressions from us.
Like as a father pities his children,
  so Yahweh pities them that fear Him.
For He knows our frame;
  He remembers that we are dust.
As for man, his days are as grass;
  as a flower of the field, so he blossoms.
For the wind passes over it, and it is gone;
  and its place knows it no more.
But the kindness of Yahweh is for ever,
  and His righteousness unto children's children;
To them that fear Him, that keep His covenant,
  and to those that remember His precepts to do them.

Yahweh has established His throne in the heavens;
  and His kingdom rules over all.
Bless Yahweh, ye His angels,
  that are mighty in strength, that fulfil His **word**,
Bless Yahweh, all ye His hosts,
  ye ministers of his, that do His pleasure.
Bless Yahweh, all ye His works,
  in all places of his dominion:
Bless Yahweh, O my soul. (Ps. 103)[1]

---

[1] The companion psalm, Ps. 104, celebrates God's glory in the work of creation, following apparently the creation story of Gen. 1. It has such close affinities to a solar hymn of Pharaoh Amenhotep IV (*ca.* 1370 B.C.) that it would seem that the psalm was

Among the individual psalms there are not only prayers for help and forgiveness and hymns of praise, but also many spiritual songs and meditations on fundamental themes, which throw light on the religious life of the people, especially in postexilic times.   We may consider first some psalms on the omnipresence of God, His providence, and His righteous rule.   Psalm 139 is a meditation on God's omnipresence and omniscience.   This psalm is unique in the Psalter. It shows that the belief in monotheism necessitated an understanding of the problems connected with it.   There is real philosophical thinking in this meditation, although the form is not speculative but poetic: the poet sinks down in adoration of the great wonder of the one omnipresent and omniscient God who is not bound by space and time, and his meditation becomes a hymn.

> O Yahweh, Thou hast searched me, and known me,
>> Thou knowest my downsitting and mine uprising;
>> Thou understandest my thought afar off.
> Thou searchest out my walking and my lying down,
>> and art acquainted with all my ways.
> For there is not a word in my tongue,
>> but, lo, O Yahweh, Thou knowest it altogether.
> Thou hast beset me behind and before,
>> and laid Thy hand upon me.
> Such knowledge is too wonderful for me;
>> it is high, I cannot attain to it.
>
> Whither shall I go from Thy Spirit?
>> or whither shall I flee from Thy presence?
> If I ascend up into the heaven, Thou art there:
>> if I make my bed in Sheol, behold, Thou art there.
> If I choose the wings of the dawn,
>> and dwell in the uttermost parts of the sea;
> Even there would Thy hand seize me,
>> and Thy right hand would hold me.
> If I say, Surely the darkness shall screen me,
>> and the light about me shall be night;
> Even the darkness is not too dark for Thee,
>> but the night shines as the day:
>> the darkness and the light are both alike to Thee. (Ps. 139 $^{1-12}$)

deliberately patterned after the Egyptian hymn which is translated in J. H. Breasted, *A History of Egypt*, 2 ed., 1912, pp. 371ff.   But here as elsewhere the peculiar genius of Israel shows itself in such a complete assimilation of the foreign material that the psalm appears as a thoroughly Jewish composition with all the distinctive Israelite belief in the personal Creator.   See also G. A. Barton, *Archæology and the Bible*.

After considering the divine mystery of his own formation and birth
the psalmist exclaims, overwhelmed by the wonder of it all,

How precious are Thy thoughts to me, O God!
  how great is the sum of them!
If I should count them, they are more in number than the sand,
  if I should define them, my lifetime would have to be like Thine. (139 [17f.])

Then suddenly he bursts forth into an almost unaccountable denun-
ciation of the enemies of God, whom he hates as if they were his own
personal enemies too. In his fanatic devotion to God it seems in-
comprehensible to him that any one should not worship and serve
Him, that any one should persist in wickedness and defy Him. He
wants all such to be destroyed, in order that God may be everywhere glorified:

Oh that Thou wouldst slay the wicked, O God!
  and that bloodthirsty men would depart from me!
Who defy Thee with wicked intent,
  and take Thy name in vain.
Do not I hate them, O Yahweh, that hate Thee?
  and do not I loathe them that rise up against Thee?
I hate them with a perfect hatred:
  they are become mine enemies. (139 [19—22])

So completely has he identified himself with God's cause that he
hates God's enemies as his own. And so little does he realize the
essential heinousness of his fanaticism that he prays to God with
utter sincerity,

Search me, O God, and know my heart,
  try me, and know my thoughts;
And see if there be any wicked way in me,
  and lead me in the way everlasting. (139 [23f.])

The thought never occurred to him that his hatred was a wicked
way, which must lead to sorrow and pain. He was still far from
the teachings of Him who said, "Love your enemies . . . that
ye may be sons of your Father who is in heaven," for He loves His
enemies too (Matt. 5 [44f.]).

Psalm 91 is a meditation on the providence of God. After a
forceful introductory statement of the theme (vv. [1f.]) the poet
addresses and instructs the believer by celebrating the security
enjoyed by him that trusts in God in the midst of danger (vv. [3—43]).

At the conclusion Yahweh Himself speaks and confirms this magnificent exposition with a personal promise (vv. [14-16]).

> He that dwells in the secret place of the Most High,
>> that abides under the shadow of the Almighty,
> Shall say to Yahweh, " My refuge and my fortress ;
>> my God, in whom I trust."
>
> For He will deliver thee from the snare of the fowler,
>> and from the pit of destruction.
> He will cover thee with His pinions,
>> and under His wings shalt thou take refuge,
>> His truth is a shield and a buckler.
> Thou shalt not be afraid for the terror by night,
>> nor for the arrow that flies by day ;
> For the pestilence that walks in darkness,
>> nor for the destruction that wastes at noonday.
> Though a thousand fall at thy side,
>> and ten thousand at thy right hand ;
>> it shall not come nigh thee.
> Only with thine eyes shalt thou behold,
>> and see the reward of the wicked.
> For as for thee, Yahweh is thy refuge,
>> thou hast made the Most High thy stronghold ;
> There shall no evil befall thee,
>> neither shall any plague come nigh thy tent.
> For He will give His angels charge over thee,
>> to keep thee in all thy ways.
> They shall bear thee up in their hands,
>> lest thou dash thy foot against a stone.
> Thou shalt tread upon the lion and adder :
>> the young lion and the serpent shalt thou trample under foot.
>
> Because he has set his love upon Me, I will deliver him :
>> I will set him on high, because he has known My name.
> He shall call upon Me, and I will answer him ;
>> I will be with him in trouble :
>> I will deliver him, and honor him.
> With long life will I satisfy him,
>> and show him My salvation.

It is a religious quietism that is celebrated here, the passive trust in God's protection and care, rather than the active overcoming of danger and the conquest of evil. This is the ideal of the meek and the poor, the quiet in the land, who trust in God for everything.

There are, of course, also songs of virile strength, such as Psalm 101, where a man of high authority, a ruler, promises to God not only a personal life of integrity but also a righteous administration of the city of Jerusalem, which favors the just and punishes the wicked:

> Morning by morning will I destroy
>   all the wicked of the land;
> To cut off from the city of Yahweh
>   all the workers of iniquity. (Ps. 101 [8])

But ordinarily the establishment of righteous conditions is only expected from the divine interference (cf. Ps. 58). In the eschatological hymns we witnessed the eager anticipation of Yahweh's assumption of the government of the world. The poet of Psalm 82, who was also a prophet, saw Yahweh standing among the unjust judges of the earth and rebuking them:

> How long will ye judge unjustly,
>   and respect the persons of the wicked?
> Judge the poor and fatherless,
>   do justice to the afflicted and destitute!
> Rescue the poor and needy,
>   deliver them out of the hand of the wicked!

But these judges have so little ethical discernment that the moral foundations of the earth are endangered. Yahweh must therefore interfere, and in passionate plea the psalmist prays,

> Arise, O God, judge the earth,
>   for Thou art the heir [1] of all nations. (Ps. 82)

Only thus can righteousness be established in the world.

Righteousness was the fundamental requirement of Yahweh for all. Its paramount importance was brought out in a number of psalms. We saw how as a result of the prophetic emphasis on righteousness the sacrificial cult in the temple was ethicized by the priests, and how the prophetic Psalm 50 criticised the whole sacrificial system. In Psalm 15 we have a song which has sometimes been called a catechism for the proselytes, but which was later taken into the public cult (cf. Ps. 24). It answers the question of the conditions of true communion with God by an exclusive emphasis on social morality:

[1] *I.e.* the rightful lord.

Yahweh, who may be a guest in Thy tent?
who may dwell in Thy holy hill?

He that walks uprightly, and works righteousness,
and speaks truth in his heart;
He that slanders not his neighbor,
nor does evil to his friend,
nor takes up a reproach against his neighbor,
In whose eyes a reprobate is despised,
but who honors them that fear Yahweh.
He that swears to his own hurt, and changes not,
he that puts not out his money to interest
nor takes a bribe against the innocent.
He that does these things without ever wavering. (Ps. 15)

Quite justly did an eminent Jewish commentator remark on this psalm: "If Israel had accepted this conception . . ., the religion of Yahweh would have become the religion of the world" (Ehrlich).

But it was not accepted, the law became supreme, the religion of Yahweh became legalistic, and no legalistic form of religion, however exalted its ethics, can ever be a true expression of the religion of the spirit. Moreover, the Jewish law insisted on ceremonies as well as on morals. Besides the danger of externalizing religion there was thus also the danger of placing the primary, fundamental moral requirements on the same level with the ceremonial. And the wearisome burden of this mass of legal details, which never allowed one to gain peace, rested as a heavy yoke upon many people. It required much knowledge too; one had to study the law day and night, as Psalm 1 says, if one intended to be truly righteous. We are therefore surprised to read such legal psalms as Psalm 19 [7ff.] and especially the long alphabetical Psalm 119, with their extravagant praises of the law.

The law of Yahweh is perfect, refreshing the soul:
The testimony of Yahweh is trustworthy, making wise the simple.
The precepts of Yahweh are right, rejoicing the heart:
The commandment of Yahweh is pure, enlightening the eyes.
The fear of Yahweh is clean, enduring for ever:
The ordinances of Yahweh are true and righteous altogether.
More to be desired are they than gold, yea, than much fine gold:
Sweeter also than honey and the droppings of the honeycomb. (Ps. 19 [7-10])

> Oh how love I Thy law!
>   it is my meditation all the day. (Ps. 119 [97])

> How sweet are Thy words to my palate!
>   sweeter than honey to my mouth!   (Ps. 119 [105])

This intense love of the law was due to the fact that it had become to these earnest men a guide to God.   In the study of it they experienced a mystic fellowship with Yahweh, who had here expressed His will.   The law became to them a means of direct communion with God.

The longing for fellowship with God has found tones so deep and so human in some psalms of intimate communion that they still touch responsive chords in human hearts.   The condition of the exiled singer who wrote Psalm 42f., harassed by enemies and pained by his own bitter grief, may be quite his own ; his delight in the festal procession and the worship in the temple may even be quite foreign to us, yet his cry for the living God comes out of the far depths of the soul and seems like the cry of our own souls, whose yearning it has awakened.

> As the hind cries for the water brooks,
>   so cries my soul for Thee, O God.
> My soul thirsts for God, for the living God,
>   when shall I come and appear before God?   (Ps. 42 [1f.] cf. also Ps. 63 [1,3])

The sorrow over interrupted fellowship with God mourns in the penitential psalms.   And the blessedness of forgiveness is sung in Psalm 32,

> Blessed is he whose transgression is forgiven,
>   whose sin is covered.
> Blessed is the man to whom Yahweh imputes not iniquity,
>   and in whose spirit there is no guile. (Ps. 32 [1f.])

Happy, thrice happy is he who can sing with all his heart the shepherd psalm, that most beloved of them all :

> Yahweh is my shepherd ; I shall not want.
>   He makes me to lie down in green pastures:
> He gently guides me unto still waters.
>   He refreshes my soul.
> He leads me in paths of righteousness
>   for His name's sake.

Yea, though I walk through a valley of deep gloom,
    I will fear no evil,
For Thou art with me. Thy rod and Thy staff,
    they comfort me.

Thou preparest a table before me
    in the sight of mine enemies: [1]
Thou hast anointed my head with oil,
    my cup is well filled.

Only goodness and kindness shall follow me
    all the days of my life;
And I shall dwell in the house of Yahweh
    for length of days. (Ps. 23)

In the strength of this personally experienced communion with
God some psalmists faced the hardest problems of life and solved
them: death was the one, God's moral government of the world the
other. We saw how long the Jews were in coming to a satisfying
conception of the life after death. The psalmists too queried as a
rule, since

There is no remembrance of Thee in death,
    who shall give Thee thanks in Sheol? (Ps. 6 [5] cf. also 30 [8f.])

But there were some who through the inherent power of their experience of divine fellowship transcended death by their victorious faith that this communion could never be broken. Thus the
believer of Psalm 16, to whom God was his highest good, was so secure in the joy and peace of his intimacy with God that it seemed
utterly incredible to him that this should ever come to an end. He
knows that death must come, and he sees no way of escape, but he is
nevertheless serene,

For Thou wilt not leave my soul to Sheol,
    neither wilt Thou allow Thy devoted one to see the pit.
Thou wilt show me the path of life:
    in Thy presence is fulness of joy;
    in Thy right hand there are pleasures for evermore. (Ps. 16 [10f.])

He has no clearly thought out doctrine of resurrection or immortality. He does not know the way, but God will show it to him. If he
were the author of Psalm 17, as is not unlikely, the great test of
suffering came to him also, but it did not shake him in his faith:

[1] The mention of the enemies spoils a little the beauty of this psalm. This and
the close connection of religion with the temple are limitations of the psalmist.

As for me, I shall behold Thy face in righteousness,
  I shall be satisfied, when I awake, with (beholding) Thy form. (Ps. 17 [15])

He had experienced the grace and love of God too profoundly, and he believed in His righteousness too implicitly to doubt that God owns him forever.

The righteousness of God constituted, however, for some a serious problem. They could not harmonize the experiences of life, the prosperity of the wicked, and the suffering of the righteous with their faith in God's moral government of the world. True enough, there were some who would quiet the misgivings of the thoughtful with a strong reiteration of the old doctrine of retribution, as *e.g.* the aged, wise, and orthodox saint in Psalm 37, who tried to steady the doubters by his counsel,

Fret not thyself because of evil-doers,
  neither be envious against them that work unrighteousness.
For they shall soon be mown down like the grass,
  and wither as the green herb.
Trust in Yahweh, and do good;
  dwell in the land, and follow after faithfulness:
So shalt thou have thy delight in Yahweh,
  and He will give thee the desires of thy heart. (Ps. 37 [1-4])

For this is the result of his prolonged observation,

I have been young and now I am old,
  yet have I not seen the righteous forsaken,
    nor his seed begging bread. (Ps. 37 [25])

But others had different experiences; notably the author of Psalm 73. At the very beginning he states the outcome of his soul struggle:

Surely God is good to the upright,
  to such as are pure in heart.

Now he knows this, now he is certain of it, but for a while this seemed to him incredible. The facts of life were so strongly opposed to it, that he had almost suffered shipwreck in his faith. The good fortune of the wicked, their security, arrogance, and brazen denial of any divine government of the world were so impressive to him who had to suffer so much in spite of his passionate devotion to righteousness that he almost came to the conclusion,

Surely in vain have I cleansed my heart,
  and washed my hands in innocency;

> For all the day long have I been plagued,
>   and chastened every morning. (Ps. 73 [13f.])

It was only his regard for the pious community that kept him from uttering these thoughts; he must be loyal to his friends, for they must not suffer through his scepticism. But the problem pressed all the harder upon his mind and seemed completely insoluble, until he went into the sanctuary where he received the solution in a spiritual illumination. He considered the latter end of the wicked and understood.

> Surely Thou settest them in slippery places;
>   Thou castest them down to destruction.
> How are they become a desolation in a moment!
>   they are utterly brought to an end by sudden terrors! (Ps. 73 [18f.])

He had not seen this before, he had suffered all this mental agony because of his own stupidity. It is somewhat amazing that he should have regarded this as a tenable solution of his problem. To us, as well as to the author of Job, this is totally unsatisfactory. But it is not the whole of the poet's illumination. He realizes with sudden gladness that he, in striking contrast to the wicked, has found in his communion with God the solution of life, a compensation for all its sorrows.

> Yet I am continually with Thee;
>   Thou holdest my right hand.
> Thou wilt guide me with Thy counsel,
>   and afterward receive me with glory.
> Whom have I in heaven but Thee?
>   and having Thee, there is naught on earth that I desire.
> My flesh and my heart fail:
>   but God is the strength of my heart
>   and my portion forever.

Those who faithlessly depart from God are destroyed,

> But as for me, to draw near unto God is good for me;
>   I have made the Lord my refuge,
>   that I may tell of all Thy works. (Ps. 73 [23-28])

The intellectual solution by the terrible end of the wicked is untenable, but the practical solution by his communion with God is as true to-day as ever. Faith triumphs over doubt because of its experience of direct fellowship with God. Here are the roots out of which the belief in immortality could grow.   When communion with God was combined with the brave sense of righteousness, so characteristic of Israel, it was bound to develop into this hope.   Without the one or the other of these a vital faith in an eternal life of union with God is difficult to attain.   These psalmists may not have reached a doctrine of immortality, but they are not far from it, for they experienced, what the later prophet so clearly defined, that knowledge of God is eternal life (cf. John 17 [3]).[1]

It is just this element of profound trust that makes the Psalter still so full of spiritual power : a trust so deep that it can say,

> Yahweh is my light and my salvation,
>   whom shall I fear?
> Yahweh is the strength of my life,
>   of whom should I be afraid?   (Ps. 27 [1])

a trust so strong that it can burst into the powerful psalm (46) which gave to Martin Luther his Reformation hymn, "A mighty fortress is our God, a bulwark never failing"; a trust so serene that it can sing the shepherd psalm (Ps. 23); a trust so jubilant that it can shout,

> Whom have I in heaven but Thee?
>   and having Thee there is naught on earth that I desire. (Ps. 73 [25])

It is this warmly pulsating religious life that makes the psalms of perennial value.   Much of the Psalter is antiquated and superseded ; much of it is inferior poetically and spiritually ; yes, much of it is positively immoral and therefore to be discarded ; and yet there is so much of it that still voices deep human longings, that kindles spiritual devotion, that teaches pure moral religion, so much of it that is of such poetic excellence and spiritual insight that

---

[1] It seems that a reader who had made the solution of Ps. 73 his own pondered over Ps. 49 which is a didactic poem teaching that the rich in spite of their wealth and glory cannot escape death,

> Man that is in honor abides not :
>   he is like the beasts that perish (49 [12])

and inserted the great conviction,

But God will redeem my soul from the power of Sheol ; for He will receive me. (49[15]) It may be that he also changed the refrain at the end of the psalm by modifying a single letter so that it reads,

> Man that is in honor *and understands* not
>   is like the beasts that perish (49 [20]).

If man had true understanding, he would not perish like the beasts.

the Psalter still deserves, in spite of its imperfections, crudities, and barbarities, to be used, with discrimination, as a book of public and private devotion.

The Psalter is a religious book.   Among all its psalms there is only one secular song (Ps. 45), a wedding ode composed by a court poet for the marriage festival of a king with a foreign princess. Which king is meant is a matter of debate.   But we are fortunate in having a whole book of secular songs in our Bible, for the Song of Songs is nothing else but a collection of love and wedding songs. During the seven days of the wedding feast the bridegroom and bride were king and queen, as they still are in the vicinity of Damascus in our days.   They sat on an improvised throne, all sorts of dances and games were performed before them, and love and wedding songs were sung.   Among these were songs celebrating the physical beauty of the groom and especially of the bride.   To-day the most elaborate and detailed of them is sung by the bride herself, as she dances a sword dance in her full wedding adornments.   Now our Book of Canticles contains a collection of such love and wedding songs. The love of man and woman for each other is celebrated here with all the freshness, beauty, and abandon of Oriental love poetry.   There is nothing in these songs that speaks of the sanctity of the marriage relation, or of its moral and religious aspects.   It is all about human love, deep and passionate, "strong as death," a very flame of Yahweh.   One of the most beautiful and chaste of the songs deals with the springtime of love.

> Hark, my beloved! behold, he comes,
>   leaping upon the mountains,
>   skipping upon the hills.
> See, there he stands behind our wall.
>   I look through the windows,
>   I glance through the lattice.
>
> My beloved spoke, and said to me,
> Rise up, my love,
>   my fair one, and come away.
> For, lo, the winter is past,
>   the rain is over and gone;

> The flowers appear on the earth,
>   the time of singing is come,
>   and the turtle-dove's voice is heard.
> The figtree ripens her fruit,
>   the vines are in blossom,
>   they give forth their fragrance.
> Rise up, my love,
>   my fair one, and come away.
>
> O my dove, that art in the clefts of the rock,
>   in the covert of the steep place,
> Let me see thy countenance,
>   let me hear thy voice;
> For sweet is thy voice,
>   and thy countenance is comely. (Cant. 2 [8–14])

This is all exquisite in form and in sentiment. But behind much of the imagery of other poems there is an erotic suggestiveness that is offensive to an Occidental mind. When the maiden invites her lover,

> Let my beloved come into his garden,
>   and eat his precious fruits (Cant. 4 [16]),

and he accepts the invitation:

> I came into the garden of my sister,[1]
> I gathered my myrrh with my balsam,
> I ate my honeycomb with my honey,
> I drank my wine and my milk,

the implication of sexual enjoyment is quite clear, even without the additional exhortation,

> Eat, O friends, drink,
>   drink abundantly of love. (Cant. 5 [1])

No Oriental needs an interpretation of the song,

> How fair and how pleasant art thou,
>   O love, O daughter of delights!
> Thy stature is like a palm-tree,
>   and thy breasts like its clusters.
> I said, I will climb up into the palm-tree,
>   I will lay hold of its branches:
> Let thy breasts be as clusters,
>   and the smell of thy breath like apples,
>   and thy mouth like the best wine. (Cant. 7 [6–9])

[1] Sister is a term for the sweetheart in love songs also in Egypt. There is now added in the received text the variant "my bride."

No Occidental would have misunderstood the allusions either, if the song had not been in the sacred scriptures. But how did such a collection of love and wedding songs ever get into the canon? Because it was interpreted allegorically: it was not human love that was celebrated here, but Yahweh's love and Israel's: Yahweh was the bridegroom, Israel the bride. Tradition regarded Solomon as the author of these songs, and it was felt that he could not have composed them as mere love songs, for men of these later ages looked on him not only as a paragon of wisdom but also of piety. An allegorical interpretation was therefore all but inevitable.

The tradition that Solomon was the author had grown up because he is mentioned several times in the songs. In the imagination of the poets the bridegroom is king during the wedding feast, yea, King Solomon, the most magnificent of all kings, just as his beloved is the Shulamite, the most beautiful of all women! Tradition had told that Solomon had composed 1005 songs (1 Kings 4 [32]). And now it was thought that this particular collection of songs had been handed down, because it was the most beautiful of all of Solomon's songs, "*the* song of Solomon's songs." In reality neither Solomon nor any other single poet was the author of these songs, for they are folk-songs, composed by unknown men and sung by the people. How old they are, no one can tell, for such songs must have been sung in all ages of Israel's history in the North and the South. But the particular recension in which we have our collection comes from Jerusalem and is from a late period. The language shows this. Most probably it belongs to the third century B.C., but many of the individual songs are much older, some appear to come from the time before the exile, and their local allusions are all to the North.

Although the allegorical interpretation [1] prevailed and the little book was finally accepted as canonical in spite of much opposition, its secular character was still remembered even after its canonization and its songs were sung in the wine houses, which incensed Rabbi Akiba so much that he declared that "he who sings from the Song of Songs in the wine houses and makes a (secular) song of it, has no part in the world to-come." The Christian Church accepted the allegorical interpretation, but regarded Christ as the bridegroom, and the Church or the soul as the bride.

[1] Some saw in it a celebration of Solomon's passionate love for wisdom.

Lyrical poetry had accompanied Israel all through the centuries, and its flow did not cease in the second century B.C. We still have a collection of psalms composed by Pharisees at the end of the Maccabæan age, in the years shortly before and after Pompey's capture of Jerusalem in 63 B.C., which are called "Psalms of Solomon," [1] but they were written too late to be taken into the canon. And the *Magnificat* and *Benedictus* in the Gospel of Luke (1 [46-55.] [68-79]) are so thoroughly psalm-like in form and content that they might have stood in the Old Testament; they are entirely Jewish in character.

[1] Cf. R. H. Charles, *The Apocrypha and Pseudepigrapha* (1913), vol. II, pp. 625–652.

CHAPTER XXI

LATER POSTEXILIC PROPHETS

How profoundly the priests influenced religious life and thought after the exile we have witnessed more than once even among the prophets. But in Joel we meet a prophet who believed that the most terrible catastrophe that could befall the people was the cessation of the daily sacrifices, for through them the mysterious yet real union between God and His people was daily renewed. If they were not brought, there was no longer any vital contact possible with God. Joel was the sacramentarian among the prophets. A great locust plague, worse than anything that the oldest inhabitant could remember, roused him to prophetic activity. We do not know his date, it may have been toward the end of the fifth or the beginning of the fourth century. He was not a great prophet, but a remarkable poet. In a forcible and telling manner he described the vast army of the locusts and pictured their rapid advance, their destructive activity, and their attack upon the city so vividly that we can see them with our mind's eye as they come on in serried ranks. Passionately he called the people to repentance, for only thus could the plague be averted. This first address is now contained in 2 [1a 2b–10. 12–14]. But one swarm after another appeared. An accompanying drought made matters worse and brought the country face to face with ruin, spiritual as well as material, for "the meal-offering and the drink-offering are cut off from the house of Yahweh." So Joel in an address, in which his poetical and oratorical ability are finely blended, called for fasting and mourning and for a penitential assembly of the entire population in the temple at Jerusalem. This address is contained in 1 [2–14. 16–20]. And all of them came, from the youngest to the oldest, and prayed with the interceding priests for mercy. Yahweh heard and answered their plea and promised to them new fertility (2 [15–20. 25–27]).[1] At

[1] The narrative portion began originally in v.[15] not in v.[18]. The imperatives were originally historical tenses.

this the prophet burst forth, in the midst of Yahweh's speech, into beautiful strains of joy (2 $^{21-24}$). It is quite likely that this little lyrical poem belonged originally after 2 ^{27}.

Perhaps this is all that Joel wrote. If so, he can hardly be called a prophet. His poetic ability, however, would stand forth even then. His clear and fluent style, his rhythmic lines so swift and beautiful, his graphic and dramatic descriptions, and his stirring appeals mark the poet and the orator.

But it is quite probable that Joel foresaw another crisis, far greater and more terrible even than the locust plague: the awful judgment day of Yahweh on the world. He foretold the great excitement that would seize all classes; all would be in ecstasy.

> And it shall come to pass afterwards,
>   that I will pour out My Spirit upon all flesh;
> And your sons and your daughters shall prophesy,
>   your old men shall dream dreams,
>   your young men shall see visions:
> And also upon the servants and upon the handmaids
>   in those days will I pour out My Spirit. (Joel 2 $^{28f.}$)

The pouring out of the Spirit is not followed by a moral transformation but by ecstatic states, not by deeper spiritual knowledge of God but by prophetic trances, all of them having for their contents, we must assume, the coming of the day of Yahweh. Young and old, male and female, high and low, all will experience them among the Jews, for only they are meant by "all flesh." [1]

> And I will show wonders in the heavens and in the earth,
>   blood, and fire, and pillars of smoke.
> The sun shall be turned into darkness,
>   and the moon into blood,
> Before the great and terrible day
>   of Yahweh comes. (Joel 2 $^{30f.}$)

But those that call on Yahweh's name shall be delivered, whether they are in Jerusalem and Judah, or elsewhere (2 ^{32}).

The judgment will be on the nations. Yahweh will gather them into the valley of "Jehoshaphat," which means "Yahweh judges."

---

[1] Joel has sometimes been called the Prophet of Pentecost, and indeed Peter quotes this passage in his sermon on Pentecost. But Joel did not predict the enjoyment of fuller illumination or of spiritual transformation, which Christians associate with the coming of the Spirit.

All will be summoned in a most stirring fashion to prepare for war,

> Beat your plowshares into swords,
> and your pruninghooks into spears!

Come all of you to the Valley of Jehoshaphat, "for there will I sit
to judge all the nations round about." Then the command will
be given to the heavenly reapers to put in the sickle and reap
the harvest and tread the winepress of the nations.

> The sun and moon are darkened,
> and the stars withdraw their shining.
> And Yahweh roars from Zion,
> and utters His voice from Jerusalem:
> And the heavens and the earth shall shake,
> but Yahweh will be a refuge unto His people,
> and a stronghold to the children of Israel.

He will forever protect them against foreign invaders (3 [9—17]).
Nothing but Israel's "sacred egoism" runs through these prophecies. To us it is not sacred but utterly profane.

Later on an editor combined the two originally different parts,
the locust speeches and the day of Yahweh addresses, and inserted
at various places in ch. 1 and 2 references to the day of Yahweh, so
that it now seems as if the locusts were the precursors and heralds
of the day of Yahweh or even the executors of Yahweh's wrath.
It is due to these interpolations (1 [15] 2 [1b. 2a. 11]) that the locusts have
frequently been regarded not as real locusts but as apocalyptic
beasts. The first who interpreted them thus was the author of the
Revelation of John (9[3ff.]).

The editor added also at the end a beautiful, though not original, description of the wonderful fertility of Judah and the wonderful spring that would flow out of the temple, watering the Valley of
Shittim, and predicted, quite in the manner and spirit of Trito-
Isaiah and Isaiah 34f., the ruin of Egypt and Edom on account of
pogroms that had taken place in their land (3 [18ff.])

It seems that it was a still later writer who inserted in the
prophecy of the judgment in the Valley of Jehoshaphat an oracle
against the Philistines and Phœnicians, for whom he expected this
judgment especially, because at the time of the conquest of Jerusalem by Artaxerxes Ochus they had robbed the Jews and sold Jewish
captives to the Greeks. Yahweh will bring them back from cap-

tivity and then they shall requite the Philistines and Phœnicians with like punishment (3 ²ᵇ⁻⁸).

In the time of Artaxerxes Ochus belong very probably two other oracles, which are now preserved in the Book of Isaiah, the one against Sidon (Isa. 23 ¹⁻¹⁴), the other against Egypt (Isa. 19 ¹⁻¹⁵). The terrible destruction of Sidon by Artaxerxes in 348 B.C. is described here in a poem that paints the dismay in the great commercial centres over the fall of Sidon, that "mart of nations," the ancient joyful city, "whose feet carried her afar off to sojourn."

> Yahweh of hosts has purposed it,
>> to stain the pride of all glory,
>> to bring into contempt all the honorable of the earth. (Isa. 23 ⁹)

Later on, after Alexander the Great's capture and destruction of Sidon's sister city Tyre, this poem was augmented by vv. ¹⁵⁻¹⁸ and interpreted as referring to the fall of Sidon and Tyre. For seventy years Tyre will be forgotten, but then Yahweh will visit her again and she will be again the great merchant of the world.

> And her merchandise and her hire shall be holy to Yahweh; it shall not be treasured nor laid up; for her merchandise shall be for them that dwell before Yahweh, to eat sufficiently, and for durable clothing. (Isa. 23 ¹⁸)

This means that the profit of her commerce shall go to the Jews! There is no hint of any spiritual relation of Tyre to Yahweh or of any spiritual benefit for her. It is nothing but political slavery to the Jews that is expressed by the figure of her income being holy to Yahweh. Trito-Isaiah had similar ideas of the heathen as the workers for the Jews, who were to be the gentlemen priests.

The prophecy against Egypt was written apparently when Artaxerxes marched against her in 343 B.C. The writer predicted the invasion and the spread of civil war in Egypt. She will be forsaken by all her idols.

> And I will give over the Egyptians
>> into the hand of a cruel lord,
> And a fierce king shall rule over them,
>> says the Lord, Yahweh of hosts. (Isa. 19 ⁴)

This fierce king was in all probability Artaxerxes Ochus. The Nile will be dried up and all Egyptian industries will be ruined. The princes and counsellors will not know how to advise the Pharaoh.

Neither shall there be for Egypt any work, which head or tail, palm-branch
or rush (*i.e.* high or low) may do. (Isa. 19 [15])

When in the next decade Alexander the Great entered upon his
mighty career, when he defeated nation after nation and conquered
the Persian empire, a prophet in Jerusalem was strongly stirred by
the mighty commotions and his mind was filled with images of a far
greater catastrophe, the final judgment of the world by Yahweh.
He was no ordinary prophet but an apocalyptic writer, who had his
predecessors in Ezekiel, Zechariah, and Joel.   Like them he saw the
hidden secrets of the heavenly realm and revealed the spiritual
forces that were shaping the destiny of the world according to God's
plan.   He looked to the future, for it held the key that unlocked all
problems, solved all the mysteries and inequalities, and harmonized
all contradictions.   Different from the prophets, these apocalyptists
were not orators who appeared before the people and gave to them
the divine revelation with the full backing and responsibility of their
own personality, but writers who unfolded the great panorama of
the future, as it had come to them by study, meditation, and vision.
They remained, as a rule, anonymous, or used pseudonyms, frequently the great names of antiquity, in order to enhance the authority of their writings.   The author of Isaiah 24–27 was one of these
apocalyptic writers whose name we do not know.   His little apocalypse comprised Isaiah 24. 25 [6–8] 26 [20]–27 [1]. 27 [12f.].   A number of
songs were later combined with it.   The theme of his book is the
Judgment of the World and the Kingdom of God.
The whole earth will be laid waste and turned upside down and
all classes of people will be affected.   They have broken "the
eternal covenant" which God had made with men at the time of
Noah (cf. Gen. 9 [1ff.]), in which certain fundamental laws were laid
down as binding on all mankind, among them especially the prohibition of murder.   The symptoms of the coming catastrophe are
already visible in the general fading and weariness of the world: all
lose their vital power and joy of living; only few will be left in the
general upheaval.   Some indeed are full of good cheer because of
some event, which we unfortunately cannot identify, which makes
them rejoice and sing: "Glory to the righteous!"   But our prophet
feels differently:

> I said, I pine away, I pine away, woe is me!
>   the treacherous have dealt treacherously,
>   yea, the treacherous have dealt very treacherously.
> Fear, and the pit, and the snare
>   are upon thee, O inhabitant of the earth. (Isa. 24 [16])

And now begin the terrible convulsions that will introduce the great judgment.

> The windows on high are opened,
>   and the foundations of the earth tremble.
> The earth is utterly broken,
>   the earth is rent asunder,
>   the earth is shaken violently.
> The earth shall stagger like a drunken man,
>   and shall sway to and fro like a hammock.
> And its transgression shall be heavy upon it,
>   and it shall fall and not rise again. (Isa. 24 [18–20])

The picture is painted in a most impressive way in the original, where the word-pictures and assonances heighten the power of the co-lossal convulsions, till finally the moral cause of this chaos is laid bare.

The first act of the judgment will be the imprisonment of the heavenly patrons and of the earthly kings of the nations, both of whom direct their peoples' affairs. Their imprisonment in the subterranean pit will last a long time before they are finally judged.[1] This imprisonment and judgment of the angels is elaborated in other apocalypses, e.g. that of Enoch. In our apocalypse there follows directly the beginning of the Kingdom of God in Zion in visible glory. The sun and moon will pale before His glory, and as in days gone by the elders saw the glory of God on Mount Horeb, so they shall see it on Mount Zion. There is no mention of a Messiah. God Himself is enthroned.

In connection with His assumption of universal sovereignty Yahweh will give a coronation feast on Mount Zion to which all peoples without exception are invited:

> And Yahweh of hosts will make
>   to all peoples in this mountain
> A feast of fat things, a feast of wines on the lees,
>   of fat things full of marrow, of wines on the lees well refined.

---

[1] Later, e.g. in the Revelation of John, the time was specified as a thousand years, the millennium, for to God a thousand years are like a day.

And He will destroy in this mountain
  the face of the covering that covers all peoples,
And the veil that is spread over all nations.
  He has swallowed up death forever; [1]
And the Lord Yahweh will wipe away tears
  from off all faces;
And the reproach of His people will He take away
  from off all the earth:
For Yahweh has spoken it. (Isa. 25 [6-8])

Great joy will prevail at the banquet, where all will be in direct communion with God. All the secret tears will be dried by Yahweh Himself, never again shall the people weep, for death itself will be destroyed and eternal felicity will rule in all hearts. This is one of the most beautiful passages in the Old Testament. Its large-hearted catholicity and human tenderness single it out. Its music has sung itself into the sorrowing heart of mankind. Zion, it is true, is still the centre of the world, and the Jews are still considered especially by Yahweh, yet not in order to give them a higher place. It is surprising, however, to notice how little stressed, how incidental is the significant idea of the abolition of death. As if it were by no means new and astounding. Perhaps it was not so new to the people as we think. The author does not speak of the resurrection of the dead, but of the immortality of the living.

The final judgment of mankind and of the heavenly host is still to come, if indeed the order of the text is chronological. But His people are called by Yahweh to hide themselves "for a little moment, until the indignation is overpast."

For behold Yahweh comes out of His place
  to punish the inhabitants of the earth for their iniquity:
The earth also shall disclose her blood,
  and shall no more cover the slain.
In that day will Yahweh punish
  with His hard and great and strong sword
Leviathan the swift serpent,
  and Leviathan the crooked serpent,
And He will slay the monster that is in the sea. (Isa. 26 [21]-27 [1])

These seem to be the constellations *serpens*, *draco*, and *hydra*, the

---

[1] In 1 Cor. 15 [54] the Hebrew word for "forever" is translated, under the influence of the Aramaic, by "in victory."

heavenly patrons of the nations. Not only man and nature, but also angels are included in the judgment of the world.

After this is past, the gathering of every one of the dispersed Jews takes place. A trumpet will be blown,

> And they shall come that were ready to perish in the land of Assyria,
>   and they that were outcasts in the land of Egypt ·
> And they shall worship Yahweh
>   in the holy mountain at Jerusalem. (Isa. 27 [13])

This had become one of the tenets of the Jewish hope of the future, and even this author could not help emphasizing it. But he had felt the sorrow and suffering of humanity and voiced the hope of the final joy of all mankind so beautifully that in their sorrow men still turn to his words and read of the time when there shall be no more tears.

In one of the poems which have been combined with the apocalypse and in which the historical allusions are so tantalizingly elusive that we cannot make out their date, there is a passage of great significance in which the hope of the resurrection is expressed. Although there had been some events that had raised the spirit of the people, the death of some overlords and the enlargement of the country, yet in all the pains and efforts of bringing something new to life they had failed, "we have not wrought deliverance in the land, neither have inhabitants of the world been born." The smallness of the population of the country worried the poet, but he gives voice to this hope,

> Thy dead shall live,
>   their corpses shall arise ;
> They that dwell in the dust
>   shall awake and sing,
> For Thy dew is as the dew of lights,
>   and the earth shall bring forth the shades. (Isa. 26 [19])

Yahweh's dead, faithful saints will be raised, their actual bodies will come back, not only their ghosts. Yahweh has a life-giving dew, the dew of lights, which will be dropped down on the graves and revivify the corpses. It is not the resurrection of all that is hoped for here, only the resurrection of Yahweh's dead, perhaps of the martyrs and other saints. At last this hope had come. The brief reference to it here suggests that it was not entirely new among the people for whom the author wrote.

The large-hearted catholicity of the apocalyptist of Isaiah 24–27 has filled us with grateful admiration. Fortunately, he was not the only one of those universal spirits among the Jews that understood the full import of monotheism. One was even greater than he. Sometime during the Greek period, perhaps between 300–200, he wrote the story of Jonah, which belongs to the finest and highest that the Old Testament writers have produced and which reveals the prophetic spirit in the purest and truest way. Most deservedly was it included among the prophetical books of the canon, although it was not a prophecy of Jonah, but a story about the prophet. Long ago, in the time of Jeroboam II of Israel (784–744), Jonah had lived and prophesied victory and national aggrandizement to that brilliant king. None of his prophecies are preserved, but he was most probably a thoroughly nationalistic prophet. That and his name Jonah, which means "dove" and was used as a symbolical name for Israel,[1]—perhaps also his father's name Amittai, which is connected with *emeth* = truth so that Jonah could easily be interpreted as the son of truth, *i.e.* the possessor of the true God and the true religion,—may have suggested Jonah to the author as the most appropriate figure for his story. He used him as the representative of the narrow, nationalistic tendency among the Jews, according to which they alone were Yahweh's peculiar people and the sole object of His love and care, while the heathen were not only their enemies but also Yahweh's and merited nothing but punishment and destruction.

Yahweh had commanded Jonah to go to Nineveh and prophesy God's punishment on account of her wickedness, but the prophet refused to go and fled from Yahweh's presence, *i.e.* from the land of Israel, taking ship at Joppa, to escape Yahweh's anger. But Yahweh sent a terrific storm, which the mariners at first tried to calm by prayer, while Jonah slept. When this proved of no avail, Jonah was discovered, rudely awakened from his sleep, and ordered to pray to his God. Then the lot was cast to find out on whose account God had sent the storm, and it fell on Jonah. He confessed that he had fled from Yahweh and advised them to cast him

---

[1] Compare Ps. 74 [19] where the synonym "turtle dove" is applied to Israel, "Oh, deliver not Thy turtle dove to the wild beast; forget not the life of Thy poor for ever."

into the sea. But only after renewed endeavors to save the ship had been in vain and after an earnest prayer for Yahweh's mercy did they throw him into the sea, which at once became calm; whereupon the sailors, overcome by awe, offered a sacrifice and vowed vows to Yahweh. Meanwhile a great fish had been ordered by Yahweh to swallow Jonah, who spent three days and three nights inside of the fish before he was ejected upon the dry land. This part of the story has caused much difficulty and ridicule, because the whole story was taken as a historical tale recounting events that had actually happened. But it was no narrative of historical facts but a prose poem with a purpose, and the fish story, far from being unique, has turned out to be quite common the world over. Such tales of miraculous deliverance, with many variations of detail, were told by many peoples; maritime people spoke of a huge fish or a sea monster, inland people of a wolf or a dragon or bear. And just at Joppa the Greeks located the story of Perseus and Andromeda, with his fight inside of the sea monster. The author took this bit of folklore and used it as a means of transporting Jonah back to the land. He never thought that readers would be so much without poetical imagination as to strip it of its fantastic beauty and nullify the wonderful lesson he had to teach in the sequel. At Yahweh's repeated command Jonah went to Nineveh, an immense city of three days' journey in diameter. Going in a day's journey he cried to the astonished Ninevites, "Yet forty days, and Nineveh shall be overthrown!" At once they repented, proclaimed a fast, and sat in sackcloth and ashes. Even the king joined them and published a decree of fasting in his own and his nobles' name, calling upon the people to repent and turn from their evil ways in order to gain God's favor. And they all fasted and repented. Surely, this was a more astounding miracle than the miracle of the fish! Moved by their penitence Yahweh did not execute His threat. This angered Jonah, who remonstrated with Him: he had known that Yahweh was too gracious to carry out His threat; that was why he had refused to go on His mission and had fled to Tarshish. "Therefore now, O Yahweh, take my life from me, for it is better for me to die than to live." But Yahweh taught him in a most effective way the superlative folly of his behavior. A kindly humor without sting or bitterness runs through the rest of the tale. Jonah had made a booth for himself outside of the city, where he had waited for the destruction of Nineveh. There Yahweh caused a gourd to grow, whose shade was highly welcome to the prophet. But Yahweh destroyed the gourd through a worm and sent one of those terrible sultry east winds, which with the scorching sun made Jonah so faint that he asked again for his death. So angry was he over the withering of the gourd! But Yahweh said to him,

Thou hast had regard for the gourd, for which thou hast not labored, neither madest it grow, which came up in a night and perished in a night; and I should not have pity on Nineveh, that great city, in which are more than 120,000 persons that cannot discern between their right hand and their left; and also much cattle? (Jonah 4 10f.)

With this question the story closes. The author does not tell whether Jonah was convinced by the irresistible argument. It is not Jonah, but every reader that must answer the question. All must learn that Yahweh is not the God of the Jews only but the God of all men, who pities and cares for all, even for Israel's worst enemies and who wants all to repent and be forgiven.

"*For the love of God is broader than the measure of man's mind,*
And the heart of the Eternal is most wonderfully kind;
But we make His love too narrow by false limits of our own,
And we magnify His strictness by a zeal He will not own."
(F. W. Faber)

If the Jews had but listened to this appeal, they would have become the great missionaries of the world carrying the gospel of the one God to all the world until they had established the universal religion. That was Deutero-Isaiah's vision and this writer's hope. He summoned Israel to its task. But the people did not respond.

A pious reader missed the prayer which Jonah had uttered in the fish and so inserted a psalm which he regarded as an appropriate prayer for Jonah to make (2 2-9). It would have been more fitting as a prayer of thanksgiving after his deliverance, but the story had said nothing of Jonah's praying at that time.

During the Greek period the horizon of many Jews widened, and it is with delight that we come upon such prophecies as those that were added to the oracle against Egypt in Isaiah 19 18-25, of which the first predicted,

In that day there shall be five cities in the land of Egypt that speak the language of Canaan, and swear by Yahweh of hosts; one shall be called The city of the sun. (Isa. 19 [18])

When the Jewish temple at Leontopolis was founded by the fugitive high priest Onias in the first half of the second century this prophecy was quoted in justification of it.

The second prediction reads,

In that day shall there be an altar to Yahweh in the midst of the land of Egypt, and a pillar at its border to Yahweh. And it shall be for a sign and for a witness to Yahweh of hosts in the land of Egypt; for they shall cry to Yahweh because of oppressors, and He will send them a savior, and a defender, and He will deliver them. And Yahweh shall be known to Egypt, and the Egyptians shall know Yahweh in that day; yea, they shall worship with sacrifice and oblation, and shall vow a vow to Yahweh, and shall perform it. And Yahweh will smite Egypt, smiting and healing; and they shall return to Yahweh, and He will be entreated of them, and will heal them. (Isa. 19 [19-22])

The third prophecy foretold,

In that day shall there be a highway out of Egypt to Assyria, and the Assyrian shall come into Egypt, and the Egyptian into Assyria; and the Egyptians shall worship with the Assyrians. (Isa. 19 [23])

The fourth prediction was,

In that day shall Israel be the third with Egypt and with Assyria, a blessing in the midst of the earth; because Yahweh of hosts has blessed them, saying, Blessed be Egypt My people, and Assyria the work of My hands, and Israel Mine inheritance. (Isa. 19 [24f.])

Other universal prophecies, which looked forward to a restoration of the nations, were inserted in the prophetic books. For instance, Zephaniah 3 [9f.] contains now the beautiful hope, not shared by Zephaniah but inherent in his message,

> For then will I turn to the peoples
> a pure language,
> That they may all call upon the name of Yahweh,
> to serve Him with one consent. (Zeph. 3 [9])

In Jeremiah 12 [14-17] Yahweh now says after the punishment of the "evil neighbors" of Israel,

I will return and have compassion on them; and I will bring them again, every man to his heritage, and every man to his land. And it shall come to pass, if they will diligently learn the ways of My people, to swear by My name, As Yahweh lives; even as they taught My people to swear by Baal; then shall they be built up in the midst of My people. But if they will not hear, then will I pluck up that nation, plucking up and destroying it, says Yahweh (Jer. 12 [15b–17]).

The last two passages never were independent prophecies, but were written for these particular places and inserted by editors.

The activity of the editors of the prophetic books was of great significance and far-reaching influence. None of the books has escaped editorial revision. The words of the prophets were not their own but Yahweh's. His authorship was paramount, even if there had already been a conception of the rights of the authors of literary works. Thus there were bound together with the Book of Isaiah not only the Books of the Second and Third Isaiahs (Isa. 40–55; 56–66), but also the apocalypse in Isaiah 24–27, and many other single chapters or passages. To the Book of Zechariah were added the Books of the Second and Third Zechariah (Zech. 9–11 and 12–14), originally apparently also the Book of Malachi. Many prophecies by men of various times, whose names had been forgotten, were circulating among the people. They were put into the prophetic collection, to which they seemed to belong according to their subject, if not by their authorship. Thus a number of anonymous Oracles against the Nations were collected with Isaiah's Oracles against the Nations in one book (Isa. 13–23), another series of such prophecies with Jeremiah's in another book (Jer. 46–51). Prophecies of hope were gathered together in a Little Book of Comfort with Isaiah's (Isa. 32–35) or with Jeremiah's prophecies of hope (Jer. 30–33) as a nucleus. It happened that such booklets were not always inserted in the same place and order in the various manuscripts so that e.g. Jeremiah's Book of Oracles against the Nations (Jer. 46–51) is in a different place in the Greek Bible, which inserts it after 25 [13].

But all this is but one phase of the editorial activity of the Jews. God had a message for every age. He still spoke through His prophets of old, but the times changed and the needs varied. So with changing times and varying needs these books were constantly adapted to the new conditions. We saw how Judæan editors brought the books of Amos and Hosea up to date in order that they might serve as guides and warnings to Judah, lest it also be engulfed in

408 THE LITERATURE OF THE OLD TESTAMENT

ruin. After the Babylonian exile had brought the fearful catastrophe which the prophets had predicted, and new prophets, especially the great Deutero-Isaiah, had written their predictions full of hope and glory, the earlier prophets were edited afresh and words of hope and restoration were added. It seemed not quite true in the light of events that Amos should have predicted nothing but absolute destruction for all Israel, so there was added in 9 $^{8-10}$,

> Save that I will not utterly destroy the house of Jacob, says Yahweh. For, lo, I will command, and I will sift the house of Israel among all the nations, like as grain is sifted in a sieve, yet shall not the least kernel fall upon the earth. All the sinners of My people shall die by the sword, who say, The evil shall not overtake nor meet us.

Similarly in Jeremiah the little clause was inserted, "yet will I not make a full end" (4 ^{27} 5 $^{10. 18}$). But not only sentences and clauses but whole new oracles were added. Thus the glowing prediction at the end of the Book of Amos (9 $^{11-15}$ cf. p. 252), which totally modified the impression of the message of that powerful prophet of doom.

The restoration of Israel in its various aspects forms the theme of many such additions (e.g. Mic. 7 $^{8ff.}$ Zeph. 3 $^{14ff.}$). Sometimes a nucleus was expanded as in Obadiah and Joel, sometimes the whole was new. Again and again there were inserted the hopes of the return of the scattered people from exile (e.g. Mic. 2 $^{12f.}$ 4 $^{6-8}$ Jer. 23 $^{3f.}$), of the reunion of Israel and Judah under the leadership of a Davidic king (e.g. Hos. 1 $^{10f.}$ 3^5, the single phrase "and unto David their king"), of the larger city (Jer. 31 $^{38ff.}$), of the reconquest of all the former territory (e.g. Zeph. 2 $^{7a. 9b}$ Ob. $^{18-21}$), of Yahweh's visible dwelling in Zion (Isa. 4 $^{5f.}$), of the punishment of the nations (Isa. 19 $^{16f.}$), of Israel's lordship over the heathen (Isa. 14 $^{1-4a}$), occasionally of the restoration of the nations (Zeph. 3 $^{9f.}$ Jer. 46 ^{26b} 48 ^{47} 49 $^{6. 39}$).

Sometimes it was liturgical matter that was inserted, as e.g. the little poems on Yahweh's greatness in nature in Amos 4 ^{13} 5 $^{8f.}$ 9 $^{5f.}$ to enhance the power of the prophetic appeal, or a psalm was added to furnish a suitable ending for a book, e.g. Isa. 12, or poems were inserted as in Isa. 25–27, or a prayer where it seemed to be called for (e.g. Jer. 32 $^{17ff.}$), or a call to reverent silence in worship (Hab. 2 ^{20}).

Again, didactic portions were supplied especially on the folly of idolatry (Hab. 2 ^{18} Jer. 10 $^{1ff.}$) and appeals to the wise and reasonings with them (Hos. 14 ^{9} Jer. 9 $^{12ff.}$).

To the Books of Isaiah and Jeremiah historical chapters were affixed (Isa. 36–39, Jer. 52).

By all this the appearance of the original books of the prophets was modified considerably. Rarely was a prophetic text itself changed as in Zech. 6 [9ff.], where the royal oracle was altered into a priestly one (cf. p. 240). This was more frequently done by additions as in Jeremiah 33 [18–22]. An eager and intensive study of the prophetic books is revealed by this editorial activity of so many earnest men. In Micah 5 [3] there is an interesting illustration of an addition which is based on a study of the Immanuel passage in Isaiah 7 [1ff.]. It is interpreted messianically. Immanuel (with us is God) and Shearjashub (a remnant shall return) are utilized here.

These editors were sure that God spoke through the prophets to their time in ever fresh manner and that He had kindled His light in their own souls too. But not all of them understood the greatness and originality of the prophets. The law had gained its dominant place, God's will was revealed through it. He sent no more His living original spokesmen. So a writer added at the end of the Book of Malachi, "Remember ye the law of Moses My servant." To him the prophets had been nothing but interpreters of the law. This view unfortunately prevailed. The annotator of Malachi believed that only one other prophet might be expected: Elijah, who, strikingly enough, was not a literary prophet!

CHAPTER XXII

THE LAST PROPHETS

AFTER a century-long conflict between the Seleucid kings of Syria and the Ptolemies of Egypt Palestine had finally come into the hands of Antiochus III the Great through his victory at Paneas in 198 B.C. Under his reign Hellenistic civilization with its ideas and practices influenced the Jews in Judea more profoundly than before. The rich and cultured Jews especially felt the irresistible attraction of the Hellenistic view and mode of life. The conflict between them and the followers of the law became more bitter all the time. At last the very life of Hebrew religion seemed to the faithful to be at stake, when Antiochus IV Epiphanes (175–164 B.C.) tried to force Hellenistic culture and religion upon the Jews. A strife for the high priesthood brought about his interference in Jewish affairs, which led to the Maccabæan wars. Jason, the brother of the high priest Onias III, a Hellenizer as his Greek name shows, had succeeded in persuading Antiochus by the promise of immense sums of money to give to him the high priesthood. Onias had to flee. Jason began at once with his Hellenistic schemes, a Greek gymnasium was built in Jerusalem, and Greek customs were introduced. Two years later Jason was displaced by Menelaus, who was not even of high priestly blood. He had promised the king even greater sums, which he took out of the temple treasury after his appointment. Antiochus was at this time warring in Egypt, and the rumor came to Jerusalem that he had fallen in battle. Jason tried to regain the high priesthood and a sanguinary fight took place in the city. Menelaus fled to Antiochus, for the rumor was false, and Antiochus returned to reinstate Menelaus and to punish the city (170 B.C.). The temple treasury was looted and the costly furniture, including the golden candlestick and table, was taken. When two years later Antiochus marched once more against Egypt, Rome interfered through her legate Popilius Laenas, who commanded him peremptorily to withdraw on peril of war with Rome. He retreated in an ugly mood and now determined to proceed with his program of Hellenizing the Jews in earnest. On its homeward march his army stopped awhile in Jerusalem. After an ostensibly peaceful entrance they attacked the people, killed some, and then began to plunder. The city walls were razed, and a Syrian garrison was placed in the strongly fortified Akra, the old city of David. A little later the observance of the Sabbath and of circumcision was forbidden, the temple services and sacrifices were stopped, the sacred books were destroyed, and much damage was done to the temple. Even this was not enough. On the 15th day of Kislev (December, 168) there was planted to the horror of the Jews an altar of Zeus on the sacred altar of burnt-offering, and on the 25th of the month a sacrifice of swine was brought on this heathen altar in Yahweh's temple! Everywhere in the country altars and images were erected and the Jews were ordered to pay homage to them and to sacrifice swine. Then the smouldering rage of the Jews burst forth into hot flame. In the little country town of Modin Mattathias, a priest, with his five sons, chief among them the lion-hearted Judas Maccabæus, led the revolt, and in the next few years they won incredible victories. In 165 Jerusalem, except only the citadel, was in their hands, and on the 25th of Kislev (December, 165) the temple was cleansed and rededicated. But after all, how could the small host withstand in the long run the power of a world-empire like Syria? It seemed impossible, and in many hearts hope died and the look of despair came into many eyes.

Just at this crisis there appeared the Book of Daniel throbbing with the power of an unconquerable faith. Like a trumpet it sounded the call to loyalty and trust. Hold fast, be faithful to your God! The time of salvation is at hand! Soon, very soon complete and glorious delivery will be yours! In order to infuse his own high spirit into his hearers, the author told of men who in like perilous situations had been loyal to Israel's religion: of Daniel and his three friends, who kept the ritual laws concerning food and drink and became fairer, wiser, and more honored than others (ch. 1); of Shadrach, Meshach, and Abednego, who refused to worship the golden image of Nebuchadrezzar and were thrown into the fiery furnace, where they were shielded by God's angel (ch. 3); of Daniel, who fearlessly performed his daily prayers and was thrown into the lions' den, but wonderfully saved by the angel of God (ch. 6). So gloriously did God help His faithful saints that even the heathen kings were astounded and compelled to bless the God of these men, "who had sent His angel and delivered His servants that trusted Him," and to declare,

He is the living God, and steadfast forever. . . . He delivers and rescues, and He works signs and wonders in heaven and in earth, who has delivered Daniel from the power of the lions. (Dan. 6 ^{26f.})

God helped His faithful saints most marvellously out of the direst perils. Will He not do so still? Only trust in Him and be loyal to Him and to His cause! And as for the tyrant? Read what God did to King Nebuchadrezzar, when in godless pride he boasted, how He reduced him to the level of a beast, that ate grass in the open field, where "his body was wet with the dew of heaven, till his hair was grown like eagles' feathers, and his nails like birds' claws," until he finally came to acknowledge the sovereignty of God. Or listen to what He did to King Belshazzar, when he mocked Him by drinking from His sacred temple vessels at one of his banquets, how that awful mysterious hand wrote "mene, mene, tekel, upharsin" upon the wall, which Daniel interpreted as meaning,

Mene, God has numbered thy kingdom, and brought it to an end;
Tekel, thou art weighed in the balances, and found wanting;
Peres, thy kingdom is divided, and given to the Medes and Persians. (Dan. 5 ^{26ff.})

In the same night Belshazzar was slain! God is not mocked with impunity. Do you think that Antiochus, who has plundered the temple and taken the sacred vessels (1 Macc. 1 ^{21–24}), will escape without punishment? The author does not say this with so many words, but he wants his readers to infer it. Yahweh alone is God, and He alone is King. The various kings have their kingdoms only by His grace. So far He has given the dominion of the world to different nations in turn, but the time is at hand when He will give it to His saints. There is a definite divine plan in the history of the world. The heathen sages do not understand it, but God has revealed it to His servant Daniel in dreams and visions.

The first revelation was given in a dream to Nebuchadrezzar

in ch. 2, but only Daniel understood it. It was the dream of the image whose "head was of fine gold, whose breast and arms were of silver, whose belly and thighs were of brass, its legs of iron, its feet part iron and part clay." It was broken in pieces by "a stone cut out without hands," which "became a great mountain, and filled the whole earth." The image represented the four world-empires, the Babylonian, Median, Persian, and Greek. The Babylonian is the head of gold, the Greek composed of iron and clay, strong in part, weak in part, not firmly welded together. The stone is Israel.

In the days of those kings (*i.e.* the Greek kings) shall the God of heaven set up a kingdom which shall never be destroyed, nor shall its sovereignty be left to another people; but it shall break in pieces and consume all these kingdoms, and itself shall stand forever. (Dan. 2 44.)

At the time when this book appeared, men were living in the fourth kingdom, in the Greek period. How soon will its end be here? Will it be soon or will it be delayed? This question is answered in the visions of Daniel.

In Daniel's vision of the four beasts in ch. 7 only the fourth or Greek kingdom is described more in detail and the final judgment on Antiochus IV Epiphanes is foretold. Of the four great beasts that Daniel saw coming out of the sea the lion with eagle's wings represented the Babylonian, the bear the Median, the leopard with four bird wings on its back the Persian, and the terrible, strong beast with iron teeth and ten horns the Hellenistic kingdoms. The ten horns represented the ten kings of Syria from Alexander the Great to Demetrius.[1] The other horn, which came up as the prophet looked, the "little one before which three of the first horns were plucked up by the roots," was no one else but Antiochus Epiphanes, who had "a mouth speaking great things." The three horns were his immediate predecessors, Seleucus IV, Heliodorus, and Demetrius, who "were plucked up by the roots" in 176 B.C. With Antiochus IV the end is reached.

I beheld till thrones were placed, and one that was ancient of days sat down: His raiment was white as snow, and the hair of His head like pure wool; His

---

[1] Alexander 336–323
Seleucus I 312–280
Antiochus I 280–261
Antiochus II 261–247
Seleucus II 246–226

Seleucus III 226–222
Antiochus III 222–187
Seleucus IV 186–176
Heliodorus 176
Demetrius 176

throne was fiery flames, and its wheels burning fire. A fiery stream issued and came forth from before Him: thousands of thousands were ministering to Him, and ten thousand times ten thousand were standing before Him: the judgment (the judge) was seated, and the books were opened. I beheld at that time because of the voice of the great words which the horn spoke; I beheld even till the beast was slain, and its body destroyed, and it was given to be burned with fire. And as for the rest of the beasts, their dominion was taken away: yet their lives were prolonged for a season and a time.

I saw in the night-visions, and, behold, there appeared coming with the clouds of heaven one like a son of man, and he came even to the ancient of days, and they brought him near before Him. And there was given him dominion, and glory, and a kingdom, that all the peoples, nations, and languages should serve him: his dominion is an everlasting dominion, which shall not pass away, and his kingdom that which shall not be destroyed. (Dan. 7 $^{9-14}$)

In the interpretation which the angel gave to Daniel it is made perfectly clear that "the one like a son of man" who came with the clouds of heaven and to whom was given eternal dominion was the representative of the kingdom of the saints of the Most High.

These great kings, which are four, are four kings that shall arise out of the earth. But the saints of the Most High shall receive the kingdom, and possess the kingdom for ever, even for ever and ever. (7 $^{17f.}$)

It may be that "the one like a son of man" was Israel's patron angel and representative Michael (Dan. 12 ^{1}), who is the conqueror of the dragon in Rev. 12 ^{7}. In any case, our author did not identify him with the Messiah. That was done in the Book of Enoch (e.g. 46. 48. 62. 63. 69), which was written before 64 B.C. and in the Fourth Book of Ezra (ch. 13) under Domitian (81–96 A.D.). Daniel was especially interested in the little horn which represented Antiochus IV, although of course he never mentioned him by name. This cryptic veiling in the unveiling is characteristic of apocalypses.

Thus he said, The fourth beast shall be a fourth kingdom upon earth, which shall be different from all the kingdoms, and shall devour the whole earth, and shall tread it down, and break it in pieces. And as for the ten horns, out of this kingdom shall ten kings arise: and another shall arise after them; and he shall be different from the former ones, and he shall put down three kings. And he shall speak words against the Most High, and shall afflict the saints of the Most High; and he shall think to change the times and the law; and they shall be given into his hand until a time and times and half a time. But the judgment shall be seated, and they shall take away his dominion, to consume and to destroy it unto the end. And the kingdom and the dominion, and the greatness of the kingdoms under the whole heaven, shall be given to the people of the saints of the Most High: his kingdom is an everlasting kingdom, and all dominions shall serve and obey him. (Dan. 7 23–27)

The vision of the ram and the he-goat with the four horns out of which came a little horn (ch. 8) is a variation of the preceding vision. The ram with the two horns is definitely explained as the Medo-Persian empire, the he-goat as Alexander the Great.

The ram which thou sawest, that had the two horns, they are the kings of Media and Persia. And the rough he-goat is the king of Greece, and the great horn that is between his eyes is the first king (*i.e.* Alexander the Great). And as for that which was broken, in whose place four stood up, four kingdoms shall stand up out of the nation, but not with his power. (Dan. 8 20–22)

They were the kingdoms of Alexander's successors, (1) Cassander's in the west, Macedonia and Greece, (2) Lysimachus' in the north, Asia Minor as far as Pontus and Paphlagonia, (3) Seleucus' in the east, Asia as far as the Indus but with Asia Minor excepted, and (4) Ptolemy's in the south, Egypt with Phœnicia and Cœlesyria.

But in the latter time of their kingdom, when the transgressors are come to the full, a king of fierce countenance, and understanding dark sentences shall stand up,

that is, Antiochus Epiphanes. He is the "little horn."

And out of one of them came forth a little horn, which waxed exceeding great, toward the south, and toward the east, and toward the beauteous land. And it waxed great, as far as the host of heaven; and some of the host and of the stars it cast down to the ground, and trampled upon them. Yea, it magnified itself, even to the prince of the host; and it took away from him the daily sacrifice, and the place of his sanctuary was cast down. And the temple service was abandoned together with the daily sacrifice through transgression; and truth was cast down to the ground, and it (the horn) carried out its purpose successfully. (Dan. 8 9–12)

And his power shall be mighty, but not by his own power; and he shall utter astonishing things and shall accomplish his purpose, and he shall destroy the mighty ones, and against the holy ones is his policy, he shall succeed by means of deceit, and he shall magnify himself in his heart, and unawares shall he destroy many: he shall also stand up against the prince of princes; but he shall be broken by no (human) hand. (Dan. 8 24f.)

But how soon will his end come?

Then I heard a holy one speaking; and another holy one said unto the one who spoke, How long shall the vision be that the daily sacrifice shall be taken away and an appalling transgression be set up and the sanctuary and the temple service be trodden under foot? And he said to me, For two thousand and three hundred evenings and mornings; then shall the sanctuary be restored to its rightful use. (Dan. 8 13f.)

On the 25th of Kislev, 168, the altar had been defiled; on the same day three years later, 165, the temple was cleansed and rededicated. One thousand one hundred and fifty days are 3 years and 55 days. Had the author already witnessed the rededication? If so, he wrote in December, 165, or January, 164. But this is not quite certain. That he expected the end early in 164 he says unmistakably.

The question of the exact time of the end gave him no rest. He studied the writings of the older prophets and found in Jeremiah's book the prophecy of the seventy years. After much fasting and prayer the correct understanding of this prediction was given to him by the angel Gabriel. The seventy years are not simply years, but weeks of years, *i.e.* 490 in all.

Know therefore and discern, that from the going forth of the commandment to restore and to build Jerusalem unto the anointed one, the prince, are seven weeks, and threescore and two weeks: it shall be built again, with street and moat. And at the end of times, even after the sixty-two weeks [1] shall the anointed one be cut off, without judicial trial, and the city and the sanctuary shall be destroyed together with a prince and the end shall come with a flood, and even unto the end shall be war . . . and the covenant shall be annulled for many for one week: and in the midst of the week shall the sacrifice and the oblation cease; and in its place shall be an appalling abomination until the determined ruin shall be poured out upon the appalling thing. (Dan. 9 25–27)

The end is due in June, 164!

The most elaborate and detailed vision is given in ch. 10f., in which the history of the Greek kingdoms and especially of the time of Antiochus IV is given so accurately that ch. 11 can be used as a reliable historical source of the period. The author did not know much about the history of Babylonia and Persia. About the time of Nebuchadrezzar and his successors, in which Daniel is supposed to have lived, he is so poorly informed that he commits serious historical blunders, but his own time he knows very well and the history of the preceding century also. He gives interesting and reliable details of the conflict of the Seleucids with the Ptolemies, of

---

[1] The author makes here a mistake of about 70 years, for 62 weeks are 434 years, which would give the year 103, if deducted from 537. Demetrius (*ca.* 200 B.C.) and Josephus made a similar mistake in their chronology of this period.

their wars and their marriages, until he finally comes to the accession of Antiochus Epiphanes.

And in his place shall stand up a contemptible person, to whom they had not given the majesty of the kingdom: but he shall come unawares, and shall obtain the kingdom by intrigues. And the forces shall be completely overwhelmed from before him, and shall be broken; yea, also the prince of the covenant. And after the league made with him he shall work deceitfully; and he shall come up, and shall become strong, with a small people. Unexpectedly shall he come even upon the fattest places of the province; and he shall do that which his fathers have not done, nor his fathers' fathers; he shall scatter among them prey, and spoil, and substance: yea, he shall devise his devices against fortresses and that until a time. And he shall stir up his power and his courage against the king of the south with a great army; and the king of the south shall war in battle with an exceeding great and mighty army; but he shall not stand; for they shall devise devices against him. Yea, they that eat of his delicacies shall destroy him, and his army shall be swept away; and many shall fall down slain. And as for both these kings, their hearts shall be to do mischief, and they shall speak lies at one table: but it shall not prosper; for yet the end shall be at the time appointed.

And he shall return into his own land with great substance; and his heart shall be against the holy covenant; and he shall execute his purpose, and return to his own land. At the time appointed he shall return, and come into the south; but it shall not be in the latter time as it was in the former. For ships of Kittim shall come against him; therefore he shall be cowed, and return, and have indignation against the holy covenant, and shall execute his purpose: he shall even return, and have regard unto them that forsake the holy covenant. And forces sent by him shall stand, and profane the sanctuary, even the fortress, and shall take away the daily sacrifice, and they shall set up the appalling abomination. And such as do wickedly against the covenant shall he pervert by flatteries; but the people that know their God shall be strong, and do exploits. And they that are wise among the people shall instruct many; yet they shall fall by the sword and by flame, by captivity and by spoil, many days. Now when they shall fall, they shall be helped with a little help; but many shall join themselves to them with false protestations. And some of them that are wise shall fall, to refine them, and to purify, and to make them white, even to the time of the end; because it is yet for the time appointed.

And the king shall do according to his will; and he shall exalt himself, and magnify himself above every god, and shall speak astonishing things against the God of gods; and he shall prosper till the indignation be accomplished; for that which is determined shall be done. Neither shall he regard the gods of his fathers, nor the desire of women, nor regard any god; for he shall magnify himself above all. But in his place shall he honor the god of fortresses; and a god whom his fathers knew not shall he honor with gold, and silver, and with precious stones and costly things. And he shall procure for the strongest fortresses adherents of a foreign god : whosoever acknowledges him he will increase with glory; and he shall cause them to rule over many, and shall divide the land for a reward. (Dan. 11 $^{21-39}$)

So far the author is in strict accord with history. But now he begins to predict, and here he proves to be mistaken, for he believed that Antiochus would make another campaign against Egypt and lose his life there. In reality he died at Tabæ in Persia in 164. The author was right, therefore, as far as the year of Epiphanes' death is concerned. But was he right also in regard to the end? Did it come at that time? Let us see what he says about this.

And at that time shall Michael stand up, the great prince who stands for the children of thy people; and there shall be a time of trouble, such as never was since there was a nation even to that same time: and at that time thy people shall be delivered, every one that shall be found written in the book. And many of them that sleep in the dusty ground shall awake, some to everlasting life, and some to shame and everlasting abhorrence. And they that are wise shall shine as the brightness of the firmament; and they that turn many to righteousness as the stars for ever and ever. (Dan. 12 $^{1-3}$)

This is the most important passage concerning the resurrection in the Old Testament. Not all the dead will be raised, only many, most probably the martyrs and the especially wicked, the ones to eternal life, the others to eternal shame and contempt. Let the people but be loyal to Yahweh, even if they should be killed for their faithfulness, for they will be raised and enjoy eternal felicity! But "how long shall it be to the end of these wonders?" The answer is given, "for a time, two times and a half" which means three years and a half, *i.e.* till June, 164.

There is a fire burning in this book, a faith throbbing in its pages of such intensity and power that we must believe that it met with instantaneous acceptance. But a question was certainly going to be asked when it appeared, unless the author anticipated it. The book went out under the name of the ancient saint Daniel, of whom Ezekiel had spoken as one of the great holy figures of the past in conjunction with Noah and Job. Our author believed that Daniel lived in the latter part of the Babylonian exile and in the following years. If that was so, why then had nobody ever heard of his book or seen it before? Because Yahweh had commanded that it should be kept secret until the time of the end and that was now!

"Shut thou up the vision, for it belongs to many days to come" (8 26), and "go thy way, Daniel, for the words are shut up and sealed till the time of the end." (Dan. 12 9)

Why did the author resort to this fiction? Because he would never have gained a hearing for his great and stirring message which burnt in his soul, if he had appeared in person before the people or had sent out his book under his own name. For the time of the prophets was at an end, the law was the revelation of God's will, the people believed that prophetic inspiration had ceased. So he used this literary device not in order to deceive, but in order to make his book a real vehicle for his message. That men did not think that this was a fraud is clear from the fact that most apocalypses used this same device after him.

There was an astonishing boldness in his faith that dared to fix the exact time of the end in the immediate future. But the popularity and influence of the book was such that even when the calculated time had passed, it survived. The author himself added, by new calculations, at first half a month, 1290 days instead of 1277, and again a month and a half, 1335 days instead of 1290. And finally closed with the resigned statement, "but go thou thy way till the end be, for thou shalt rest and stand in thy lot, at the end of the days" (12 13), he shall participate in the final bliss. Later, after the Hellenistic kingdom of Syria had been overthrown, the fourth kingdom was interpreted as referring to Rome (cf. Baruch, ch. 36–40, ca. 90 A.D.), and still later it was ever again adapted to new times by new interpretations of the figures and symbols, for it seemed impossible that the prophet could have been mistaken.

The author had intended his book to be popular and had written the first part (ch. 1–7) in Aramaic, the language which the people spoke at the time. But later he wrote in the sacred language, the Hebrew (ch. 8–12), and when he combined the two parts he translated the first chapter (1 1–2 4a) into Hebrew. Most probably he intended to do this for the rest of the first part too, but he was prevented by some reason or other, perhaps by death, from carrying out his aim.

The victories of the Maccabees, to which the author of Daniel had referred as "a little help" (11 34), had strengthened the national sense of the Jews and raised the hope of future glory afresh. A prophet, whose prophecies are preserved in Zechariah 9–11. 13 [7–9] and whom we may therefore call the Second or Deutero-Zechariah, voiced these hopes at this time, it would seem.[1] He saw all Syria, Phœnicia, and Philistia subjected and part of the Jewish domain.

> Yahweh is in the land of Hadrach,
>   and Damascus is His resting place,
> For the cities of Aram belong to Yahweh,
>   Hamath also which borders thereon,
>   Tyre and Sidon, because they are very wise. (Zech. 9 [1f.])

Yahweh has already occupied all these lands. The strong fortifications of Tyre and her wealth cannot save her from it. The Philistine cities also are conquered and incorporated in the domain of Judah.

> And I will take away his blood out of his mouth,
>   and his abomination from between his teeth;
> And he also shall be a remnant for our God;
>   and he shall be as a clan in Judah
>   and Ekron as a Jebusite. (Zech. 9 [7])

The incorporation of Philistia in Judah involves the acceptance of the laws concerning clean and unclean food and especially concerning the eating of blood. One misses the insistence on circumcision as one of the conditions, inasmuch as the Philistines had always been referred to contemptuously as the uncircumcised. But it is not a religious and certainly not a moral and spiritual conversion to which our author looks forward, but a political subjugation, which insisted on conformity to certain external ritual requirements, in the spirit of the Priest Code.

The Messianic hope is aroused in the prophet. He knows that Yahweh will defend His own city against all attacks by foreign foes, but he looks forward to an ideal king, Yahweh's agent and vicegerent in Jerusalem, whom he predicts in a second poem:

> Rejoice greatly, O daughter of Zion,
>   shout, O daughter of Jerusalem;
> Behold, thy king comes to thee,
>   he is vindicated and victorious;

---

[1] He appears to have used an older oracle as the basis of his own.

> Lowly, and riding upon an ass,
>> even upon a colt, the foal of an ass.[1] (Zech. 9 [9])

As a victorious conqueror he returns from the war in which Yahweh has vindicated his cause and saved him.   But the ideal king is not only a brilliant warrior, but especially a prince of peace.   He does not come back on his battle-horse, but on an ass that had never yet been used, for he belongs to the pious, devoted adherents of Yahweh, the lowly.   And as such he will reign:

> He will cut off the chariot from Ephraim,
>> and the horse from Jerusalem;
> And the battle bow shall be cut off;
>> and he shall dictate peace to the nations:
> And his dominion shall be from sea to sea,
>> and from the River to the ends of the earth. (Zech. 9 [10])

It is a thoroughly national idea, involving a world empire and its peaceful enjoyment for Israel.

In a third poem (Zech. 9 [11–17]), the author predicts the return of the exiles.   Yahweh has regard for the blood of the covenant, by which Israel is bound to him, and calls on "the prisoners of hope" to return, for the Israelites and Judæans together will fight against the Greeks.

> And Yahweh shall be seen over them,
>> and His arrow shall go forth as the lightning;
> And the Lord Yahweh will blow the trumpet,
>> and will go with the whirlwind of the south. (Zech. 9 [14])

Thus aided by the ancient war god, they will gain a decisive victory, which is described in bloodthirsty fashion.   One is reminded of Psalm 149, which at this same time exhorted the saints to exult:

> Let the high praises of Yahweh be in their mouth
>> and a two-edged sword in their hand,
> To execute vengeance upon the nations,
>> and punishments upon the peoples. (Ps. 149 [6])

In a fourth poem in which Yahweh's sheep have become war horses the battle is once more described, and the return of the exiles from Egypt and Syria predicted (Zech. 10 [3–12]).   The author used Assyria for Syria.   It is remarkable that the hope of a return of North Israel

---

[1] Matthew, overlooking the parallelism, took "even" in the sense of "and," and so spoke of two asses on which Jesus rode, in order to conform the scene altogether to the prediction (Matt. 21 [5]).   Mark and Luke speak only of a colt.

was never given up, although there was no chance for it, after North Israel had been irrecoverably lost among the nations of Assyria.

Perhaps we may insert here in our discussion of Deutero-Zechariah the prophecy of Isaiah 33, which seems to come from this same period, more precisely from the years 162–1. It cannot be attributed to Isaiah, but it fits apparently quite well with the conditions of this time. In 162 Antiochus V, or rather his general Lysias, had made peace with the Jews, after his defeat of Judas at Bethzechariah and a long siege of the temple hill. He had granted to them religious liberty, but on condition that they recognize Syrian suzerainty, submit to the razing of the fortifications of the temple hill and to the occupation of the citadel by a Syrian garrison. He did however not acknowledge the rule of the Maccabees, and after a while he put Alkimus of high priestly family over them as ethnarch. From the standpoint of the Maccabees and their adherents it was a poor peace, and the installation of Alkimus was treachery pure and simple. Our author describes this condition.

> Behold, the valiant ones cry without,
> the ambassadors of peace weep bitterly.
> He has broken the covenant, despised the cities,
> and regarded not man. (Isa. 33 [7f.])

A woe had already been pronounced upon the treacherous tyrant, but now Yahweh declares that He will rise and consume the peoples. Then the sinners in Zion will be afraid, because they will realize that they cannot live in the presence of the devouring fire, the eternal burnings of Yahweh's appearance. Only the righteous may dwell in His presence, and will be protected and provided for by Yahweh. A little while before the defender of the temple had to capitulate, but soon,

> His place of defence shall be the munitions of rocks,
> his bread shall be given him, his waters shall be sure. (Isa. 33 [16])

Then the golden time will come.

> Thine eyes shall see the King in His beauty,
> they shall behold a land that reaches far.
> Thy heart shall muse on the terror;
> where is he that counted, where is he that weighed?
> Zion shall be a quiet habitation, which shall never again be disturbed,

For Yahweh is our judge, Yahweh is our lawgiver,
Yahweh is our King; He will save us. (Isa. 33 [17f. 22])

No sickness or sin shall plague the people that live in it.

We return to Deutero-Zechariah and find that his high hopes give way in the following poems. It appears that in the meantime Judas had fought his last battle, in which he was killed (161): a dirge is sung over his death, it would seem, in Zechariah 11 [1–3].

The prophet now enacts two allegories in the presence of the people. They understood their significance at once; to us, however, they are by no means clear, even if we are right in assuming that they represent the time after Judas' death. The prophet is to act the shepherd, *i.e.* the ruler of his oppressed people, who are a veritable "flock of slaughter," sold and killed. His two policies of government are represented by two staffs, the one symbolizing "graciousness" or friendship, the other "union" or harmony. But soon he becomes impatient for no reason, at least none is given, and the people of course reciprocate his feelings. He will no longer rule them with "graciousness," and leaves them to their fate. He breaks the staff "graciousness" and demands his wages from the traffickers of the people whose hired "shepherd" he had been. They give him the paltry sum of 30 shekels, which Yahweh commands him to cast into the temple treasury. Then he breaks the other staff "union," symbolizing that the union between Israel and Judah is at an end. The whole is enigmatic. Did the author represent Alkimus, his recognition as high priest by the pious, and the split between the parties in Jerusalem and Judah? It is quite probable, but we do not know it for certain.

The second allegory would fit Alkimus well. He is called "the man that is My fellow," which shows that a high priest is meant (cf. Zech. 3 [7]). The prophet represents him as the "foolish shepherd," who does not care for his sheep but maltreats and devours them. A woe is pronounced upon him and Yahweh declares,

I will smite the shepherd,
and the sheep shall be scattered. (Zech. 13 [7])

The people will suffer terribly, but out of this punishment will come a purified remnant who will be Yahweh's devoted people (11 [15–17] 13 [7–9]). If this interpretation is correct, at least part of the prediction was speedily fulfilled, for according to 1 Macc. 9 $^{54ff.}$ Alkimus died soon afterwards (160) from a stroke.

The remaining chapters of the Book of Zechariah (12–14 except 13 $^{7-9}$) were probably written by another, later prophet, whom we may call the Third or Trito-Zechariah. He wrote, if we interpret the historical allusions correctly, about 135, after Simon had been murdered by his son-in-law Ptolemy, when the war between John Hyrcanus and Antiochus VII Sidetes had begun and the siege of Jerusalem was impending. It was a desperate situation. The prophet foresees that all the surrounding peoples and even the country of Judah will take part in the siege of the capital. But Jerusalem will prove too strong, the besiegers will only suffer themselves. Then the Judæan chieftains will perceive that Yahweh is with Jerusalem and they will turn against the invaders, and defeat them and thus save Jerusalem. Through this it will come about "that the glory of the house of David and the glory of the inhabitants of Jerusalem be not magnified above Judah." The Jerusalemites would have succeeded even without the help of their countrymen, "for he that is feeble among them at that day shall be as David; and the house of David shall be as God, as the angel of Yahweh before them," so strong and so powerful! The house of David is here the Hasmonean royalty, which many, among them our prophet, regarded as the legitimate successor of the Davidic dynasty, although they were not related at all.

After the successful defence of the city, "the house of David and the inhabitants of Jerusalem" will engage in solemn and bitter mourning for the murdered Simon, who had won their affections so that "they will mourn for him, as one mourns for his only son, and be in bitterness for him, as one that is in bitterness for his first-born." The war had apparently come so quickly upon them that they had not had time for a solemn mourning before the siege. Now "the land shall mourn, every family apart" in strict accord with the established ceremonies for such an occasion.

Then all sin of the ruling family and of the people will be washed off in a fountain that will be opened in Jerusalem, all idolaters and prophets and the unclean spirit itself will be removed from the land. The prophets whom our author condemns are the professionals, who wear the prophet's hairy mantle and make incisions between their hands, as the frenzied prophets of Baal in Elijah's time had done.

> And it shall come to pass that, when any shall yet prophesy, then his father and his mother that begat him shall say to him, "Thou shalt not live; for thou speakest lies in the name of Yahweh;" and his father and his mother that begat him shall thrust him through when he prophesies. And it shall come to pass in that day, that the prophets shall be ashamed every one of his vision, when he prophesies; neither shall they wear a hairy mantle to deceive: but he shall say, "I am no prophet, I am a tiller of the ground; for I have been made a bondman from my youth." And one shall say to him, "What are these wounds between thine arms?" Then he shall answer, "Those with which I was wounded in the house of my friends." (Zech. 13 3–6)

When the siege of Jerusalem had begun and the situation appeared quite hopeless, Trito-Zechariah published an apocalyptic vision, in which he predicted that the attack of the nations would at first be successful, Jerusalem would be captured and one half of her population would be carried into exile. But then Yahweh Himself would appear to fight against the enemies. He will stand on Mount Olivet, which will be split, and through the chasm thus formed the people will escape. Thereupon Yahweh will enter Jerusalem with His holy angels and the Kingdom of God on earth will begin. The climate will be changed, so that there will be no more extremes of temperature, "neither heat nor cold nor frost." Perpetual light will shine, night shall never come again, even "at evening time there will be light." Perennial streams will flow from Jerusalem eastward and westward, irrigating the whole country, which will become a veritable paradise. The sovereignty of Yahweh will be recognized by the whole earth; and the political unity of the world under a theocracy, Yahweh being the sole king, will be combined with the religious unity of the world in the recognition of Yahweh as the one God.

> Yahweh shall be King over all the earth: in that day shall Yahweh be one, and His name one. (Zech. 14 9)

The spiritual preëminence of the religion of Jerusalem will be accompanied by the physical elevation of the city. The whole country is to be levelled down to a plain as low as the Jordan valley, but Jerusalem will be on a high mountain visible from everywhere.

After the nations that had attacked the holy city have been destroyed by an appalling plague and by a panic in which they will fight against one another, their remnant shall come to recognize Yahweh and make a yearly pilgrimage to the universal sanctuary at Jerusalem, the religious centre of the world, to pay homage to the King of the world by celebrating the great harvest thanksgiving festival, the feast of tabernacles, in Jerusalem. That will be their stern duty. If any do not come, they will be punished by Yahweh with drought, or if it should be Egypt, with the plague, since Egypt did not depend on rain for its harvests. It is not the love of God that has conquered their hearts, it is not the free, spontaneous worship of their spirits that they bring, but the outward acknowledgment of Yahweh's deity and kingship. When they all come, "in that day there shall be upon the bells of the horses 'Holy unto Yahweh,'" for they will be consecrated, since they bring pilgrims not warriors. And there will be so many thousands of worshippers that the temple vessels will not suffice, and

Every pot in Jerusalem and in Judah shall be holy to Yahweh of hosts, and all they that sacrifice shall come and take of them, and boil therein (their sacrificial meals). And in that day there shall be no more a trader in the house of Yahweh of hosts. (Zech. 14 21)

Ritual sanctity is this prophet's ideal. There is not much left of the great teaching of the preëxilic prophets. How far we have travelled from Amos and Hosea, Isaiah and Micah and Jeremiah! How external the universal ideal of Deutero-Isaiah has become, and how exclusive his monotheism in the messages of these prophets! But the time was not so distant, only a century and a half later, when prophetic religion was revived in its original purity by the Prophet of Nazareth, through whom it was given its truest and highest expression.

CHAPTER XXIII

CANON AND TEXT OF THE OLD TESTAMENT

WHY were only the books which are at present in the Old Testament included in the final collection? The Old Testament was meant to contain only sacred writings, secular books were therefore excluded on principle; if some were nevertheless admitted, as the Book of Esther and the Song of Songs, they had to be interpreted in a religious or allegorical manner in order to be acceptable. But there were other religious books, some of them of high value and even written in the sacred Hebrew language, that were not admitted. What was the reason for this apparently strange procedure? A brief survey of the formation of the canon will show this.

The canon of the law, containing the so-called five books of Moses, had been fixed between the time of Ezra and the founding of the Samaritan church, for when the rival organization on Mount Gerizim was established, the law was taken over by the Samaritans as their sacred book. The principle of canonization was divine inspiration, i.e. these books were regarded as sacred, because they contained the word of God; and as such they were the final authority, the fundamental law of the Jewish community. Moses had been merely God's spokesman, His mouthpiece, nothing else; the real author was God. There had been several stages in the process of canonization; the most notable were the adoption of the Deuteronomic law at the time of Josiah's reformation and the recognition of the Priest Code at the time of Ezra. When all the various laws together with the narratives belonging to the sources of which they formed a part were combined, — the Torah of Moses, — the Pentateuch was complete, the canon of the law was perfect. It has remained the highest Jewish authority ever since.

The canon of the prophets, comprising the so-called "Former Prophets," i.e. the Books of Joshua, Judges, Samuel, and Kings; and the "Latter Prophets," i.e. Isaiah, Jeremiah, Ezekiel, and the Twelve, was fixed by 200 B.C., but its authority never was as great as that of the law. True enough, the prophets had been God's spokesmen too, and this gave to their words divine sanction. But they were regarded, especially after the formation of the canon of the law, as mere expounders of the law, and as such not in the same class with Moses (cf. Num. 12 $^{6f.}$), in spite of their divine inspiration. Indeed the Book of Ezekiel had difficulty in gaining admission to the canon because it contained some statements which could only with difficulty be harmonized with the law.

The canon of the prophets was already closed when the Book of Daniel appeared, so that it could not be included in it, although it was a prophetic book. It was placed in the third collection, "the writings" or "hagiographa." A number of religious books, some of which were in existence before the canon of the prophets was closed, could not be put among the prophets on account of their character. But they were much used and appealed to as authoritative alongside of the law and the prophets. There was quite a number of them, and at first no sharp distinction regarding their authority was made among them. The Greek Version which was made by Jews in Egypt contained some that never gained access to the Palestinian Jewish Bible. They were later on called Apocrypha.[1] The Alexandrian Jews believed that the Spirit of God was still active and still inspiring writers. The Palestinian Jews believed that the period of divine inspiration had come to an end with Ezra and Nehemiah. And when they finally fixed the extent of the canon or of the authoritative collection of Holy Scripture, the application of their fundamental principle of the divine inspiration of any

---

[1] The *Apocrypha* are 1 and 2 Esdras, Tobit, Judith, the Additions to the Book of Esther, the Wisdom of Solomon, Ecclesiasticus or the Wisdom of Jesus the son of Sira, Baruch with the Epistle of Jeremy, the Additions to the Book of Daniel (The Song of the Three Holy Children, the History of Susanna and the Elders, and the Destruction of Bel and the Dragon), Prayer of Manasses, and 1 and 2 Maccabees.

Besides these Apocrypha there were a number of books of great interest and importance which never gained official recognition by the Synagogue. They are called *Pseudepigrapha* or works written under an assumed name. The most significant of these are the Book of Enoch, the Book of the Secrets of Enoch, the Apocalypse of Baruch, the Assumption of Moses, the Ascension of Isaiah, the Sibylline Oracles, the Testament of the Twelve Patriarchs, the Book of Jubilees, and the Psalms of Solomon. For an understanding of the Judaism immediately before and at the time of Jesus they are of the greatest possible value.

book was determined by the test whether it was written, or believed to have been written, before divine inspiration had ceased, in other words, at or before the time of Ezra and Nehemiah. Any book which was, or was supposed to have been, composed later, however valuable and important it might be, could not be admitted to the canon. For this reason, only the Psalms, Proverbs, Job, Canticles, Ruth, Lamentations, Ecclesiastes, Esther, Daniel, Ezra, Nehemiah, and Chronicles found their way into the canon of "the writings"; all the rest were excluded. There was much dispute about Canticles and Ecclesiastes. But the belief that they had been written by Solomon finally overcame all opposition. Esther also was disputed, but in the end it also won its place in the canon. At a convention of Rabbis at Jamnia (*ca.* 100 A.D.) the authoritative list of sacred writings was definitely fixed and the entire canon was closed.[1]

---

[1] The Christians, outside of Palestine, had used the Old Testament in the Greek Version from the beginning, and though they learned, of course, of the rejection of the first and second Books of Maccabees, Tobit, Judith, Ecclesiasticus, Wisdom, Baruch, and the Additions to the Books of Esther and Daniel, they continued to use them in their church worship and in religious instruction, although some scholars made a distinction between them and the books received by the Jews, and Jerome even declared that "whatever is not included in this list [of the Jewish canon] is to be classed as apocrypha." But the church in general was not influenced by them.

Martin Luther, however, made this distinction pronounced. Only the books of the Jewish canon were to him the word of God. His translation of the other books he entitled, "Apocrypha; that is, books that are not equally esteemed with the Holy Scripture, but nevertheless are profitable and good to read." 1 and 2 Esdras he omitted.

The Roman Catholic Church thereupon defined its position sharply at the Council of Trent (1546), including the Apocrypha among the books of the Old Testament, "If any man does not accept as sacred and canonical these books, entire, with all their parts, as they have customarily been read in the Catholic Church and are contained in the ancient common Latin edition . . . let him be anathema!"

The Reformed Churches took at first the Lutheran position in general, but the Westminster Assembly (1643), following the lead of the Synod of Dort (1618), reverted completely to the official Jewish position, and declared, "The books commonly called Apocrypha, not being of divine inspiration, are no part of the canon of Scripture; and therefore are of no authority in the church of God, nor to be otherwise approved, or made use of, than other human writings." The full effect of this radical position was attained when the British and Foreign Bible Society in 1827 decided after a severe controversy to exclude from its publications the Apocrypha, "those unhallowed productions of the wisdom and folly of men that have been so presumptuously associated with the sacred oracles of God."

The canonization of the books necessitated an authoritative, standard text. The need for this was felt all the more keenly, because the Christians in their arguments with the Jews appealed also to the Old Testament. In order to have a firm basis for the defence, an official text must be made and all the other text-forms must be removed. This was done at the beginning of the second Christian century, soon after the canonization.

There existed a number of copies of each book, and the text of these manuscripts varied in many particulars. One may safely say that there were no two manuscripts of the same book whose text was exactly alike. And we can easily see how this had come about. Let us sit down in imagination by the side of Amos, for instance, as he writes his prophecies. We note first of all that he does not use the Hebrew script with which we are familiar from the Hebrew Bible, but the older Hebrew characters, which are more different from the later ones than the German script is from the English. And what a curious way of writing he has! At times he runs his words together, he does not always indicate periods, nor even long paragraphs. And to make it still more puzzling to us, he puts down only consonants, not a single vowel. How eager he is! The divine fire burns in his soul as he writes. He hurries on and abbreviates a word now and then in his haste. This is how an old Hebrew manuscript looked, written in the earlier Hebrew script, often without word or verse or chapter divisions, without vowels, and here and there with abbreviations.

Of course, the authors could read their own manuscripts well, and a skilled scribe need not have had too much difficulty either in reading them. But it was sometimes possible to read a sentence in two different ways, either of which would give good sense, the difference depending merely on the vowels which were to be supplied. Shall we read, *e.g.*, *hereb* or *horeb* in Deut. 28 ^{22}, "Yahweh will smite thee with consumption, and with fever, and with inflammation, and with fiery heat; and with the *sword* [or, with *drought*] and with blasting, and with mildew"? The official text reads *sword*, but is the other reading not required by the context? Again, shall we read in Judg. 15 ^{16}, "with the jawbone of an ass *a heap, two heaps* (RV. heap upon heaps), with the jawbone of an ass have I smitten a thousand men"? or shall we not rather read, "with the jawbone of an ass *I have piled them in heaps*," etc.? The difference is merely a matter of vocalization, and the original text was written only in consonants.

Sometimes two words might be read as one, as happened, *e.g.*, in Am. 6 [12], where the text now reads, "Do horses run upon the rock? does one plow *with oxen?*" The argument of Amos demands a negative answer to both questions. But people do plow with oxen! The English translators inserted therefore the little word *there*, but that is not in the text. Originally the text of Amos read two words *bbḳr ym*, "does one plow *the sea with an ox?*" Of course not! How absurd that would be! Well, your behavior which turns justice into gall is just as absurd. The copyist took the two words as one, for together they formed the plural of ox, *bbḳrym*. It was therefore very easy to make this mistake.

Occasionally two words were not correctly divided. Thus in Hos. 6 [5] the text now reads, "and *thy judgments are* light which goes forth," whereas the original meant, "and *My judgment is as* the light that goes forth." This was occasioned by taking the first consonant of the second word as the last of the first. A little reflection would have obviated the mistake.

Abbreviations might not be understood as such and be read as a single unabbreviated word, or a scribe might think he had an abbreviation before him, when in reality this was not so. In 2 Sam. 6 [7] there is an unusual word which the English translators render in the connection, "and God smote him there *for his error*" (RV. margin *for his rashness*). The Chronicler took it as an abbreviation and translated it correctly enough, "and He smote him *because he put forth his hand to the ark*" (1 Chr. 13 [10]). The Greek Version in Num. 23 [3] understood the Hebrew word which is translated in the English Versions, "and he went to *a bare height*," as an abbreviation for "and he went *to seek the oracle* (literally, the *mouth*) of *Yahweh.*" This is so much better than the other that it probably represents the original text. The name Yahweh was sometimes abbreviated and the initial Y, when attached to the preceding word, would be the personal pronoun of the first person, and, for instance, "the wrath of *Yahweh*" would become "*my* wrath," as in the Greek of Jer. 6 [11] 25 [37].

Such variant readings do not necessarily reflect on the exactness or ability of the scribe. But not all copyists were scrupulously exact, and indeed, correct copying is not always easy, even if the manuscript is reasonably legible. It was all but inevitable that a great many mistakes should be made by the scribes, and most of them quite accidentally.

Some letters looked very much alike in Hebrew and could easily be mistaken for each other, *e.g. r* and *d*. In Ps. 18 [10] we read, "And He rode upon a cherub and flew, yea, He *soared* upon the wings of the wind." In the parallel text of 2 Sam. 22 [11] the scribe mistook the *d* for an *r*, and read, "yea, He *was seen* upon the wings of the wind."

Some words sounded alike. In Ps. 100 [3] the author wrote, "It is He that made us, and we are *His*"; a scribe who copied this mistook *lō = to him* for *lō' = not* and thus gave it as, "It is He that made us, and *not* we ourselves."

It happened that letters were transposed. In Noah's blessing of Shem, Gen. 9 [26], the original read, "Bless, O Yahweh, *the tents* of Shem," but the copyist thought (quite excusably too!) that *'ŏhŏlê* directly after Yahweh was the ordinary *'elohê* = God, and so changed the meaning to "*Blessed* [with a different vocalization] be Yahweh, *the God* of Shem." In Ps. 2 [11f.] several letters were mixed up, so that the text now reads,

> Serve Yahweh with fear,
> *and rejoice* with trembling.
> *Kiss the son*, lest He be angry, etc.

Originally it was,

> Serve Yahweh with fear,
> *and kiss His feet* with trembling,
> Lest He be angry, etc.

The words ordinarily translated *rejoice* and *the son* were originally one word, but they had become accidentally severed and dislocated. At times even whole clauses or sentences were transposed. Thus the first part of the sentence in Ps. 18 [45] has changed places with the second part in the parallel, 2 Sam. 22 [45].

Sometimes a letter was left out. In Isa. 53 [8] the omission of a single *t* occasioned the queer reading, "for the transgression of my people *to whom the stroke* (was due)." Originally it read, "for the transgression of my people *was he stricken to death*."

Carelessness was responsible for the omission of entire words. In 1 Sam. 13 [1] the number of years is left out, "Saul was . . . years old when he became king."   In 1 Chr. 6 ^{28} the name of the first-born (Joel) is omitted; we can supply it from 1 Sam. 8 ^{2}.   From the context we can easily fill up a lacuna in Josh. 22 ^{34}, they "called the altar *Ed:* because it is a witness (*'ed*) between us that Yahweh is God."

Whole clauses and sentences even were omitted by copyists, especially when their eyes could glide from one or more words to the same word or words a line or two la‛ ‛.   Greek manuscripts help us to restore the omitted portion, *e.g* in 1 Sam. 14 $^{41 f.}$, where the scribe omitted everything from the first to the third Israel: "And Saul said to Yahweh, the God of Israel, *Wherefore dost Thou not answer Thy servant to-day?   If this guilt be in me or my son Jonathan, O Yahweh, God of Israel, give Urim; and if this guilt be in Thy people Israel*, give Tummim."

It also occurred that a word or a clause or even whole sentences were repeated.   For example, in Lev. 20 ^{10}, "And the man that commits adultery with the wife of (*the man that commits adultery with the wife of*) his neighbor."   Or in 2 Sam. 6 $^{3 f.}$, "And they set the ark of God upon a new cart, and brought it out of the house of Abinadab that was in Gibeah: and Uzzah and Ahio, the sons of Abinadab, drove the (*new*) cart (*and brought it out of the house of Abinadab that was in Gibeah*) with the ark."   The eye of the scribe glanced back to the first occurrence of *cart* and then repeated thoughtlessly the following clause.   The parallel in 1 Chr. 13 ^{7} does not contain the repetition.

Also other mistakes were made by the scribes, *e.g.* in Jer. 27 ^{1} the text now reads, "In the beginning of the reign of *Jehoiakim*" instead of *Zedekiah*, as the contents of the whole chapter requires, cf. the margin of the Revised Version.   But all mistakes thus far noted were more or less accidental.

There are, however, also some intentional changes of the original text.   Indelicate expressions were removed and euphemisms were substituted.   Thus in Job 1 ^{5} we now read, "Perhaps my children have sinned and *blessed God* in their heart" for an original *cursed God;* so also in Job 2 ^{9}, "His wife said to him . . . *bless God* and die!" for "*curse God* and die!"   In 1 Sam. 25 ^{22} it seemed improper to let David curse himself in his oath, so *the enemies* of David were inserted, "God do so to (*the enemies of*) David, and more also, if I leave of all that pertain to him by the morning light so much as one man-child." Cf. also 2 Sam. 12 ^{14}.

Hosea's declaration, "I will take away the names of the Baalim out of her mouth, and they shall no more be mentioned by their name" (Hos. 2 ^{17}), was taken quite literally later on and applied to the occurrences of Baal even in proper names. Instead of reading *baal* they read *bōsheth = shame*. Thus the name of Saul's son Eshbaal, as it is still given in 1 Chr. 9 ^{39}, was changed to *Ishbosheth* in 2 Sam. 2 ^{8} etc.; the name of Jonathan's son Meribbaal (1 Chr. 9 ^{40}) was read *Mephibosheth* in 2 Sam. 9 ^{6}, etc.; and even Gideon's name Jerubbaal (Judg. 6 ^{32}) became *Jerubbosheth* in 2 Sam. 11 ^{21}.

In the interest of theology *Elohim = God* was substituted later frequently for Yahweh. The most significant illustration of this we saw in the Elohistic Psalter. Other dogmatic changes were made, *e.g.* in Hab. 1 ^{12} the prophet had said, "Art Thou not from everlasting, O Yahweh my God, my Holy One *that shall not die?*" It seemed blasphemous even to utter such a thought, and so the text was slightly changed (only one letter is involved) to "*we shall not die.*"

The substitution of Mount Ebal for Mount Gerizim in Deut. 27 ^{4} we noticed in our discussion of the Samaritan controversy (cf. p. 285). It wrested from the Samaritans their strongest scriptural support.

Besides these accidental and intentional changes the text was altered also by the introduction of marginal notes which had originally nothing to do with it. The fortunate possessor of a manuscript copy of a book or a reader of it sometimes wrote notes in the margin, and a later copyist inserted them in the text, sometimes in the right, sometimes in the wrong place. One illustration may suffice for a multitude. In 1 Ki. 22 the prophet Micaiah the son of Imlah is the central figure of a fascinating story. A reader thought that he was the same prophet as Micah, the contemporary of Isaiah, and so he wrote in the margin a reference to Micah's book by quoting the first words of it, "Hear, ye peoples, all of you," and a copyist inserted them in the text, v. ^{28}!

Occasionally a reader wrote remarks in the margin which explained the passage; they also found their way into the text later on. Thus someone annotated Isa. 7 ^{17}, "Yahweh will bring upon thee and upon thy people, and upon thy father's house, days such as have not come, since the day that Ephraim departed from Judah," by *the king of Assyria*. This is correct, of course, but it certainly was not written by Isaiah himself. Similarly, somebody noted on Ezek. 4 [1], "Thou also, son of man, take thee a tile, and lay it before thee, and portray upon it a city," *Jerusalem*. This is again quite correct, but the construction in Hebrew shows that it is an addition in the text.

Again, critical readers made notes in the margin which corrected sometimes merely the reading, sometimes the sense. These also were inserted later in the body of the text, side by side with the word or sentence whose place they were meant to take. If now a copyist had a number of manuscripts which he compared when he made a new copy, mixed readings or conflations were inevitable. How much the texts varied occasionally may be seen from the fact that the Hebrew manuscripts from which the books of Jeremiah and of Job were translated into Greek were much shorter than the official text which we now have in our Hebrew Bible.

It is clear that the text of the various books, after all these changes had been introduced, looked different from the original texts which the author had written. Unfortunately, the originals are lost beyond all hope of recovery, and all ancient copies likewise. We have no Old Testament manuscripts that can be dated with certainty before the tenth Christian century, and all manuscripts that we do have represent one text. When the official standard text of the Synagogue was fixed, all other texts were removed. Any that might have been saved were destroyed in the great Jewish war (132–135 A.D.). This standard text was handed down with extreme care. Formerly changes could be made, but this was possible no longer. A few obvious mistakes might still be corrected, some indelicate or anthropomorphic or profane expressions might still be removed, but those were minor matters. Scholars were now intent on fixing and guarding the text with scrupulous care. They counted every letter, and preserved carefully also the tradition of how the text was to be read. This they finally fixed by inserting vowel points and other diacritical signs, not indeed in the official texts of the Synagogue, but in those intended for private use. The scholars who thus guarded the text were called Massorites, because they were guardians of the *Massora = tradition*, and their text is called the Massoretic

Text.   It is the official Textus Receptus or Received Text of the Synagogue.

If this minute, detailed, and loving attention had been given to the text by the copyists of the original manuscripts, we should now have absolutely correct and reliable texts.   As it is, we have only the official text dating from the beginning of the second Christian century, with all its mistakes and corruptions carefully and accurately preserved.   Fortunately, the ancient Versions, especially the Greek Septuagint, help us quite frequently to restore a more original text, since they were made from manuscripts that antedated the received text.   Often also, a critical conjecture gives us the original, but quite frequently we do not know nor shall we ever know what the original reading was.

For practical purposes this is not as serious as it sounds, for in spite of numerous mistakes in the Hebrew text and many mistranslations in ancient and modern versions, the Old Testament has exerted its living power and will exert it as long as men, thirsting for the revelation of the living God, read the pages of this book, which together with the New Testament has become The Bible of Mankind, Israel's priceless literary bequest to the world.

SELECTED BIBLIOGRAPHY

In conformity with the character of this book the following bibliography is for the student and general reader rather than for the specialist, and for this reason only few German books have been mentioned. Many other good titles might have been given, but a selection had to be made for practical reasons.

GENERAL INTRODUCTION

The larger questions of the critical study of the Bible are ably treated by C. A. Briggs, *General Introduction to the Study of Holy Scripture. The Principles, Methods, History, and Results of Its Several Departments and of the Whole* (1899).

W. R. Smith, *The Old Testament in the Jewish Church* (1882, 2d ed., 1902). A classical treatment, still valuable.

A. S. Peake (editor), *The People and the Book* (1925). The latest treatment by members of the Society for Old Testament Study.

W. E. Barnes, *A Companion to Biblical Studies* (1916), and A. W. T. Perowne, *Helps to the Study of the Bible* (1931) are most valuable handbooks.

SPECIAL INTRODUCTION

The problems of literary criticism concerning the composition, date, authorship, and genuineness of the various books are handled in a number of volumes, of which the following are the most important in English:

S. R. Driver, *Introduction to the Literature of the Old Testament* (1891, 6th ed., 1897, and later reprints). This has long been the standard book on the subject. It deals with the problems in a most careful, critical manner; a conservative bent marks the author's extraordinary power of judgment. Although critics have passed beyond many of his positions, his book remains one of the best treatises on special introduction.

C. H. Cornill, *Introduction to the Canonical Books of the Old Testament*. Translated from the fifth German edition by G. H. Box (1907). Briefer and less detailed but critically more advanced than Driver. It is concisely and interestingly written and deserves to be the most popular critical Introduction.

E. Sellin, *Introduction to the Old Testament* (1923). A translation from the German edition which, however, has since had several revised editions. Sellin is stimulating and suggestive, even when he is not convincing.

H. Creelman, *An Introduction to the Old Testament Chronologically Arranged* (1917). A valuable reference book, a veritable encyclopedia, in which the differing results of literary critics are arranged in chronological order.

437

Besides these larger works there are two excellent brief Introductions, which give a quick and authoritative orientation to the student:

G. F. Moore, *The Literature of the Old Testament* (1913).

G. B. Gray, *A Critical Introduction to the Literature of the Old Testament* (1913).

The following three books are more popular, but scholarly and most interesting:

W. F. Badè, *The Old Testament in the Light of To-day* (1915).

H. M. Battenhouse, *The Bible Unlocked: A Study of the History, Literature, and Religious Teachings of the Bible* (1928), includes the New Testament.

E. R. Trattner, *Unravelling the Book of Books* (1929).

HISTORY OF THE LITERATURE

The results of the literary investigations have been woven into a history of the literature: by E. Kautzsch, *An Outline of the History of the Literature of the Old Testament* (1899), a very brief but valuable sketch; and by H. T. Fowler, *A History of the Literature of Ancient Israel* (1912), written with admirable skill.

I. G. Matthews, *Old Testament Life and Literature* (1923).   Very good.

C. E. Noyes, *The Genius of Israel: A Reading of Hebrew Scriptures Prior to the Exile* (1924).   Brilliantly written.

Besides these, two very important German works should be consulted:

K. Budde, *Geschichte der althebräischen Litteratur* (1906), written by one of the greatest Old Testament scholars and embodying many original results.

H. Gunkel, *Die israelitische Litteratur* (1906) in Hinneberg's *Kultur der Gegenwart*.   It presents a new and fruitful way of approach by focussing the attention upon the literary categories and forms.

COMPARATIVE LITERATURE

Much light has been cast on the Old Testament by a comparison with other literatures, especially Babylonian, Assyrian, and Egyptian, and much more light will come from this study.   The most useful general books for this are:

R. W. Rogers, *Cuneiform Parallels to the Old Testament* (1912).

G. A. Barton, *Archaeology and the Bible* (1916, 4th ed., 1925).

I. M. Price, *The Monuments and the Old Testament* (1925).

H. Gressmann, *Altorientalische Texte und Bilder zum Alten Testament*, 2 vols. (1909, 2d enlarged ed., 1926–27).

H. Zimmern und H. Winckler, *Die Keilinschriften und das Alte Testament*, 3d ed. (1903).

A. Jeremias, *The Old Testament in the Light of the Ancient East*, 2 vols. (1910).   Translated from the second German edition, revised and enlarged. The fourth German edition appeared in 1930.

TRANSLATIONS

American Revised Version: Standard Edition (1901).

R. G. Moulton, *Modern Readers Bible* (one vol. 1924).

P. Haupt (editor), *The Sacred Books of the Old Testament*, Polychrome edition (1898–99). A new translation, based on a critically restored text and differentiating by colors the various sources of the books, accompanied by introductions and exceedingly valuable notes. Only the Books of Leviticus, Judges, Joshua, Isaiah, Ezekiel, and Psalms have appeared, and the publication of the remainder has been suspended.

James Moffatt, *The Old Testament, a New Translation* (1924).

J. M. P. Smith (editor), *The Old Testament: An American Translation* (1927).

G. C. Martin and T. H. Robinson (editors), *Books of the Old Testament in Colloquial Speech*.

TEXT WITH COMMENT

C. F. Kent, *Students' Old Testament*, 6 vols. (1904–27). The results of Old Testament criticism are here embodied in a new edition of the books, the composition of the sources is clearly brought out, a new critical translation is given with textual and exegetical notes; lucid introductions and instructive tables and lists enhance the significance of this work, which is without question one of the most valuable contributions to the study of the Old Testament.

E. Kautzsch (editor), *Die Heilige Schrift des Alten Testaments*, 2 vols. (3d ed., 1922–23, by A. Bertholet). A number of German scholars have collaborated in this great work, which is much more than a translation. Its fine introductions to the various books, its headings, summaries, and critical comments both of a historical, exegetical, and textual nature, make it almost a commentary.

E. Czarnomska, *The Authentic Literature of Israel*, 2 vols. (1924–28). The texts are arranged in their chronological order, with introductions and notes.

THE HEXATEUCH

J. E. Carpenter and G. Harford-Battersby, *The Hexateuch According to the Revised Version*, 2 vols. (1900). The first volume of this standard work contains an excellent Introduction to the Hexateuch; the second gives the text in such a skilful arrangement of the sources that the reader at once sees to which document a particular passage belongs; the reasons are stated in footnotes. The first volume was republished by Carpenter in separate form under the title *The Composition of the Hexateuch*, in 1902, but it is greatly to be regretted that the second volume could not be reprinted; it is unfortunately now quite rare.

E. S. Brightman, *The Sources of the Hexateuch* (1918). The documents J, E, and P are printed separately as continuous stories so that the student may get a clear and comprehensive view of each of them. Brief but pointed introductions, headings, and cross-references augment the value of this book.

A. T. Chapman, *Introduction to the Pentateuch* (1911) in the *Cambridge Bible*. It is a very good brief introduction, interestingly and lucidly written.

F. C. Eiselen, *The Books of the Pentateuch* (1916). Able and clear.

D. C. Simpson, *Pentateuchal Criticism* (1924). Cautious, thorough, valuable.

J. Wellhausen's *Prolegomena to the History of Israel* (1885) is still in many respects unrivalled and brings home to the student as no other book the real significance of the literary criticism of the Pentateuch. It must not be confused with Wellhausen's *Composition des Hexateuch und der historischen Bücher* (1885, with additions in 1889 and later), which is also of fundamental importance, but more technical and detailed, and not translated into English.

J. B. Harford, *Since Wellhausen: A Brief Survey of Recent Pentateuchal Criticism* (1926). An important little book.

O. Eissfeldt, *Hexateuchsynopse* (1922). The latest analysis in German.

HISTORICAL LITERATURE

G. F. Moore, "Historical Literature" in the *Encyclopædia Biblica*, Vol. II (1901), gives a masterly survey of the historiography to the time of Josephus.

H. Schmidt, *Die Geschichtsschreibung im Alten Testament* (1911) is a very brief but interesting and suggestive sketch for the general reader. It is one of the little booklets of the *Religionsgeschichtliche Volksbücher*.

LEGAL LITERATURE

S. R. Driver, "Law" [in the Old Testament] in Hastings' *Dictionary of the Bible*, Vol. III (1900).

G. B. Gray, "Law Literature" in the *Encyclopædia Biblica*, Vol. III (1902).

J. M. P. Smith, *The Origin and History of Hebrew Law* (1931).

All three are excellent. Smith gives in the appendix the Hammurapi, the Assyrian, and the Hittite Codes.

PROPHETICAL LITERATURE

W. R. Smith, *The Prophets of Israel* (1882, 2d ed., 1895). Still vital and most valuable.

C. H. Cornill, *The Prophets of Israel* (1895). This brilliant sketch, full of fine religious feeling and insight, is perhaps the best brief introduction to the understanding of the prophets and their messages.

A. B. Davidson, "Prophecy and Prophets" in Hastings' *Dictionary of the Bible*, Vol. IV (1902) and his *Old Testament Prophecy* (1903) are characterized by the luminous, stimulating, and profound exposition of which Davidson was a master.

A. C. Knudson, *Beacon Lights of Prophecy* (1914).

M. Buttenwieser, *The Prophets of Israel* (1914).

J. M. P. Smith, *The Prophet and His Problems* (1914). A series of fine and important essays on certain fundamental problems of the prophets.

—— *The Prophets and Their Times* (1925).

K. Fullerton, *Prophecy and Authority* (1919). A truly remarkable book on the history of interpretation, which cannot be too warmly recommended.

A. R. Gordon, *The Prophets of the Old Testament* (1916). A popular presentation with many quotations from the prophets in a fine new translation. Sound scholarship is here combined with great literary charm.

B. Duhm, *Israels Propheten* (1916). A book by the greatest modern authority on the Prophets; illuminating, stimulating, and fascinating alike by its thought and its diction.

F. C. Eiselen, *Prophecy and the Prophets in Their Historical Relations* (1909).

—— *The Prophetic Books of the Old Testament* (1923). Both fine books, written in Eiselen's clear and able manner.

T. H. Robinson, *Prophecy and the Prophets in Ancient Israel* (1922). Suggestive, interesting, valuable.

N. Micklem, *Prophecy and Eschatology* (1926). Able and stimulating.

W. H. Bennett, *The Religion of the Postexilic Prophets* (1907). Very good.

J. Skinner, *Prophecy and Religion* (1922). A great book, dealing mainly with Jeremiah.

POETICAL LITERATURE

On Hebrew Poetry there are two excellent articles : by K. Budde, "Hebrew Poetry" in Hastings' *Dictionary of the Bible*, Vol. IV (1902), and by B. Duhm, "Political Literature" in the *Encyclopædia Biblica*, Vol. III (1902).

G. A. Smith, *The Early Poetry of Israel in its Physical and Social Origins* (1912), deals with the subject of our first chapter in an admirable manner.

A. R. Gordon, *The Poets of the Old Testament* (1913). A companion volume of his *Prophets*, characterized by the same qualities.

F. C. Eiselen, *The Psalms and Other Sacred Writings, Their Origin, Contents, and Significance* (1918).

H. Gunkel's work, see above, is fundamental for a new understanding and treatment of the Psalms, especially his article on *Psalmen* in *Die Religion in Geschichte und Gegenwart*, Vol. IV (1913, 2d ed., 1930).

H. Schmidt, *Die religiöse Lyrik im Alten Testament* (1912), a companion volume of his little *Geschichtschreibung*, but even briefer, illustrates Gunkel's method very happily.

COMMENTARIES

For technical and detailed critical study the volumes of the *International Critical Commentary*, published under the chief editorship of Briggs and Driver, are best. *The Cambridge Bible for Schools and Colleges*, chief editor A. F. Kirkpatrick, and the *New Century Bible*, chief editor W. F. Adeney, are much briefer and omit all technical matters, but they are very good on the whole, some are excellent. The *Westminster Commentaries*, chief editor W. Lock, are fuller; some are of a high order.

A. S. Peake (editor), *A Commentary on the Bible* (1920) is a series of commentaries on the whole Bible by many scholars, bound in one volume. Its introductions and special articles, together with its very brief comments, make it a most useful handbook for the general reader.

Charles Gore (editor), *A New Commentary on Holy Scripture, Including the Apocrypha* (1928). One vol. Very useful.

F. C. Eiselen, E. Lewis, D. G. Downey (editors), *The Abingdon Bible Commentary* (1929). One vol. Very useful.

H. Gressmann, H. Gunkel, and others, *Die Schriften des Alten Testaments in Auswahl übersetzt und für die Gegenwart erklärt*, in 7 vols. (1910-15). It is a thoroughly modern, critical commentary, without the technical matter, to be read and enjoyed from beginning to end.

C. F. Kent, *Historical Bible*, in 4 vols., on the Old Testament (1908-11). He gives selected texts in a new translation and brief suggestive comments. It is intended especially for Bible Classes, but it is also a most delightful and stimulating guide for the general reader.

Of the *Clarendon Bible*, three excellent volumes have been published so far:
L. E. Binns, *From Moses to Elijah* (1929).
T. H. Robinson, *The Decline and Fall of the Hebrew Kingdoms* (1926).
W. F. Lofthouse, *Israel after the Exile, Sixth and Fifth Centuries B.C.* (1928).

ON GENESIS

J. Skinner, in the *International Critical Commentary* (1910); very able and thorough.

S. R. Driver, in the *Westminster Commentaries* (1903, 12th ed., by G. R. Driver, with an Appendix, 1926); more popular than Skinner, with fine introductions and a careful, discriminating, and reliable interpretation. The finest volume of the series. *Additions and Corrections in the Seventh and Eighth Editions* appeared separately in 1910.

W. H. Bennett, in the *New Century Bible* (no date); a fine little book.

H. E. Ryle, in the *Cambridge Bible* (1914), is also good.

The outstanding commentary on Genesis is by H. Gunkel, *Genesis übersetzt und erklärt* (1901, 4th reprint, 1922). It is unrivalled for its suggestiveness and literary beauty. It opened up a new era in the interpretation of Genesis and is a really great commentary. Its fascinating introduction was translated into English under the title *The Legends of Genesis* (1901). The bulk of the commentary without its technical matter was published in *Die Schriften des Alten Testaments in Auswahl*, see above, under the title *Die Urgeschichte und die Patriarchen* (1911).

ON EXODUS

The best book is by S. R. Driver in the *Cambridge Bible* (1911), but A. H. McNeile, in the *Westminster Commentaries* (1908), and W. H. Bennett, in the *New Century Bible* (1908), are also good.

On LEVITICUS

A. R. S. Kennedy, in the *New Century Bible* (1911), and Chapman and Streane, in the *Cambridge Bible* (1914).

On NUMBERS

G. B. Gray, in the *International Critical Commentary* (1906), is a remarkably thorough and judicious work, one of the best volumes in the series. A. H. McNeile, in the *Cambridge Bible* (1911), A. R. S. Kennedy, in the *New Century Bible* (1911), and L. E. Binns, in the *Westminster Commentaries* (1927), are also good.

On DEUTERONOMY

S. R. Driver, in the *International Critical Commentary* (1895), has rightly been the standard ever since its publication, but G. A. Smith has carried the critical investigation further than Driver, in his fine commentary in the *Cambridge Bible* (1918).

A. C. Welch, *The Code of Deuteronomy. A New Theory of Its Origin* (1924).
—— *Deuteronomy, the Framework to the Code* (1932).

See, on this and similar theories, J. B. Harford, *Since Wellhausen* (cf. above); and J. A. Bewer, G. Dahl, L. B. Paton, "The Problem of Deuteronomy," in the *Journal of Biblical Literature and Exegesis*, Vol. XLVII (1928).

On JOSHUA

H. W. Robinson, in the *New Century Bible* (no date), and more recently G. A. Cooke, in the *Cambridge Bible* (1918). Both good.

J. Garstang, *The Foundations of Bible History: Joshua, Judges* (1931), lays particular stress on the data of archeology.

On JUDGES

G. F. Moore, in the *International Critical Commentary* (1898), is a masterpiece and rightly the standard book on Judges, although C. F. Burney's commentary on *The Book of Judges* (1918) takes high rank by its thoroughness and ability.

G. A. Cooke, in the *Cambridge Bible* (1913). Good.

On RUTH

G. W. Thatcher and more recently G. A. Cooke on Judges and Ruth in the *New Century* (no date) and *Cambridge Bible* (1913), respectively. Both good.

On SAMUEL

H. P. Smith, in the *International Critical Commentary* (1899), is the most thorough in English.

A. R. S. Kennedy, in the *New Century Bible* (1905), is excellent.

A. F. Kirkpatrick, in the *Cambridge Bible* (1930), is the latest and best in English.

On Kings

J. Skinner, in the *New Century Bible* (no date), is excellent.

W. E. Barnes, in the *Cambridge Bible* (1911), is very good.

On Chronicles

E. L. Curtis and A. A. Madsen, in the *International Critical Commentary* (1910), is the most thorough and the best in English.

W. R. Harvey-Jellie, in the *New Century Bible* (1906).

W. A. L. Elmslie, in the *Cambridge Bible* (1916).

On Ezra-Nehemiah

H. E. Ryle, in the *Cambridge Bible* (1893).

T. W. Davies, in the *New Century Bible* (1909).

On Esther

L. B. Paton, in the *International Critical Commentary* (1908), is the best.

A. W. Streane, in the *Cambridge Bible* (1907).

H. Gunkel, *Esther*, in *Religionsgeschichtliche Volksbücher* (1916), is a most suggestive little book.

On Job

A. B. Davidson, in the *Cambridge Bible* (1884, many reprints), long the standard, revised by H. C. O. Lanchester.

A. S. Peake, in the *New Century Bible* (1905), is excellent.

The great commentary on Job is by B. Duhm, *Das Buch Hiob* (1897).

Morris Jastrow, Jr., *The Book of Job* (1920), is a very interesting work, with a new translation.

G. B. Gray, in the *International Critical Commentary*, 2 vols. (1921), is very thorough, cautious, and reliable.

E. C. S. Gibson, in the *Westminster Commentaries* (1899).

H. W. Robinson, *The Cross of Job* (1916), is very suggestive and fine.

On the Psalms

T. K. Cheyne, *The Book of Psalms* (1884 and subsequent impressions). This earlier work of the great Oxford scholar is still very valuable. Its exquisite translations and beautiful interpretation single it out as a truly noble book.

A. F. Kirkpatrick, in the *Cambridge Bible*, 3 vols. (1897–1901), also in one vol. (1902 and subsequent impressions), is on the whole the most useful commentary in English. It is characterized by deep religious sympathy and understanding, great learning, and true expository power. In its literary criticism it is, however, too conservative.

W. F. Cobb, *The Book of Psalms* (1905), is a good corrective to Kirkpatrick at this point, and an able, suggestive and interesting commentary with a minimum of technical matter.

C. A. Briggs, in the *International Critical Commentary*, 2 vols. (1906–7), is a work of great learning, but too technical for the general reader.

The translations of Cheyne (see above), S. R. Driver, *The Parallel Psalter*

(1898), J. Wellhausen in the *Polychrome Bible* (1898; see above), and J. E. McFadyen, *The Psalms in Modern Speech* (1916), are most valuable.

A new direction was given to the interpretation of the Psalms by H. Gunkel, *Ausgewählte Psalmen* (3d ed., 1911), and *Die Psalmen übersetzt und erklärt* (1925-26), W. Stärk in *Die Schriften des Alten Testaments in Auswahl* (1912), and R. Kittel, *Die Psalmen übersetzt und erklärt* (1914). These books are of great importance and destined to influence all subsequent interpretation of the Psalms.

W. E. Barnes, in the *Westminster Commentaries*, 2 vols. (1931), is the latest; it combines careful scholarship with spiritual insight.

Three small but valuable books on the Psalms are:

D. C. Simpson (editor), *The Psalmists. Essays on their Religious Experience and Teaching* (1926).

A. C. Welch, *The Psalter in Life, Worship and History* (1926).

J. M. P. Smith, *The Religion of the Psalms* (1922).

ON PROVERBS

C. H. Toy, in the *International Critical Commentary* (1899), is very valuable.

G. C. Martin, in the *New Century Bible* (1908).

W. O. E. Oesterley, in the *Westminster Commentaries* (1929), is the most up-to-date, utilizing the latest discoveries and discussions.

ON ECCLESIASTES

P. Haupt, *The Book of Ecclesiastes*. A new metrical translation with an introduction and explanatory notes (1905).

G. A. Barton, in the *International Critical Commentary* (1908), is excellent.

Morris Jastrow, Jr., *A Gentle Cynic; Being a Translation of the Book of Koheleth, Commonly Known as Ecclesiastes* (1919), is an interesting and charming exposition of the critical position, with stimulating and illuminating discussions and a new translation.

A. L. Williams, in the *Cambridge Bible* (1922).

H. Odeberg, *Qohaelaeth, a Commentary on the Book of Ecclesiastes* (1929).

ON CANTICLES

A. Harper, in the *Cambridge Bible* (1907). The standard work is by K. Budde, *Das Hohelied* (1898). P. Haupt, *Biblische Liebeslieder* (1907), and W. Stärk (1912, see above, "On the Psalms"), are also most suggestive and valuable.

M. Jastrow, Jr., *The Song of Songs* (1921).

ON ISAIAH

G. B. Gray, on Isaiah I–XXVII in the *International Critical Commentary* (1912), is very thorough, detailed, and technical.

J. Skinner, in the *Cambridge Bible*, 2 vols. (last edition, 1915), and O. C. Whitehouse, in the *New Century Bible* (1905-8), are both excellent.

G. A. Smith, in the *Expositor's Bible*, 2 vols. (1889–90, 2d ed., 1927), is a work of great attractiveness and charm, and indispensable to the general reader for a fresh, vital exposition of this great book.

B. Duhm, *Das Buch Jesaia* (1892, 4th ed., 1923), an epoch-making book, greatly advancing the critical understanding, full of originality, depth of insight and sympathy, the greatest commentary on Isaiah in any language.

G. W. Wade, in the *Westminster Commentaries* (1911).

C. C. Torrey, *The Second Isaiah. A New Interpretation* (1928).

J. E. McFadyen, *Isaiah in Modern Speech* (1918).

On Jeremiah

A. S. Peake, in the *New Century Bible*, 2 vols. (1910–12), is excellent.

A. W. Streane, in the *Cambridge Bible* (1913).

L. E. Binns, in the *Westminster Commentaries* (1919).

The finest commentaries are by B. Duhm, *Das Buch Jeremia* (1901), and by C. H. Cornill, *Das Buch Jeremia* (1905).

S. R. Driver, *The Book of the Prophet Jeremiah. A Revised Translation with Introductions and Short Explanations* (1906).

J. E. McFadyen, *Jeremiah in Modern Speech* (1919).

The following books on Jeremiah are all remarkably able, at times inspiring. The greatest is the first:

J. Skinner, *Prophecy and Religion* (1922).

G. A. Smith, *Jeremiah* (1922).

W. F. Lofthouse, *Jeremiah and the New Covenant* (1925).

H. W. Robinson, *The Cross of Jeremiah* (1925).

A. C. Welch, *Jeremiah* (1928).

R. Calkins, *Jeremiah, the Prophet: A Study in Personal Religion* (1930).

T. C. Gordon, *The Rebel Prophet: Studies in the Personality of Jeremiah* (1931).

On Lamentations

A. S. Peake, together with Jeremiah in the *New Century Bible* (1912).

A. W. Streane, together with Jeremiah, in the *Cambridge Bible* (1913).

On Ezekiel

J. Skinner, in the *Expositor's Bible* (1895).

A. B. Davidson, in the *Cambridge Bible*, revised by A. W. Streane (1916).

H. A. Redpath, in the *Westminster Commentaries* (1907).

W. F. Lofthouse, in the *New Century Bible* (1907).

—— *The Prophet of Reconstruction* (1920).

C. H. Toy's admirable translation of the *Book of the Prophet Ezekiel* (1899) in the *Polychrome Bible* is more than a translation, it is almost a commentary.

On Daniel

S. R. Driver, in the *Cambridge Bible* (1901), is excellent.

R. H. Charles, in the *New Century Bible* (1913), is brief but good.

J. A. Montgomery, in the *International Critical Commentary* (1927), and R. H. Charles, *A Critical and Exegetical Commentary on the Book of Daniel* (1929), are both able, thorough, and satisfying.

ON THE TWELVE MINOR PROPHETS

G. A. Smith, in the *Expositor's Bible*, 2 vols. (1896–98, new ed., 1928), is deservedly the most celebrated book in English on the Prophets. It arouses enthusiasm and admiration by its brilliance and power. No one can afford to miss it, if he wants to enter into the spirit of the Prophets.

Harper, J. M. P. Smith, Ward, Mitchel, Bewer, in the *International Critical Commentary*, 3 vols. (1905, 1911, 1912); very thorough, detailed, and technical.

S. L. Brown, on Hosea, in the *Westminster Commentaries* (1932).

R. S. Cripps, *A Critical and Exegetical Commentary on the Book of Amos* (1929).

G. A. Cooke and E. A. Edgehill, on Amos, in the *Westminster Commentaries* (1913).

S. R. Driver, on Nahum, Habakkuk, Zephaniah, Haggai, Zechariah, Malachi, in the *New Century Bible* (1906), and on Joel and Amos, in the *Cambridge Bible* (1898); excellent throughout.

G. W. Wade, on Micah, Obadiah, Joel, Jonah, in the *Westminster Commentaries* (1925).

H. C. O. Lanchester, on Obadiah and Jonah, in the *Cambridge Bible* (1918), revision of A. B. Davidson's Nahum, Habakkuk, Zephaniah (1920).

G. G. V. Stonehouse, *The Book of Habakkuk* (1911).

W. E. Barnes, on Haggai, Zechariah, and Malachi, in the *Cambridge Bible* (1917).

B. Duhm, *The Twelve Prophets. A Version in the Various Poetical Measures of the Original Writings* (1912). Translated from the German (1910) by A. Duff.

ON THE APOCRYPHA AND PSEUDEPIGRAPHA

R. H. Charles (chief editor), *The Apocrypha and Pseudepigrapha*, 2 vols. (1913) is the standard work.

ON CANON AND TEXT

H. E. Ryle, *The Canon of the Old Testament* (1892, 2d ed., 1895, and later reprints).

K. Budde, "The Canon of the Old Testament" in the *Encyclopædia Biblica*, Vol. I (1899).

F. H. Woods, in Hastings' *Dictionary of the Bible*, Vol. I (1898).

F. C. Burkitt, "Text of the Old Testament" in the *Encyclopædia Biblica*, Vol. IV (1903).

T. H. Weir, *A Short History of the Hebrew Text of the Old Testament* (2d ed., 1907), is excellent for readers who know Hebrew.

C. A. Briggs, *General Introduction to the Study of Holy Scripture* (1899), Chaps. V–X.

James Baikie, *The English Bible and Its Story; Its Translators and Their Adventures* (1928).

H. L. Willett, *The Bible through the Centuries* (1929).

GEOGRAPHY AND HISTORY

G. A. Smith, *The Historical Geography of the Holy Land* (with maps, 1894, 25th ed., 1931).

—— *Atlas of the Historical Geography of the Holy Land* (1915).

C. F. Kent, *Biblical Geography and History* (with maps, 1911).

A. T. Olmstead, *History of Palestine* (1931).

A. S. Rappoport, *History of Palestine* (1931).

W. F. Albright, *The Archaeology of Palestine and the Bible* (1932).

R. L. Ottley, *A Short History of the Hebrew People to the Roman Period* (1901).

H. P. Smith, *Old Testament History* (1903).

N. H. Baynes, *Israel amongst the Nations. An Outline of Old Testament History* (1927, 2d ed., 1928).

T. H. Robinson and W. O. E. Oesterley, *History of Israel*, 2 vols. (1932).

CULTURE AND RELIGION

A. Bertholet, *A History of Hebrew Civilization* (1927, German original 1919).

J. Pedersen, *Israel, Its Life and Culture* (1926).

A. Lods, *Israel from Its Beginnings to the Middle of the Eighth Century* (1932, French original 1930).

R. L. Ottley, *The Religion of Israel* (1905).

A. B. Davidson, *Theology of the Old Testament* (1904).

H. P. Smith, *Religion of Israel* (1914).

J. P. Peters, *Religion of the Hebrews* (1914).

H. W. Robinson, *Religious Ideas of the Old Testament* (1913).

A. C. Knudson, *Religious Teaching of the Old Testament* (1918).

E. Pace, *Ideas of God in Israel* (1924).

INDEX OF OLD TESTAMENT PASSAGES

INDEX OF OTHER PASSAGES

INDEX OF SUBJECTS

RECORDS OF CIVILIZATION

SOURCES AND STUDIES

Edited under the auspices of the

DEPARTMENT OF HISTORY, COLUMBIA UNIVERSITY

XX. THE EARLIEST NORWEGIAN LAWS. Translated, with introduction, annotations, and glossary, by Laurence M. Larson. xi + 451 pages, maps. $5.00.

XXI. THE CHRONICLE OF THE SLAVS, BY HELMOLD. Translated, with introduction and notes, by Francis Joseph Tschan. vii + 321 pages, map. $4.00.

XXII. CONCERNING HERETICS; AN ANONYMOUS WORK ATTRIBUTED TO SEBASTIAN CASTELLIO. Now first done into English by Roland H. Bainton. xiv + 342 pages, illustrations. $4.00.

XXIII. THE CONQUEST OF CONSTANTINOPLE, FROM THE OLD FRENCH OF ROBERT OF CLARI. Translated by Edgar H. McNeal. vii + 150 pages, map. $2.75.

XXIV. DE EXPUGNATIONE LYXBONENSI (THE CONQUEST OF LISBON). Edited from the unique manuscript in Corpus Christi College, Cambridge, with introduction, notes, and an English translation, by Charles Wendell David. xii + 201 pages, maps, illustrations. $3.75.

XXV. THE WARS OF FREDERICK II AGAINST THE IBELINS IN SYRIA AND CYPRUS, BY PHILIP DE NOVARE. Translated, with notes and introduction, by John L. La-Monte, and with verse translation of the poems by Merton Jerome Hubert. xii + 230 pages, illustrations, maps, and table. $3.75.

XXVI. SEVEN BOOKS OF HISTORY AGAINST THE PAGANS: THE APOLOGY OF PAULUS OROSIUS. Translated, with introduction and notes, by Irving Woodward Raymond. xii + 436 pages, map. $4.50.

XXVII. THE EDUCATION OF A CHRISTIAN PRINCE, BY DESIDERIUS ERASMUS. Translated, with an introduction on Erasmus and on ancient and medieval political thought, by Lester K. Born. xii + 277 pages. $3.75.

XXVIII. THE PHYSICAL TREATISES OF PASCAL . . . Translated by I. H. B. and A. G. H. Spiers, with introduction and notes by Frederick Barry. xxviii + 181 pages. $3.25.

FORTHCOMING WORKS

ABELARD: SIC ET NON. By Richard McKeon, Dean of the Division of the Humanities, University of Chicago, and Mary Sweet Bell.

ADAM OF BREMEN: HISTORY OF THE BISHOPS OF HAMBURG. By Francis Joseph Tschan, Professor of History, Pennsylvania State College.

CORRESPONDENCE OF BISHOP BONIFACE. By Ephraim Emerton, Late Professor Emeritus, Harvard University.

ENGLISH TRANSLATIONS FROM MEDIEVAL SOURCES: A BIBLIOGRAPHY. By Austin P. Evans, Professor of History, Judith Bernstein, and Clarissa P. Farrar, Columbia University.

EUDES OF ROUEN: THE DIARY OF A BISHOP. By Sidney M. Brown, Professor of History, Lehigh University.

HERESY AND INQUISITION IN THE MIDDLE AGES. By Anna M. Campbell, Associate Professor of History, New Jersey College for Women, and Austin P. Evans, Professor of History, Columbia University.

MEDIEVAL HANDBOOKS OF PENANCE. By John T. McNeill, Professor of the History of European Christianity, University of Chicago, and Helena M. Gamer, Instructor in Latin, Mt. Holyoke College.

MEDIEVAL UNIVERSITIES AND INTELLECTUAL LIFE. By Lynn Thorndike, Professor of History, Columbia University.

THE SOURCES FOR THE EARLY HISTORY OF IRELAND. Volume Two: Secular. By Dr. James F. Kenney.

THREE COPERNICAN TREATISES: THE "COMMENTARIOLUS" AND THE "CRITIQUE OF WERNER'S TRACTATE" BY COPERNICUS AND THE "PRIMA NARRATIO" BY RHETICUS. By Eduard Rosen, Instructor in History, College of the City of New York.

WILLIAM OF TYRE: HISTORY OF THINGS DONE IN THE LANDS BEYOND THE SEA. By Mrs. Emily Atwater Babcock, Instructor in Latin, and A. C. Krey, Professor of History, University of Minnesota.